D1569916

INTRODUCTION

"That's ancient history," someone might say today in dismissing a topic that's stale or irrelevant. But in fact ancient history is neither of those things. This volume was undertaken in the belief that the Greek historians are exciting to read in their own right; accessible to all, once certain obstacles have been overcome, and of great importance to us as we navigate our own times and our own historical evolution. They wrote for *our* benefit as much as for their readers (or, more accurately, listeners) in the classical Greek world or the high Roman Empire.

Thucydides, writing at the end of the fifth century BC, understood clearly that the story he told—the war between Spartan and Athenian coalitions, what we know as the Peloponnesian War—would provide paradigms for future ages. In his prologue he addressed "those who wish to have an accurate knowledge of what happened and, because of human nature, will likely happen to be the same as, or similar to, these events." He would no doubt be pleased to know that his first English translator was Thomas Hobbes, the Enlightenment political philosopher who went on to write *Leviathan* and other influential works, including one entitled *Human Nature;* or that his book is still required reading at the West Point military academy; or that policy makers speak today of a "Thucydides trap," in which an established superpower (as Sparta once was) feels it must fight to avoid being overtaken by a rival (like Athens). Thanks to its exploration of the deepest levels of human nature, the work has become what its author intended—an everlasting possession.

Human nature stands at the center not just of Thucydides' work but of all Greek historical writing. Thus the Greek historians, in contrast to modern ones, weave speeches, conversations, and even, in one famous case—Thucydides' account of negotiations between Melos and Athens—a dialogue into their narratives. These speech acts give us access to the minds and thoughts of historical actors, whether individuals or city-states (the latter can "speak" collectively through their ambassadors and envoys). They serve to put human beings, rather than impersonal or abstract forces, squarely at the center of historical change; they engage our emotions and our moral sense in the same way that the epic poems of Homer do, for indeed those poems, the *Iliad* in particular, were the primary model with which the first Greek historian, Herodotus, worked.

This centrality of speeches and conversations may surprise modern readers, who live in an age of audio recording devices and of careful documentation of quotes. When Herodotus reveals to us, in his very first episode, an exchange between a king and his chief bodyguard, held in a private room of a palace several centuries before his own time, we may feel that the rules of historical writing, as we understand them, are being broken. But Herodotus played by a different set of rules, as did his successors. In the next generation, Thucydides, writing about events of his own day, addresses the question of the veracity of his speeches, but even while acknowledging the validity of the question, he still claims the right to put words in people's mouths based on what he thinks they ought to have said in particular situations.

It's hard to conceive of an ancient historical narrative without such inserted speeches and comments, just as it's difficult to conceive of a modern one that *has* them. (An experiment of this kind, attempted several decades ago by a biographer of Ronald Reagan, featuring imagined dialogue that had not been recorded or witnessed, was met with widespread outrage and disdain.) This bright dividing line helps define larger differences in the ways ancient and modern historians conceived of their roles. Whereas today's historians seek the truth of facts, their ancient Greek counterparts sought the truth of story. They shaped the presentation of events to create unity and coherence, amplified crucial points by the inclusion (or, in some cases, invention) of speeches, and highlighted emblematic figures while ignoring those whose lives offered fewer insights. In some cases (as in those of Xenophon and Plutarch) they might shift focus toward leaders and states they considered admirable, giving their writing a strong moralistic or ethical slant. (Both Xenophon and Plutarch were students of moral philosophy as well as historical writers.)

Part of the moral dimension of these works is their awareness or inclusion of the gods, an element they share with Greek epic and tragic literature. Of the four authors presented in this volume, three show explicitly how the divine plays a role in the working out of human history, bringing low those who transgress or who strive for too much power. The fourth, Thucydides, avoids all direct reference to the gods and expresses skepticism about some aspects of traditional religion, but he hews so closely to tragic narrative patterns—for example, juxtaposing the greatest disaster that befell Athens, the defeat in Sicily, with the city's greatest moment of hubris, its annihilation of the population of Melos—as to imply, perhaps, that divine forces operate even in his universe. Both he and Herodotus clearly learned much from the tragic playwrights whose works were first staged in their lifetimes—Aeschylus, Sophocles, and Euripides. (Sophocles in fact seems to have been a friend of Herodotus.) Xenophon too saw many of those plays performed, and he remained deeply convinced, as he says at one point, that "the gods do not ignore the impious and those who commit impious acts" (see p. 291, *Hellenica* 5.4).

Plutarch lived a full five centuries after the great age of tragic drama had ended, yet he too drew on the plays of the Athenian tragedians, which he encountered on papyrus scrolls rather than in the theater, to bring out the cosmic context of historical action. He quotes liberally from the plays to reflect on events in his *Lives*, as when he imports an extended passage of *Menelaus*, a play he attributed to Sophocles, to give a larger dimension to the career of Demetrius the Besieger (see p. 402). Such quotes are more than mere adornment or literary erudition. They invoke the imaginative world of tragedy, a world in which the human is deeply enmeshed with the divine. Plutarch's frequent allusions to dreams, oracles, and portents governing the lives of his subjects, or signaling their deaths, are further evidence that we mortals are not the captains of our fate, however high we may rise.

This overlap between Greek tragic drama and Greek historical narrative helps explain how we, the editors of Modern Library's *The Greek Plays*, have come to compile *The Greek Histories*, and also accounts for the choices we have made as to what authors to include here. Many historical writers we might have included have been left to one side. The four we have chosen are those who most belong to the broad mainstream of Greek literature, a tradition steeped in mythic and tragic patterns and in an awareness of the larger context in which historical action is set. The same spirit, we believe, that makes the Greek epics and tragedies so meaningful today, and so stirring to the human soul, is very much in evidence in the authors presented here. Their themes are eternal, their portraits of character are indelible, and they convey with moving clarity their sense of the larger cosmos that gives meaning to human events.

Our selections have been made with one eye on these aspects of the genre, the other on the need for continuity and completeness. We hope that our volume tells a coherent story of the evolution of Greece between the sixth and early third century BC—that is, from the late archaic age through the whole of the classical period and far enough into the Hellenistic world to illustrate the shape that world would take as the Successors of Alexander the Great donned crowns and claimed kingdoms. Naturally there are gaps in continuity where our four sources are silent, especially in the mid-fifth century (covered in summary fashion by Thucydides but in a passage not included here) and the mid-fourth (a period only partially accessible here through Plutarch's *Demosthenes* and the first segments of *Alexander*). We have supplied italicized summaries as a way of bridging these gaps, so that the reader seeking a grand tour of Greek history, or the student in a history survey course, will have a reasonably comprehensive account of crucial eras and events.

The time spans covered by our selections are in no way consistent with or proportional to their length. The Athenian expedition to Sicily, occupying just two years (415–413 BC), takes up nearly 15 percent of our volume, for the simple reason that Thucydides' account of it is riveting and intense, in our opinion, the most compelling piece of historical writing that survives from the Greek world. By contrast, the period between the end of that expedition and the rise of Thebes in the 370s, a span of four decades, is represented here by a single brief selection from Xenophon's *Hellenica* (the fall of Theramenes in 403), reflecting our much lower regard for that work as compared with the others that bracket it. We have sought a sensible compromise between the comprehensiveness required of a historical survey and the very different demands of a "greatest hits" anthology, which means we will inevitably disappoint readers seeking one or the other exclusively.

A word should be said to explain our inclusion of several selections from Xenophon's *Anabasis*. The episode this work deals with is peripheral to the main narratives of Greek history; its action takes place in Asia and has little impact (at least in the portions sampled here) on the balance of power among the city-states of Hellas. But the story it tells is a fascinating one, and Xenophon, who was both its author and its main character, here produced his most vivid, most compelling prose work. So we have given as much space to this absorbing digression as to the *Hellenica,* Xenophon's more central but less successful account of events in Greece between 411 and 362 BC.

Our decision to include selections from Plutarch's *Parallel Lives*—works of historical biography rather than history proper—was also not an easy one, as discussed in our prefatory comments introducing those selections. Plutarch approached history as an ethicist, exploring the characters of men who had played leading roles in history and arranging them in pairs to contrast Greek with Roman figures. His goals were thus very different from those of the other three authors presented here, and unlike them he wrote about events in the distant, not recent, past. But he preserves important details found nowhere else in our sources and offers a uniquely personal glimpse of his subjects. His *Lives* have thus made an important contribution to our understanding of the ancient world, and they are hugely influential in the Western literary tradition.

GLOSSARY OF NAMES, PLACES, PEOPLES, AND MILITARY TERMS

All dates are BC unless otherwise indicated.

AEGAE: Important Macedonian city (modern Vergina), originally the capital of the country, where Philip II, father of Alexander III, was assassinated and where members of the royal family were interred. Recent excavations have brought to light a tomb there that may well be that of Philip.

AEGINA: An island off the coast of Attica, frequently at war with Sparta, Athens, or both.

AGESILAUS: Long-lived Spartan king whose aggressive pursuit of power dominated Spartan policy throughout the first four decades of the fourth century. After his accession in 400, Agesilaus led an expedition into Asia in the 390s, the forerunner of Alexander the Great's campaign, before Sparta recalled him to confront opposition at home. He later targeted the Thebans, who had increasingly drifted out of Sparta's orbit. He invaded Boeotia twice in the 370s and pressed for the campaign of 371 that ended in defeat at Leuctra. He died in 360 in his eighties.

AGIS II: Spartan king during most of the Peloponnesian War and its immediate aftermath. Succeeded by Agesilaus when his eldest son, Leotychides, fell under suspicion of being the illegitimate son of Alcibiades.

ALCIBIADES: Athenian general and politician who rose to prominence at an early age in about 420. A former disciple of Socrates, he was a man of enormous charm and great wealth. His diplomacy created an anti-Spartan coalition that threatened Sparta, but failed to defeat it, at the Battle of Mantinea in 418. He helped persuade the Athenians to make their ill-fated expedition to Sicily and was appointed one of its three generals. After he was removed from command of the expedition and indicted for impiety, he fled to the Spartans and gave them vital information on conducting the war against Athens in both Attica and Sicily. He returned to the Athenian side in 411 but was exiled in 406 and died two years later, the target of a Spartan-organized assassination.

ALCMAEONIDS: A wealthy family whose members (including Cleisthenes, Pericles, and Alcibiades) exerted great political influence at Athens.

ALEXANDER I: King of Macedon at the time of Xerxes' invasion of Greece, when he generally supported the Persians; ancestor of Alexander III.

ALEXANDER III, "THE GREAT": Born to Philip II and Olympias in 356, he ascended the throne after his father's murder in 336. He inherited from his father the most powerful army in the world, along with a plan to use it in an invasion of Asia. His conquests ultimately far surpassed anything his father had dreamed. From 334 to 326, Alexander conquered all the territories that had comprised the Persian Empire, moving as far east as the Indus river system before his mutinous troops called a halt. He returned westward as far as Babylon but fell ill and died there in June 323, aged thirty-two. His failure to plan for a succession led to the breakup of his empire and a long period of warfare among his generals.

ALEXANDER OF PHERAE: A tyrant who took power in Thessaly in the 360s, the nephew of Jason of Pherae. Like his uncle, he used mercenary troops to dominate the Thessalians but also terrorized them with cruel abuses.

AMMON: Egyptian deity generally identified with Zeus. Alexander III consulted the oracle of Ammon in Egypt in 331 and claimed, possibly out of sincere belief, that he was descended from the god.

AMPHIPOLIS: City in Thrace in northern Greece that was of strategic importance because it guarded access by river to major sources of timber (for shipbuilding) and precious metals. Originally settled by Thracians, it was made a colony of Athens in 437, but was lost to the Spartans in 424. The historian Thucydides held a command in the area at the time of its loss; he was held accountable and exiled. After this time, Amphipolis maintained its independence until Philip of Macedon (Alexander's father) took it in 357.

ANTIGONUS (NICKNAMED ONE-EYE): Macedonian officer detailed by Alexander the Great to govern conquered Phrygia, starting in 333 BC. He entered the rivalry for Alexander's realm in 323 and controlled much of Asia for several years, using his son Demetrius as his top general and representative. Battles with Ptolemy and his ally Seleucus ate away at Antigonus' power and territory. In 301 he was killed at the Battle of Ipsus, in his eighties, after his foes united against him.

ANTIPATER: Father of Cassander, Alexander's boyhood friend; appointed by Alexander to govern Macedonia's European empire while the Asian campaign was under way.

ARCHIDAMUS: Spartan king during the first phase of the Peloponnesian War, the so-called Archidamian War (431–421).

ARISTIDES: Athenian political leader during the early fifth century, nicknamed "the Just" because of his reputation for fair dealing. Aristides' conservative politics and aristocratic background contrasted sharply with those of the more populist Themistocles, with whom he often clashed and competed.

ARISTOTLE: Greek philosopher and head of the Peripatetic school, appointed Alexander's tutor for two years starting near the end of 343.

ARTABANUS: Persian noble at the time of Xerxes' invasion of Greece (480); brother of Darius and uncle of Xerxes; depicted by Herodotus as an elder sage.

ARTAXERXES II: Also known as Artaxerxes Mnemon, king of Persia from 404 to 358. His long reign spanned from the end of the Peloponnesian War through the series of confrontations between Thebes and Sparta. Artaxerxes played arbiter of Greek affairs after the signing of the Peace of Antalcidas in 387.

ARTEMISIA: Carian queen who ruled Halicarnassus on behalf of the Persians and accompanied Xerxes on his invasion of Greece in 480.

ASPASIA: Milesian woman living at Athens who became the consort of Pericles. Her influence over Pericles was said to have helped spark the Peloponnesian War.

ASSEMBLY: The primary decision-making body of the Athenian democracy. Any citizen could attend its meetings, where speakers addressed the policy choices the city faced and votes were taken. Over time the

Assembly took on greater powers, especially after the constitutional reforms of Ephialtes in 462 and 461.

ATTALUS: Macedonian noble from the fourth century and son-in-law of Parmenio and uncle of Cleopatra, Philip II's last wife. Alexander perceived him as an enemy and had him assassinated shortly after coming to power.

BABYLON: Mesopotamian city that became one of the capitals of the Persian Empire after its conquest by Cyrus the Great in the sixth century. Alexander captured it after his victory at Gaugamela in 331 and celebrated the rites of Bel, its chief deity. He returned there in 324 and died there in June 323.

BACTRIA: Northeastern province of the Persian Empire encompassing modern northern Afghanistan and southern Uzbekistan and Tajikistan. The strengths of the region in cavalry horses and skilled riders made it an important military asset for the Persians and, later, for Alexander the Great and his Successors.

BESSUS: Satrap of Bactria and fierce foe of Alexander the Great. Bessus led one wing of Darius' line at Gaugamela in 331 and fled with the king after the Persian defeat in that battle. When Alexander seemed poised to overtake the king's party, Bessus assassinated Darius and assumed the kingship himself. Bactrian peoples who feared Alexander's retribution turned Bessus over to the Macedonians, who had him killed in 329.

BOEOTARCH: Officer of the Boeotian League, elected for a one-year term. A board of boeotarchs, usually seven in number, directed affairs of the league, a regional hegemony headed by Thebes.

BOEOTIA: Region of central Greece dominated by Thebes. The ethnic and cultural unity of the Boeotians made possible their union in the Boeotian League, a regional federation that existed at various points in the fifth and fourth centuries.

BOULĒ: The executive board at Athens that supervised the agenda and schedule of the Assembly. At first four hundred in number, the Boulē was expanded to five hundred in the fifth century, and its powers increased as Athens's constitution evolved.

CASSANDER: Son of the Macedonian general Antipater and, after his marriage to Alexander the Great's half-sister Thessalonicē, self-proclaimed ruler of Macedonia. Cassander established control over

Athens in 317, with the help of a Piraeus garrison on the hill of Munychia. Demetrius the Besieger took over the hill in 307 and evicted Cassander's forces.

CHAERONEA: City in Boeotia, the site of a battle that in 338 ended an attempt by Thebes and Athens to prevent Philip II from dominating mainland Greece. Alexander led the decisive cavalry charge that smashed the Theban infantry and defeated the Sacred Band.

CHERSONESE: Long peninsula in the eastern Aegean, modern Gallipoli; largely dominated by Athens starting in the mid-sixth century; ruled by Miltiades (the younger) before his escape to Athens.

CHIOS: Eastern Aegean island that remained loyal to Athens until 413, after which it resisted Athens until the end of the war. Chios was one of very few members of the Delian League that retained its own fleet.

CIMON: Athenian political and military leader who came to prominence after the Persian wars (470s and 460s). Cimon took the lead role in foreign policy after Themistocles fell from grace and advocated a more friendly and collaborative stance toward Sparta. Cimon in turn fell from favor after the Spartans revealed their mistrust of Athens at Mount Ithome.

CLEARCHUS: Spartan mercenary captain who led a large segment of the Ten Thousand, the Greek hoplite army assembled by Cyrus the Younger in 401 BC. Xenophon, who served in that army, praised him as a uniquely capable commander. He was imprisoned by the Persians after a treacherous arrest and later executed.

CLEISTHENES: Alcmaeonid politician who spearheaded a democratic reform of the Athenian constitution in 508.

CLEOMBROTUS: Spartan king of the early fourth century, killed in the Battle of Leuctra.

CLEON: Athenian politician and demagogue who rose to power after the death of Pericles. He was responsible for the brilliant Athenian success at Sphacteria in 425 but was killed soon afterward at the Battle of Amphipolis.

CLEOPATRA: (1) Last wife of Philip II of Macedon and mother of his son Caranus, whom some viewed as a rival to Alexander for the Macedonian throne; killed after Philip's death. (2) Daughter of Philip and Olympias and sister of Alexander, whose wedding festivities in 336 were the occasion of her father's murder.

COENUS: High-ranking officer under Alexander who led a decisive cavalry movement at the Battle of the Hydaspes. In the Hyphasis mutiny of 325 he served as spokesman for the troops who did not want to proceed farther eastward. He died of disease shortly thereafter.

COMPANIONS: Alexander's trusted inner circle of advisers and friends, consisting of fewer than a hundred Macedonian nobles.

CORINTH: Greek city located near the isthmus where the Peloponnese joins mainland Greece.

CRATERUS: A revered officer in Alexander's army who executed many crucial commissions for Alexander, serving virtually as second-in-command after Parmenio's death. Appointed to lead the veterans homeward from Opis and assume command of the home front from Antipater (323), he played a crucial role in the Lamian War and died in battle in 321.

CRITIAS: Leading member of the Thirty, the oligarchic regime installed at Athens by Sparta in 404 BC. A former student of Socrates, Critias became infamous for his abuses of power.

CROESUS: King of Lydia, a Hellenized but non-Greek realm in western Anatolia, in the mid sixth century BC and a major figure in Herodotus' *Histories*. He provoked war with Cyrus the Great of Persia around 560 BC and was captured, perhaps killed, in a Persian invasion of his capital city, Sardis. The Greeks mythologized his fall from power, as seen not only in Herodotus' work but on a vase painting of the late sixth century and in an ode by Bacchylides.

CUNAXA: Site near Babylon where Cyrus the Younger fought his brother, Artaxerxes, using the force of Greek mercenaries called the Ten Thousand. Cyrus was killed in that battle (401 BC).

CYRUS THE GREAT: Founder of the Persian Empire in the mid-sixth century and subject of the second half of Herodotus' first book (as well as *The Education of Cyrus* of Xenophon). Cyrus' tomb at Pasargadae, ransacked by looters, was restored by Alexander the Great in 324.

CYRUS THE YOUNGER: Brother of the Persian king Artaxerxes II and satrap of Lydia in the late fifth century. He aided Sparta in the late stages of the Peloponnesian War, then attempted to overthrow his brother, Artaxerxes II, in 401. His hired Greek soldiers included Xenophon, Clearchus, and the army of the Ten Thousand. His death at the

Battle of Cunaxa, near Babylon, left the Greek army stranded in Persian territory.

DARIUS I: King of Persia from 522 to 486. Under his leadership, Persia expanded westward into Europe, first with a crossing of the Bosporus to attack the Scythians (c. 513), later with two attempted invasions of Greece, one assigned to Mardonius (492), the other to Datis and Artaphernes (490). Both were unsuccessful, and the task of conquering Greece was left to Darius' son and successor Xerxes.

DARIUS II: King of Persia during much of the Peloponnesian War, in which he supported the Spartans. He reigned from 423 to 405.

DARIUS III: King of Persia starting in 336, the same year Alexander came to the throne; portrayed by ancient sources (perhaps unfairly) as a bungler who ran from battle and lost the engagements with Alexander at Issus and Gaugamela. Assassinated in exile by a group of usurpers led by Bessus, Darius was given burial with full royal honors by Alexander.

DATIS: Persian general and a leader in the invasion of Greece culminating in the Battle of Marathon (490).

DECELEA: Area of the Attic countryside fortified and used as a year-round base by Sparta, at the urging of Alcibiades, starting in 413. With a permanent presence at Decelea, Sparta was able to deny the Athenians the use of much of their agricultural land and also draw off escaped slaves and deserters.

DELIAN LEAGUE: Alliance of Greek city-states led by Athens, formed in 477 as a counterweight to Persian power after the Greek victories at Salamis and Plataea. Though it began as a strictly cooperative venture, the league became dominated by Athens to a degree that effectively made it an Athenian empire.

DELOS: Sacred Greek island at the center of the Cycladic islands, supposedly Apollo's birthplace. Delos was from 477 to 454 the repository of funds collected by Athens for common defense of the Aegean; the contributing states were therefore known as the Delian League (q.v.).

DELPHI: Greek oracular shrine where the priestess of Apollo, known as the Pythia (q.v.), answered questions posed by visitors. Thanks to the offerings by those seeking the oracle's favor (Croesus in particular), and to the tithes of wartime plunder offered by victorious powers,

Delphi accrued enormous wealth, most of which was squandered after the Phocians took over the shrine in the 350s and 340s.

DEMADES: Athenian politician of the late fourth century; an advocate of collaboration with Alexander and the Macedonians.

DEMETRIUS (NICKNAMED THE BESIEGER): Son and successor of Antigonus One-eye, on whose behalf he fought numerous battles with Ptolemy, Lysimachus, and Seleucus. Together with his father he took a royal crown in 306 BC, signifying his family's ambition to control most or all of Alexander's realm. His rivals teamed up against him, though, and defeated him at the Battle of Ipsus (301), killing his father and ending his Asian dominion. He established himself in Athens and later in Macedonia but continued to press his claims on Asia, leading to his capture by Seleucus.

DEMETRIUS OF PHALERON: An Athenian orator and philosopher, appointed to rule Athens in 317 as the puppet of Cassander. He was exiled in 307 when Demetrius the Besieger took control of Athens and expelled Cassander's garrison.

DEMOSTHENES (SON OF ALCISTHENES): Athenian general during the Peloponnesian War. His initiative at Pylos allowed the Athenians to capture nearly three hundred Spartan prisoners at Pylos. He arrived at Syracuse in 413 BC, with another general (Eurymedon), in command of several thousand reinforcements. He led the assault on Epipolae that failed terribly and led to the defeat of the entire expeditionary force. During a forced retreat he surrendered to the Syracusans along with his portion of the force and was later executed.

DEMOSTHENES (SON OF DEMOSTHENES): Leading Athenian orator and politician in the third quarter of the fourth century. Led the opposition to Philip II's expansion, and then, after Philip's death, worked quietly behind the scenes to oppose Alexander. After the defeat of Athens in the Lamian War, he was exiled and hunted as an enemy of Macedonia; he killed himself in 322.

EPAMINONDAS: Theban general who led the military and political resurgence of Thebes in the 370s and 360s. His brilliant tactics, and the newly constituted infantry forces he had helped train (together with his co-leader Pelopidas), enabled Thebes to defeat Sparta at the Battle of Leuctra (371), drive deep into Spartan territory, and liberate the enslaved Messenians.

EPHIALTES: Athenian political leader who, together with Pericles, introduced a set of radical democratic constitutional reforms in 462 and 461. Ephialtes was killed shortly thereafter, evidently by conservative opponents.

EPIPOLAE: Strategic height overlooking Syracuse, site of the night battle that turned the tide against the Athenians in 413.

EUBOEA: Long island off the north coast of Attica. Athenian military and economic strategy depended on retaining control over Euboea.

GEDROSIA: Desert region spanning the coast of modern Pakistan and eastern Iran. Alexander marched his army through this land on his return from India in 325, at huge cost.

GYLIPPUS: Spartan general sent by Sparta to organize the Syracusan resistance to Athens in 414 BC. His arrival turned the tide of battle against the Athenians. He received the surrender of Nicias and his troops to end the Athenian campaign.

HARPALUS: Boyhood friend of Alexander who was appointed to the important post of royal treasurer on the Asian campaign. He defected and fled to Greece in 333 but was welcomed back by Alexander and granted amnesty. During the satrapal purge of 324 he again decamped from Babylon, where he had been spending lavishly out of purloined funds, and tried, unsuccessfully, to stir up a revolt against Alexander in Greece. Exiled from Athens, he was murdered by an associate on Crete in 323.

HELLESPONT: Modern strait of Dardanelles and surrounding region, used as a crossing point between Europe and Asia, first by Xerxes marching his armies toward Greece in 480, then by Alexander in 334 leading his forces in the opposite direction.

HEPHAESTION: Macedonian officer and intimate friend from childhood of Alexander the Great. Hephaestion accompanied Alexander throughout the Asian campaign of 334–323 and died in its final year, apparently of illness. Alexander's grief over Hephaestion's death was extreme; a pyre constructed in his honor was said to have cost ten thousand talents, a huge sum.

HERACLES: Son of Zeus by Alcmene, a mortal; by legend, an ancestor of Alexander as well as the kings of Sparta. The mythic labors of Heracles (called Hercules by the Romans) were echoed in Athenian legends about Theseus, and Heracles was thought to have befriended and helped Theseus on numerous occasions.

HERODOTUS: Greek historian of the mid-fifth century, originally from Halicarnassus in Asia Minor. His work, today known as the *Histories,* gives an account of the Persian Empire from about 560 to 479, focusing on its conflicts with the Greeks.

HOPLITES: Heavy-armed infantry who formed the backbone of Greek armies during the Classical Age. As they were expected to pay for their own armor, hoplites, in most cases, were moderately well-off citizens.

HYPERIDES: Athenian orator and politician known for his opposition to Macedonian power in the era of Philip and Alexander the Great. After teaming with Demosthenes in support of the failed 322 Athenian revolt from Macedon, Hyperides fled Athens but was arrested and executed by agents of Antipater.

INDIA: To the Greeks, an indistinct realm of unknown extent, east of the Hindu Kush mountain range. Herodotus considered it a wealthy region where much gold was harvested; other authors wrote of its wonders, monsters, and bizarre races of humankind. Alexander the Great invaded it in 327 BC and, after defeating Porus, swept down through the Indus valley in a campaign that inflicted huge casualties. Soon thereafter, Chandragupta reclaimed the region for an indigenous dynasty, the Mauryas.

IONIA: A term usually used to refer to the Greek-populated coast of Asia Minor. The uprising of the Greek cities on that coast in 499 is known as the Ionian Revolt.

JASON OF PHERAE: A tyrant who rose to power in eastern Thessaly in the 370s, with the help of a mercenary army paid for by inherited wealth. Xenophon considered him the foremost man of that era. After attaining to the *tageia,* or unified command, of all Thessaly, he seemed poised for great enterprises, but assassins cut him down in 370.

THE KING'S PEACE (OR PEACE OF ANTALCIDAS): The first Greek attempt at a Common Peace, a security framework governing all mainland states. It was arranged by Artaxerxes, Great King of Persia, in 387 and sworn at Sparta by most of the Greeks the following year. It guaranteed autonomy to all signatories and banned attempts at coercion or unilateral use of force. The Spartans used it as a pretext to break up the leagues of other Greek states and to undermine their foes.

LACEDAEMON: Southeastern region of the Peloponnese, centered on and politically dominated by Sparta. "Lacedaemonians" is the normal Greek term for the nation commonly (though less precisely) called Spartans (since in fact most of the "Spartan" army was composed of people not living in Sparta itself).

LAMACHUS: Athenian general, one of three who were given shared command of the Sicilian expedition, with Nicias and Alcibiades, in 415. Seemingly the most capable of the three, he was killed in battle in 414.

LAMIA: A famously desirable Athenian courtesan of the late fourth century, with whom Demetrius the Besieger carried on a public love affair that scandalized Athens.

LEONIDAS: Spartan king who led the famous three hundred Spartans at Thermopylae, in a futile attempt to prevent the Persian penetration of central Greece. He died in the pass with nearly all the rest of the three hundred (480 BC).

LESBOS: The largest of the islands off the coast of Asia Minor. Its main city is Mytilene. In the second half of the fifth century it was one of the only states in the Athenian Empire that retained its own navy and thus a degree of autonomy.

LYCURGUS: Legendary Spartan lawgiver, credited with the constitutional reforms that produced Sparta's uniquely closed and militarized society. If he in fact existed, Lycurgus can best be dated to the eighth century.

LYDIA: Non-Greek kingdom in western Anatolia; imperial master of various Ionian Greek cities starting in the mid sixth century. Croesus brought it to a new level of power and wealth in the early sixth century.

LYSANDER: Spartan admiral during the last phase of the Peloponnesian War (late fifth century), victor at the Battle of Aegospotami and arbiter of the terms of Athenian surrender. Lysander attained power not through royal birth but through the patronage of King Agesilaus, reportedly his former lover.

LYSIMACHUS: One of Alexander the Great's high-ranking officers and, after Alexander's death, a rival for portions of his empire. Based in Thrace, Lysimachus sided with Ptolemy and Seleucus to limit the ambitions of Antigonus One-eye and his son Demetrius, though neither of his allies trusted him. He took part in the victory over Antigonus in the Battle of Ipsus (301 BC).

MACEDONIA: Hellenic or Hellenized kingdom situated in the north of mainland Greece.

MALLI: An Indian people usually identified with the Malavas mentioned in Sanskrit literature. Their fierce resistance to Alexander during his trip down the Indus in 325 resulted in much bloody fighting, including one siege in which Alexander, trapped almost alone within a town's walls, was badly wounded by an arrow in the chest.

MARATHON: Coastal plain about twenty-five miles northeast of the city of Athens; site of the battle in 490 in which Athenian troops defeated the invading Persians.

MARDONIUS: Persian noble who commanded the land army of Darius in the invasion of Xerxes (480–479).

MEDES: An Asian people who became powerful starting in the seventh century, participating in the defeat of the Assyrians at Nineveh in 612, thereafter masters of the northern and eastern segments of the Assyrian empire; subjugated by the Persians in 550, they became integrated into Persian society to the extent that Greek authors often call the Persians "Medes."

MEGARA: City located between Athens and Corinth and a member of the Peloponnesian League. The Megarian Decree of the Athenians barred Megara from commerce with Athens and its empire and was one of the causes of the Peloponnesian War.

MELOS: Small island in the central Aegean, founded by colonists from Sparta but neutral in the Peloponnesian War until Athens required it to join its empire. The so-called Melian dialogue of Thucydides is set on the island.

MESSENIANS: Inhabitants of Messenia, the district of the Peloponnesus west of Sparta. Conquered by Sparta in the eighth and seventh centuries, most of the Messenians were forced to work their own land for Spartan landlords. Something between serfs and sharecroppers, they were known as helots.

MILETUS: Ionian Greek city located on the coast of Asia Minor; intellectual and economic capital of the Asian Greeks prior to its destruction by Persia in 494.

MILTIADES (THE YOUNGER): Athenian nobleman who ruled the Chersonese peninsula on behalf of Athens in the late sixth and early fifth centuries; escaped Persian pursuit and arrived at Athens in time to serve as one of ten generals at the Battle of Marathon. His son Cimon became an important Athenian leader.

MYTILENE: Principal city of Lesbos and the center of a revolt from the Athenian Empire in 428 BC.

NICIAS: Athenian politician and general. He helped negotiate the peace treaty of 421 between Athens and Sparta that bears his name. Opposed to the expedition against Sicily, he was nevertheless made one of its three commanders in 415, becoming principal commander after the defection of Alcibiades.

OLYMPIAS: Philip II's fourth or fifth wife, a princess of the kingdom of Epirus east of Macedonia and mother of Alexander the Great. She vied for control of Macedon after Alexander's death and gained it for a time but was overthrown and killed by Cassander in 316.

OSTRACISM: Ten-year banishment and disenfranchisement inflicted occasionally on a leading Athenian by popular referendum. Themistocles and Cimon were both removed from power by this method.

PARMENIO: Senior Macedonian general and right-hand man to both Philip and Alexander until 331, when Alexander posted him to a lesser command in Media; murdered in 330 on Alexander's orders after his son Philotas had been executed.

PAUSANIAS: Spartan regent and general during the Persian invasion of 480. He led the Spartan forces that defeated the army of Mardonius in 479 at Plataea. Later he was accused of colluding with Persia and died resisting arrest by Spartan authorities.

PELOPIDAS: Theban political and military leader who teamed up with Epaminondas to lead Thebes in its brief sojourn as superpower of Greece. Pelopidas helped defeat the Spartans on several occasions starting in 379 and tangled with Alexander of Pherae, a Thessalian tyrant. He died in a heated charge against Alexander in 364 BC.

PELOPONNESE: Peninsula comprising the southern portion of mainland Greece, dominated militarily and politically by Sparta with the exception of Argos, an independent democracy.

PELOPONNESIAN WAR: The name conventionally given to the war between Spartan and Athenian coalitions, lasting from 431 to 404 (with a partial hiatus from 421 to 415). It should be understood as "the war against the Peloponnesian states," the point of view being that of the Athenians.

PERICLES: Leader of Athens during the period of its greatest expansion and most explosive cultural developments. After coming to prominence in 462 as a supporter of Ephialtes, Pericles assumed leadership of the democratic political wing after Ephialtes' death. Athens looked to Pericles to set policies toward Sparta that were uncompromising enough to provoke war in 431. Pericles died of illness in the second year of the war.

PERSEPOLIS: One of several capital cities of the Persian Empire, site of magnificent palaces built under Darius I and Xerxes. The central palace of the complex was destroyed by fire while occupied by Alexander's forces in 331.

PERSIANS: An Iranian people who seized power from their kinsmen, the Medes, in the mid-sixth century. Under the so-called Achaemenid dynasty established by Cyrus the Great, the Persians built an immense empire, which by 500 encompassed all of Asia from Turkey to the Indus River, Egypt and North Africa, and parts of eastern Europe. Their attempts to conquer Greece in 490 and 480 were unsuccessful, however. By the fourth century their empire was thought to be in decline, tempting Agesilaus of Sparta to lead a partly successful invasion in 396; later Alexander succeeded in capturing the entire empire and ending the Achaemenid dynasty.

PHALANX: Rank-and-file formation of infantry soldiers designed to present a solid wall of weaponry to an opponent in battle. Devised by the Greeks, perhaps in the ninth century, the phalanx was radically altered in the fourth century, first by Thebes, which experimented with its size and configuration, and then by Macedonia, which armed its soldiers with long *sarissas* (lances) and small shoulder-hung shields.

PHILA: Eldest daughter of Antipater, wed first to Craterus and later to Demetrius the Besieger (though she was much older than he). She stayed loyal to Demetrius despite his many infidelities and reportedly committed suicide when his prospects began to fade.

PHILIP II (OR PHILIP OF MACEDON): Born in 382, he assumed the Macedonian throne in 359. A gifted leader, diplomat, and military strategist, Philip transformed his country from a weak provincial backwater to superpower status in two decades. Philip was assassinated by a junior officer in 336, two years after his victory over Athens and Thebes at Chaeronea, and was succeeded by his son Alexander III, "the Great."

PHILOTAS: Son of Parmenio and senior officer in Alexander's army, executed for treason in Bactria in 330 following his failure to report a conspiracy against Alexander's life.

PHOCION: Athenian general and statesman whose life spanned most of the fourth century. A famous moderate with regard to policy toward Macedon, Phocion was appointed one of two puppet leaders of the government imposed on Athens by Antipater in 322.

PHOEBIDAS: Spartan general of the early fourth century who led an unprovoked attack on the Theban stronghold called the Cadmeia. By seizing this fort, Phoebidas and his Spartan troops gained control over Thebes, until they were overthrown in a revolt led by Pelopidas and others.

PHOENICIANS: Seafaring people inhabiting the cities of the Levantine coast (principally Tyre, Sidon, and Gaza) as well as parts of North Africa and the western Mediterranean. Phoenicians served the principal naval arm of the Persian Empire, but did so without great loyalty to Persia; many deserted to Alexander's side during the early phase of the Asian campaign.

PIRAEUS: Port system on the west coast of Attica; after 493, the harbor serving Athens.

PISISTRATUS: Tyrant of Athens starting around 560, after the reforms of Solon had failed to resolve class conflicts. Ejected and returned to power numerous times, he died in 527, leaving power to his sons.

PLATAEA: Greek city on the border between Attica and Boeotia.

PLUTARCH: Greek essayist and biographer of the late first and early second centuries AD who composed *Parallel Lives of the Greeks and Romans* as well as many short ethical treatises, dialogues, and speeches collectively known as the *Moralia*.

PNYX: Hill in Athens on which the Athenian Assembly met.

PORUS: Indian ruler of territories between the Hydaspes and Acesines rivers; Alexander's last great opponent, defeated in 326 at the Battle of the Hydaspes.

PTOLEMY, SON OF LAGUS: Boyhood friend of Alexander and member of the Companions, he held various minor commands during the Asian campaigns. After Alexander's death he established himself as ruler of Egypt, where he was crowned king in 305 and ruled as Ptolemy Soter ("Savior"). His battles with Demetrius and Antigonus eroded the power of their dynasty, though his defeat in the Battle of Gaza (306) was a severe setback. He participated in the Battle of Ipsus (301) on the winning side and died in old age in 283. His dynasty controlled Egypt for centuries.

PYTHIA, THE: Greek term for the priestess through whose mouth the oracular responses were given at Delphi (q.v.).

ROXANE: Iranian princess, daughter of Oxyartes (ruler of the so-called Sogdian Rock, a formidable stronghold). Alexander married her in 327, and she bore him a son, Alexander IV, after his father's death in 323. Cassander had both Roxane and her son killed in 310 or 309.

SACRED BAND: Elite infantry corps created at Thebes in the 370s, finally destroyed by the Macedonians at the Battle of Chaeronea in 338. The band consisted of 150 male homosexual couples, on the theory, propounded in Plato's *Republic*, that men would fight more vigorously if their lovers were fighting beside them.

SALAMIS: Island in the gulf offshore from Attica, site of the sea battle in which the Greek navy defeated the navy of the invading Persians in 480.

SAMOS: Island off the coast of Asia Minor not far from Miletus. A strong member of the Delian League, Samos tried to quit in 440 but was brought to heel by Pericles. In the second phase of the war, after 412, Samos became a major Athenian naval base.

SELEUCUS: A midlevel officer under Alexander the Great, he established himself in Babylon after Alexander's death but was forced out by Antigonus. With the help of Ptolemy he retook Babylon in 312 and began a long struggle with Antigonus and his son Demetrius. He helped defeat those two at the Battle of Ipsus in 301, bringing to bear a war corps of elephants he had acquired from the Maurya dynasty in India. He later married a daughter of Demetrius, but the alliance was an uneasy one, and Demetrius ended up his prisoner. His dynasty, the Seleucids, controlled much of Asia for more than two centuries.

SOGDIANA: One of the two "upper satrapies" of the Persian Empire (along with Bactria). Both were subdued by Alexander the Great in the years 330–327, at considerable cost.

SOLON: Athenian moralist and poet whose political role commenced (probably) in 594, when he was empowered to alter the constitution of Athens to address strife between rich and poor. He carved out a famously moderate path between the two factions, hoping Athens might avoid a tyranny (often the result of class strife). He traveled abroad after instituting these changes, though whether he visited Croesus in Lydia, as Herodotus represents, is doubtful. He lived long enough to see the tyranny he dreaded come into being, under Pisistratus in 561.

SPARTA: Leading Greek city in the Peloponnese and for centuries (until the rise of Athens) the military superpower of the Greek world. Its constitution preserved a monarchy (actually a diarchy, with two kings sharing rule) until well past the time when other Greek cities had rejected that institution. A system of military training and strict social discipline, the *agōgē*, was ascribed by Spartans to an early leader they called Lycurgus.

SPHACTERIA: Tiny island offshore of Pylos on the west coast of the Peloponnese, site of a Spartan defeat in 425 that resulted in a large contingent of prisoners being brought to Athens.

SPHODRIAS: Spartan general of the fourth century who led a failed raid on the Athenian port at Piraeus.

STRATĒGOS: "General," a military officer elected annually at Athens by a vote in the Assembly. Ten generals served at any one time, sometimes acting together as a board, other times leading separate expeditions or assignments. Because the *stratēgoi* were chosen from among the leading citizens, they also exercised great influence in the Assembly and other political bodies.

SUSA: One of the imperial capitals of Persia, and the only one known to Greek writers of the fifth century (Herodotus and Aeschylus). It was captured, with its vast wealth, by Alexander in 331.

SYRACUSE: Colony of Corinth and the most powerful of the Greek cities on the island of Sicily. By the 420s it had begun to threaten other Sicilian cities including allies of Athens, Leontini and Egesta among them. It became the main target of Athens's ill-fated expedition of 415–413, a campaign recounted in remarkable detail by Thucydides (books 6 and 7).

THEBES: Principal city of Boeotia and head of the Boeotian League. Though allied with Sparta in the Peloponnesian War, Thebes changed allegiance and leaned toward Athens in the postwar period. Thebes became the superpower of the Greek world in the 370s and 360s, thanks to the military innovations of Epaminondas and the generalship of Pelopidas. After teaming up with Athens in a last-ditch effort to stop Philip II of Macedon, Thebes was defeated by Philip II at the Battle of Chaeronea and thereafter secured by a Macedonian garrison. Finally Thebes was destroyed by Alexander the Great to quell a revolt in 335.

THEMISTOCLES: Athenian statesman in the early fifth century who charted the course that led to Athens becoming a naval power. Themistocles led the Athenian contingent of the Greek fleet at Salamis and engineered the Greek victory there almost single-handedly. Despite this victory, Themistocles later fell into disfavor at Athens, was ostracized, and fled to Asia, where he became a satrap of the Persian Empire.

THERAMENES: Athenian moderate politician and military leader, nicknamed Cothurnus after a kind of shoe that could fit either foot (from his habit of switching sides).

THERMOPYLAE: Narrow pass leading into central Greece from the north. In a battle in 480, a small Greek force, led by Leonidas and three hundred Spartans, defended the pass of Thermopylae against the invading Persian army. After a Greek guide revealed to the Persians a way around to the rear of the pass, the Spartans were trapped and entirely destroyed.

THE TEN THOUSAND: A mercenary army gathered by Cyrus the Younger in 401, as his principal means of unseating his brother, Artaxerxes II. The force included Xenophon, serving at first as a common soldier but later as commander after the entire leadership was wiped out by the Persians. After enduring a difficult march through Media and Armenia in harsh winter weather, most of the corps made it back to the Black Sea and regions settled by Greeks.

THE THIRTY: Oligarchs put in power at Athens by Sparta following Sparta's victory in the Peloponnesian War.

THIRTY YEARS' PEACE: Treaty that kept a kind of peace between the Athenians and the Lacedaemonians and their respective allies from 446/5 to 432/1 (approximately fourteen years), when the Spartans voted to go to war.

THRACE: Tribal region to the northwest of Macedonia, stretching across the northern Aegean to the Danube. Athens had strong strategic interest in Thrace and curried favor with its monarchs. Later the Thracians were subdued by Philip of Macedon and contributed a cavalry contingent to the Macedonian army.

THUCYDIDES: Athenian general and historian of the late fifth century, born about 460, exiled from Athens in 424 for a military lapse that led to the loss of Amphipolis from the Athenian Empire. His historical narrative *The Peloponnesian War,* partly or wholly written while in exile, covers the period 432–411 in remarkable detail. The date of his death is not known, but he certainly lived to see the defeat of Athens in 404.

TRIREME: Large Greek warship of the Classical period. A trireme carried a crew of two hundred, of which most were rowers, plus a few hoplites and officers. Triremes fought either by ramming each other at high speed or by placing themselves close enough to other vessels that the hoplites on board could fire off javelins, arrows, or slings.

XENOPHON: Athenian general, mercenary captain, historian, and essayist of the late fifth and early fourth centuries. In his late twenties he took part in the campaign of the Ten Thousand and was elected one of the army's leaders following the arrest of its general staff. He got most of the Ten Thousand home after a grueling march, later described in his work *Anabasis.* A confirmed Spartophile who was exiled by his native Athens, Xenophon served under Agesilaus in the 390s, then retired to an estate in the western Peloponnese, where most of his works were written. His *Agesilaus* and *Hellenica* are valuable but deeply flawed records of the times in which he lived. He returned to Athens before his death in the 350s.

XERXES: Persian king from 486 to 465. He commanded the great land-and-sea invasion of Greece in 480, resulting in the sacking of Athens and the terrible defeats at Salamis and Plataea. Herodotus portrays him as an unsteady and distracted ruler prone to being manipulated by his advisers.

HERODOTUS

HERODOTUS

(C. 485–C. 425 BC)

As Homer was to poetry, so Herodotus was to history: a writer of enormous scope and vision who, working from small, discrete stories largely circulated by word of mouth, created a monumental work unlike anything before it. And just as with Homer, Herodotus seemed, to later readers, to be a darling of the Muses: After his death the nine books into which his work was divided were given the names of the nine Muses, as though they had taken shape from divine inspiration.

For lack of any title or genre label to describe his creation, Herodotus introduced it to his audience with his declarative opening words: "This is the display of the historiē *of Herodotus of Halicarnassus." The Greek word* historiē *meant "inquiry" at the time Herodotus deployed it, but because of its prominence in his opening sentence, it took on new layers of meaning. Within a century, Aristotle would use it to mean "a written account of the past." Thus was the word "history," in the sense we give it today, created, at the same moment as the genre itself.*

Though he is today called a historian, Herodotus was much more than that. His work focuses on the wars between the Greek world and a vast Persian empire that stretched from the Aegean to what is now Pakistan and included Egypt as well. Those conflicts began in earnest in 499 BC, but Herodotus casts his eye further back in time, only reaching the start of hostilities at about the midpoint of his work. He has much else to discuss: the origins of great Asian monarchies and Greek tyrannies; the customs of various non-Greek peoples, especially the Egyptians, builders of an immensely old and complex civilization; the geography of the oikoumenē *or "inhabited world," the span of the earth known from human report; and above all the influence of the divine on human life, whether through dreams, oracles, natural phenomena, or the strange freaks of chance that we might chalk up to blind luck but which the Greeks always linked to the gods.*

The main story line of Herodotus' work, the Persian Wars as we call them, serves as a connecting thread on which many tales are hung, the units Herodotus calls logoi *("stories," "accounts," "discussions"). Some of these larger* logoi *contain smaller ones within them, as for example the* logos *of Croesus, king of Lydia, span-ning the first half of book 1. To put this monarch in his proper historical context, Herodotus first describes how his great-great-grandfather Gyges established his dynasty by seizing the Lydian throne, and how each successive king expanded Lyd-ian power. Then comes a dialogue between Croesus and Solon, an Athenian wise man, and, as a result of the arrogance Croesus there displayed, a family drama in-volving the king's ill-fated son. Only at this point, halfway into the Croesus* logos, *do we reach Lydia's attack on Persia, and the connection to our major theme—the rise and fall of the Persian Empire—begins to emerge.*

This loose, digressive structure defies our expectations for linear narrative. We seem to be in a "web" of stories, hitting "hyperlinks" everywhere that take us in new directions. In book 2 we veer off the main path to explore Egypt, a land thick with marvels, in enormous depth. Yet the main thrust of the work is always discernible: Egypt matters because the Persians conquered it in the 520s BC, another stage in their relentless growth. The same imperial drive will take us later to India, Arabia, Scythia, Thrace, indeed nearly every part of the world known to the Greeks. For each new region that falls to the Persian advance, Herodotus tells us all he knows about the people and their customs and notes any "wonders" of which he has heard. His work is thus a compendium of geography and anthropology as much as a nar-rative history.

There are other ways in which Herodotus does not behave as a historian "should." He repeats stories that he himself disbelieves, simply because they are going around—"to tell what is told" is a goal he at one point claims for himself. He puts speeches and dialogues in the mouths of historical actors, even at points where he cannot possibly have known what was said. He attributes events of global importance—a massive invasion, say, of one nation by another—to the personal or whimsical motives of an individual, not to the broader geopolitical factors we might look for today. For this reason he often seems to be writing something closer to myth than history, employing the same kind of thinking by which the Trojan War was traced to one man's abduction of one woman—Helen, the wife of Menelaus.

Yet Herodotus also recognizes a boundary between myth and history, and in his opening paragraphs he places himself squarely on the historical side. He declines to discuss the Trojan War, or other early accounts of East-West conflict, but moves to a starting point with "the man who I myself know was the first to begin unjust deeds against the Greeks"—namely, Croesus. The stress on personal knowledge—"I myself"—is important. Herodotus lived well after Croesus had died, but he could talk to his grandfather, perhaps even his father, about the fall of the Lydian king. Nearly all the events of the Histories *could be attested by eyewitnesses or by those who had talked with eyewitnesses in an older generation—that is, Herodotus heard* them either at first or at second hand. He could himself assess the reliability of his informants, sorting out which ones to trust and what motives each one had for distorting the record. He could make an "inquiry," the starting point of historical writing in the Greek world.

But Herodotus does not always stick to his own methodology. He sometimes accepts reports that can't be inquired into or expresses belief in things that can't be seen. When he speaks of the Hyperboreans—a legendary arctic race thought to dwell "beyond the North Wind"—he says that if such people exist, then there must be men beyond the South Wind too. So also in matters of religion: In cases where some thought the gods were at work but others looked to human or natural causes, Herodotus tended to side with the believers. When the question arises, at the court of Xerxes, whether dreams come from the divine or simply from our own minds, an experiment proves that they do have a divine source (see pp. 83–86 below). Perhaps more important than this pious conclusion, however, is the fact that Herodotus allows the question to be raised, and the experiment to be made, in the first place.

Even the gods can be interrogated in the world into which Herodotus ushers us. Croesus, whose logos comes first in the Histories, serves as a model in this respect as in so many others. When his fate seems to run counter to what the oracles had foretold, Croesus is given leave to ask Apollo to account for the gap and for the god's seeming abandonment of a generous worshipper. Remarkably, Apollo answers—not in verse, as an oracle normally would, but in plain prose, Herodotus' own medium. The reply satisfies Croesus, and Herodotus expects it will also satisfy us. Historical events can in the end be explained, even when the gods, and other mysterious forces, help steer them to their resolution.

THRACE

MACEDONIA

Abdera

Amphipolis

Methone
CHALCIDICE
Thasos
Samothrace
Chersonese
Lampsacus
Aigospotamos
Imbros
Abydos

Ainos

Larissa

Tenedos

MYSIA

Lemnos
Antandros

Dodona

EPIRUS

THESSALY
Pagasae
Lesbos
AEOLIS

Pharsalus

Aegean Sea
Mytilene

AETOLIA
BOEOTIA
Scyrus

Naupactus
Delphi
Thebes
Euboea
Chios
SARDIS
LYDIA

Plataea
Delion
IONIA

ACHAEA
Megara
Notion
Ephesus

ELIS
Corinth
ATHENS
Andros
Samos
Magnesia

Olympia
Mantinea
Argos
Piraeus
Tenos
Miletus
CARIA

Ionian
Sea
ARCADIA
Troezen
Keos

MESSENE
SPARTA
Paros
Naxos
Cos

LACONIA

Melos

Rhodes

Crete

Mediterranean Sea

Strymon

SELECTIONS FROM
HERODOTUS' *HISTORIES*

TRANSLATED BY SAMUEL SHIRLEY AND JAMES ROMM

A. HERODOTUS' INTRODUCTION

[1.1] This is the display of the inquiry of Herodotus of Halicarnassus, done so that human events may not become faded with time, and so that great and wondrous achievements, some put forward by Greeks and others by non-Greeks, may not lose their measure of fame. I include other things and the reason why they made war on one another.

[1.5.3] I'll go forward in my account by pointing out the man who I myself know was the first to begin unjust deeds against the Greeks. I'll recount equally the small and the great cities where men dwell, for many that were great long ago have since become small, and those that were great in my time were small before. I'll pay equal attention to both, since I know that human prosperity never stays long in the same place.

B. THE RISE AND FALL OF CROESUS, KING OF LYDIA (MID-SIXTH CENTURY BC) (*HISTORIES* 1.6–94)

[1.6] Croesus, king of Lydia, reigned over the peoples west of the river Halys, which flows from the south between the Syrians and the Paphlagonians and runs northward into the Black Sea.* He was the first foreigner, as far as we know, to have contact with the Greeks, subjugating some by forcing payment of tribute and forming friendships with others. He subjugated the Ionians, Aeolians, and Dorians who dwell on the Asian seaboard and made a treaty of friendship with the Spartans.† Before the time of Croesus' reign, all the Greeks were free.

---

* That is, Croesus ruled over the western portion of the Anatolian or Turkish peninsula.

† The Greek says "Lacedaemonians," meaning the people of Lacedaemon in the Peloponnese—the region that included, principally, the city of Sparta; our translations will use "Spartan" instead of this more cumbersome term. The Spartans were the military superpower of the Greek world and hence valuable allies for Croesus; Herodotus explains at 1.69, a passage not included in this volume, that the Spartans had been won over to friend-

[1.7] Now sovereignty over Lydia had once belonged to the descendants of Heracles, and I shall describe how it came to pass into the hands of the Mermnads, the ancestors of Croesus. The Heraclids* had held power for twenty-two generations, or 505 years, each son succeeding his father in turn, until the throne came down to Candaules, son of Myrsus.

[1.8] This Candaules was utterly devoted to his wife, whom he considered to be by far the most beautiful woman on earth. Among his bodyguard was a man named Gyges, who was the king's particular confidant, and Candaules not only discussed state matters with this man but expounded to him many praises of his wife's beauty. One day the king, who was destined to come to a bad end, spoke to Gyges thus: "Gyges, I am not sure that you fully believe me when I speak of my wife's beauty. Well then, since a man is inclined to trust his eyes more than his ears, I will arrange for you to see her naked." Gyges gave a cry of horror. "Master," he said, "what a shocking idea. Do you bid me look on my queen when she is naked? When a woman puts off her clothes, she puts off her modesty. We should obey the rules of morality devised for mankind ages ago, and one of these rules requires us to look only on what is our own. I am convinced that she is the fairest of women, and I beg you not to ask me to do what is wrong."

[1.9] Thus did he try to resist the king, dreading what harm might ensue for himself. But the king replied: "Be of good cheer, Gyges, and have no fear that I am making a trial of you, or that any injury will befall you from my wife. I will surely contrive that she won't know that you have seen her. I will station you in our bedroom behind the door as it opens. When I have entered, my wife too will follow me to bed. Near the door is a chair. On this she will lay her garments one by one as she takes them off. You will have plenty of opportunity to see her. Then, when she walks to the bed with her back to you, take care to slip through the door without her seeing you."

[1.10] Gyges made ready to do what he could not avoid. Candaules brought him into the bedroom and was soon followed by the queen.

---

ship with Croesus by a gift of Lydian gold. The "Ionians, Aeolians, and Dorians" referred to here are the Greek colonists who had settled the coast of Turkey (often called Asia by Herodotus), who, being far less powerful and also near neighbors of the Lydians, were easy prey.

* The suffix "-ids" means "descendants of," hence "Heraclids" = "descendants of Heracles." Herodotus believed that the god Heracles had sired children by a Lydian slave girl and had thus begotten a line of kings.

Gyges watched her enter and place her clothes on the chair, and when she turned her back to him and moved toward the bed, he quietly slipped out. But the queen caught sight of him. Realizing what her husband had done, she neither gave vent to her shame by screaming nor gave any other indication that there was anything amiss, but she resolved to take revenge on Candaules. For with the Lydians, as with almost all foreign peoples, it is reckoned a shameful thing even for a man to be seen naked.

[1.11] For the time being she gave no sign and kept quiet. But as soon as morning came, she made ready those of her servants whom she knew to be most devoted to her and summoned Gyges. Not suspecting that she knew anything of what had happened, he came at her bidding, for it was quite usual for him to be called to attend on the queen. "Gyges," she said, "I offer you the choice of two courses that are open to you, and you may choose whichever you please. Either kill Candaules and take the throne, with me as your wife, or you must die on the spot, so that never again will you give such unquestioning obedience to Candaules as to see what is forbidden. Either he who plotted this must die, or you, who have broken our laws by beholding me naked."

Gyges was at first astounded and fell to begging the queen not to force him to make such a dreadful choice. But his pleadings were in vain, and he realized that he was, in truth, faced with the necessity either of slaying his master or of losing his own life. He chose to live. "Since you compel me against my will to kill the king," he said, "come, tell me how we are to attack him." "The assault will come from the very place where he displayed my nakedness," she said, "and you will strike while he is asleep."

[1.12] There was no escape possible for Gyges; either he or Candaules must perish. When night fell, he followed the queen into the bedroom. She gave him a dagger and concealed him behind the very same door. Then, when Candaules was asleep, Gyges slipped out of his hiding place, struck, and took possession of both queen and kingdom. [1.13] His hold on the throne was confirmed by the oracle at Delphi. For when the Lydians, angered at the fate of Candaules, took up arms, and when civil strife seemed inevitable between Gyges' partisans and the rest of the population, they agreed to consult the oracle and abide by its decision as to whether Gyges should rule or the throne be restored to the Heraclids. The answer favored Gyges, but the Priestess* also added this: that the

---

* Oracles at Delphi were thought to originate from Apollo but were actually spoken by a priestess, sometimes called the Pythia.

Heraclids would be avenged in the fifth generation from Gyges. This prophecy was disregarded by the Lydians and their kings until it was fulfilled.

———

Once in power, Gyges began to make forays against his Greek neighbors to the west, especially the Ionian city of Miletus, the principal Greek settlement in Asia Minor. After his death his son Ardys and grandson Sadyattes continued to harass Miletus and other Greek cities until the throne at last came to Alyattes, father of Croesus, about 600 BC.

———

[1.17] Alyattes used to make annual inroads into Milesian territory in the following way. He made his invasions when the crops were ripe, accompanied by the sound of pipes, harps, and flutes. He never destroyed the farmhouses or burned them or tore off their doors but left them undamaged, destroying only the trees and crops before withdrawing. It was pointless to lay siege to the city because the Milesians commanded the sea. Now the reason why he refrained from demolishing the dwellings was this: so that the Milesians would be encouraged to sow seed and work the land, thereby providing a source of plunder for his future invasions.

[1.18–19] This went on for eleven years, in the course of which the Milesians were twice defeated in battle. But in the twelfth year the burning of the crops had an unusual sequel. As soon as the crops were set on fire, a strong wind drove the flames onto the temple of Athena at Assesus, which burned down to the ground. At the time this caused little stir, but when the army returned to Sardis, Alyattes fell ill. As his illness continued, he sent messengers to the Delphic oracle to inquire about it, either on somebody's advice or on his own initiative. The Priestess refused to make any reply to the messengers until the Lydians should rebuild the temple of Athena of Assesus in Milesian territory. This is what I myself have gathered from the Delphians, but the Milesians add the following details to the story: They say that Periander of Corinth, a close friend of Thrasybulus who at that time was ruler over Miletus, got to know of the oracle's reply and sent a message giving Thrasybulus prior information, so that he could take appropriate measures.

[1.21] Alyattes, on receiving the oracle's reply, sent a messenger to Miletus, proposing a truce that would last until he could rebuild the temple. Anticipating through his foreknowledge what Alyattes was likely to do, Thrasybulus adopted the following plan: Gathering together in the public square all the grain in the city from both public and private sources, he instructed everyone, at a given signal, to start drinking and holding parties. His purpose was this: to induce the messenger reporting to Alyattes to make mention of the immense pile of grain and the high spirits of the populace. And this, indeed, was what came about. The messenger marked what was going on, delivered his message, and returned to Sardis. A peace treaty was then signed, and it was for this reason alone, as I judge, that Alyattes, expecting to find the Milesians oppressed by famine and the populace reduced to extreme suffering, was informed by the messenger that the situation was quite the reverse of what he had thought.

Thereafter peace was established, the two sides becoming friends and allies. Alyattes built two temples instead of one to Athena of Assesus and recovered from his illness. This was the way that Alyattes concluded his war with the Milesians and their leader, Thrasybulus.

[1.23–24] This Periander, the one who gave information about the oracle to Thrasybulus, was the son of Cypselus and ruler over Corinth.* During his lifetime there occurred a very great wonder, as the Corinthians say (and the Lesbians agree with them): Arion of Methymna, by far the foremost lyre-player of his period—the man who first, as far as we know, composed the dithyramb, gave it its name, and taught it at Corinth†—was carried on a dolphin's back to Taenarum. Arion, they say, after spending a great part of his life at Periander's court, felt an urge to sail to Italy and Sicily. There he amassed a great fortune and eventually decided to return to Corinth. Having faith in Corinthians above all others, he hired a Corinthian vessel to sail from Tarentum. But when they were at sea, the crew formed a conspiracy to throw Arion overboard and seize his wealth. Realizing what they were about, he gave them his money and begged for his life. But the sailors, unmoved, ordered him to take his own life if he wished to be buried on land, or else to leap overboard forthwith. Faced with this painful dilemma, Arion asked the crew to

---

* Here and elsewhere in this volume, the word "ruler" translates the Greek *tyrannos*, a term that has no good English equivalent. A *tyrannos* holds absolute power in a Greek city, but his authority is not grounded either in tradition or in constitutional legitimacy, as is that of a king. Usually a *tyrannos* wields power and hands it on to his sons only because he has enough armed support to defend himself against any challenges. But that does not make him a despot, as the English word "tyrant," derived from *tyrannos*, might imply. Indeed, many such "rulers" were beloved by their fellow citizens, especially the lower classes, whose cause they often championed. Periander of Corinth is the first of several Greek *tyrannoi* we meet in Herodotus' work; Polycrates of Samos is another (see 3.39ff.).

† The dithyramb is a kind of choral poetry especially used for hymns in honor of the god Dionysus.

allow him to stand on the quarterdeck, dressed in his full musician's robes, and to sing for the last time, after which he undertook to do away with himself. The sailors, pleased at the prospect of hearing a performance by the best musician in the world, gathered amidships, and Arion, donning his full attire, took up his lyre, stood on the quarterdeck, sang a stirring air, and then flung himself into the sea, fully robed just as he was.

The sailors continued their voyage to Corinth, but the story goes that a dolphin swam up, took Arion on his back, and carried him to Taenarum. Arion reached land, made his way to Corinth in his musician's attire, and related what had befallen him. The incredulous Periander would not release him but kept him under strict guard while he watched for the crew's arrival. When at last they did arrive, he summoned them and asked them if they had any news of Arion. "Yes," they replied, "he is in Italy; we left him safe and well at Tarentum." Thereupon Arion made his appearance, attired just as he had been when he leapt overboard. The sailors were dumbfounded and could make no further denial. This is the story as told by the people of Corinth and Lesbos, and there is at Taenarum an offering made by Arion, a small bronze figure of a man riding a dolphin.

———

Alyattes having died, Croesus now came to the throne of Lydia, the man who, as Herodotus has claimed (1.5), was "the first . . . to harm the Greeks."

Croesus is said to have been thirty-five years old at the time of his accession.

———

[1.28–30] Under Croesus' rule nearly all the peoples west of the river Halys were added to the Lydian empire, except the Cilicians and Lycians. When Croesus had subjugated all these and added them to his empire, there came to his capital, Sardis, then at the height of its wealth, all the most distinguished teachers of that period throughout the length and breadth of Greece, and one of these was Solon of Athens. The Athenians had entrusted to him the task of drawing up a code of laws for them, having bound themselves with mighty oaths to make no change in it for a period of ten years without his permission. Solon carried out this task and then went abroad, so as not to be compelled to alter any of his laws—but giving out as a pretext that he wanted to see something of the world. First he visited the court of Amasis, ruler of Egypt, and then the court of Croesus at Sardis.*

———

* Solon is a historical figure who did indeed draw up new laws for Athens, probably in 594, and who might well have traveled the world thereafter. That he actually met with

Solon - Athenian poet

He was welcomed and hospitably entertained at Croesus' palace, and in three or four days' time, at Croesus' bidding, servants escorted Solon around the royal treasuries to display the magnificence of Croesus' wealth. When Solon had had the opportunity to view and examine all that was there, Croesus said to him, "My Athenian friend, much talk of you has reached us, both in respect of your wisdom and of your extensive travels in search of knowledge. Now I have a great desire to put this question to you: Who is the happiest man you have ever seen?" He was, of course, expecting to be named the happiest of humankind, but Solon was not flattered. With strict regard for the truth he replied, "O king, it was Tellus the Athenian." Croesus, amazed at that reply, asked with some sharpness, "And how do you arrive at this judgment?" "In the first place," said Solon, "living at a time when his native city was flourishing, he had fine, handsome children and got to see children born to *them,* all of whom survived. Secondly, after enjoying a prosperous life, as we judge of prosperity, he came to a most glorious end. In a battle between the Athenians and their neighbors of Eleusis, he played his part in the battle, put the enemy to flight, and died most nobly. The Athenians granted him a state funeral at the very place where he fell and paid him great honor."

[1.31] Solon's account of the many blessings of Tellus spurred Croesus on to ask who it was whom Solon judged the happiest of men after Tellus, doubtless expecting that he, Croesus, would at least be placed second. But Solon replied, "Two young men of Argos, Cleobis and Biton. Their means were quite sufficient for their needs, and they were blessed with remarkable physical strength. They were both prizewinners in athletic contests, and the following tale is told of them: When the Argives were holding the festival of Hera, it was an urgent religious duty for the mother of these men to be conveyed to the temple in a special carriage, but the oxen had not returned from the fields in time to pull it. In this emergency the two sons got into the harnesses and pulled the wagon themselves, with their mother aboard, a distance of almost six miles to the temple. After this remarkable feat, witnessed as it was by the entire assembly, their lives came to a most wonderful close, whereby the deity revealed how much better for humankind is death than life. The Argives were crowding around the two young men, congratulating them on their

---

Croesus, though, who came to power around 560, is doubted. The scene that follows should therefore be read not as a record of fact, even though it involves two historical figures, but as a kind of philosophic dialogue.

strength, and the women were rejoicing with their mother on having such sons. Overjoyed at the public recognition of their achievement, their mother stood before the statue of the goddess and prayed to her to grant Cleobis and Biton, the sons who had brought her such honor, the greatest blessing that can befall mortals. After her prayer, when they had sacrificed and feasted, the two sons lay down to sleep in the temple and never rose again. They were finished. The Argives had statues made of them and set them up at Delphi—to show that they honored them first among humankind."

[1.32] To these, then, did Solon award second place for happiness. In his exasperation Croesus said, "My Athenian friend, do you so despise my happy state that you rank me beneath common folk?"

To this Solon replied, "Croesus, you are questioning one who understands how the divine power is envious of human good fortune and never leaves it long undisturbed. Over a lengthy period of time one sees much that one would wish not to see and undergoes much one would wish not to. Let us take seventy years as the space of a man's life. This period, if you disregard the intercalary months, contains 25,200 days. If you add a month every other year so as to make the seasons come around at their due time, you have thirty-five extra months, that is, 1,050 days. So the full total comes to 26,250 days.* Of these days not a single one is like another in what it brings forth. So you see, Croesus, the extent to which people are at the mercy of chance. I hold you to be exceedingly rich and the ruler over many peoples. But I will not answer your question until I learn that you have reached the end of your life in the same state of happiness. The man who is immensely rich is no better off than the man who just makes ends meet, unless he has the good fortune to reach the end of his life in the same happy state. Many wealthy men are unlucky, while many in moderate circumstances are blessed by fortune. The man who is very rich but unlucky has only two advantages over the man who is merely lucky, but the latter has many advantages over the former: The rich man is better able to fulfill his desires and to cope with disaster when it befalls him, but the poor and lucky trumps him: Though he cannot manage desires and disasters as easily, his good luck dispels the need to do so, for he avoids injury, disease, and calamity and is blessed in children and good-looking. If, beyond these boons, he also comes to a good end of life, then

---

* Intercalary months were inserted by the Greeks to realign their lunar calendar with the solar, though they did not occur quite as often as Herodotus (or Solon) here supposes.

this is the man you are seeking, the man who merits the title 'happy.' But until his death you should withhold the title 'happy'; he is merely temporarily fortunate.

"No human being can possess all blessings, just as no single country can produce all that it needs; it will possess one thing and lack another. Similarly, no man is entirely self-sufficient; he will surely lack something. But whoever possesses the greatest number of blessings and retains them until he reaches the end, and then dies happily, he is the one, in my opinion, who should be awarded the title. In every matter you should look to the ending. To many men the god grants but a glimpse of blessedness, only to bring them to utter ruin."

[1.33] This view found no favor with Croesus, and he contemptuously dismissed Solon, regarding as a fool a man who urged him to look to the ending of every matter and who paid no heed to present prosperity.

[1.34] After Solon's departure, terrible punishment, sent by the gods, fell upon Croesus, probably because he considered himself the happiest of men. It began with a dream that seemed to indicate that disaster was about to befall his son. Croesus had two sons, of whom one was a cripple, being deaf and mute, while the other, named Atys, surpassed all other young men of his time. Croesus dreamed that Atys would be killed by a blow from an iron weapon. When he awoke and reflected on his terrifying dream, he took action. He arranged a marriage for his son and no longer permitted him to take the field with the Lydian soldiers whom he used to command. He banished all warlike weapons—javelins, spears, and so on—from the men's quarters and had them gathered together in the women's apartments, lest any weapon hanging on the wall should chance to fall on his son.

[1.35] While he was busy with arrangements for the marriage, there came to Sardis a man in the grip of misfortune, with blood on his hands, a Phrygian by birth and of royal lineage. Presenting himself before Croesus, this man begged the king to cleanse him from the blood-guilt according to the laws of the land, and this Croesus did. (The Lydian method of purification is very similar to that of the Greeks.)* After the ceremony, Croesus questioned the man. "Stranger, who are you? From what part of

* According to ancient religious practices, a murderer, especially one who kills his own kin, becomes stained with pollution or blood-guilt and cannot take part in normal social relations until he is ritually cleansed or "purified." Note the parenthetic sentence in which Herodotus opportunely inserts an anthropological note concerning Lydian purification rites.

Phrygia do you come to seek my protection? What man or woman have you slain?" "Sire," replied the man, "I am the son of Gordias, whose father was Midas, and my name is Adrastus.* I accidentally slew my own brother, and I have been driven into exile, destitute." "You are descended from a family with friendly relations to mine," said Croesus, "and you have come among friends, where you shall lack for nothing. I urge you to bear your misfortune as best you can." Thus did Adrastus come to reside with Croesus.

[1.36] At about this time there was a monstrous wild boar on Mount Olympus in Mysia. Issuing forth from its mountain lair it used to ravage the Mysians' crops. Many an expedition did the Mysians make against it, but inflicted no injury on it while themselves sustaining many injuries. Finally their messengers sought audience with Croesus and spoke as follows: "Sire, a monster of a boar has appeared in our land, destroying our crops. Our efforts to catch it have all been in vain. Now we beg you to send us your son with a chosen band of young men and hunting dogs, so that we may drive it out of our land." Bearing in mind his dream, Croesus answered with these words: "Let there be no more mention of our son. I could not send him because he is newly married and has much to occupy him. However, I will send you a select band of men with hunting equipment, and I will urge them to show the utmost zeal in ridding your land of this beast."

[1.37] The Mysians were all satisfied with this answer, but then Atys, who had heard of the Mysians' request, came in. Seeing that Croesus declined to send him, Atys spoke to him as follows: "Father, it was once thought most noble and most honorable for me to win renown in war and hunting. Now you have cut me off from both these pursuits, although you have seen no cowardice or lack of spirit in me. What will people think of me when I appear in public? How will the citizens regard me, how will my bride regard me? What kind of man will she think she has married? Either let me take part in the hunt or give me reason for your refusal."

[1.38] "My son," said Croesus, "it is not because I have seen cowardice or any other fault in you that I act in this way. It is because of a dream I had that you had not long to live, and that you would perish by an iron weapon. It was that dream that made me hasten your wedding and makes me reluctant to send you off on this enterprise. I am taking these precau-

---

* The name Adrastus is significant; one possible meaning of it is "he who cannot be escaped."

tions so I may keep you out of death's reach during my lifetime. You are my only son, for I cannot look on that other one, with his defect, as my son."

[1.39–40] "It is understandable, Father," replied Atys, "that you should take precautions after being visited by such a dream. But there is a point in that dream that has escaped your notice, and it is not improper for me to mention it. You say that the dream indicated that I would be killed by an iron weapon. But what sort of hands does a boar have? How can it use an iron weapon? Had the dream foretold that I would be killed by a boar's tusk or the like, you would be doing your duty. But it is a weapon that is in question, and since I shall not be fighting against men, let me go." "My son," replied Croesus, "I own myself vanquished in the matter of the dream's interpretation, and, being vanquished, I change my decision and permit you to go to the hunt."

[1.41–43] Thereupon the king sent for Adrastus the Phrygian and said to him, "When you came to me, Adrastus, smitten by dire disaster—for which I do not reproach you—I cleansed you, received you into my household, and provided for all your needs. Now I call upon you to re-quite good with good. I charge you to be my son's guardian when he goes forth to this hunt, to protect him against robbers or evildoers who may come upon you. Furthermore, you too have the duty of going where you may win distinction by your deeds. That is your heritage, and you do not lack strength." "Sire," replied Adrastus, "I would not normally wish to go on this expedition. It is not proper for one who is smitten with misfortune to seek the company of more fortunate young men, nor do I desire it, and I would hold back on many accounts. But since you ask me to do so and it is my duty to please you—for I owe you a great debt of gratitude— I am ready. Your son, whom you bid me protect, shall be unharmed as far as his protector can ensure it, and you may look for his safe return." Such was Adrastus' answer, after which the party set out with a chosen band of men and dogs. They came to Olympus, sought out the boar, sur-rounded it, and hurled their spears. It was then that the stranger named Adrastus, the man who had been purified from blood-guilt, hurling his spear missed his mark and hit Croesus' son; struck by an iron blade, Atys fulfilled the prophecy of the dream.

[1.44] A messenger hastened to tell the father of his son's fate. The shock of his son's death was dreadful but was made more horrible by the fact that he had been killed by one whom Croesus himself had purified of blood-guilt. In the excess of his grief Croesus called upon Zeus as the god of purification, asking him to bear witness to his sufferings at the hands of the stranger whom he had purified; he called upon Zeus as the god of the hearth, because in welcoming the stranger into his home he had unwittingly entertained the slayer of his son; he called upon Zeus as the god of comradeship, in that the man whom he had charged to guard his son had been found to be his greatest enemy.

[1.45] Soon the Lydians arrived, bearing the body and followed by the slayer. Standing before the body he submitted himself to Croesus, stretching forth his hands and bidding Croesus to slaughter him on top of the corpse. To crown his previous trouble, he said, he had ruined the man who had cleansed him, and he could no longer bear to live.

At these words, in spite of his own domestic sorrow, Croesus took pity on Adrastus. "Since you condemn yourself to death," he said, "justice makes no further demands on you. You are not to blame for this calamity, except that your unwitting hand did the deed. No, it was some god, who long ago gave me warning of what was to be."

So Croesus buried his son with fitting ceremony. But when all was quiet about the grave, Adrastus, son of Gordias, and grandson of Midas, the man who had destroyed his own brother and then had destroyed he who had granted him purification, knowing himself to be the most ill-fated of humankind, slew himself upon the tomb.

[1.46–47] For two years Croesus continued in deep mourning for his son and was roused from grief only by the rapidly increasing power of the Persians on his eastern border, a power founded by Astyages, son of Cyaxares, and greatly increased by Cyrus, son of Cambyses.* It occurred to Croesus to take the initiative by attacking the Persians before they could grow even stronger; in pursuit of this plan, Croesus contrived to make trial of the various oracles in both Greece and Libya. To this end, he dispatched messengers to the oracles at Delphi, at Abae in Phocis, at Dodona, to the oracles of Amphiaraus and Trophonius, to the oracle of Branchidae in Milesia, and, not content with Greek oracles, to the oracle of Ammon in Libya. He sent these messengers as a test of the knowledge of the oracles: If one oracle was found to know the truth, then he would send a second time to ask if he should undertake a campaign against the

---

* The Persians at last enter the narrative; soon they will become its primary characters. The war between Croesus of Lydia and Cyrus of Persia is here described as an episode of Lydian history, but later in book 1 (108ff.) Herodotus will deal in more detail with Cyrus, treated this time as the founder of the Persian Empire.

Persians. These messengers were instructed to consult the different oracles on the hundredth day after leaving Sardis and to inquire what Croesus, King of Lydia, was doing at that moment. They were to write down the reply and bring it straight back to Croesus. What the rest of the oracles replied is not told by any of my sources, but at Delphi, as soon as the Lydians arrived in the enclosure and put their question to the god, the Pythia said as follows, speaking in hexameter verse:

> *I can count the grains of sand on the beach, and I can measure the sea.*
> *I understand the speech of the dumb, and I hear the voiceless.*
> *There has come to my nostrils the odor of the hard-shelled tortoise*
> *Boiling together with lamb's flesh in a brazen cauldron,*
> *With a base of bronze and a bronze cover.*

[1.48–50] These words the Lydians recorded and carried back to Sardis. At last all the replies came back to Croesus, who opened and read them, and it was the Delphic reply that he accepted with deep reverence, declaring that it was the only true oracle in the world, for after dispatching his messengers Croesus had devised an action least open to guesswork. On the appointed day he had cut up a tortoise and a lamb and boiled them together in a brazen cauldron with a brazen lid. Croesus now proceeded to offer the most sumptuous sacrifices to Apollo of Delphi.

[1.53–54]* The messengers who conveyed these gifts were to put the following question to the oracle: "Croesus, King of Lydia and other nations, convinced that you are the only true oracle in the world, has sent you these gifts and asks you if he should march against the Persians, and also whether he should make allies of some other army." In reply the oracle prophesied that if Croesus marched against the Persians he would destroy a great empire. As to an alliance, he should seek the friendship of the most powerful of the Greeks. Croesus was overjoyed at this reply, confident that he would destroy the power of Cyrus. He bestowed further presents on Delphi, two gold staters for every citizen, having first inquired how many there were. In return the Delphians granted to Croesus and to all Lydians, in perpetuity, the right to become citizens of Delphi, exemption from taxes, priority in access to the oracle, and front seats at all state functions.

---

* A lengthy catalog of Croesus' offerings at Delphi has been omitted here.

[1.55–56] Being now eager to extract full value from an oracle of whose genuineness he was firmly convinced, Croesus sent one more question— would his reign be a long one? The Priestess made the following reply:

When a mule shall sit on the Median throne, then stay not,
Tender-footed Lydian, but flee by the many-pebbled stream
Of Hermus, and think no shame of being a coward.

This reply gave Croesus more satisfaction than any other. Was it likely that a mule would become king of the Medes?

[1.71] Croesus, having missed the meaning of the oracle, now prepared to invade Cappadocia,* confident that he could destroy the power of Cyrus and his Persians. While he was making these preparations a certain Lydian named Sandanis, already renowned for his wisdom, gave him the following advice, thereby greatly increasing his reputation with the Lydians. "Sire," he said, "you are preparing to fight against men who are so poor that they dress in leather, breeches and all. Their country is so rough that they eat what they can manage to get, never as much as they want. They have no wine to drink, only water. They have no luxuries, not even figs for dessert. If you conquer them, what will you take from them, seeing that they have nothing? If they conquer you, think what you will lose. Once they have tasted our good things, they will hold on to them and will not ever let go. Indeed, as it is, I am grateful to the gods for not putting it into the minds of the Persians to attack the Lydians."† Croesus rejected this advice, yet Sandanis was right on one point. The Persians had no luxuries of any sort before they conquered Lydia.

[1.73–74] Croesus made the invasion of Cappadocia because he wanted to extend his territories and, more important, because he trusted the oracle. But there was this further reason—he wanted to take revenge on Cyrus on behalf of Astyages. Astyages, formerly king of Media, had been conquered and held in subjugation by Cyrus.‡ Astyages was Croesus'

---

* Cappadocia is the eastern portion of the Anatolian peninsula, across the river Halys from Croesus' realm. It was at this time part of Persian territory.

† Another thematic keynote of the text is sounded here: the contrast between wealthy, advanced, luxury-loving aggressors and the poorer, tougher, hardier nations they attack. Though the Persians here fall into the latter category, they will shortly develop the attributes of the former, as Sandanis here predicts.

‡ The story of Cyrus' overthrow of Astyages will be told at length by Herodotus further on in book 1 (see below, 1.107ff.).

brother-in-law, and the marriage connection came about in this strange way: A band of Scythians, a nomadic people, left their country as a result of internal strife and immigrated to Media. They were at first welcomed by Cyaxares, at that time ruler over Media, who treated them kindly as suppliants. He even entrusted to them the education of some boys, who they were to teach their language and the use of the bow. As time went on, the Scythians, who continually went out hunting and returned with game, on one occasion returned empty-handed. Cyaxares, a man of quick temper, received them with harsh words and abuse. Resenting this undeserved ill treatment, the Scythians resolved to kill one of their pupils, chop him up, prepare the pieces like game, serve them to Cyaxares as a side dish, and then make their escape to the court of Alyattes at Sardis. And that is indeed what happened. Cyaxares and his guests ate some of the meat. The Scythians escaped to Alyattes and sought his protection. Cyaxares demanded their return. Alyattes refused, and war broke out between Lydia and Media. It lasted five years, with victory going first to one side, then to the other. After all this indecisive fighting, in the sixth year, there was a battle during which day suddenly turned into night. (This change from daylight to darkness had been foretold to the Ionian Greeks by Thales of Miletus, who even fixed the year in which it did in fact occur.)* When the Lydians and the Medes saw day turn into night, they became awestruck and broke off the engagement, and both sides became anxious to make peace. Certain mediators (Syennesis the Cilician and Labynetus the Babylonian) were responsible for bringing about a reconciliation and for making a peace treaty reinforced by a marriage connection. These men persuaded Alyattes, king of Lydia and father of Croesus, to give his daughter in marriage to Astyages, Cyaxares' son, for agreements do not usually remain strong unless backed up by strong assurances. (These nations have the same form of oath-taking as the Greeks, but in addition they make an incision in the skin of their arms and lick each other's blood.)

[1.75] I will explain further on why Cyrus had overthrown, and now was holding prisoner, his grandfather Astyages. But it was this insult that Croesus held against Cyrus, leading him to ask the oracle whether he should attack the Persians; and when he received a double-edged answer, he assumed the oracle was on his side and invaded Persian territory.

---

* Modern astronomers have fixed two possible dates for this eclipse, one in May 585 and the other in September 582. The idea that a Greek scientist had enough skill to predict a solar eclipse, at this early stage, is remarkable but not unthinkable. Thales was a legendary wise man of Greek lore, like Solon; another anecdote about his cleverness is related below.

When Croesus reached the river Halys, he crossed it, in my opinion, by the existing bridges. But there is a version widespread in Greece that it was Thales of Miletus who took the army across. They say that the bridges did not exist at this time, and that Thales, who was present in Croesus' camp, solved the difficulty by splitting the river into two channels. This he did by digging a deep crescent-shaped channel from a point above the camp around to the rear of the camp, so that the river ran for a space in two channels, each of which could be forded. Some even say that the river was entirely rerouted and the old channel left dry. But this I cannot accept; for how would the army have crossed again on their return journey?*

[1.76] Be that as it may, Croesus crossed the river with his army and reached the district called Pteria in Cappadocia. He ravaged the properties of the Syrians who lived there, captured the town of the Pterians, enslaved the inhabitants, seized the outlying settlements, and drove out the Syrians, though they were uninvolved in the quarrel.

Cyrus meanwhile had assembled his army and marched to meet Croesus, recruiting more men on his way. Before marching out he had already sent messages in an attempt to persuade the Ionians to throw off their allegiance to Croesus, but the Ionians had not heeded him. When he had encamped opposite Croesus, the two armies met in a sharp struggle. There were heavy losses on both sides, but the result was indecisive, and night broke off the engagement.

[1.77–78] Croesus' army was somewhat inferior in number to Cyrus' forces, and it was to this that he attributed his lack of success. When Cyrus did not advance to attack on the following day, Croesus decided to withdraw to Sardis. He intended to reinforce his army by calling on his allies, the Egyptians (for he had made an alliance with Amasis, king of Egypt),† and also the Babylonians (for he had made an alliance with these too, who were at this time ruled by Labynetus), and the Spartans. These were to join him at an appointed time, and then he proposed to wait until the winter was over and attack Cyrus in the following spring. So he sent out messengers, requesting his allies to assemble at Sardis in four months'

---

* It is noteworthy that Herodotus retells the story of Thales' engineering feat, in two variations, though he himself deems it unreliable.

† Amasis will become an important character in books 2 and 3 (see below, 2.162–74 and 3.39–43). The alliance between him and Croesus demonstrates that the rapid growth of Cyrus' power had scared all the other Near Eastern powers into aligning their interests against him.

time, and meanwhile he disbanded his mercenaries, for he did not imagine that Cyrus would venture to march on Sardis after the even fortunes of the recent battle.

At this time an unusual incident occurred. Snakes swarmed in the suburbs of Sardis, and horses, leaving their customary pastures, came and devoured them. Croesus regarded this as an omen, as indeed it was, and he sent messengers to Telmessus, where there were seers skilled in interpretation. These messengers were told the significance of the omen, but they had no opportunity to report back to Croesus, who became a prisoner before they could complete the return voyage to Sardis. The interpretation of the Telmessian seers, which they gave before knowing that Croesus was captured, was as follows: Snakes were natives of the soil, horses were beasts of war and foreigners. Croesus must expect the coming of a foreign army that would subdue the natives of Sardis.

[1.79] When Croesus retired toward Sardis after the Battle of Pteria, Cyrus found out that he was going to disband his army. So he took counsel and resolved that his best plan was to march on Sardis as swiftly as possible before the Lydian forces could gather again. No sooner said than done, and Cyrus made such good speed that he reached Sardis as his own messenger.* This unexpected development put Croesus in a dilemma, but he nevertheless led out his Lydians to battle, for at this time there were no braver nor stouter warriors than the Lydians, nor better horsemen.

[1.80] The armies met on a level plain before Sardis. When Cyrus viewed the battle-array, he was very apprehensive of the Lydian cavalry, and he adopted the suggestion made to him by a certain Mede named Harpagus. He gathered together all his camels that were used as pack-animals to carry stores and provisions, unloaded them, and mounted men on their backs to act as cavalry. These he ordered to advance against Croesus' cavalry, to be followed by the infantry, while his own cavalry brought up the rear. The reason for this maneuver was the instinctive fear that camels inspire in horses, who cannot endure the sight or smell of them. In this way the Lydians' cavalry, their greatest source of confidence, would be rendered useless. Having made these dispositions, Cyrus gave a general order to his army to kill all the Lydians they encountered except Croesus, whom he wanted taken alive even if he offered resistance.

---

* A colorful phrase, meaning that he arrived so swiftly that no advance report had preceded him.

Cyrus:
Persian
leader?

When battle was joined, as soon as the Lydian horses smelled and saw the camels, they turned and fled, and Croesus found his hopes dashed to the ground. But there was no cowardice on the part of the Lydians. Seeing what was happening, they leapt from the saddle and fought as infantry. There were heavy losses on both sides, but finally the Lydians were forced to give way and retreat within their walls, where they were besieged by the Persians.

[1.81] Thus began the siege of Sardis, and Croesus, believing it would be a lengthy affair, sent messages from the besieged city to his allies, this time begging for assistance, not in four months' time but immediately, to relieve the siege. He applied to all his allies, among them the Spartans.

[1.82] The Spartans were at this time engaged in a quarrel with Argos over some border territory called Thyreae, which had belonged to Argos but had been cut off and seized by the Spartans. The Argives marched out to recover it, and a conference was held at which it was decided that the fighting should be restricted to three hundred men on each side and Thyreae should belong to the victors. The main body of each army should not stay to watch the fighting, but retire each to its own homeland, so as to avoid the temptation of coming to the assistance of their own men if they were being defeated. On these terms they retired, and the chosen three hundred on either side joined the battle.

So equally balanced was the contest that out of six hundred men only three were left alive—two Argives, Alcenor and Chromius, and one Spartan, Othryades; these survived only because night fell. The two Argives hastened back to Argos, claiming victory, but the Spartan Othryades remained on the field of battle, stripping the dead and carrying back their spoils to the Spartan camp.

On the following day both sides returned to discuss the outcome. For a while both sides claimed victory, the Argives because they had the greater number of survivors, and the Spartans because, while the Argives had run away, the Spartans' own man had remained on the battlefield and stripped the dead. The argument led to blows, and then to a general engagement in which both sides suffered heavy losses, with the Spartans finally victorious. From that day onward the Argives, who were previously required to wear their hair long, began cutting it short and made a vow that no Argive man should wear long hair, nor any Argive woman wear gold jewelry, until Thyreae was reclaimed. Meanwhile the Spartans did the opposite. They began wearing their hair long, which had not been their custom before. It is said that the single Spartan survivor of the three hundred, being ashamed to return to Sparta after the death of his companions, killed himself there at Thyreae.

[1.83] Such were the circumstances in which the Spartans found themselves when the messenger from Sardis arrived, seeking assistance for the besieged Croesus.* Nevertheless, when the Spartans heard his message, they were eager to send help. But by the time they had completed their preparations and the ships were ready to sail, a second message brought news that the city had fallen and that Croesus was taken prisoner. The Spartans were greatly distressed, but there was nothing they could do.

[1.84] This was how the city of Sardis was taken: On the fourteenth day of the siege, Cyrus sent cavalrymen to ride through his army, proclaiming a rich reward to whoever should be the first to scale the walls. This was followed by a concerted assault, which met with no success. While the others were resting, a Mardian named Hyroeades resolved to make an attempt at a point in the fortifications that was left unguarded because there appeared to be no danger of its ever being scaled. There was a sheer drop there, which made it inaccessible. (Many years before these events a former king of Sardis, named Meles, had a concubine who gave birth to a lion. The seers of Telmessus declared that if the lion were carried around the walls of Sardis, the fortress would be impregnable. Meles followed their advice and carried the lion around the entire circuit of the walls except for this part, which he considered impossible to scale.) This Hyroeades had observed one of the Lydians climbing down the precipice to retrieve a helmet that had rolled down. This put the idea into his head. He made the ascent himself, was followed by many others, and finally by a great mass of the Persians. Thus was Sardis taken, and the city was sacked.

[1.85] What was Croesus' fate? I have already mentioned[†] that he had a son, a fine enough young fellow except for being mute from birth. In the days of his prosperity, Croesus had spared no effort to help the lad and had consulted the Delphic oracle. The Priestess replied,

---

* Having completed his digression on the Spartan-Argive war, Herodotus now returns us to the main story, the fall of King Croesus.

† The mute son will be recalled from the story of the death of Atys (1.34). Cross-references like this one reveal the care Herodotus took to tie together the many originally separate stories that went into his work, but it is worth noting also that he sometimes errs, referring ahead to stories that are not in fact found in his text.

divine

> *O Lydian, king over many peoples, thou foolish Croesus,*
> *Seek not to hear the longed-for sound of thy son's voice*
> *In thy palace. Far better were it otherwise,*
> *For his first words will be spoken on a day of great sorrow.*

When the city was taken, a Persian soldier advanced on Croesus to slay him, not knowing who he was. Croesus saw him. But, sunk in misery, he paid no heed, not caring whether he lived or died. But this son, the mute one, was so appalled by the danger that he gained speech and cried, "Fellow, do not kill Croesus." These were the first words that he uttered, and he retained the power of speech for the rest of his life.

[1.86] So Croesus was captured alive after a reign of fourteen years and a siege of fourteen days. He had indeed fulfilled the oracle by destroying a great kingdom—his own. He was brought before Cyrus, who had him put in chains and placed on a pyre that he had constructed, and with him fourteen Lydian boys.* Perhaps he intended making an offering to some god, perhaps he was fulfilling some vow, or perhaps he had heard tell that Croesus was a pious man and wanted to find out if some divine power would save him from being burned alive. As Croesus stood upon the pyre, in spite of his miserable condition he remembered the saying of Solon, surely divinely inspired, that no man could be called happy during his lifetime. Remembering this, he sighed bitterly, and breaking a long silence, he uttered a deep groan and thrice called Solon's name: "Solon, Solon, Solon."

On hearing this, Cyrus bade his interpreters ask Croesus upon whom he was calling. For some time Croesus maintained an obstinate silence, but when they forced him to speak he replied, "One who should speak with every ruler in the world—if only my riches could buy this." As this answer seemed mysterious and they continued to question him, pressing him hard and giving him no rest, he told how Solon the Athenian came to Sardis and was unimpressed by all the magnificence he saw there, and how everything he said, meant generally for all humankind but especially for those who deemed themselves happy, had come true in his case exactly as Solon had said.

---

* Well before Herodotus wrote, the Greeks were already captivated by the idea of Croesus ending his reign on a flaming pyre. A vase painting from about 500 and an ode of Bacchylides from a few decades later depict the very same event. In Bacchylides, however, Croesus had climbed the pyre himself to commit suicide, and the same is likely true of the figure in the vase painting.

While Croesus was still speaking, the fire had been kindled and was burning around the sides. Then Cyrus, listening to the interpreters, had a sudden change of heart. He reflected that he himself, a mere mortal, was burning alive another man who had once been equally as prosperous as he. This thought, and the thought of retribution, and the realization of the instability of the human condition, persuaded him to order his men to extinguish the fire as quickly as possible and to bring Croesus and those with him safely down. But the fire had got a hold and in vain did his men try to extinguish it.

A Greek vase painter, several decades before Herodotus' time, depicted this scene of Croesus on the pyre, the earliest known image on a vase of a historical figure. In this version of the story, Croesus appears to be committing suicide, pouring a libation to the gods as the pyre is kindled. WIKIMEDIA COMMONS

[1.87] Now the Lydians tell* that when Croesus realized that Cyrus had had this change of heart and when he saw that every man was engaged in a vain attempt to extinguish the fire, he called loudly upon

---

* It is typical of Herodotus to cite a source when his stories become implausible or fantastic, as if to shore up their credibility.

Apollo. "If any of my gifts have found favor in thy sight, come to my aid, rescue me from this present peril." Thus did he, with tears, <u>call upon the god</u>, and although the day had been clear with hardly a breeze, the sky was suddenly darkened with clouds, and <u>a storm broke with such a violent downpour of rain that the flames were extinguished.</u>*

In this way Cyrus learned that <u>Croesus was a good man and a friend to the gods</u>, and when he had brought him down from the pyre he questioned him. "Croesus, who of humankind induced you to march against my country and become my enemy rather than my friend?" Croesus made answer, "O king, what I did has proved to be for your good fortune and for my own ill fortune. The fault lies with the <u>gods of the Greeks who encouraged me to embark on this campaign</u>. No one is so foolish as to choose war instead of peace. <u>In peacetime children bury their fathers, in wartime fathers bury their children. It must be by divine will that this has come upon me.</u>" Cyrus set him free, seated him at his side, and treated him kindly, gazing at him in wonder, as did all his attendants.

divine mention {

[1.88–89] Croesus sat deep in thought; then, turning around and seeing the Persians sacking the city, "O king," he said, "shall I tell you what is in my mind or ought I to keep silent?" Cyrus bade him speak frankly without fear. "This vast crowd of men," said Croesus, "what are they so busily doing?" "Why, they are plundering your city and carrying off your treasures," said Cyrus. "Not my city, nor my treasures," was the reply. "They are no longer mine. It is you they are robbing." These words gave Cyrus food for thought and, dismissing his attendants, he asked Croesus what his advice was under these circumstances. "<u>Since the gods have made me your slave</u>," said Croesus, "<u>it is right for me to advise you for your good</u>. Persians are proud by nature, and poor. <u>If you suffer them to accumulate great wealth from sacking the city, you can expect that whomever gets the most will rebel against you.</u> If you will be advised by me, you will station men of your personal guard at every gate and let them take all the valuables as men bring them out, saying that a <u>tenth part of the spoil must be given to Zeus.</u> They will not resent this act of piety and will willingly surrender their spoil."

→ Zeus {

[1.90] Cyrus was highly pleased at what seemed to him good advice, and, after giving the orders Croesus had recommended, he said to Croe-

---

* This miraculous redemption is closely echoed by Bacchylides' poem on the subject of Croesus' pyre, in which Apollo whisks the king away from the flames and gives him a happy immortality among the mythical Hyperboreans.

sus, "I see that you are willing to do me service. Ask me for any gift you please in return." "The greatest boon you can bestow on me," said Croesus, "is to allow me to send these chains to the god of the Greeks whom I have most honored, and to ask him if it is his custom thus to reward those who serve him." And he explained to Cyrus how he had come to trust the oracle, the magnificent gifts he had sent, and the oracle's reply. Cyrus laughed. "This request is granted, and anything else you may ask." So Croesus sent to Delphi and instructed his messengers to lay the chains on the floor of the temple and ask the god if he was not ashamed of having encouraged Croesus to make war against the Persian Empire, in the belief that he would end the power of Cyrus, from which venture had come such "rewards" (here he bade them point to the chains). Was it usual (he bade them ask) for Greek gods to be so ungrateful?

[1.91] It is said that the Priestess replied to these reproaches as follows: "Even the gods cannot escape allotted destiny. In the fifth generation, Croesus expiated the crime of his ancestor, a soldier in the body-guard of the Heraclids, who succumbed to a woman's treachery, slew his master, and seized a throne that was not his.* Nevertheless Apollo wanted the fall of Sardis to be postponed to the time of Croesus' son but failed to persuade the Fates. They did, however, make some concession to him: They put off the fall of Sardis for three years, and Croesus should understand that his fate caught up to him three years late. Then again, Apollo came to his rescue when he was on the pyre. As to the oracle, Croesus does wrong to blame it, for Apollo foretold only this, that if he took the field against the Persians, he would destroy a great empire. Croesus should have made a further inquiry as to whether the empire was that of the Persians or his own. But he failed to understand the reply, made no further inquiry, and was himself to blame. Again, when he consulted the oracle on the last occasion and Apollo's answer made reference to a mule. This too Croesus misunderstood. The mule meant Cyrus, for he is the offspring of parents of different races,† an aristocratic mother and a base-born father. His mother was a Mede, daughter of Astyages, king of Media, while his father was a Persian, at that time subject to the rule of the Medes, and in every way inferior to his wife." When the Lydian messengers returned with this reply, Croesus had to admit that the fault was his, not the god's.

---

* Referring to Gyges' murder of Candaules (1.8ff.).

† A mule being the offspring of a horse and a donkey.

where is Lydia?

Throughout the first half of his work, Herodotus gives brief descriptions of the lands and cities his account has dealt with and the customs of the peoples who dwell there. These ethnographies, as they are called, can be as short as a few sentences or very, very long; indeed, most of book 2, one of the longest of the nine books of the Histories, consists of a detailed ethnography of Egypt. This volume presents excerpts from a few of his more important ethnographies, and that of the Lydians is included in its entirety below.

[1.93] The country of the Lydians has few remarkable features in comparison with other countries, except for the gold dust carried down by the river from Tmolus. It does, however, show the greatest work of human hands except for those wrought by the Egyptians and Babylonians. I refer to the tomb of Croesus' father, Alyattes, the base of which is built of huge stone blocks surmounted by a huge mound of earth. It was constructed by the joint efforts of three classes: tradesmen, craftsmen, and prostitutes. Five stone pillars stood on the summit even up to my own days, with inscriptions engraved on them showing the contributions of each class; calculations reveal that the prostitutes' share was the largest. The daughters of the common people of Lydia all ply the trade of prostitute to collect money for their dowries, and they continue to do so until they marry, choosing their own husbands. The tomb is nearly three-quarters of a mile in circumference and about a quarter mile wide; there is a large lake near it called Gyges' Lake, which the Lydians say is never depleted.* And that's what the tomb is like.

[1.94] The Lydians' way of life is not unlike our own, except for the prostitution of their daughters. They were the first people we know of to adopt silver and gold coinage[†] and to engage in trade, and they also claim to have invented the games now played by them and the Greeks. This invention they date back to the time when they colonized Tyrrhenia in Italy. In the time of King Atys the whole of Lydia suffered a terrible famine, which they endured as best they could. But as the famine continued, they devised various ways to alleviate their misery, including games of dice, knucklebones, and ball games. In fact, they claim to have invented all games except checkers. On one day they would play all day long, hop-

---

* Both the tomb and the lake have been located by modern archaeologists.

† Archaeology again bears out Herodotus' information here.

ing to banish all thought of food, and the next day they would eat and not play. This mode of life continued for eighteen years. Finally, as their sufferings went on unabated and even grew worse, the king divided the population into two groups and decided by lot which group should emigrate and which should remain. He himself took charge of the group chosen to stay where they were, while the emigrants were commanded by his son Tyrrhenus. After the lots had been drawn, the departing group went down to the coast at Smyrna and fashioned boats and, after loading on all the equipment needed for the voyage, sailed away in search of land and livelihood. They passed by many peoples and finally settled in Umbria in northern Italy, where they remain to this day. But they have changed their name from Lydians to Tyrrhenians, after their great leader Tyrrhenus.*

C. THE MARVELS OF EGYPT

After taking the story of the Persian Empire as far as the death of Cyrus, Herodotus enters into a long description of the land and people of Egypt, comprising about one-eighth the length of the entire Histories. *This section, like the other ethnographies contained in the work, is connected to the main story by the organizing pattern of Persian expansion: Herodotus opens book 2 by telling us that Cyrus' elder son Cambyses inherited his father's throne and made ready to attack Egypt; at that point he "pauses" the story to relate everything he knows about that ancient land. Then he restarts the narrative "clock" with the account of the Persian invasion of Egypt, at the beginning of book 3. Each of the earth's regions is dealt with in turn by Herodotus as it becomes a target of Persian imperialism.*

   The Egyptian material divides roughly into three sections: the geography of the country, especially its great river, the Nile; the customs and religious rites of the people; and the history of the land under successive kings going back to Min, the first Egyptian ruler of whom Herodotus has knowledge (c. 3000 BC), and ending with King Amasis, a contemporary of Croesus and Cyrus. The brief excerpts below are designed to give a sampling of each of the three sections of this remarkable Egyptian account.

———

* "Tyrrhenians" are known to us as Etruscans, a mysterious people who ended up in central Italy but whose origins are widely debated.

[2.2] Before the reign of Psammetichus,* the Egyptians used to think that of all the peoples of the world they were the most ancient. But ever since Psammetichus came to the throne and made up his mind to inquire into this matter, the Egyptians have believed that the Phrygians are the more ancient and that they themselves take second place. Psammetichus, finding that all his inquiries into this question proved fruitless, devised the following plans: He took two newborn babes at random from their parents and gave them to a shepherd to bring up among his flocks, with strict orders that no one was to utter a word in their presence. They were to live on their own in a lonely cottage. At times goats were to be brought in to them to provide them with milk, and their other needs were to be supplied.

In giving these instructions, Psammetichus had this in mind: to find out what word they would first utter when they had outgrown their meaningless babbling. In this he was successful. For two years the shepherd continued to carry out his orders; then once, as he opened the door and entered the cottage, both children ran up to him with outstretched hands, uttering the word *becos*. The first time this happened, the shepherd kept silent; but when this word continued to greet him whenever he visited the children to minister to them, he informed his master and at his bidding brought the children to him. When Psammetichus himself heard this word spoken, he sought to discover what language this word belonged to and found that this was the Phrygians' word for "bread." So the Egyptians gave way and agreed that the Phrygians were a more ancient people than they. That this is what really happened I was assured by the priests of Hephaestus at Memphis.† But the Greeks, in a number of other absurd versions, say that Psammetichus arranged for the children to be reared by women whose tongues he cut out.

———

One of the unique features of Herodotus' Egyptian account is the insight it displays into scientific questions, especially those concerned with geography, geology, and climate. These questions were hotly debated by the Ionian thinkers of the previous

* Psammetichus, or Psamtik, reigned from about 664 to 610. According to Herodotus' later account of his reign, he was the first pharaoh to hire Greek mercenaries to augment his army and even gave a grant of land for these newcomers to settle on.

† These priests were Herodotus' principal informants during his stay in Egypt. The city of Memphis had been home to Greek settlement in Egypt ever since the time of Amasis, so many Egyptians spoke Greek there and some, even the priests charged with upkeep of sacred shrines, profited from the Greek tourist trade. The god that Herodotus calls Hephaestus is in fact the Egyptian deity Ptah.

generations, and Herodotus often brings new and remarkably astute observations into the attempt to find solutions. Note, for example, his keen eye for physical evidence in the discussion below of how the land of Egypt was formed.

———

[2.4–5] The priests at Memphis told me that in the time of Egypt's first king, Min,* the whole country was swampland except the district around Thebes, and that none of the land north of Lake Moeris, to a distance of seven days' journey up the Nile, was then above water. And they seem to me quite correct. For it's clear to anyone who sees firsthand and who has understanding, even if he has not been told in advance, that Egypt—I mean the land to which the Greeks now voyage—is newly made land and the gift of the river; and I know this is true also of the region south of Lake Moeris for an additional three days' sail, even though the priests said nothing to me about this tract. For the quality of Egypt is such that if you sail as far as a day's journey off the coast and drop a plumb line into the sea, you will bring up silt from the bottom and find the depth to be only eleven fathoms. This evidence shows how far out the soil is carried by the river's flow.

[2.10–11] It seems to me that Egypt is indeed newly made land, as the priests claim. I believe that the whole region in between the mountain ranges south of Memphis was once a gulf of sea. There is another such gulf in Arabian territory, projecting out of the Red Sea, which is so long that a ship under oars would need forty days to traverse it, though its width is only a half-day's sail at its widest point; and in it each day the tide ebbs and flows.† I believe that Egypt was once a gulf like this one, extending from the northern sea to the Ethiopian, almost merging with the other one that extends from the southern sea to Syria, with only a small strip of land separating them. If someone diverted the Nile so that it flowed into this eastern gulf, who's to say it would not fill it up with silt in the course of twenty thousand years? I myself suspect that even ten thousand years would suffice. So isn't it likely that in the vast stretch of time before my birth, a gulf even larger than this one would be filled in, given that such a huge and productive river flows into it?

[2.12] Therefore, I trust the priests in what they tell me about Egypt, and what is more, I am confident for my own part that they are right, for I have seen that Egypt sticks out into the sea, compared with the land

---

* About 2,500 years before Herodotus' time.

† Herodotus here describes what we call the Red Sea.

around it; I have seen seashells discovered in the mountains; I have seen salty extrusions that corrode even the pyramids; and I've noted that the mountains south of Memphis are the only ones in Egypt containing sand, and that Egypt, unlike the countries of Arabia and Libya that border it, has a blackish and clod-filled soil, as though it were formed from mud and silt carried down by the river. Libyan soil is redder and sandier, as I have observed, while that of Arabia and Syria is more clayey and almost rocky.

———

The river Nile especially interests Herodotus, being the defining feature of the land of Egypt and a geographic anomaly in that it floods in the summer rather than (as all Greek rivers do) in the rainy winter. Herodotus goes to great lengths to explain this bizarre summer flooding and also to trace the source of the Nile, a geographical mystery that remained unsolved until the nineteenth century. (He himself had explored the upper Nile but had gotten no farther south than the city of Elephantine, near the edge of Ethiopian territory.) Reasoning from the general principle that the southern half of the globe mirrors the northern half, he theorized that the Nile followed a course that parallels that of the Danube, the great northern river whose mouth lies at approximately the same longitude as the Nile Delta. That hypothesis then governs his observations on the customs of the Egyptian people, as seen below.

———

[2.35] Just as the Egyptians have an opposing climate and a river whose nature is different from that of other rivers, so they have established customs and ways of life entirely opposite to the rest of humankind. For example, the women go to the market and do business, while the men stay at home and weave cloth. Men carry loads on their heads, women on their shoulders. Men urinate while sitting, women while standing. They go to the bathroom indoors and eat outside in the streets, explaining that they feel they must perform necessary but embarrassing functions in a hidden place but other, less embarrassing things in public. No woman can be a priest there, either of a male or female deity, but all gods are served by men.

[2.36] Priests in other countries let their hair grow long, but in Egypt the priests shave their heads. Other peoples keep their domestic animals outside the home, but the Egyptians live with theirs. Others make wheat and barley the staples of their diet, but Egyptians who do this are greatly ridiculed; they make bread out of rye, which some of them call *zeia*. They knead their dough with their hands but clay with their feet. Whereas the Greeks write their letters and add numbers going from left to right, the

Egyptians go from right to left, and in doing so they claim they are in the "right," while the Greeks are just "backward."

———

About half of book 2 is devoted to a history of Egypt, surveying the reigns of twenty major kings going back to Min, around 3000 BC. Herodotus provides thumbnail sketches of each ruler in turn, ending with the most recent and the most colorful, Amasis (who reigned from 570 to 525). At the outset of this mini-biography, Amasis is not yet king but the trusted subordinate of the reigning pharaoh Apries, whose poor leadership of the army has provoked an insurrection.

———

[2.162] When King Apries learned of the rebellion against him, he sent Amasis to negotiate with the rebels and stop the uprising. While Amasis was speaking to the rebels and urging them to stop, someone standing behind him put a helmet on his head and, as he did so, declared he was crowning a king. Amasis was not displeased by this move, as soon became evident, for when the rebels did in fact choose him to be king, he prepared to lead them into battle against Apries. Meanwhile Apries, learning of this treachery, sent to Amasis a trusted servant whose name was Patarbemis, with orders to capture Amasis alive and bring him before Apries. But when Patarbemis arrived at the camp and summoned Amasis, Amasis rose in his saddle (for he was at that moment mounted on horseback) and, letting out a fart, said "Take *this* back to Apries!"

[2.169] Battle finally broke out near the city of Memphis, with Apries leading a body of foreign mercenaries and Amasis leading native Egyptians. The foreigners fought well but were not nearly as numerous as the natives and so were defeated. Apries is said to have entertained the notion that not even a god could overthrow him, so secure was his rule; yet, for all that, he was defeated in battle and taken as a prisoner to Sais.

[2.172] And so with Apries deposed, Amasis came to the throne, a man from the region of Sais, from a town known as Siouph. At first the Egyptians looked down on their new king and held him in contempt, since he had formerly been a common man from an undistinguished background. But Amasis used his cleverness to win them over rather than reacting out of arrogance. He possessed many fine things, among which was a golden vessel in which he and his guests used to wash their feet. He broke this vessel apart and used it to make a statue of a god, and erected this statue in a convenient spot in the city, where the Egyptians, as they passed before the statue, stopped to pay it great reverence. Learning how things had gone, Amasis called the Egyptians together and revealed that the statue had been made from a footbath, into which the Egyptians used to vomit, urinate, and wash the filth off their feet; and now, he said, they revered it as a god! "I myself," he told them, "am just like that footbath; though I was once humble, I am now your king; honor and respect me as you do the statue." In this way he seduced the Egyptians into accepting his mastery.

[2.173] Here was the way he conducted his business: In the morning, up to the time when the marketplace fills up, he pursued zealously whatever affairs were pressing; but after this time he drank, laughed with his drinking buddies, and became a useless jokester. His friends grew annoyed with this behavior and admonished him: "Sire, you conduct yourself badly, always indulging in what is base; you should act in accordance with the solemn throne on which you sit, and stay by your tasks throughout the day. Then the Egyptians would know they are ruled by a great man, and you would be better spoken of by your subjects. What you do now is not the least bit royal." Amasis replied as follows: "Men who wield bows and arrows string their bows when they need them and unstring them when they don't. If the bows remained strung all the time, they would break and could no longer be used when needed. Such also is the way of human conduct. If we remain always dutiful and never relax with revelry, we would, before we know it, go insane or have a breakdown. Since I understand this principle, I give equal time to each pursuit." Thus he answered his friends. [2.174] It is said that Amasis, while he was still a commoner, was a big drinker and prankster and in no way a person of substance. Indeed, when he had finished drinking and enjoying himself he would go around stealing things. If people accused him of taking their property, he denied it, and they would haul him off to some oracle or other; sometimes the oracle convicted him, other times it exonerated him. After he became king, he did the following: He ignored the oracles that had let him off the hook and made no provision for their upkeep, and never made sacrifices there, seeing that they were false and worthless; but he took special care of the ones that had convicted him, since these were true oracles and spoke on behalf of the gods.

D. REIGN OF CAMBYSES OF PERSIA
(LATE SIXTH CENTURY BC)

Having surveyed Egyptian history up to the time of Amasis—the narrative present—Herodotus returns to the main story of the development of the Persian

Empire. Cambyses, son of Cyrus, assumed the throne in the 520s BC, conquered Egypt with ease, and, while based there, began plotting further invasions of surrounding territories.

—

[3.17–19] Cambyses planned three different campaigns: one against the Carthaginians, one against the Ammonians, and a third against the Long-Lived Ethiopians, who inhabit the part of Libya nearest the southern sea.* Against the Carthaginians he sent his navy, and against the Ammonians a select part of his army; but to the Ethiopians he first sent spies, to see whether there really was such a thing as the so-called Table of the Sun and to spy on the country generally. He gave these spies gifts to present to the Ethiopian king as a pretext for their visit. (The Table of the Sun, reportedly, is something like this: In front of the Ethiopian city there is a meadow, and it is filled with cooked meats from every type of animal; state officials go there every night to set out these meats, and in the daytime, anyone who wishes can come and partake of them. But the Ethiopians say that these meats spring forth from the earth itself.)† Having decided to use spies, then, Cambyses immediately sent for some of the Fish-eaters who live in Elephantine,‡ since these men understand the Ethiopian language.... When they arrived, he sent them on their mission, giving orders what to say and loading them up with gifts: a purple cloak, a necklace and bracelets of gold, a container of myrrh, and a jar of Phoenician wine. [3.20] The Ethiopians to whom Cambyses sent these men are said to be the tallest and most beautiful of all peoples. Their customs are unlike those of other peoples, especially as concerns the kingship: They select as king whomever they deem to be the tallest and to have strength commensurate with his size. [3.21] So, the Fish-eaters arrived and presented the king with their gifts, saying: "Cambyses, king of the Persians, has sent us to negotiate with you and to give you these gifts, items that he himself most

* By the term "southern sea" Herodotus probably meant the waters off southernmost Africa, though neither he nor his audience had more than the vaguest idea where this was or how far from Egypt. Both the name of the tribe, "Long-Lived Ethiopians," and their location are intended to convey a sense of extreme remoteness and unfamiliarity, like Herodotus' later phrase "at the ends of the earth."

† An interesting example of rationalization: Though treading perilously close to the borders of fairy tale, Herodotus keeps from stepping over by offering a plausible account of how the meats are replenished.

‡ Elephantine, or "Ivory City," was a real locale, at the southernmost boundary of Egypt. Nothing is known of the Fish-eaters prior to Herodotus' account; later, they appear in Greek lore as a fairy-tale race of happy primitives.

delights in, in the hopes of becoming your ally and visiting you in person."
The Ethiopian king realized that they were spies, however, and spoke as
follows: "It's not true that the Persian king has sent you here because he
hopes to become my guest; nor do you fellows speak the truth (for it's obvious you're spying on my realm); nor is your king a righteous man, for if
he were, he would not feel tempted to conquer land outside his own territory, nor would he enslave men who have done him no wrong. Here, give
him this bow and say to him, 'The king of the Ethiopians advises the king
of the Persians thus: If the Persians can draw bows as big as these with as
much ease as we do, then let them come in full force against the Long-
Lived Ethiopians; if not, let them give thanks to the gods, who have never
inspired in the children of the Ethiopians any desire to gain lands beyond
their own.'" Then he picked up a bow, unstrung it, and handed it to them.*

[3.22] Then, picking up the purple clothing, he asked what it was and
how it had been made. The Fish-eaters gave him a true account of how
purple cloth is dyed, to which he replied: "Disguised clothing for disguised men." Next he asked about the gold necklace and bracelets; when
the Fish-eaters explained that they were jewelry, he laughed, thinking
they meant shackles. "We have shackles in our land far stronger than
this," he said. Then he asked about the myrrh, and when they described
its manufacture and its use as a perfume, he said the same thing he had
said about the clothing. Finally he came to the wine; after learning how
it was made and drinking some, he declared himself delighted. Then he
asked what the Persian king ate and how long the oldest Persians lived.
They described the making of bread out of grain and said that eighty
years was the greatest complement of years allotted to their race. To this
the Ethiopian replied that he was not surprised they lived such a short
time while feeding on dung;† moreover, he said, they would not live even
as long as eighty years if not for their drink (pointing to the wine); in this
alone, he said, the Ethiopians were outdone by the Persians.‡

* Later we learn, in a passage not presented here, that only Cambyses' brother, Smerdis,
proved strong enough to draw this bow, and even he could draw it only a little way. Jealous
of Smerdis' superior strength, Cambyses sent his brother back to Persia and later ordered
his murder.

† Being the product of a nonagricultural society, the king is disgusted by the idea of eating foods that grow out of the fertilized earth.

‡ Though innocent of wine, like all nonagricultural peoples, the Ethiopians do not seem
vulnerable to its effects. By contrast, Cambyses, though he belongs to a wine-drinking race,
is said to have become deranged by alcoholism (see 3.34 below).

[3.23] Now the Fish-eaters asked in their turn about the Ethiopian way of life, and the king told them that many Ethiopians lived to 120 years, and some even longer than that, eating meat and drinking milk. When the spies expressed amazement at their longevity, the king led them to a spring, whose water made their skin glisten just as if it were olive oil and gave off a smell of violets. The spies later reported that this water was so light that nothing would float on it; even wood, or things lighter than wood, would sink to the bottom. (If this water is really such as they described, then it must be through their constant use of it that they have become long-lived.) Next after the spring, he showed them the prison, where all the prisoners were bound with shackles of gold. (Bronze is the rarest and most precious substance among these Ethiopians.)* After their visit to the prison, he also showed them the so-called Table of the Sun.

[3.24] Finally the king showed them the Ethiopian tombs, which are said to be made of crystal and used in the following manner: After embalming the corpse (either in the Egyptian manner or some other way), they whiten it with gypsum and paint on it as close a likeness of the living person as they can. Next they surround the body with a pillar of crystal, hollowed out to form a chamber (this crystal is mined easily and in great quantities in their land). In the middle of the pillar stands the corpse, where it can be clearly seen from outside; no unpleasant smells or anything else unseemly can be sensed; the image of the corpse is not distorted in any way by the crystal. For the space of a year, the nearest and dearest of the dead person keep the pillar in their home, bringing it sacrifices and offering it the finest foods; after that they carry it outside and set it up in a circuit around the city.

[3.25] Having seen all this, then, the Fish-eaters departed and, returning to Egypt, made their report to Cambyses. Immediately Cambyses, enraged, marched against the Ethiopians, without first ordering provision of food or reckoning with the fact that he was setting out for the ends of the earth; when he heard what the Fish-eaters had to say, he became maddened and no longer in his right mind, and he marched. He ordered the Greeks who were with him† to remain there in Egypt and took with

---

* Unlike gold, bronze is an alloy and must be smelted; presumably the Ethiopians get their bronze through trade and lack the knowledge to produce it, just as they are ignorant of the other manufacturing and agricultural processes described to them by the Fish-eaters.

† As subjects of the Persian Empire, the Greeks of Asia Minor were compelled to take part in Cambyses' military expeditions, even against other Greek cities. In this case the Greeks serving in Egypt constituted part of his navy.

him his entire infantry corps. When he came to Thebes in the course of his march, he split off five myriads* from the army and sent them to attack the Ammonians,† enslave them, and to set fire to the local oracle of Zeus, while he himself took the remaining forces and proceeded against the Ethiopians.

When Cambyses had not yet completed even a fifth of the march, his food supplies began to fail. Next the pack-animals gave out, for they were devoured by the soldiers. If under these circumstances Cambyses had come to his senses and turned the army around, he would have been a wise man despite his original error, but in fact he paid no heed to his difficulties and pressed ahead. As long as the soldiers could, they foraged grass and plants from the ground, but soon they came to the desert sand, and there some of them did a terrible thing: Drawing lots, they chose one man out of ten and the rest ate him. When Cambyses learned of this, and shaken by the spectacle of his men devouring one another, he at last gave up his Ethiopian campaign and turned around, getting back to Thebes after having lost most of his army. From there he went north to Memphis and discharged the Greek fleet.

[3.26] Thus fared the campaign against the Ethiopians. As for those who were detached to attack the Ammonians: These troops set out from Thebes, with guides in the lead, and are known to have arrived at the city of Oasis, a seven days' journey across the desert (Oasis is settled by Samians, reportedly of the Aeschrionian tribe).‡ This place has a name that translates to "Islands of the Blessed." The army is said to have arrived at this place, but neither the Ammonians nor their neighbors nor any other sources know what happened thereafter. The men never reached the Ammonians and never returned home. This much, however, is told by the Ammonians: When the men were midway between Oasis and themselves on their journey through the desert, they stopped to prepare a meal and a violent south wind arose and buried them under heaps of sand; in this way they disappeared forever. So the Ammonians say regarding the expedition against them.

---

* A myriad is a company of ten thousand men.

† The Ammonians were a real people, inhabiting the oasis of Siwa in the deserts west of Egypt. There was found the famous oracle of the Egyptian god Amun (identified with Zeus by the Greeks), from whom their tribal name is derived.

‡ The term "oasis" has obviously been misinterpreted by Herodotus as a proper name. Nothing else is known of the Samians said to live here—Greek islanders dwelling in the Sahara?

Herodotus shows how Cambyses, already behaving irrationally in his proceedings against the Ethiopians, completely lost his sanity after his return to occupied Egypt. According to Herodotus, he antagonized Egyptian religious feeling by trying to kill a holy calf called the Apis after mistaking a festival in honor of the calf for a celebration of his African defeats. Next he turned on his own closest kin, sending his trusted aide Prexaspes to murder his brother, and killing his own sister himself, after first incestuously marrying her. As this portrait of cruelty and paranoia reaches nightmarish proportions, Herodotus pauses to speculate on the cause of Cambyses' madness, which the Egyptians attributed to divine revenge for the wounding of the Apis calf.

[3.33] Such were the crimes that Cambyses, in his madness, committed against his closest kin, whether it was because of the Apis or for some other reason, for many are the ills that humankind is subject to. Indeed Cambyses is said to have suffered since his birth from the disease some call "sacred," a great affliction.* And it seems reasonable that a man whose body was thus diseased would also be sick in his mind.

[3.34] Other Persians too suffered as a result of his derangement: Prexaspes was a man most honored by him, one who used to bring him his dispatches and whose son was the king's cupbearer, a post of considerable distinction. It is said that one day Cambyses addressed him thus: "Prexaspes, what sort of man do the Persians consider me to be, and how do they speak of me?" "My lord," said Prexaspes, "in all other respects they lavish praises on you, but they say that you are overmuch fond of wine." Cambyses flew into a rage. "So now the Persians think I am crazy and out of my mind," he said. "What they previously said, then, was not the truth." For on some previous occasion, when the Persians were sitting in council with him along with Croesus, he had asked them how they thought he compared with his father, Cyrus. They answered that he was a better man than his father, for he had extended Cyrus' empire by acquiring dominion over Egypt and the sea. Croesus, however, was not satisfied with this judgment, and said, "Son of Cyrus, in my opinion you are not the equal of your father. For as yet you do not have a son such as he left us." Cambyses was delighted and praised Croesus' judgment.†

---

* The "sacred disease" is generally thought to be epilepsy.

† Croesus of Lydia, having been appointed by Cyrus to look after his son, is depicted by Herodotus as Cambyses' senior counselor in occupied Egypt. But this, like the earlier passage in which the Greek sage Solon visited Croesus, may well be a thematically convenient fiction.

[3.35] It was with these events in mind that Cambyses, in hot temper, said to Prexaspes, "Learn now whether the Persians are speaking the truth or whether what they say is an indication of their own madness. If I shoot your son, standing there at the door, right through the heart, I shall prove that the Persians are talking nonsense. If I miss, then it can be said that the Persians are right and I am not of sound mind." So speaking, he drew his bow and shot the boy. Then he ordered the fallen body to be cut open and the wound examined. When it was found that the arrow was lodged in the heart, he laughed and gleefully said to the boy's father, "Prexaspes, it must now be clear that I am not mad and that it is the Persians who are out of their minds. Tell me, have you ever seen anyone shoot so straight?" Prexaspes, realizing that the man was deranged, feared for his own safety, and replied, "My lord, I do not believe that [the] god himself can shoot so straight."*

[3.36] On another occasion, Cambyses arrested twelve high-ranking Persians for no good reason and had them buried alive upside down.† When he did this, Croesus the Lydian ventured to give the following advice: "O king, do not always give way to your youthful impetuosity; hold yourself in check and keep control over yourself. It is a good thing to look ahead and a wise thing to have regard to the future. For no good reason you arrest and kill men who are your own subjects; yes, and you kill children too. If you continue to act thus, beware lest the Persians revolt against you. Your father, Cyrus, bade me many a time to give you my counsel and my suggestions for your own good."

It was with all goodwill that Croesus delivered this advice, but Cambyses replied, "So you dare give me advice, you who were such a fine ruler over your own country, you who gave such good advice to my father! You urged him to cross the Araxes and attack the Massagetae, when they were willing to cross over to our territory.‡ You destroyed yourself by your misgovernment of your own country and destroyed Cyrus, who listened to you. But you will not get away with it. I have long been looking for an excuse to pay you out."

With these words, he seized his bow to shoot him, but Croesus leapt

---

* Remarkably, Prexaspes never sought revenge for the murder of his son, according to Herodotus, but continued to serve Cambyses faithfully until the monarch's last days. Later, when the Magi priests usurped the Persian throne by installing a pretender, Prexaspes reportedly denounced the conspiracy from the top of a high tower and then leapt to his death.

† The Greek phrase might also mean "buried them up to their necks."

‡ See 1.207ff.

up and rushed from the room. Failing to shoot him, Cambyses ordered his servants to seize him and kill him. But his servants, knowing their master's ways, concealed Croesus with this intention: that if Cambyses should change his mind and ask for Croesus, they would bring him forth and be rewarded for saving his life; but if the king should not change his mind or miss Croesus, they could then do away with him. And indeed, not long afterward Cambyses did miss Croesus; and when the servants saw this, they announced that he was still alive. Cambyses said he was glad to hear it, but those who had saved Croesus would not escape; he would kill them. And so he did.*

[3.37] These are examples of the utter madness that Cambyses exhibited in his conduct toward the Persians and his allies. And during his stay at Memphis he broke open ancient tombs and examined the bodies and even went so far as to enter the temple of Hephaestus and jeer at his statue. (This statue of Hephaestus is very like the Pataici of the Phoenicians, which they take around with them on the prows of their warships. For those who have never seen one, I can tell you that it is like a pygmy.) He also entered the temple of the Cabiri, which only the priest is permitted to do. He scoffed at the images and even burned them. (These images resemble those of Hephaestus and are said to be his sons.)

[3.38] This indicates to me that Cambyses was completely out of his mind; otherwise he would not have poured ridicule on holy things and sacred traditions. For if one were to ask men of any nation to choose the traditions that they think best in the world, after examining each of them, they would choose the traditions of their own country; such is the reverence in which all hold their own traditions.† So it is only a madman who would make a laughingstock of such things.

One can conclude on the basis of many different indications that this is the universal sentiment of humankind toward their own customs, and the following anecdote is but one example: When Darius became king of Persia, he summoned the Greeks who were at his court and asked them what it would take to persuade them to eat the dead bodies of their fathers. They replied that nothing could persuade them to do such a thing. Thereupon Darius summoned some Indians of the tribe called Callatiae,

* This is the last we hear in the *Histories* of Croesus, Herodotus' most fully developed character. The story of his life remains curiously open-ended.

† Herodotus here ignores the many instances he himself gives of a people adopting foreign customs when they regard them as better than their own.

who do actually eat their parents' corpses,* and in the presence of the Greeks (who understood through interpreters what was being said), he asked the Indians what it would take to persuade them to *burn* their fathers' dead bodies. With a cry of horror they urged him not to speak of such a thing. Such, then, is the force of tradition, and I think that Pindar was right in saying "custom is the king of all."

E. A GREEK TYRANT, POLYCRATES OF SAMOS

[3.39] While Cambyses was making his expedition against Egypt, the Spartans sent a force to Samos against Polycrates, son of Aeaces, who ruled Samos as the result of a coup.† Originally he had divided the realm into three, sharing rule with his brothers Pantagnotus and Syloson, but thereafter he slew the former, banished the younger brother, Syloson, and ruled the whole of Samos. He then formed a close friendship with Amasis, king of Egypt, confirmed with an exchange of gifts. It was not long before his extraordinary good fortune became the talk of Ionia and the rest of Greece. Wherever he chose to campaign, he met with marked success. He had a fleet of a hundred penteconters and a thousand archers. He raided and plundered without discrimination, for he used to say that a friend would be more grateful for the restoration of what had been taken from him than if it had not been taken in the first place. He captured quite a number of islands and many towns on the mainland as well. Among other successes, he defeated at sea and captured the Lesbians, who were coming with full force to the help of the Milesians. They were put in chains and made to dig the ditch that surrounds Samos's walls.‡

[3.40] Amasis the Egyptian§ became aware of Polycrates' remarkable good fortune, but it made him uneasy, and as Polycrates' successes still mounted, he wrote the following letter and sent it to Samos: "Amasis to

---

* The neutral tone of Herodotean ethnographies, even when subjects like incest or cannibalism are being described, is noteworthy.

† Polycrates is one of the Greek *tyrannoi*, or unconstitutional rulers, whose careers Herodotus follows in the *Histories*. During his reign (c. 535–522 BC), the island of Samos established a naval empire in the Aegean.

‡ Samos was famous for its vast and ingenious engineering projects.

§ This highly successful monarch has been encountered twice now, once as an ally of Croesus (1.77) and again as the colorful "party boy" who overthrows Apries to gain the Egyptian throne (2.162ff.).

Polycrates. It is a pleasure to hear of the prosperity of a close friend and ally; but knowing as I do the jealousy of the gods, your striking successes do not bring me joy. What I would like for myself and for those I care for is to meet with good fortune in some things and ill fortune in others, and to pass through life with alternating good and ill fortune rather than with continuous good fortune. For I have never heard of any man who, after enjoying continuous good fortune, did not in the end meet with utter disaster. Take my advice and deal with the problem of your extraordinary successes as follows: Consider what it is you value most, something whose loss would cause you the greatest grief, and throw it away, so that it will never be seen again. If thereafter you do not find good fortune alternating with misfortune, then continue to follow my suggestion until you do."

[3.41] On reading the letter, Polycrates accepted as sound the advice it contained and began to consider which of his treasures it would grieve him the most to lose. He decided on a signet ring he wore, an emerald set in gold, the work of a Samian named Theodorus, son of Telecles. Being resolved to throw it away, he acted as follows: He manned a penteconter, went aboard, and ordered it to put to sea. When he had gone a good way from land, taking the ring from his finger, in full view of all on board, he hurled it into the sea. Thereupon he rowed back to land, returned to his home, and lamented his misfortune.

[3.42] Five or six days later, this is what befell him. A fisherman who had caught a perfectly fine, large fish thought it would make a suitable present for Polycrates. He went to the palace gates, sought an audience with Polycrates, and when this was granted, he presented him with the fish, saying: "O king, when I caught this fish I did not think it proper to take it to market, though I am but a poor laboring man. It seemed to me worthy of you and your greatness, so I have brought it as a present for you."

Pleased with the fisherman's words, Polycrates replied as follows: "You have done very well, and I thank you twice, both for your words and for the gift. Take supper with us." The fisherman, proud of this invitation, went home. Meanwhile the servants cut up the fish and found Polycrates' ring in the belly. On seeing this, they took it and hastened with great jubilation to Polycrates, gave him the ring, and related how it had been found.

[3.43] Seeing in this a divine hand, he wrote a letter to Amasis in Egypt, recounting all he had done and what had befallen him. On reading the letter from Polycrates, Amasis realized how impossible it is for one man to save another from what is destined for him, and that Polycrates, a man who was so constantly favored by fortune that he even found what he had thrown away, would meet a miserable end. He sent a herald to Samos to announce the dissolution of their alliance. His purpose in so doing was to avoid the distress he was bound to feel for one who was a friend and ally when a terrible calamity should finally overtake Polycrates.*

While Cambyses was losing his sanity in Egypt, a pair of Magi priests seized the Persian throne, exploiting the coincidence that one of them resembled and had the same name as Cambyses' royal brother, Smerdis. In Herodotus' account, a messenger from the Magi found Cambyses, with his army, at Ecbatana in Syria and delivered a proclamation that royal power now resided not in Cambyses but in Smerdis—implying the royal Smerdis, Cambyses' brother. But Cambyses had in fact had his brother secretly killed some time before this, and he now correctly deduced that Smerdis the Magus had taken the throne under a false identity. Distraught, Cambyses leapt onto his horse to ride to Susa, the Persian capital, and expose the impostor, but in his haste he wounded his thigh on his own sword, in the same spot, significantly, where he had once struck the sacred Apis calf. Realizing that he was fated to die from this wound and that he had in fact not only lost the throne but destroyed the only legitimate heir, Cambyses, as depicted by Herodotus, uttered these last words to the assembled Persian nobles:

[3.65] "Persians, I am forced to reveal to you now what I have most of all kept hidden. While I was in Egypt, I had a dream that I wish I had never had. I dreamed that a messenger arrived from the palace and announced to me that Smerdis was sitting on the royal throne and that his head was touching the sky. In fear lest my brother rob me of my crown, I acted more in haste than in wisdom: For though men cannot avert what is to be, I rashly sent Prexaspes to Susa to kill Smerdis. With this foul deed done, I lived at peace, never imagining that, with Smerdis out of the way, any other challenger could arise. Alas! I failed to see anything of what was coming; I killed my own brother when there was no point in doing so, and now I am losing my crown anyway. It was Smerdis the Magus whose revolt the god warned me of in the dream! Yet the deed is done; you must recognize that Smerdis, son of Cyrus, is no longer living. The Magi rule your realm, both the one I left in charge of my house and his brother,

---

* The "calamity" is described in the sequel to this story, 3.128ff.

Smerdis. The man who could best have avenged this outrage against my rule, my brother, is dead—foully murdered by those who were closest to him. But with him gone, Persians, it is you who must stand in for him and carry out my dying wishes.

"I command you, with the gods of my royal house as my witness: All of you here, but especially those of the Achaemenid line,* do not allow sovereign power to revert back to the Medes. If they use trickery to get it, take it back from them by trickery; if they seize it by force, protect it with even greater force. If you do this, I pray that the earth bear fruit for you, and your wives and flocks bear young, and that you stay forever free. But if you fail to preserve our power or do not even try to do so, I lay this curse on you: May you get the opposite of all this and also suffer a death as bad as mine, each of you."

[3.66] As he spoke, Cambyses began to weep for all his misdeeds, and the Persians, when they saw him crying, began as one to tear the clothes they had on and to wail and groan piteously. After that, his leg wound having become infected and rotten, the end came for Cambyses, son of Cyrus, who had ruled seven years and five months altogether and who died completely childless.†

F. REVOLUTION IN PERSIA

Soon after this, the Magi, exposed as pretenders to the throne, were killed by a band of seven Persian nobles, among them Darius, son of Hystaspes. This left a power vacuum in the palace, with no direct descendant of Cyrus still surviving. In this crisis the seven conspirators who had killed the Magi held a conversation that modern scholars have dubbed the Debate on Government or Constitutional Debate. Despite Herodotus' protestations, it is almost certainly fictitious, an early experiment in what would later become political philosophy.

———

[3.80] The Persians who had overthrown the Magi took counsel among themselves, reviewing the whole situation before them. Certain speeches

* The Achaemenid clan was the highest in rank among the Persian nobility.

† A somewhat different account of Cambyses' death, and the events surrounding the Magi conspiracy, is given in a stone inscription found in 1836 in a place called Behistun. The inscription was set up by Darius as part of a propaganda campaign to legitimize his rule. It describes the revolt of a Magus named Gaumata and claims that Cambyses died by his own hand.

were made that some Greeks find incredible but were nevertheless made.* Otanes, speaking as follows, recommended that all Persians should share in the government: "I do not think it right that any one of us should become the sole ruler, for that is neither a happy nor a good thing. You have seen to what lengths the intoxication of power carried Cambyses, and then you had to endure the same thing from the Magus. How can monarchy be a well-adjusted system when the monarch can do whatever he wants unchecked? Even the best of men, placed in such a commanding position, would change from his previous way of thinking. His elevation breeds arrogance in the man, while jealousy is instinctive in all men. With these two qualities he possesses every form of vice. Many of his acts of savagery are due to a surfeit of arrogance, others to jealousy. Absolute power ought to render a man free from jealousy, possessing as he does all that he could wish for, but the opposite proves to be the case in respect of his conduct toward his subjects. He is jealous of the best of the citizens for surviving and continuing to live, and he rejoices in the worst; thus, he is always ready to welcome slanderers. Of all people he is the most awkward to deal with. If you show him reasonable reverence, he is angry that you do not utterly abase yourself; if you do the latter, he resents your servility. But I am just coming to the worst of his excesses—he disregards our traditional customs, violates women, and puts men to death without trial.

"Now the advantages of majority rule are, first, it possesses the fairest of all names, *isonomia,* or equality before the law;† second, it is not guilty of any of the excesses of monarchy. Magistrates are appointed by lot; they are accountable to the people, and all their deliberations are in public. I therefore recommend that we abolish monarchy and give power to the people. For in the many lies the totality of the state."

[3.81] Such was the opinion put forward by Otanes, but Megabyzus was in favor of establishing an oligarchy and spoke as follows: "What Otanes has said in criticism of monarchy I agree with entirely, but in speaking in favor of democracy he has missed the mark. There is nothing more stupid and more violent than an ignorant mob. It would be quite intolerable for men, in seeking to escape the unbridled violence of a despot, to fall

* Paradoxically, Herodotus insists on the historical veracity of a closed-door debate that took place nearly a century before and about which he could not have had any accurate report.

† This word, denoting the idea that all citizens were equal in legal terms, preceded the more familiar *dēmokratia* in Greek usage but means much the same thing.

victim to that of an undisciplined rabble. The despot, in all that he does, at least acts with understanding, but the mob does not even have the ability to understand. How can it, when it has not been taught nor does it know what is its own good? It rushes blindly into decisions, sweeping all before it like a river in flood. No, let those who bear ill will to the Persians embrace democracy, but let us choose a number of the best men and entrust the government to them. We shall be among them, and from the best men the best policies are likely to emerge."

[3.82] Such was the opinion of Megabyzus. Darius was the third to speak, and he spoke as follows: "I agree with what Megabyzus has said about democracy, but not with his advocacy of oligarchy. Of the three suggested forms of government—democracy, oligarchy, and monarchy—if we examine the best example of each kind, I maintain that monarchy takes first prize without contest. There can be nothing better than the one best man. Gifted with such character, his care for the people would be beyond criticism, and being sole ruler he would find it easiest to keep secret the measures he plans against his enemies. In an oligarchy, many who distinguish themselves in public service are wont to develop bitter private feuds. Each desirous to achieve pre-eminence and have his counsels accepted before others, they fall to bitter quarreling, which leads to party strife, which leads to bloodshed, and bloodshed ends in monarchy, thus proving how much this is the best form of government. As for democracy, this form of government cannot avoid corruption, and when this develops in the public service, those who are corrupt do not engage in feuds but in close associations, the malefactors making common cause with one another. And so it goes on, until somebody comes forward as the people's champion and puts a stop to all this. As a result, he is much admired by the people, and from being admired he finds himself established as a monarch—which again shows that monarchy is the best form of government.

"The essence of the matter is this: Where did we get our freedom from, and who gave it to us? Was it from the people, an oligarchy, or a monarch? In my opinion, we gained our freedom through one man.* Furthermore, we ought not discard our ancestral traditions, which have served us well. To do this would not be the better course."

With these three opinions set before them, the remaining four of the seven men voted in favor of monarchy.

---

* Meaning Cyrus, who liberated the Persians from the Medes as described in book i.

———

A contest was held to determine which of the seven would rule; Darius prevailed by means of a cunning ploy and assumed the throne.

Herodotus now provides a remarkable survey of the entire Persian Empire under Darius, divided into twenty provinces, or "satrapies," each paying a fixed amount of yearly tribute into the Persian treasury. The account is remarkably detailed and must have come directly from some written document, which Herodotus somehow or other obtained and had translated into Greek. At the end, he gives the grand total of annual Persian revenue as 14,560 talents of silver—a fantastic sum, ten times as much as Athens, which grew to be the wealthiest Greek city, received at the height of its imperial power.

The largest single contribution to Persia's wealth comes from its Indian subjects, who pay tribute out of the vast quantities of gold found in their country. The idea of India's gold deposits then leads Herodotus into the following observation:

G. THE EDGES OF THE WORLD

[3.106] The farthest reaches of the inhabited world have been blessed with the finest things, just as Greece has been blessed with the best mixture of hot and cold weather. For example, India is the easternmost of inhabited lands, as I have described, and in it are creatures of all kinds, both land animals and birds, whose size far exceeds those in other lands (except for their horses; for the Indian horses are smaller than those called Nesaean, raised by the Medes). And India has gold in great quantities... and its trees produce a kind of fruit that, in beauty and quality, surpasses sheep's wool; they get their clothing from these trees.*

[3.107] Then again in the south, Arabia is the farthest land in the inhabited world, and alone of all countries it has frankincense, myrrh, cassia, cinnamon, and a gum called ledanon. However, all these, except the myrrh, are very hard for the Arabians to harvest. For instance, they must burn storax (the same stuff that the Phoenicians import into Greece) in order to get at the frankincense; for the trees where frankincense grows are surrounded by flying snakes, small creatures with mottled skin that swarm in great numbers around each tree. They can't be driven off except by smoking them with the burning storax.

---

* Herodotus refers here to cotton, a substance almost totally unknown to Greeks of his era.

[3.108] The Arabians also say this: Their whole land would be filled with these flying snakes, except that something happens to reduce their numbers—the same thing that, as I have learned, happens to vipers. It seems that the divine mind, which plans wisely (as by all indications it does), has arranged that creatures that are timid and make easy prey are also very prolific in the bearing of young, so that they are not preyed upon to the point of extinction; while fierce and menacing creatures bear few young. So, on the one hand, we have the hare, a creature hunted by every other animal as well as men and birds, which is so prolific that, of all the animal kingdom, it alone can conceive while already pregnant; in its womb you can find the furry fetuses beside the ones still hairless, or the embryos already developing beside the ones just starting.* On the other hand, we have the lioness, strongest and fiercest of beasts, which bears only once in its lifetime, and then only one cub; for when it gives birth, it ejects its womb along with its offspring.† The cause of this is the following: When the unborn cub begins to move around in its mother's womb, its sharp claws—sharpest of any creature—begin to scratch, and the more the cub grows, the more he scratches. By the time of delivery there is no womb left intact at all.

[3.109] Similarly, vipers and the flying snakes in Arabia, were they able to reproduce as freely as nature allows, would soon make human life unlivable. But in fact, during mating, when the male is fertilizing the female, just as he releases his seed, she grabs him by the neck with her teeth and doesn't let go until she bites clean through. Thus the male snake dies; but later his death is avenged on the female, in the following way: The young in her womb pay her back for their father's death by eating a hole through their mother—gnawing through her belly until they gnaw their way out.

Other kinds of snakes, which are not harmful to humans, reproduce simply by laying eggs, and they have huge broods. Vipers, by the way, can be found everywhere, while the flying snakes are concentrated in Arabia and nowhere else. That's why they seem so numerous.

[3.114] In the southwest, the farthest country in the inhabited world is Ethiopia; this land has much gold, elephants everywhere, all sorts of wild

---

* Entirely untrue, though Herodotus expresses the idea with remarkable force and conviction.

† Also untrue. Simple mathematical logic refutes this idea, since with such a low birth rate the race of lions would soon be extinct.

trees, ebony wood, and the tallest, loveliest, and most long-lived races of men.

[3.115] Such are the farthest lands of Asia and Africa. As for those of Europe, toward the extreme west, I cannot say anything with certainty. For I don't accept that there is a river called Eridanus by foreigners, which flows into a northern sea and which, as legend has it, carries amber in its stream; nor do I know whether the Tin Islands, which supply us with tin, exist. As for the Eridanus, the very name testifies against it, for it comes from Greek and not a foreign tongue; some poet invented it. Also I have never been able to find anyone, though I have tried, who has seen that this part of Europe is bordered by sea. In any case, tin and amber *do* come to us from the earth's edge.*

[3.116] The northernmost part of Europe seems to have a huge amount of gold. How it is extracted I can't say with certainty either. There's a story that Arimaspians, one-eyed men, steal it away from griffins, but I can't accept the idea that men can be one-eyed, yet normal humans in every other way.

So then, the farthest parts of the earth, which enclose the rest in a circle and hem it around, seem to have the things we deem most beautiful and hardest to find.

H. THE END OF POLYCRATES

After these pronouncements on the global distribution of resources, Herodotus returns to the story of the growth of Persian power. At this point he turns the clock back slightly in order to recount the conclusion of the tale of Polycrates, the ruler of Samos who had tried but failed to discard his ring (3.39ff.).

———

[3.120] At about the time of Cambyses' illness, the following events occurred: A Persian named Oroetes had been appointed by Cyrus as governor of Sardis. This man conceived a most unholy project. Although he had never received injury by word or deed from Polycrates of Samos and had never even met him, he planned to seize him and kill him. The

---

* Herodotus disclaims knowledge of *specific* places in the far west, but still uses the tin and amber said to come from these places as evidence that precious goods belong to the farthest countries.

reason generally accepted for his determination is as follows: Oroetes and another Persian named Mitrobates, governor of the province of Dascyleium, were sitting at the gates of the royal palace when they fell into quarreling, Mitrobates claiming to be the better man. "What kind of man do you call yourself?" said he. "Although the island of Samos lies close to your province, you have not added it to the King's dominions.* Yet it is so easy to subdue that one of the natives with fifteen soldiers gained mastery over the island and now rules it." The story goes that Oroetes was nettled by his reproach, but instead of seeking revenge on the speaker for this insult, he sought the utter destruction of Polycrates as being the cause of his disgrace.

[3.121] There is a less well authenticated account, that Oroetes sent a herald to Samos to make some request (what that was is not clear), and Polycrates happened to be sitting in the men's apartments in company with Anacreon of Teos. Now, it is not sure whether this was deliberate or a chance occurrence, but when the herald advanced and spoke, Polycrates, who happened to be turned away from him facing the wall, did not bother to turn around and made no reply. Both of these stories are told to account for the death of Polycrates, and you may take your choice.

[3.122] Oroetes, residing at Magnesia on the river Maeander, now sent Myrsus, son of Gyges, a Lydian, with a message to Samos. Oroetes knew of Polycrates' ambitions, for Polycrates was the first Greek we know of to plan to become master of the seas—if we except Minos of Cnossus and prior to him any others who may have been rulers of the seas. But as far as authentic history goes, Polycrates was the first,[†] and he had great hopes of becoming ruler over Ionia and the islands. Knowing of his intentions, Oroetes sent him the following message: "I know that you have great enterprises in mind and that your resources do not match your designs. If you act as I suggest, you will achieve greatness for yourself and safety for me, for I have it on good authority that Cambyses is plotting my death. Get me away from here and share my wealth with me; with such resources you will rule the whole of Greece. If you doubt my wealth, send your most trustworthy emissary, and I will reveal to him what I possess."

* In this volume the word King is capitalized when it refers to the Great King of Persia.

† Herodotus here makes a crucial distinction between Polycrates, who belongs to the recent past and so to investigable history, and Minos, who belongs to mythology and fable.

[3.123] Polycrates, who had a great desire for money, received this proposal with joy and accepted it. He first sent his secretary, a townsman named Maeandrius, son of Maeandrius, to investigate on his behalf. (Not long afterward, this Maeandrius sent as an offering to the temple of Hera all the magnificent furniture of Polycrates' men's quarters.) Learning of his approach, Oroetes filled eight chests with stones, almost all the way to the brim and then put gold on top of the stones; then he fastened the chests securely and kept them in readiness. Maeandrius arrived, beheld the gold, and reported back to Polycrates.

[3.124] In spite of the earnest protests of his soothsayers and his friends, Polycrates now prepared to depart. His daughter too tried to dissuade him because of a vision she had seen in a dream. She saw her father suspended in the air, washed by Zeus, and anointed by the sun god. Because of this vision, she did all she could to prevent her father from leaving the country to visit Oroetes. She even pursued him to the ship with words of ill omen. He replied with this threat: That if he returned safe he would put off her marriage for many a year. She then prayed that his threat would be fulfilled; she would rather remain a virgin for a longer space of time, she said, than be bereft of her father.

[3.125] But Polycrates, disregarding all good counsel, sailed to meet Oroetes, taking with him among other companions Democedes of Croton, son of Calliphon, the most distinguished physician of his time.* On reaching Magnesia, Polycrates met a dreadful end, quite unbefitting his own distinguished life and ambitions—for with the exception of the rulers of Syracuse, no other Greek ruler† can be compared with Polycrates for splendor. Having killed him in a manner that does not bear repeating, Oroetes hung the body on a cross. Of his followers, he released the Samians, bidding them thank him for their freedom; the foreigners and slaves he held as prisoners of war. The crucifixion of Polycrates brought to fulfillment his daughter's vision. He was washed by Zeus when it rained, and he was anointed by the sun god when moisture dripped from his body. This was how Polycrates' long run of good fortune came to an end.

---

* Soon to play an important role in world events.

† As stated earlier, the term "ruler" here translates the Greek *tyrannos*, the term for someone who holds absolute power without constitutional authority. Syracuse is a city in Sicily, an island widely colonized by Greeks at this time.

I. LEADERSHIP CRISIS IN SPARTA

The Persian Empire continued to expand throughout the late sixth century BC, *but the Greeks on its western fringe, the Aegean coast of Turkey, became restive. In 499 the cities of this coast, and the islands offshore, mounted a revolt that succeeded in sacking and burning the western Persian capital of Sardis. Athens sent a small squadron of ships that took part in this revolt, as did another city of European Greece, Eretria. This participation of the European Greeks in the affairs of those in Asia broadened the Greco-Persian conflict and created a pretext for the massive showdown that lay ahead. In the short term, the Athenians quickly withdrew their forces from Asia, and the revolt collapsed after five years. The city that had led it, Miletus, was destroyed by the Persians, its population enslaved and deported deep within Central Asia.*

The reconquest of the Ionian Greeks by Persia left the mainland Greeks deeply unsettled. Since Athens and Eretria had taken a small but significant part in the burning of Sardis, Darius determined to have revenge on those two cities at least. Beyond that, the Persians faced the larger question of whether their rule over Ionia could ever be secure as long as the mainland Greeks remained free. Perhaps supposing that it would be safer to conquer all the Greeks than only some, Darius began in the years 494 and 493 to lay plans for the subjugation of the Greek mainland. Many Greek cities were all too willing to surrender without a fight.

———

[6.48–49] After this, Darius began to make trial of the spirit of the Greeks, to see whether they would offer resistance or submit to him. He therefore sent heralds to various places throughout Greece to demand earth and water* for the King. At the same time, he sent other messengers to the coastal towns already under his dominion, requiring them to provide warships and cavalry transports. These vessels were duly provided, and many of the mainland cities of Greece gave the tokens demanded by the King, as did all the islanders whom the heralds visited.

Among the latter who gave earth and water were the Aeginetans. This act of submission immediately aroused the anger of the Athenians, who believed that the Aeginetans intended to join Darius in attacking Athens. Gladly seizing on this as a pretext, the Athenians put the matter before the Spartans, accusing the Aeginetans of having betrayed Greece by their action.

---

* Vessels of earth and water were demanded of those accepting Persian sovereignty, as signs that both land and sea were at the disposal of the Great King.

[handwritten margin notes: "conflict / disagreement between 2 Persian kings"]

[6.50] In response to this accusation, Cleomenes, son of Anaxandrides and king of Sparta,* crossed over to Aegina with the intention of arresting those Aeginetans who were most responsible for policy. But when he was attempting to do so, he found himself opposed by many of the Aeginetans and particularly by Crius, son of Polycrites. This man declared that Cleomenes would be made to rue it if he tried to carry off a single man, and that he was acting without the authority of the Spartan government, being bribed by the Athenians; otherwise he would have been accompanied by the other king. (These words had been supplied to him by Demaratus, the other Spartan king, in a letter.)† Cleomenes, on quitting Aegina, asked Crius his name, and, when he was told it, "Get your horns tipped with brass as soon as you can, Crius,"‡ he said, "for you are going to meet with much trouble."

[6.51–52] Meanwhile, Demaratus, who had remained behind at Sparta, was making accusations against Cleomenes. He was the other of the two Spartan kings but of the inferior house—not that it is inferior in any respect (for they have a common ancestor) other than the esteem due to the house of Eurysthenes as being the elder.

For the Spartans, diverging from all the poets, maintain that it was Aristodemus himself who, as their king, brought them into territory that they now possess,§ and not the children of Aristodemus.¶ Soon thereafter, his wife, Argeia, gave birth to twins. Aristodemus lived long enough to see his children but then fell sick and died. The Spartans of that time were resolved, in accordance with their custom, to make the elder of the two children their king but were unable to choose between them, the

---

* Cleomenes reigned roughly from 520 to 490 and, his reluctance to help the Ionians notwithstanding, pursued a strongly anti-Persian policy throughout. Herodotus here begins a series of tales involving his bitter rivalry with Demaratus, who was his coregent from about 515 to 490. The peculiar Spartan institution of dual kingship often led to such power struggles.

† That is, Demaratus had conspired with Crius in an effort to embarrass Cleomenes by instructing the Aeginetan how best to undermine Cleomenes' authority. It's not clear whether Demaratus was motivated by policy differences with Cleomenes, i.e., a more pro-Persian outlook, or simply by personal antagonism.

‡ Cleomenes puns on the name Crius, which is Greek for "ram."

§ Herodotus here turns back the clock to the earliest phase of Spartan history, several centuries in the past, at a time when the kingship had not yet become dual.

¶ Here Herodotus makes a digression from his main story, the feud between Cleomenes and Demaratus, to explain the origin of the dual kingship at Sparta. No other Greek state of Herodotus' day had two kings sharing power.

children being the same in size and exactly alike. Finding themselves in this difficulty, they questioned the mother, but she insisted that she herself could not distinguish between them. No doubt she knew very well but said this in the hope that both might become kings.

The Spartans, in this dilemma, sent to the oracle at Delphi to inquire how they should deal with this situation. The Priestess replied that they must make both children kings but give the greater honor to the elder. This answer did nothing to solve the difficulty confronting the Spartans as to which was the elder, but the following suggestion was made by a Messenian named Panites: The Spartans should keep watch to see which of the babes the mother washed and fed first. If she always kept to the same order, this would tell them what they wanted to know; if she varied, giving preference to the one and then to the other, it would be clear that she knew no more than they, and they must then resort to another plan.

The Spartans accepted the Messenian's suggestion and, by keeping watch over the mother, who had no idea that she was being watched, they found that in feeding and washing the babes she did indeed give preference to one over the other. So they accepted the child that was preferred by the mother as being the elder and brought it up at public expense. This elder boy had the name Eurysthenes, and the younger, Procles. When the children grew to manhood, it is said that in spite of being brothers, they were always at loggerheads, and their descendants continued to feud.

[6.61] To return then to the time when Cleomenes was in Aegina, pursuing the common good of Greece: Back in Sparta, Demaratus was bringing accusations against him, prompted not by any regard for the Aeginetans but by jealousy and enmity toward his fellow king. So upon his return from Aegina, Cleomenes began to consider how he might deprive Demaratus of his kingship. And he discovered some ground for this in the following circumstance.

When Ariston was king of Sparta, he was twice married but had no children. Unwilling to recognize that he was himself the cause of failure, he married a third time.*

[6.63] His new wife, before the full term of ten months had elapsed, gave birth to this same Demaratus. Ariston was sitting in council with the

---

* At this point Herodotus tells a long story, omitted here, concerning this third wife, who was said to have been made beautiful by a supernatural apparition.

ephors* when one of his servants came to tell him that a son was born to him. Recalling the date of his marriage and counting off the months on his fingers, Ariston cried out, with an oath, "The boy can't be mine." This was said in the hearing of the ephors, but at the time they paid little attention to it. The boy grew up, and later Ariston regretted what he had said, feeling quite certain that the boy was his. (He gave him the name Demaratus for the following reason: Some time before this, the Spartans had offered public prayers, praying that Ariston, whom they esteemed as the most distinguished of all the kings who had ever reigned in Sparta, should be granted a son. Hence the name Demaratus—prayed for by the people.)

[6.64] In the course of time, Ariston died and was succeeded by Demaratus as king. But it was fated, it seemed, that the question of legitimacy would become public and would deprive him of the kingship. In this Cleomenes played the major part, being at enmity with Demaratus on two counts: That Demaratus had withdrawn the army from Eleusis, and then again in the affair of the Aeginetans when Cleomenes had crossed over to deal with those who favored the Medes.[†]

[6.65] Eager for revenge, he approached Leotychides, who belonged to the same house as Demaratus,[‡] and made an agreement with him to the effect that Cleomenes would make him king in place of Demaratus, and then Leotychides would support him in his attack on Aegina. Now, Leotychides had become the bitter enemy of Demaratus for the following reason: When Leotychides was betrothed to Percalus, daughter of Chilon, Demaratus robbed him of his marriage by carrying off the girl himself and marrying her. This was the origin of the enmity between Leotychides and Demaratus, and now Leotychides, instigated by Cleomenes, swore an oath against Demaratus, declaring that he was not the rightful king of the Spartans, not being Ariston's son. He then proceeded to a formal prosecution, recalling the words uttered by Ariston when his servant announced the birth of a child, and he, reckoning up the months, had cried, "It can't be mine." Relying on these words, Leotychides sought to prove that Demaratus was neither the son of Ariston

---

* Under the Spartan constitution, five ephors (magistrates) were charged with overseeing a wide array of state functions and even had jurisdiction over the kings in certain matters.

† Herodotus in the later books of the *Histories* often uses the terms "Medes" and "Persians" interchangeably. In Greek the verb "to medize" meant to go over to the Persian side.

‡ He was in fact Demaratus' cousin.

nor the rightful king of Sparta and furnished as witnesses the ephors who were present at the time and had heard Ariston's words.

[6.66] The matter being hotly disputed, the Spartans finally decided to send to the oracle at Delphi to ask whether Demaratus was the son of Ariston. Cleomenes, who had contrived to get the question referred to the Priestess, now won over Cobon, a man of considerable influence at Delphi, who prevailed upon the prophetess Perialla to give the answer that Cleomenes desired. So when the sacred envoys put the question to her, the Priestess replied that Demaratus was not the son of Ariston. Some time afterward, all this became known, and Cobon was exiled from Delphi, while the prophetess Perialla was deprived of her office.

[6.67] Such were the means whereby Demaratus was deposed, but it was an insult that led to his flight to the Persians. After being deprived of the kingship, Demaratus was elected to a lesser domestic office in Sparta. When the festival of Gymnopaedia came around and Demaratus took up his position as spectator, Leotychides, now king in his place, by way of insult and mockery sent his servant to ask him how it felt to be a mere magistrate after being a king. Demaratus, stung by the question, replied, "Tell him I have experienced both, and he has not. Nevertheless, this question will bring to Sparta either thousands of ills or thousands of blessings." Then wrapping his head in his cloak, he left the theater and went home, where he prepared to sacrifice an ox to Zeus and, having done so, sent for his mother.

[6.68] When she had appeared, he put into her hands a portion of the entrails* and besought her earnestly as follows: "Mother," he said, "I beseech you by all the gods, and especially by Zeus, god of the hearth, to tell me the truth. Who was really my father? Leotychides said, in the course of the dispute, that you were already pregnant by your former husband when you were married to Ariston, and others tell a more scandalous story, that you had an affair with a stable-boy and that I am *his* son. I entreat you by the gods, tell me the truth. Even if you are guilty of what is alleged, you are not alone among women. There is much talk in Sparta that Ariston was impotent; otherwise, he would have had children by his other wives."

[6.69] "My son," replied his mother, "since you urge me so insistently to tell the truth, you shall have the whole truth. On the third night after my marriage to Ariston, a phantom, closely resembling Ariston, came to

---

* As a means of making the oath more binding.

me; it lay down with me and decked me with the wreaths it had brought. Then it left, and afterward Ariston came in. When he saw me wearing the wreaths, he asked who had given them to me, and I replied that *he* had; but he denied it, though I swore a solemn oath and reproached him for his denial. When he heard me swear the oath, Ariston realized that something supernatural had happened. And the wreaths turned out to have come from the shrine adjoining the courtyard door, belonging to the hero they call Astrabacus; and it was this same hero whom the seers named, when we questioned them, as the one by whom I conceived. So, my son, you now know all that you wanted to know. Either your father is Astrabacus and you were begotten by this hero, or it is Ariston, for it was on that night I conceived. With regard to what your enemies allege, that Ariston, when told of your birth, declared in the hearing of many that you could not be his son because ten months had not elapsed, it was simply his ignorance of such matters that led him to such a heedless utterance. Children can be born not only after ten months but also after nine or seven. Indeed I bore you, my son, after seven months. Ariston himself realized soon afterward that he did wrong to speak as he did. Give no heed to any other stories about your birth; you have heard the honest truth from me. May it befall Leotychides and all who speak like him to have wives who bear children fathered by stable-boys."

[6.70] Now that he had learned all he wanted from his mother, Demaratus took with him provisions for a journey and made his way to Elis on the pretext that he was proceeding to Delphi to consult the oracle. The Spartans, however, suspecting that he intended to flee the country, pursued him, but Demaratus crossed from Elis to Zacynthus before they caught up. The Spartans continued their pursuit and got their hands on him and deprived him of his servants; but as the Zacynthians refused to give him up, he escaped and thereafter crossed over to Asia and presented himself before Darius. The king welcomed him generously, giving him lands and cities. Such, then, was the fate that brought Demaratus to Asia, a man who had won distinction among the Spartans both for his deeds and for his wisdom in counsel, and who was moreover the only Spartan king to have gained victory in the four-horse chariot race at Olympia.

[6.71–72] After the deposition of Demaratus, Leotychides succeeded to the kingship. But for him too there was no peaceful old age at home in Sparta, for he suffered a punishment whereby Demaratus was fully avenged. Commanding the army in an expedition to Thessaly, when success was within his grasp he accepted a large bribe. He was caught in the act, sitting in his tent on a glove stuffed with money, and was brought to trial and banished, and his house was demolished. He took refuge in Tegea, and there he died. All these events, however, took place later.*

[6.73] Having thus succeeded in his scheme against Demaratus, Cleomenes, still incensed by his previous rebuff and accompanied this time by Leotychides, lost no time in proceeding against Aegina. Confronted by both kings, the Aeginetans thought it best to offer no further resistance. The kings selected out of the Aeginetans ten men pre-eminent by wealth and birth, among them Crius and Casambus, the ones who wielded the most influence. These men they carried to Attica and handed them over to the Athenians, their bitterest enemies, as hostages.

[6.74] Some time later, when the evil devices that Cleomenes had employed against Demaratus became generally known, he became fearful of the Spartans and fled to Thessaly. From there he passed to Arcadia, where he began to make trouble, seeking to unite the Arcadians against Sparta. He made them swear to follow him wherever he might lead them and was especially eager to take the leaders of the Arcadians to Nonacris, so as to make them swear by the waters of the Styx.†

[6.75] When the Spartans heard what Cleomenes was contriving, in their alarm they brought him back home on the understanding that he would be restored to his former office. Even before this he had exhibited some strange behavior, and now he was seized with outright madness that assumed this form, that whenever he met a Spartan of the citizen class he rapped him on the face with his scepter. His kindred, seeing that he was quite out of his mind, restrained him in the stocks. Being so bound and finding himself with but a single guard, he asked the man for a knife. At first the man refused, but in the face of Cleomenes' repeated threats as to what he would do to him when freed, he gave him a knife.‡ As soon as the knife was in his hand, Cleomenes began to mutilate himself, beginning with his legs, and, slicing his flesh, he advanced from his legs to his thighs, hips, and loins until he reached his belly, and, cutting this into strips, he died.

The Greeks in general say that he incurred this fate because he had bribed the Priestess to pronounce against Demaratus, but the Athenians

---

* As much as twenty years later, long after the events described in the *Histories* had ended. On this and several other occasions, Herodotus turns the clock forward to show us how retribution for a wrong works itself out over the course of decades or even generations.

† An especially binding oath; in Greek myth the gods themselves swear by the Styx.

‡ Herodotus further notes here that the guard was a helot or serf, who would therefore be at the mercy of all of Cleomenes' punishments.

attribute it to his destroying the sacred precinct of the goddesses Demeter and Persephone when he invaded Eleusis,* while the Argives ascribe it to the occasion when he took them from their refuge in the temple of the god Argus those Argives who had fled from battle and executed them, and also set fire to the sacred grove itself, giving no heed to its sanctity.†

[6.84] But the Spartans, for their part, deny that Cleomenes' madness was a punishment from heaven; they say that it was caused by his habit, acquired from the Scythians, of drinking his wine without adding water. It seems that the nomadic Scythians, eager for revenge on Darius for his invasion of their country, had sent ambassadors to Sparta to propose an alliance. It is said that when the Scythians arrived on this mission, Cleomenes was continually in their company, much more so than was seemly, and from them he learned to drink his wine without water—and this, the Spartans believe, led him to insanity. (From this episode, the Spartans say, comes the phrase they use when they want strong drink: "Scythian style.")

For my own part, I think that Cleomenes' death was a punishment for what he did to Demaratus.

———

With Cleomenes dead, the Aeginetans mended their dispute with Sparta in an effort to get back their leading citizens who were being held hostage in Athens, but the Athenians refused to give these men back, prompting a series of hostilities between Athens and Aegina.

The Persians now prepared a major assault on Athens and Eretria, the two states that had helped the Ionians in the sack of Sardis. An initial invasion, launched in 492 under the general Mardonius, Darius' son-in-law, failed before getting halfway to its targets. The plan had been for the army and navy to proceed toward Greece together, such that the fleet could land supplies for the men as they marched down the coast. But the army, moving westward across Thrace, was badly mauled in a night battle with the Brygi tribe, while the fleet incurred heavy damage

---

* This was in 506, during Cleomenes' last, abortive attempt to intervene in Athenian politics and prevent Cleisthenes from coming to power. Eleusis is a shrine near Athens; the Athenians naturally prefer to see the sacrilege done on their turf as the cause of Cleomenes' madness.

† Herodotus goes on to tell the story of this campaign (494) in some detail, but the main outlines are clear from the passage excerpted here. The city of Argos had long been Sparta's bitterest enemy, and this episode only deepened the antagonism. In the Persian wars that would follow, Argos refused to take part in any defense of Greece organized by Sparta and thus stayed neutral. It was considered a violation of religious law to execute those who have taken refuge at a holy shrine.

*from a storm as it rounded the peninsula of Athos. Mardonius returned in disgrace,
having conquered only Macedonia and the Greek island of Thasos. But Darius
decided to try a new approach, with new generals, two years later.*

J. THE FIRST PERSIAN INVASION OF GREECE (490 BC)

[6.94] While war continued between Athens and Aegina, Darius, the Persian king, carried on with his own designs, being exhorted every day by his servant to "remember the Athenians," and urged on by the Pisistratids,* who never ceased to slander the Athenians. At the same time, he was himself pleased to have this pretext for reducing to submission those Greeks who refused him the symbolic totems of earth and water. In view of the failure of the previous expedition, he relieved his general Mardonius of command and appointed other generals to lead the attack on Eretria and Athens: Datis, a Mede, and Artaphernes, his own nephew and son of Artaphernes. Their orders were to reduce to slavery Athens and Eretria and to bring the slaves before the king.

[6.95] These new commanders, leaving the king's presence, made their way to the Aleian plain in Cilicia, accompanied by a strong and well-equipped force of infantry. Here they were joined by the entire naval force requisitioned from various communities and also by the horse transports that Darius had commanded his tributaries to prepare the previous year. The horses were embarked on the transports, the troops on their ships, and together with six hundred triremes they set sail for Ionia. From there, instead of keeping a straight course parallel to the coast toward the Hellespont and Thrace, they sailed westward from Samos across the Icarian Sea through the islands. In my opinion, the reason for this was their fear of the passage around Athos, which had been the cause of a fearful disaster the previous year. A further compelling reason was that the island of Naxos remained as yet unconquered.[†]

[6.96] When the Persians reached Naxos from the Icarian Sea (this being their first objective), the Naxians, remembering what had happened on the previous occasion, offered no resistance, but took to the

---

* That is, Hippias the exiled Athenian tyrant and his kin. Though he had been out of power for almost thirty years, the aged Hippias, now living at Darius' court, had not given up hope of regaining rule at Athens.

[†] Naxos had been the target of a joint Samian-Persian attack ten years earlier.

hills. The Persians carried off to slavery those whom they caught, burned the temples along with the town, and then sailed away to affront the other islands.

[6.97] While the Persians were thus engaged, the Delians also quit Delos and took refuge in Tenos.* As the Persian fleet first drew near, Datis, sailing ahead, commanded them not to anchor at Delos but at Rhenaea opposite. He himself, on discovering whither the Delians had fled, sent a herald to them with this message: "Holy men, why have you fled, judging me so harshly? I myself have enough understanding—even if the king had not given me specific orders—to avoid doing harm to the birthplace of the two gods, both to the land itself and those who dwell there. Return, therefore, to that which is your own and continue to dwell in your island." This was the message he sent to the Delians, after which he proceeded to heap up on the altar three hundred talents-weight of frankincense and burned it as an offering. Then he sailed with his force against Eretria first, taking with him a number of Ionians and Aeolians.

The Delians say that after his departure, Delos was shaken by an earthquake, the first and, to this day, the last shock experienced there. It may well be that this was a sign whereby the god gave warning of troubles to come, for during the successive reigns of the three kings—Darius, son of Hystaspes; Xerxes, son of Darius; and Artaxerxes, son of Xerxes—Greece suffered more woes than in the twenty generations preceding Darius, some inflicted on them by the Persians, some arising from the struggles for supremacy by their own leading states.[†] It was therefore not surprising that Delos should be shaken by an earthquake where there had never been an earthquake before. And indeed there existed an oracle containing the words "Delos too I will shake, though never before shaken." The above names can be rendered in Greek as follows: Darius—worker; Xerxes—warrior; Artaxerxes—great warrior. This would be a correct translation of the names of these kings.[‡]

---

* Delos, the legendary birthplace of Apollo and Artemis, was considered a sacred island by the Greeks, especially the Ionians (for whom it was the center of various cult rituals and festivals).

† Historians have given much attention to this sentence, since it is the one place in the *Histories* where Herodotus seems to make explicit reference to the Peloponnesian War—the great conflict between Athens and Sparta that began, officially, in 431. But the two Greek superpowers had been skirmishing long before this date, and it is possible that Herodotus' words here could refer to a period decades earlier than the war itself.

‡ These are spurious translations.

———

Eretria was a small city in western Euboea, whose only hope of resisting the Persian invasion lay in its walls. Faced with imminent attack, the citizens became fractious, with many inclined to surrender to the Persians; a contingent of support troops from Athens, learning of this divisiveness, hastened to abandon the town. At last the Persians arrived and commenced siege operations. Fighting was fierce for six days, after which two Eretrians treacherously opened the gates to the Persians, allowing them to sack and burn the city and enslave all its inhabitants. Darius had settled one of his scores with the Greeks; now Athens remained.

———

[6.102] With the subjugation of Eretria, after a few days' delay the Persians sailed for Attica,* confident that they could deal with the Athenians just as they had dealt with the Eretrians. Marathon being a place in Attica suitable for cavalry and nearest to Eretria, it was to Marathon that they were guided by Hippias, son of Pisistratus.†

[6.103] When the news reached the Athenians, they likewise marched out to Marathon under the command of ten generals,‡ of whom the tenth was Miltiades.§ Miltiades' father, Cimon, had been banished from Athens by the tyrant Pisistratus. While in exile it was his fortune to win the four-horse chariot race at Olympia, thereby acquiring the same honor as his half-brother Miltiades before him. At the next Olympiad he won the same prize with the same mares, but he surrendered his victory and caused Pisistratus to be proclaimed the victor, on the understanding that he would be allowed back to his own country. He won another Olympiad with the same mares; he was murdered by the sons of Pisistratus after their father had died. They set men to waylay him by night, and these slew him near the Council House. He was buried outside the city beyond what is called the Valley Road, and opposite the tomb were buried the mares that had won three prizes. At the time of Cimon's death,

---

* Attica is the peninsula on which Athens is situated.

† Exiled almost thirty years earlier and now an old man, Hippias nevertheless hoped to get back into power at Athens, this time as a Persian satrap.

‡ The Athenians elected ten *stratēgoi*, or "generals," annually to supervise military affairs, though usually only one or two commanded any single military expedition.

§ Herodotus here interrupts the story of the developing battle to give us background on Miltiades, who will soon be its principal hero. The point of describing the murder of Miltiades' father, Cimon, by the sons of Pisistratus becomes obvious when we consider that one of those same sons, Hippias, is now guiding the Persian attack on Athens. For Miltiades, the coming battle is not only a moment of national peril but a personal grudge match as well.

Stesagoras, the elder of his two sons, was living with Cimon's brother Miltiades in the Chersonese, while the younger, called Miltiades after his uncle, who had founded the Chersonese settlement, was with his father in Athens.

It was this Miltiades who was then elected one of ten generals of the Athenian troops. He had escaped from the Chersonese and twice come within an ace of losing his life—first when the Phoenicians, eager to seize him and carry him off to the Persian king, pursued him as far as Imbros; and then, after he had escaped that peril and reached his own country and thought himself safe, his political enemies, having lain in wait for him, arraigned him before the court and prosecuted him for his rule of the Chersonese.* This attack he likewise escaped and was appointed general by popular vote.

[6.105] But before leaving the city, the Athenians first sent off to Sparta a messenger, one Philippides,† an Athenian who was by profession and practice a courier. According to the account he later gave to the Athenians, this man, when he was in the neighborhood of Mount Parthenion above Tegea, encountered the god Pan, who called him by name and bade him ask the Athenians why they neglected him, though he was well disposed to them and had often been helpful to them in the past and would be so again. The Athenians, believing this to be a true account, when their affairs were once more in good order, set up a shrine to Pan beneath the Acropolis, and from the time they received this message, they propitiate him with yearly sacrifices and a torch-race. [6.106] So Philippides, at this time—that is, when he was sent by the generals and when, as he said, the god Pan appeared to him—reached Sparta the day after leaving Athens‡ and delivered this message to the Spartan authorities: "Men of Lacedaemon, the Athenians ask you to come to their assistance and not to permit a city that is the most ancient in Greece to be enslaved by the barbarians. Already Eretria has been reduced to slavery, and Greece is the weaker for the loss of a notable city." Thus spoke Philippides, as instructed, and the Spartans replied that although they

---

* The younger Miltiades had inherited rule over the Chersonese from his uncle of the same name.

† In some manuscripts he is called Pheidippides.

‡ Covering seventy miles per day for two days, fast running indeed! In later legends he is also said to have run the twenty-six miles to Athens from Marathon to announce the Greek victory there—the reason that our modern marathon run is set at just over twenty-six miles.

were willing to send help, they found it impossible to do so immediately because of the restrictions of their own laws. It was the ninth day of the month, and they said they could not take the field until the moon was at the full.* So they waited for the full moon.

[6.107] Meanwhile Hippias, son of Pisistratus, was guiding the Persians to Marathon. On the previous night he had dreamed a strange dream, that he was lying in his mother's arms. This dream he interpreted to mean that he would be restored to Athens, would recover his power, and would end his days peacefully in his own native country. Such were his first thoughts about the dream. Acting now as a guide to the Persians, he put the prisoners from Eretria ashore on Aegilia, an island belonging to the town of Styra, and then proceeded to lead the fleet to an anchorage off Marathon, where he landed the Persians and drew them up in formation.

As he was thus engaged, it so happened that he sneezed and coughed more vigorously than was his wont, and, since he was advanced in years and most of his teeth were loose, one of them fell out through the violence of his coughing. It fell somewhere in the sand, and in spite of all his efforts, he could not find it. He heaved a great sigh and, turning to some bystanders, said: "This land is not ours and we shall never be able to hold it. Whatever of it was my portion, my tooth possesses." So Hippias believed that this was the manner in which his dream had come true.

[6.108] The Athenians were drawn up in an enclosure sacred to Heracles when they were joined by the Plataeans in full force.†

[6.109] The Athenian generals were divided in their opinions, some arguing against risking a battle in view of their numerical inferiority, while others were in favor. Among the latter was Miltiades. Seeing that opinion was divided and that the less valiant view was likely to prevail, Miltiades resolved to approach the polemarch, who held the eleventh and decisive vote. (At this period of time, the man on whom the lot fell to be polemarch was entitled to an equal vote with the ten generals.) The polemarch on this occasion was Callimachus of Aphidna, and it was he whom Miltiades approached, speaking as follows: "It is in your hands, Callimachus, either to enslave Athens or to make her free and to leave

---

* Not necessarily a specious excuse. The Spartans were strict observers of religious ritual, and the law forbidding military maneuvers during the period in question was an ancient one. It also seems clear that the Spartans preferred to avoid a direct clash with Persia.

† Plataea was the only Greek city to come to Athens' aid in this crisis. In the sections omitted here, Herodotus describes how Plataea had become an ally of Athens decades earlier in order to escape harassment by her neighbors.

This painted cup shows the mismatch between Greek infantrymen, with their metal armor and heavy shields, and the typical Persian infantryman, dressed in cloth, wearing a headdress instead of a helmet, and carrying no shield (perhaps having lost or discarded a wicker one). MUSEUM OF SCOTLAND

behind you for all time a memory surpassing even that of Harmodius and Aristogeiton.* Never in all their history have the Athenians faced a greater peril. If they bow their necks to the Medes, no one can doubt what they will suffer when given over to Hippias; but if our native city fights and wins, it can become the leading city of all Greece. How such things can be, and how it rests with you to determine the course of events, I shall now make clear: We generals, ten in number, are divided in our opinions, some in favor of risking a battle, some against. If we do not fight now, I expect to see bitter dissension break out in Athens, which will shake men's resolution and lead to submission to Persia.† But if we join

* The illustrious "tyrant-slayers" who had assassinated one of the Pisistratids in 514 and thus ushered in the end of autocratic rule.

† Miltiades envisions Athens being destroyed by internal factionalism, just as Eretria had been. His own experience since returning to Athens had revealed to him the strength of the accommodationist faction.

battle before the rot can spread throughout the citizen body, and if the gods do but grant us fair play, we can win in the engagement. So yours is now the decisive voice; all depends on you. If you cast your vote on my side, your country will be free and the foremost city of Greece. But if you support those who are against giving battle, then the opposite of those blessings I have mentioned will be your lot." [6.110] These words of Miltiades convinced Callimachus, and with the polemarch's vote added to the others, the decision to fight was made. Thereupon the generals who had been in favor of fighting, as each one got his turn to exercise supreme command for the day, all resigned authority in favor of Miltiades. He accepted their offer but nevertheless waited until his own turn of command came around before he would join battle.*

[6.111] Then the Athenian army was drawn up for battle in the following order: The right wing was commanded by the polemarch, for it was the custom of the Athenians at the time for the polemarch to have the right wing. Then, in their regular order, the tribes were arrayed in an unbroken line; and finally on the left wing were stationed the Plataeans. Ever since this battle, whenever the Athenians offer sacrifice at their quadrennial festivals, the Athenian herald prays that the Plataeans, along with the Athenians, receive benefits. Now the way that the Athenian troops were arranged at Marathon had this result: that the extending of the Athenian front to equal that of the Medes left their center the weakest part of the line, being few ranks deep, but both wings were strengthened.

[6.112] These dispositions being made and the sacrifices being favorable, with the word being given, the Athenians charged the enemy at a run. The distance between the armies was about a mile.† The Persians, seeing them coming on at a run, prepared to receive them; they thought that the Athenians had lost their senses and were bent on self-destruction, for they were inferior in number and came on at a rush without cavalry or archers. Such were the thoughts of the barbarians, but the Athenians

* Much confusion arises from this chapter, as from other aspects of Herodotus' account of the Battle of Marathon. Why would Miltiades want to wait before attacking, given his words in the previous chapter about the creeping "rot" that threatened Athenian unity? Probably he was hoping that the Spartan army would arrive to help him—an aspect of the story that Athenian legend later "forgot."

† It is impossible to imagine men wearing heavy armor running at full speed for a mile without exhausting themselves. Legend has clearly exaggerated the distance involved. Probably the troops *did* run for a short distance, if only to avoid the hail of arrows falling on them as they advanced.

fell upon them in close order and fought in a way never to be forgotten. They were the first of the Greeks, as far as we know, to charge the enemy at a run and the first to look unafraid at Median dress and the men wearing it. Before this, the very name Mede had been a terror to the Greeks.*

The struggle at Marathon lasted a considerable time. In the center, which was held by the Persians themselves and the Sacae, the invaders had the upper hand. It was there that they broke the line and pursued the fugitives inland, whereas on the wings the Athenians and the Plataeans were victorious. Where they had prevailed they allowed the enemy to flee, and, uniting both wings, they fell upon those who had broken the center and defeated them.† They pursued the fleeing Persians and cut them down as they fled to the sea. Then, laying hold of the ships, they called for fire.

[6.114–15] It was in this phase of the battle that the polemarch Callimachus, who had fought valiantly, lost his life; and one of the generals, Stesilaus, was slain; and Cynegirus,‡ as he was laying hold of the vessel's stern, had his hand cut off by an ax and so perished. So likewise did many other notable Athenians. Nevertheless, in this way the Athenians managed to secure seven of the ships. The rest succeeded in getting away, and the Persians, after taking on board the Eretrian prisoners from the island where they had left them, sailed around Sunium, and headed for Athens, hoping to reach it before the Athenian army could return.§ In Athens the Alcmaeonids were accused of suggesting this tactic. They had, it was said, an agreement with the Persians and raised a shield to signal to them when they were embarked on their ships.¶

[6.116] So the Persians were sailing around Sunium, but the Athenians made all possible speed in returning to the city and succeeded in arriving before the Persians. Just as at Marathon they had taken up a position in

---

* A striking reminder of the novelty of this confrontation; the Greeks had not faced a barbarian threat on the mainland in all their recorded history.

† A plausible explanation of how the Greeks prevailed; the Persians allowed their "crack" troops in the center to become cut off from the wings and isolated, so that the Athenians could close in on them from both sides.

‡ Brother of the playwright Aeschylus.

§ Having failed at Marathon, the Persians attempted to take the city of Athens itself while the army was still in the field. However, this entailed a journey all the way around the Attic peninsula, since the harbor of Phalerum lay on its western coast.

¶ The Alcmaeonids were a wealthy, politically liberal family at Athens that had produced Cleisthenes, among other populist leaders. There is reason to believe that they may indeed have been involved in a collusion with the Persians.

an enclosure sacred to Heracles, so they now stationed themselves in another enclosure sacred to Heracles at Cynosarges. The Persian fleet lay off Phalerum, which was at that time the harbor for Athens, and after riding at anchor for a while sailed away for Asia.

[6.117] In the Battle of Marathon some 6,400 were killed on the Persian side, and on the Athenian side 192. In this battle a strange event took place. The Athenian Epizelus, fighting gallantly in the thick of the fray, was struck blind, though untouched either by sword or arrow, and his blindness continued to the end of his life. I am told that in speaking of this event he used to say that there stood against him a man of great stature, heavily armed, whose beard cast a shadow over his entire shield, and that this phantom passed him by and slew the man beside him. Such is his story.

[6.120] When the moon reached its full, the Spartans set out for Athens, two thousand strong, so anxious to be in time that they were in Attica on the third day after leaving Sparta. Too late to take part in the battle, they were nevertheless eager to have sight of the Medes and went on to Marathon to view the bodies. Then, bestowing praise on the Athenians for their achievement, they returned home.

A great victory demands a celebration, and Herodotus closes his account of Marathon with two of his most delightful stories, both concerning the wealthy and politically influential Alcmaeonid family. Having first tried to refute the charge that the Alcmaeonids helped the Persians at Marathon, Herodotus here traces the early history of the family, going back to the founder of its fortune, Alcmaeon.

[6.125] Even in the early days the Alcmaeonids were a family of distinction in Athens, and from the time of Alcmaeon, and of Megacles after him, they acquired particular fame. When the Lydian envoys sent by Croesus from Sardis arrived to consult the oracle at Delphi, Alcmaeon, son of Megacles, exerted himself to give them every possible assistance. Having learned from the envoys sent on this mission that Alcmaeon had rendered him such good service, Croesus invited him to Sardis and promised him as a gift whatever amount of gold he would be able to carry away on his person at one time. Confronted by this unusual offer, Alcmaeon clothed himself in a very large tunic with a bulge at the waist, put on the widest boots he could procure, and thus attired he followed his guides into the treasury. Falling upon a heap of gold dust, he first crammed into his boots right up his legs as much gold as they would hold, then he filled full the bulging front of his tunic, scattered gold dust all over his hair, stuffed some more into his mouth, and was scarcely able to stagger out of the treasury, looking barely human with his mouth stuffed full and his figure all swollen. When Croesus saw him, he was overcome with laughter and gave him all the gold he was carrying and as much again. Thus it was that the house of Alcmaeon acquired great wealth, and Alcmaeon was able to maintain a racing stable with which he won the four-horse chariot race at Olympia.

[6.126] Then, in the next generation, Cleisthenes, ruler of Sicyon,* raised Alcmaeon's family to even greater heights than they had attained before. Cleisthenes had a daughter named Agariste, whom he wished to marry to the best suitor he could find in all Greece. So at the Olympic games, where he himself had won the chariot race, he caused a proclamation to be made that any Greek who wished to become Cleisthenes' son-in-law should come to Sicyon within sixty days, or even sooner; within a year's time from the end of the sixty days, Cleisthenes would decide on the man to marry his daughter. Thereupon all the Greeks who had confidence in their own merit and in that of their country came as suitors to Sicyon, where Cleisthenes had prepared for them a racetrack and a wrestling-ground for this very purpose.

[6.127] From Sybaris in Italy (Sybaris was at that time at the height of its prosperity) came Smindyrides, a man famous above all others for the art of luxurious living; and from Siris, also in Italy, came Damasus, son of Amyris, who was called the Wise. Then there was Amphimnestus, from Epidamnus on the Ionian Gulf, and from Aetolia came Males, brother to Titormus who was the strongest man in Greece and who had sought retirement in the remotest parts of Aetolia so as to avoid his fellow men. From the Peloponnese came Leocedes. Next was Amiantus from Trapezus in Arcadia, and Laphanes, an Azenian of Paeus, and lastly Onomastus, a native of Elis. These were the four from the Peloponnese. From Athens came Megacles, the son of that Alcmaeon who had visited Croesus, and Hippocleides, the wealthiest and handsomest of the Athenians. From Eretria, which at this time was a flourishing city, came Lysanias, the only man from Euboea. From Thessaly came Diactorides, one of the Scopodae of Crannon, and Alcon from the Molossians. This was the list of suitors.

---

* Grandfather of the more famous Cleisthenes who pioneered the democratic regime at Athens.

[6.128] When they were all assembled on the appointed day, Cleisthenes first made inquiry as to each one's country and parentage, and then, keeping them with him for a year, he made trial of their many virtues, their temper, their accomplishments, and their disposition, sometimes conversing with them singly, sometimes drawing them all together. Those who were not too old he took with him to the gymnasia, but the greatest test was at the banquet table. It so came about that the suitors who pleased him best were from Athens, and of these he gave preference to Hippocleides, partly on account of his many virtues, partly because he was related far back to the Cypselids of Corinth.

[6.129] When at last the day arrived for the marriage feast and for Cleisthenes to declare his preferred suitor, he sacrificed a hundred oxen and gave a banquet for the suitors and all the Sicyonians. Dinner being over, the suitors competed with one another in music and in public speaking. As the drinking proceeded, Hippocleides, who far outclassed the others, bade the flute-player play him a tune, which the man did, and Hippocleides danced to it. No doubt he danced well to his own satisfaction, but Cleisthenes looked askance at the entire performance. After a brief pause, Hippocleides bade someone bring a table, and, the table being produced, he danced on it, first some Laconian figures, then some Attic figures, and then he stood on his head on the table, tossing his legs about in the air. Cleisthenes, although he was now quite averse to the idea of Hippocleides as a son-in-law because of his shameless display of dancing, had restrained himself throughout the Laconian and Attic figures, wishing to avoid a public outburst. But when he saw Hippocleides beating time with his legs in the air, he could no longer contain himself and cried out: "Son of Tisander, you have danced away your marriage!" "What does Hippocleides care?" came Hippocleides' reply, and that was how the proverb originated.*

[6.130] Then Cleisthenes called for silence and addressed the assembly. "Gentlemen, suitors of my daughter, I have the highest esteem for you all, and if it were possible, I would show favor to you all by not choosing one and disappointing the others. But since, with only one daughter, it is beyond my power to please all, I bestow on those of you who have failed to win the bride a talent of silver, in appreciation of the honor you have done me in wishing to marry into my house and to com-

---

* Evidently Greeks of Herodotus' day said "What does Hippocleides care?" to express disregard for conventional opinion.

pensate you for your long absence from home. My daughter, Agariste, I betroth to Megacles, son of Alcmaeon, according to Athenian law." When Megacles declared his acceptance, Cleisthenes had the marriage formally solemnized.

[6.131] Such was the Trial of the Suitors, and in this way the Alcmaeonids became famous throughout Greece. From this marriage was born Cleisthenes—named after his maternal grandfather, Cleisthenes of Sicyon—who organized the Athenians into their tribes and instituted democratic government in Athens. A second son of Megacles was Hippocrates, whose children were another Megacles and another Agariste, named after Agariste, daughter of Cleisthenes. She married Xanthippus, son of Ariphon, and, being with child, she had a dream wherein she thought she was delivered of a lion. In a few days she gave birth to a son, Pericles.*

—

Herodotus now returns to the narrative present to record the fortunes of Miltiades, hero of Marathon, in the period after the battle. Not content to rest on his laurels, Miltiades promised the Athenians he would make them rich if they gave him money and troops with which to attack an objective he refused to name. The target turned out to be Paros, a wealthy Greek island that had participated, under compulsion, in the Persian attack on Eretria and Athens. Miltiades' forces put the main city of the island under siege but failed to make any headway, and then, while conducting some sort of covert operation, Miltiades himself injured his leg jumping from the top of a fence. Incapacitated by his injury and disgraced by the failure to capture Paros, Miltiades returned to Athens to undergo a second political trial mounted by his enemies. His reputation as the hero of Marathon notwithstanding, he was fined a huge sum of money and soon thereafter died as a result of gangrene in his injured leg.

K. THE SECOND PERSIAN INVASION
OF GREECE (480 BC)

With book 7 we enter the most detailed and least fragmented portion of the Histories. *Herodotus "fast-forwards" in only a few paragraphs through the final years of Darius' reign, roughly 490–486, to arrive at the accession of King Xerxes in the fifth chapter. From that point on, his narrative pace slows dramatically; his next*

---

* The only mention in the *Histories* of the great statesman who dominated affairs at Athens during much of Herodotus' lifetime.

focus on
→ comparison of practical lessons
learned from Darius & Xerxes vs. Leonidas
→ comparison of → to previous Persian leaders
Herodotus · 75

three books cover only five years of historical time, as compared with the decades covered in the previous three books and the centuries of the first three. He follows month by month, and finally day by day, the progress of Xerxes' invasion of Greece in 480, concluding with the defeat of the last remaining Persian forces in Europe in 479. Because of its internal unity, its grand scale, and its focus on the figure of King Xerxes, this section is sometimes referred to as the Xerxiad, on the analogy of Homer's epic poem the Iliad.

The first major scene of book 7 is a debate in the Persian council chamber over the question of the proposed war on Greece. It contains some of the longest and most ornately composed speeches in the whole of the Histories, put in the mouths of the three great leaders of the day: Xerxes the king; Mardonius the army commander; and Artabanus the elder sage. The scene must be largely invented, since Herodotus could not have had much information about what was said in secret council meetings far removed from him in both time and space. But the value of these speeches for readers of the Histories goes far beyond the artistry of their composition. Herodotus here attempts an analysis of the internal workings of the Persian political system, as well as providing character sketches of the major "players" of the day. His depiction of how a major decision got made at the Persian court reveals the strengths and (mostly) weaknesses of an entire society. The comparison that can be drawn between this council meeting and two similar scenes in the Greek world, the debates of the admirals at Salamis (8.58ff.), is inescapable and highly illuminating.

—

[7.5]* After Darius' death, the throne passed to Xerxes, Darius' son.[†] At first Xerxes was in no way eager to launch an invasion of Greece; rather, he began to muster his forces to put down rebellion in Egypt. But by his side stood Mardonius (son of Gobryas), the most influential man at his court[‡]—he was Xerxes' cousin, being the son of Darius' sister—who kept advancing this argument: "Master, it doesn't look right not to punish the Athenians for the great wrongs they have done to the Persians. Go ahead and do what you are undertaking to do, teach Egypt a lesson for its inso-

* The section starting here and ending at 7.12 was translated by the editor.

† In 486; Xerxes was at this point about thirty-two years old. His succession was not assured, as Herodotus relates in the chapters omitted here. He was the youngest of Darius' sons but also the only one born of Atossa, daughter of Cyrus the Great. In the inevitable dispute over succession, Xerxes had gotten valuable advice, according to Herodotus, from the Spartan king Demaratus, now exiled and living at Susa—an authority on succession disputes, to be sure.

‡ Mardonius, it will be recalled, had led the first, abortive invasion of Greece in 493 under Darius (see pp. 62–63 above).

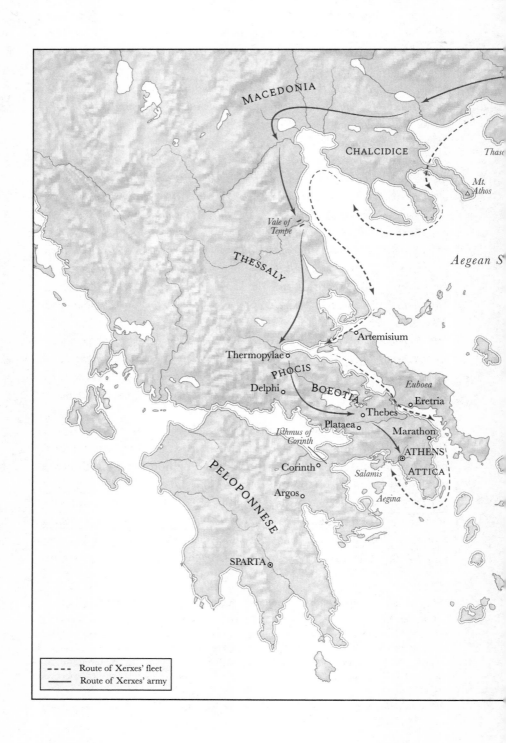

MACEDONIA

CHALCIDICE

Thas

Mt.
△ Athos

Aegean S

Vale of
Tempe

THESSALY

Artemisium

Thermopylae ○

PHOCIS

Delphi ○

BOEOTIA

Euboea

Eretria

○ Thebes

Plataea ○

Marathon

*Isthmus of
Corinth*

ATHENS

Corinth ○

Salamis

ATTICA

Argos ○

Aegina

PELOPONNESE

SPARTA ○

- - - - Route of Xerxes' fleet
———— Route of Xerxes' army

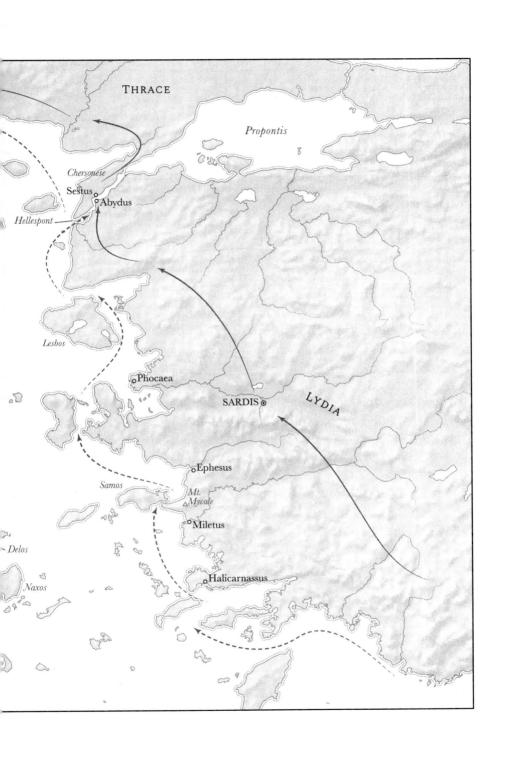

THRACE

Propontis

Chersonese

Sestus ○
○ Abydus

Hellespont

Lesbos

○ Phocaea

SARDIS ◎   LYDIA

○ Ephesus

Samos

Mt.
△*Mycale*

○ Miletus

Delos

Naxos

○ Halicarnassus

manipulated

Xerxes is easily convinced

lence; but then march on Athens, so that your countrymen will speak well of you and so that your enemies will think twice before attacking your land." Vengeance was his main theme, but he also included this as an added spur: that Europe was a very beautiful realm, excellent in every way, where all variety of trees were grown, and the king, alone among mortals, deserved to possess it.

[7.6] Mardonius spoke thus out of his restlessness for new enterprises and because he himself wished to become governor of Greece. In time, his arguments persuaded Xerxes, and other circumstances enforced his struggle to convince the king.

[7.7–8] When Xerxes had made up his mind to invade Greece, he first went through with his plan to attack the Egyptian rebels. This was in the second year after Darius' death. He quickly subdued them and made Egypt far more servile than it had been during Darius' reign, appointing his brother Achaemenes to serve as governor. (Later, a Libyan named Inaros, the son of the pharaoh Psammetichus, rose up and slew Achaemenes.) Then, after Egypt had been retaken, when he was ready to undertake the expedition against Athens, he called a council meeting of the Persian nobles to find out what they thought of it and to announce his intentions before all.

When they were assembled, Xerxes spoke as follows: "Persians, it is not I who have introduced this law of conquest among us; I follow what I have received from others. I have learned from my elders that our nation has never been at rest since we took over dominion from the Medes, when Cyrus overcame Astyages. The god has shown us this path and sees to it that our many pursuits lead always to our improvement. You know well how many nations Cyrus, Cambyses, and my father, Darius, have conquered and added to our empire; why bother to name them? As for me, ever since I have inherited this throne, I have pondered how not to fall short of the standard of honor my ancestors have set and how not to diminish the power of the Persians. And in my ponderings I have found a way we can acquire glory, along with a land every bit as large and noble as our own and indeed even more fruitful; vengeance and retribution come with it as well. Hence I have gathered you here to explain to you what I have in mind to do.

"I intend to bridge the Hellespont and take my army straight through Europe and into Greece, to punish the Athenians for what they did to the Persians and to my father. You all saw that Darius too was eager to march against these men. But he is dead, and he never got his chance at revenge.

On his behalf, and on behalf of all Persians, I vow not to stop before I capture and burn the city of Athens—those Athenians who started this with their attack on me and my father. First they marched to Sardis, together with Aristagoras the Milesian, our puppet, and they set fire to sacred groves and shrines; and then, what they did to us when we landed on their soil, in the invasion led by Datis and Artaphernes—well, I don't need to remind you.*

"For these reasons I am preparing to attack them, and in addition I reckon up the following benefits to be gained: If we subjugate these men as well as their neighbors, those who inhabit the land founded by Pelops the Phrygian,† our realm will extend to the very sky where Zeus dwells. Indeed, the sun will never look down upon a country outside our empire; you and I together, marching through the length and breadth of Europe, will make all lands one land. For I have learned that once these people I have mentioned are subdued, there will be no tribe nor city anywhere on earth able to mount a fight against us. So let the blameless ones bear the yoke of slavery along with those guilty of wronging us.‡

"Your task, if you wish to please me, is this: When I tell you that it's time to come, you must all rush to come, and whomever brings the best-prepared army, to him I will give the gifts that we Persians treasure most highly. Such is your job. But lest I appear to you to be making plans without consultation, I now put this question before the council. Let anyone who wants reveal his own opinion." With that he ended his speech.

[7.9] After this, Mardonius spoke. "Master," he said, "you have proved yourself the best of the Persians, both those who have come before and those who will follow after. Besides your other fine and true words, you have declared that you won't allow the Ionians living in Europe§ to scorn us when we do not merit their scorn. Let me now add this: It is unthinkable that we should hold in servitude the Sacae, the Indians, and the Ethiopians, and the other great and numerous peoples we have conquered, though they have done us no wrong, while not getting revenge on the Greeks who have started this fight unprovoked. What are we afraid

---

* The reference is to the Battle of Marathon some five years before this.

† "The land founded by Pelops" means the Peloponnese, the large peninsula named "island of Pelops" in Greek, dominated militarily by the city of Sparta.

‡ The "blameless ones" are the Spartans, who, unlike the Athenians, declined to take part in the Ionian attack on Sardis.

§ Another periphrasis showing how a Persian might have understood complex Greek geography and ethnic divisions. The "Ionians living in Europe" are the Athenians.

of? Why fear their numbers or their cash reserves, when we know that their style of fighting and their resources are both slight? For we can judge them by their offspring, our subjects, the Asiatic Greeks called Ionians and Aeolians and Dorians.

"I myself have made trial of these people, on an invasion ordered by your father. I got as far as Macedonia and almost to the gates of Athens without any of them opposing me in battle.* What's more, these reckless, clumsy Greeks, as I have discovered, make war in the most ill-contrived way possible: After declaring war on one another, they find a lovely, smooth plot of land and go there to fight, so that even the victors get badly roughed up, while the losers, I needn't tell you, are totally destroyed. Since they speak the same tongue, why don't they use heralds and envoys to resolve their differences, or any other means save battle? Or if they must go to war, why don't they choose ground that least favors their enemy and fight there? But no, they persist in this useless behavior and thus they never even discussed armed opposition when I drove my army right up to Macedonia.

"Who will oppose your war aims, sire, when you command the whole population of Asia and all her ships besides? I don't imagine the Greeks have so much boldness. But if I'm wrong and the Greeks bestir themselves, foolishly, to offer battle, they will learn how far beyond other men we are in the skills of war. Let us leave nothing untried, for it is by trying that men accomplish everything; nothing comes to them of its own accord."

[7.10] Thus spoke Mardonius, putting the polish on Xerxes' opinion. Then silence descended on the Persian council, no one being willing to speak in opposition. Finally, Artabanus, son of Hystaspes, brother of Darius, uncle of Xerxes, and trusted adviser to the king, spoke as follows: "It is not possible, sire, to choose the best course of action when there is no free exchange of views; one must simply follow whatever is proposed. But when both sides of the argument are expressed, the right one can be chosen, just as we test the purity of gold not by examining one sample alone but by scratching two together to see which is the purer. I am the man who once told your father, my brother Darius, not to attack the Scythians, a tribe that has no fixed dwellings anywhere on earth; but in

---

* Mardonius boldly exaggerates his achievements in 493; in fact, he was a long way from Athens when his army was thrashed and forced to retreat.

his confidence of victory he heeded me not and then went and lost the better part of his army. You, my king, are about to attack a people who are worthier by far than the Scythians, and who indeed are said to be the worthiest of all, both on the land and on the sea. It's my business to tell you just how much you have to fear from them.

"You say, my king, that you will bridge the Hellespont and march your army right through Europe and into Greece. Let's say, though, that you meet with some reverse either on land or on sea, or even on both at once—for these men are said to be valiant soldiers, as one could deduce from the way the Athenians alone defeated the large force that went with Datis and Artaphernes to Attica. But let's suppose you avoid a double defeat. What if they only bear down on you with their ships and win a naval engagement and then sail to the Hellespont and break apart the bridge there? That is a terrible thing to contemplate, my king. For my part, though, I need no special insight to guess at what would happen, since the same thing almost happened to us when your father bridged the Thracian Bosporus and then the Danube to invade Scythian land. The Scythians used all of their wiles to persuade the Ionians, who had been left as guards of the Danube crossing, to break up the bridge; and if His-tiaeus, ruler of Miletus, had followed the will of the other rulers rather than opposing them, the Persian Empire would have fallen that day.* Is it not terrible even to hear—the idea that your royal fortunes once rested entirely on one man's shoulders?

"Don't take us into such great peril when there is no need. Heed my advice, and dissolve this assembly, and then, after you've examined the matter in private, you can announce to us again what you think best to do. For the best benefit of good planning is this: If one is thwarted by some setback, nevertheless one has the sense that the plans were well laid, but bad luck intervened; whereas if one is a bad planner, but fortune turns out favorably, one has the sense of having thrown a lucky roll of the dice, but nevertheless having laid bad plans.

"Do you see how the god hurls his lightning at the outsized beasts and stops their proud displays, while the smaller creatures bother him not at all? Do you see how his bolts fall without fail on the biggest houses and trees? Thus does the god diminish all things outsized. In the same way too, a great army can be destroyed by a smaller one, when the god in jeal-

---

* See 5.133ff.

ous spite hurls thunder or puts panic into them so that they are destroyed all out of proportion to their strengths. For the god does not allow anyone except himself to think grand thoughts.*

"All things done in haste beget mistakes, and for these mistakes one usually pays a very high price. Restraint brings benefits, whether they are apparent now or only in the fullness of time. That is my advice to you, my king. As for *you*, though, son of Gobryas:† Stop making such reckless speeches about the Greeks; they do not merit your low opinion. It's obvious that you are so eager to slander the Greeks because you wish to rouse the King toward war. You must not go down this road.‡

"But if we really must fight the Greeks, then let the king stay here within Persia's borders, while you, Mardonius, lead the invasion with a force of any size you like, any men you like. And let us two put our own children up as a stake against the outcome. If things turn out for the king as you predict, then I forfeit the lives of my children and my own life on top of theirs. But if things go as I predict, then let your children suffer the same fate, and you too—that is, if you make it home. If you don't agree to this pact but lead the army to Greece anyway, then I proclaim this: Some one of those left behind here in Persia will hear that Mardonius has done great harm to our people and has left his corpse to be torn by birds and dogs somewhere in Attica or Lacedaemon—or perhaps only on the road that leads there§—and so has learned what sort of men they were whom he urged the king to attack."

[7.11] So spoke Artabanus, and Xerxes, enraged, replied as follows: "You are my father's brother, Artabanus, and so you will not pay the price your foolish words deserve. But I impose this disgrace on you for your baseness and cowardice: You will not come with me on the invasion of Greece but stay here with the women, and I shall do what I have promised without your help.

"I would be no true offspring of Darius, of Hystaspes, of Arsames, of Ariaramnes, of Teispes, of Cyrus, of Cambyses, of Teispes, and of

---

* The idea of a jealous god who destroys the proudest or happiest creatures on earth echoes the moral wisdom of Solon from the outset of the *Histories* (see 1.30ff.) along with other prominent passages (e.g., 3.39–43, 3.108–109).

† Artabanus directs the remainder of his speech at Mardonius.

‡ Two sentences have been omitted here, in which Artabanus moralizes on the evils of slander.

§ This remark contains a thinly veiled jibe against Mardonius, who in his 492 expedition had turned back before even reaching his objectives.

Achaemenes before him, if I did not pay these Athenians back. And what's more, I know well that if we don't take action, they will; they will invade our territory, to judge by what they have already set in motion when they landed on our continent and burned Sardis. There's no turning back for either side in this conflict, only the question of who strikes first and who gets struck. Either all our land will be theirs, or all theirs will be ours;* our mutual hatred allows no compromise.

"I'm glad we were the first ones wronged in this fight, so that when we take revenge I can learn what fearsome things they have in store for me—men who were conquered by my forefathers' slave, Pelops the Phrygian, and subdued so completely that their race and their land still bears the name of their conqueror today!"†

[7.12] That was the end of the discussion. But later that evening, the opinion expressed by Artabanus began to gnaw at Xerxes; and, after lying awake pondering it, the King realized that indeed it would not benefit him to attack Greece. He made a decision to cancel the war and then fell asleep, whereupon he had the following dream, according to Persian sources: A tall, beautiful man seemed to be standing over him as he slept, saying, "Persian, have you reversed course and chosen not to take your army against Greece, even after proclaiming to your countrymen to ready their troops? This change of course is the wrong thing to do, and the one standing beside you cannot condone it. Go back to your plan from the daytime; stay on that road." And then the man appeared to fly away.

[7.13] When day dawned, Xerxes dismissed the dream from his mind, recalled his council of advisers, and said: "Men of Persia, I ask your forbearance for my change of mind. I have not yet reached full maturity of understanding, and those who are urging me to this enterprise never give me any peace. When I heard the advice given me by Artabanus, my youthful spirit boiled over, and I flung at him words unbefitting an older man. But now I find that I agree with him, and I shall accept his advice. I have changed my mind regarding the invasion of Greece, so be at rest." On hearing this, the Persians rejoiced and did obedience to him.

[7.14] But when night came, the same phantom stood over him as he

---

* In the large scheme of things, Xerxes' analysis was correct, as would be demonstrated by Alexander the Great and the Greco-Macedonian invasion of Asia, 150 years down the road. But Herodotus could not have known that such an invasion would someday be possible, and he would probably have thought Xerxes' words here overblown.

† Xerxes' tone turns mocking and sarcastic at the end of his speech.

slept, and said: "Son of Darius, you have publicly renounced the expedition and made light of my words as if they had never been spoken. Now know for certain that, unless you at once go forth to war, this is what will happen to you: Just as you have in short time risen to greatness and might, so you will swiftly be brought low."

[7.15] Terrified by this dream, Xerxes sprang from his bed and, sending for Artabanus, spoke to him thus: "Artabanus, at first I acted foolishly when I gave you harsh words in return for your good advice, but then I had second thoughts and realized that I ought to do as you suggested. But now, much as I wish it, I cannot do so. Since I have turned about and changed my mind, I have been haunted by a dream that forbids me to do so, a dream that has just departed after threatening me. Now, if it is a god who sends me this dream, and it is his pleasure that we should march against Greece, the same dream will visit you and give you the same commands. And this is more likely to happen if you put on all my clothes, sit on my throne, and then go to sleep in my bed."

[7.16] Artabanus, who thought it unseemly to sit on the royal throne, was finally forced to consent, and, speaking as follows, he did what was asked: "In my belief, O king, to be wise or to be ready to listen to good advice is much the same thing. In you are united both qualities, but the counsels of evil men lead you astray, in just the same way as gales of wind assail the sea and force it to change its own nature, which is to be of the greatest service to humankind. As for me, I was not so much hurt by your abuse of me as by observing that when two courses were open to the Persians—one tending to increase their arrogance, the other restraining it and showing how wrong it is to encourage the soul always to covet more than it already possesses—you chose the course fraught with more peril to yourself and to the Persians. But now you tell me that since you have turned to the better course and renounced the expedition against the Greeks, you are haunted by a dream sent by some god, forbidding you to abandon it. But these things, my son, are not divine visitations. I, who have seen so many more years than you, will tell you what these dreams are that wander into men's minds: They are nearly always floating phantoms of what one has been thinking about during the day, and during the past few days we have been very much occupied with the question of this expedition. But if my explanation is not correct and there is something of the divine in this, you have in brief said all that needs saying about it—let it appear to me as it did to you, with the same commands. However, if it is going to appear at all, it is not more likely to appear to me wearing your clothes than wearing my own, nor sleeping in your bed than my own. For this thing, whatever it may be, that appears to you in your sleep is surely not so simple-minded as to think that I am you because it sees me clad in your dress. Still, if it pays no regard to me and deigns not to appear to me whether wearing my own clothes or yours, then this will be the inescapable conclusion: if it persists in haunting you, I would myself say that it is god-sent. Now, if you are so determined and cannot be turned from your purpose and I must sleep in your bed, very well, then; when I have carried out your instructions let it appear to me too. Until then I shall adhere to my former opinion."

[7.17–18] So spoke Artabanus, expecting to prove Xerxes wrong, and did as he was bidden. He put on Xerxes' clothes, seated himself on the royal throne, and in due course went to bed. As he slept, the same phantom that had visited Xerxes stood over him and said: "Are you the man who is dissuading Xerxes from marching against Greece, presumably out of your concern for him? For seeking to avert that which is fated to happen, you shall not escape unpunished, either now or hereafter. As for Xerxes, he has been clearly shown what will befall him if he disobeys me." These were the words the phantom seemed to utter, and it was just about to burn out his eyes with hot irons when Artabanus woke with a shriek, leapt from his bed, and ran to Xerxes. Sitting beside him, he narrated his dream and then went on to speak as follows: "O king, I am one who has seen many mighty empires struck down by lesser ones, and thus it was that I sought to prevent you from being quite carried away by your youthful spirit. I reflected what an ill thing it is to be over-covetous, remembering how fared Cyrus' expedition against the Massagetae and Cambyses' expedition against the Ethiopians. In addition, I myself took part in Darius' march against the Scythians.* With these things in mind, I was convinced that all men would deem you most blessed if you remained at peace. But since there has been this visitation from the gods, and, as it seems, a heaven-sent destruction is to fall upon the Greeks, I change my mind and reverse my judgment. Do therefore make known to the Persians the vision the god has sent us and bid them make the preparations as first instructed by you, and thus act so as to take full advantage of what the god is offering you."

---

* The three expeditions mentioned by Artabanus have all been excerpted, in whole or in part, in this volume. Significantly, all three were confrontations between the Persians and less "civilized" peoples, the nomadic Massagetae and Scythians and the hunter-gatherer Ethiopians, in which the Persians' hopes of easy conquest were dashed.

Such were his words. Now they were both encouraged by the dream. As soon as day came, Xerxes laid these happenings before the Assembly, and Artabanus, who previously had been the only dissenting voice, now heartily supported the war.

———

Once he resolved upon the invasion of Greece, Xerxes set about making elaborate preparations. Besides raising troops and preparing transport and supplies through-out the empire, he undertook two vast engineering projects to pave his way into Europe. First he employed thousands of laborers to dig a canal through the Athos peninsula, so that his fleet would not have to become cut off from his army or sail the stormy waters where the expedition of 492 BC had been wrecked. Then he laid plans for the bridging of the Hellespont (today called the Dardanelles) to enable his army to march across the gap between the continents. Egyptian and Phoenician craftsmen were set to work weaving huge, thick ropes out of flax and papyrus, to be strung across rows of ships anchored so as to span the strait. Sites for the bridgeheads were found at the towns of Abydus on the Asian side and Sestus on the European side.

———

[7.33–34] Xerxes then made preparations to move on to Abydus, where bridges had meanwhile been constructed over the Hellespont from Asia to Europe. Between Sestus and Madytus in the Hellespontine Cher-sonese there is a rocky headland running out to sea opposite Abydus. (On this spot, a little later on, the Athenians, with Xanthippus as their gen-eral, seized a Persian named Artayctes, who was tied alive to a stake.* This Artayctes had gathered women together in the shrine of the hero Protesilaus and had done perverse things.) It was to this headland that those charged with this work constructed two bridges from Abydus, one made by the Phoenicians with cables of flax, and one by the Egyptians with cables of papyrus. The distance from Abydus to the opposite shore is about three-quarters of a mile.

[7.35] When the channel had been successfully bridged, there arose a violent storm that shattered and destroyed all that had been done. On learning what happened, Xerxes was mightily angry, and he gave orders that the waters of the Hellespont should receive three hundred lashes and that a pair of fetters should be cast into them. I have even heard it said that he sent branders with irons to brand the Hellespont. Then he instructed those who scourged the waters to utter these barbarous and wicked words: "You bitter stream! Your master lays this punishment upon

* The execution of Artayctes is the final episode of the war narrated by Herodotus.

you because you have wronged him without cause, having suffered no wrong from him. Yet King Xerxes will cross you, whether you wish it or no. Well do you deserve that no man sacrifices to you, you muddy and briny river!" He not only commanded the sea to be punished but also ordered that the overseers of work on the bridge have their heads cut off.

[7.36]* Those whose business it was carried out this unpleasing task, and other engineers were appointed to bridge the channel. This is how they built the bridge: They brought ships side by side in the strait, using 360 ships to form a line on the side facing the Black Sea and 314 to form another line on the other side. Anchors of great weight were let down, two for each ship—one on the ships' eastern ends to counteract the winds blowing out of the Black Sea, the other on the western ends to counteract gales from the Aegean blowing from the south and east. They left a gap between the ships so that light craft could still sail in and out of the Black Sea. Then they stretched cables from the shore, hauling them by means of winches. They did not use flax and papyrus cables separately, as they did on the first bridge, but combined two ropes of flax and four of papyrus across each of the two lines of ships. Both types had a similar thickness and fine quality, but the flaxen rope was more dense; each yard of it weighed over a hundred pounds.†

[7.37] The work on the bridges was now completed, and news came from Athos that the canal was quite finished, including the breakwaters at both its ends to prevent the surf from silting up the entrances. Then the army, having wintered at Sardis and being now fully equipped, began its march the following spring from Sardis toward Abydus. As it was departing, the sun left its place in the sky and vanished—though it was clear and cloudless weather—and the day gave place to night. Seeing and marking this, Xerxes became anxious and inquired of the Magi as to the significance of this portent. He was told that the god was foretelling to the Greeks the eclipse of their cities, for it was the sun that gave forewarning to the Greeks, just as the moon did for the Persians. Reassured by this reply, Xerxes continued with the march.

* This chapter was translated by the editor.

† It's hard to imagine that the rope was actually this heavy, unless perhaps Herodotus gives the weight when soaked with water. These cables loom large in symbolic importance as the physical link imposed by the Persians on the space between the continents. The Greek seizure of the cables at the war's end divides the continents once more and thus provides a capstone to the story Herodotus tells; it is the last event he narrates.

[7.38] The army had begun its march when Pythius the Lydian,* taking fright at the phenomenon in the heavens and emboldened by the gifts he had got from the king, approached Xerxes and said: "My lord, please grant me a favor that is for you a light matter but would be for me something of great moment." Xerxes, expecting nothing like that which the request turned out to be, declared that he would grant it and bade him speak out freely. On hearing this, Pythius took courage and said: "My lord, I have five sons, all serving in the army with you in the campaign against Greece. Have compassion on my years, O king, and release from military duty my eldest son to take care of me and my property. Take with you the other four, and may you return in safety, having achieved your heart's desire."

[7.39] Xerxes was mightily angry and answered thus: "You wretch, do you dare to make mention of your son when I myself am marching against Greece accompanied by my sons, my brothers, and friends—you, my slave, and in duty bound to follow me with all your household, including your wife? Now mark this well: A man's spirit dwells in his ears; when it hears good things, it fills the body with delight, but when it hears the contrary, it heaves with fury. When you did me good service and offered more such, you cannot boast that you outdid the King in generosity. And now that you have turned to impudence, your punishment will be less than is deserved. Yourself and four of your sons are saved through the hospitality you gave me, but the one on whom you set most store shall pay with his life." He immediately commanded those on whom the duty lay to seek out the eldest of Pythius' sons, to cut him in half and to fix the two halves, one on the right and the other on the left of the road, so that the army could march between them. The order was obeyed.

[7.44–45] When he reached Abydus, Xerxes thought he would like to hold a review of his entire force. On a hillock a throne of white marble had already been prepared for this purpose by the people of Abydus, at the king's command. He took his seat there and, gazing down on the shore below, he beheld both his land forces and his fleet; and as he gazed he felt a desire to witness a competition between his ships. This took

---

* In an earlier episode (omitted here), Pythius, said to be the wealthiest man in the world after Xerxes, had offered to feed and billet the entire Persian army at his own expense and to give Xerxes a war subsidy as well. Determined to outdo Pythius' generosity, Xerxes instead gave money of his own to augment Pythius' fortune.

place and resulted in a victory for the Phoenicians of Sidon,* much to the satisfaction of Xerxes, who was pleased both with the race and with his forces. And, as he saw the whole of the Hellespont completely covered by his ships and all the shore and the plains around Abydus thronged with his men, he congratulated himself, but thereafter he burst into tears.

[7.46] The king's uncle Artabanus, he who originally had spoken his mind so freely in attempting to dissuade Xerxes from undertaking the Greek expedition, perceiving the king's tears, spoke to him thus: "O my king, how different is that which you are now doing from that which you did before. First you congratulated yourself, now you weep." "Yes," said Xerxes, "for there came over me a feeling of pity as I considered the brevity of a man's life, and that of all this vast host not one will be alive in a hundred years' time."

"Yet," replied Artabanus, "in our span of life there are things more pitiable than that. In our brief existence there is no one, either present here or elsewhere, who is so happy as not to wish, not once but many a time, that he were dead rather than alive. Calamities befall us, sicknesses trouble us, so as to make life, however short, seem long. Thus, our life being so burdensome, death becomes a refuge most desirable for man, and the god, who gives us but a sip of the sweetness of life, is found to be grudging even in this gift."

[7.47]† To this Xerxes replied, "Artabanus, let's talk no more of human life, which is very much as you describe; let's not be distracted by ills when we have vital matters in hand. Tell me now, if that dream had not appeared to you so unmistakably, would you now keep to your original opinion and dissuade me from marching on Greece? Or would you change your mind? Tell me truly." And Artabanus replied, "Sire, I pray that the dream may have a happy result, as we both wish it to have. But as for myself, I am still filled with fear even today and barely able to contain myself. I count many dangers, but especially this: I see that the two greatest things of all will be your worst enemies."

[7.48] Xerxes responded as follows: "You bizarre fellow! What are these two worst enemies you speak of? Do you mean the size of our land

---

* The Phoenicians, a seafaring people whose colonies were widely scattered around the Mediterranean, contributed most of the ships in Xerxes' navy. The Persians themselves had almost no experience of the sea.

† This chapter through chapter 52 were translated by the editor.

army, fearing that the Greek infantry will be far more numerous? Or that our fleet will fail to equal theirs? Or both of these things together? If you see anything lacking in our preparations, speak; there is still time to gather more forces."

[7.49] "Sire," said Artabanus, "no one in his right mind could find fault with this army, nor with the size of the fleet. But if you were to increase their size, the two enemies I spoke of would be even more opposed to you. I'm talking about the land and the sea. For on the sea there is no harbor or anchorage anywhere, I don't imagine, large enough to shelter your vessels if a storm should arise. And you won't need just one harbor, but many, all up and down the coast we're sailing. There are no such harbors—so recognize that mischances are the masters of mortals, not mortals of mischances.*

"Now I'll explain the other of the two enemies I mentioned. This land is hostile territory; even if no obstacle stops your march, it will become more hostile the farther you advance, luring you ever onward, for no one can ever get enough of success. Even with no one opposing you, the land itself will stretch out farther and farther as time goes on, until it gives rise to hunger.

"The best way for a man is this: fear everything while making plans and to suppose he will encounter every reverse, but then to act boldly in the execution of his plans."

[7.50] To this Xerxes responded, "Artabanus, everything you have said seems reasonable to me, but don't fear everything or weigh the downside equally with the upside. If one were to do this each time a new enterprise goes forward, one would never do anything at all. It's better, I think, to run every risk and pay the costs in half of them than to become paralyzed by fear and never incur any further costs. Gains go to those willing to act, never to those who reckon up all the factors and grow timid. You see how far the Persian Empire has advanced in power. Well, consider that if the kings who came before me had thought as you do, or, even if they had only had advisers like you, you would never have seen it come so far. For these kings have brought it there by being willing to roll the dice. Great undertakings go hand in hand with great risks.

"We are doing as our ancestors did. We have set out in the finest season of the year, and we shall subdue all of Europe and then return home, untroubled by hunger or any other sort of difficulty. For one thing, we're

---

* The wisdom of these warnings was borne out at Artemisium (see p. 109).

bringing much food along with us, and for another, we shall find provisions in every land and among every people we come to. It's farmers we're attacking this time, not nomads."*

[7.51] To this Artabanus said, "Sire, though you bid me dismiss my fears, nevertheless take my advice (and forgive the long discussion, but complex matters require it). Cyrus, son of Cambyses, made subjects of the Ionians, all except the Athenians, and forced them to pay tribute. Do not, I advise you, take these men with you in your attack on their fathers; we can easily prevail over our enemies without their help. If they do go with you, they must either become the most immoral of men by enslaving their own mother city, or the most upright, by helping to set her free. They will offer us little help if they become the most immoral, whereas by acting most uprightly they can do great harm to your army.

"There is an ancient expression you should take to your heart: 'Not every end can be seen in the beginning.'"

[7.52] Xerxes replied as follows: "Artabanus, you're more deceived in your fears over our Ionian conscripts than in any of your other judgments. Our opinion of the Ionians stands very high. You yourself saw, as did the others who accompanied Darius on the Scythian campaign, that when the destruction or survival of the entire Persian army rested on these men, they displayed only trustworthiness and uprightness rather than anything dishonorable. And besides, why should we fear that they will cause trouble, when their children and wives and property reside on our land?† So don't be afraid on this score. Keep your spirits up and protect my household and my crown; for to you alone out of all men I entrust my royal scepter."

So saying, he sent Artabanus back to Susa.

———

The Persian army now commenced its crossing of the Hellespont bridge, a process that, according to Herodotus, took seven days and nights to complete—and that "under the lash." Once on the European side, the troops gathered at Doriscus, where Xerxes conducted a tally by marching them in groups into a circle that holds ten thousand men, producing a total of 1,700,000 (to quote Herodotus' grossly exagger-

---

* The implicit comparison is with Darius' campaign against the Scythians (book 4), who *were* nomads and whose scorched-earth strategy caused starvation in the Persian ranks.

† The grim implication here is that the Greek cities on the coast of Asia Minor were effectively hostages; they could be destroyed if the conscripts they dispatched did not fight zealously for the Persians. Most of the Ionian troops seem to have done so, despite the efforts of Themistocles to urge them to defect or to fight poorly against their countrymen.

ated figure). A similar review is held of the fleet, which is found to contain 1,207 vessels (a more plausible number). Herodotus here catalogs the various cities and nations comprising the two Persian armed forces, including in each case a description of the indigenous style of dress and weaponry—a breathtaking roll call spanning many pages and encompassing virtually all the lands of Asia.

Herodotus now represents Xerxes, proud of his enormous might, seeking a colloquy with an adviser, as he had done at the Hellespont; this time his interlocutor is Demaratus, former king of Sparta. The dialogue that results represents Herodotus' most concerted attempt to contrast the political and military culture of Greece—in particular, Sparta—with that of Persia.

[7.101]* After he had sailed through the fleet and disembarked from his ship, Xerxes sent for Demaratus, son of Ariston, who had come with him on the march, and asked: "Demaratus, I would like to put this question to you. You're a Greek, and as I understand from you and from the other Greeks I've spoken with, you hail from a noteworthy and powerful city. So tell me now: Will the Greeks have the courage to put up a fight against me? I myself think not; for even if all the Greeks and those dwelling west of them were to join forces, they still would not be strong enough to withstand my attack, since they lack cohesion. But I want to hear what you have to say about these people." "Sire," said Demaratus, "do you want me to give a true answer or to please you?" Xerxes bade him answer truthfully, promising that he would lose none of the king's favor thereby.

"Sire," said Demaratus, "since you want the truth, and since any lie would be detected by you in time anyway, I say this: Greece has poverty as her birthright, but she has also won courage by her own merits, namely by her wisdom and the strength of her laws. With courage Greece is able to keep both poverty and despotism from her shores.

"I have high praise for all the Greeks living in Dorian lands,[†] but in what I will say next I am speaking only of the Spartans. First, they will never come to terms with you and bring enslavement to Greece. Second, they will stand up to you in battle even if all the other Greeks go over to your side. Don't bother to ask how many they are that they are able to do

---

* This section was translated by the editor.

† The "Dorian lands" are, principally, those of the Peloponnese. The Dorians were the ethnic subgroup of the Greek people to which the Spartans belonged, just as the Athenians belonged to the Ionian subgroup. Thus Demaratus' elaborate praise of Dorian values here cannot be applied to the Greeks generally, and certainly not to Athenians.

this; if there are but a thousand in the field, these will fight you; if they are fewer, or more, these will fight you just the same."

[7.103] At this Xerxes laughed and said: "Demaratus, what are you talking about—a thousand men fighting an army of this size? Come, tell me, since you claim to be a king of these men: Would you want to fight alone against ten men?... In all reasonableness, how could a thousand men, or ten thousand, or fifty thousand, stand up to an army like ours, especially free and equal men who are not under a single ruler?... If they had such a ruler, as our troops do, in fear of him they might become better fighters than their own natures allow, and under compulsion of the whip* few might hold out against many. But with the laxity that freedom allows, there's no way they could do this. For my part I don't believe that Greeks would have an easy time fighting Persians even if the numbers of forces were equal. We too possess this quality you speak of, though it's rare; but there are among our Persian lancers some who would willingly fight three Greeks at once. But you know nothing of this, and so your words are meaningless."

[7.104] To this Demaratus replied, "I knew from the outset, sire, that my answer would displease you if I spoke the truth. But it was the truth you urged me to speak, so I told you how things are with the Spartans. You know well enough that I have no love for them; they deprived me of office and privilege, of city and home, and drove me into exile. Your father took me in and gave me both a home and a living. No man of sense is likely to reject a kindness like this; rather he cherishes it more than anything else.†

"Speaking for myself, I say no, I would not be able to fight ten men, or even two; indeed I would prefer not to fight even one. But if it was necessary and there was some great conflict urging me on, I would most want to fight one of those men of yours who claim to be a match for three Greeks. The same is true of my fellow Spartans. They are the equal of any men when they fight alone; fighting together, they surpass all other men. For they are free, but not entirely free: They obey a master called Law, and they fear this master much more than your men fear you. They

---

* Herodotus later depicts the Persian commanders whipping their men to push them into the thick of battle.

† The point Demaratus is making here is that he can be trusted, since he has no reason to magnify Spartan values.

do whatever it commands them to do, and its commands are always the same: do not retreat from the battlefield even when badly outnumbered; stay in formation, and either conquer or die.

"If this talk seems like nonsense to you, then let me stay silent henceforth; I spoke only under compulsion as it is. In any case, sire, I hope all turns out as you wish."

[7.105] That was Demaratus' response. As for Xerxes, he turned the whole thing into a joke and didn't get angry, but rather sent Demaratus away with kind words.

———

The glowing portrait of Spartan military virtue given in the above passage is soon followed up by Herodotus' own personal laudation of Athens, based on that city's refusal to abandon the Greek side even under grave pressure from Persia. In this passage Herodotus assumes a knowledge of the outcome of the war, in particular the fact that the tide of battle was turned by Athenian naval power.

———

[7.138] The expedition of the Persian king, though nominally directed against Athens, had as its objective the whole of Greece. The Greeks had long been aware of this, but they were not all of one mind. Those who had given totems of earth and water were confident that they would suffer nothing unpleasant from the barbarian. Others who had refused to submit were in a panic, seeing that there were not enough battle-ready ships in Greece to meet the enemy's attack, nor were most of the Greeks willing to fight, being quite ready to accept Persian rule.

[7.139] At this point I feel myself constrained to express an opinion that most people will find objectionable, but which, believing it to be true, I will not withhold. If the Athenians, through fear of the imminent danger, had abandoned their country, or if they had remained there and made submission to Xerxes, there would certainly have been no attempt to resist the King by sea, and without any resistance at sea, by land the course of events would have been something like this: However many lines of defense should have been constructed across the Isthmus by the Spartans, they would have been deserted by their allies, not willingly but under necessity, as city after city would have fallen to the naval power of the invader. So the Spartans would have stood alone, and in their lone stand they would have performed mighty deeds and died nobly. Either that or, seeing the other Greeks going over to the Persians, they would have come to terms with Xerxes. Thus, in either case, Greece would have been subjugated by the Persians, for I cannot see what possible use it would have been to fortify the Isthmus if the King had had mastery over the sea.

So if anyone were to say that the Athenians were saviors of Greece, he would not be far off the truth, for it was the Athenians who held the scales in balance; whichever side they espoused would be sure to prevail. It was they who, choosing to maintain the freedom of Greece, roused the rest of the Greeks who had not submitted, and it was they who (apart from the gods, that is) repulsed the King. Not even the dire warnings of the oracle of Delphi, striking fear into men's hearts, could persuade them to abandon Greece.* They stood their ground and awaited the coming of the invader.

———

In the weeks following their crossing of the Hellespont, the Persian army and fleet moved relentlessly westward toward the Greek world, drinking rivers dry (in Herodotus' fanciful account, at least) as they went. Most of the northerly Greek states, which now would bear the brunt of the invasion, capitulated by giving earth and water to the king's envoys. Xerxes did not bother to send envoys to Athens and Sparta, however, remembering that both cities had murdered ambassadors sent by Darius ten years earlier. Probably he sensed as well that there was no point in seeking cooperation from either of these leading Greek cities.

At Athens there was fierce debate over what course of action the city should take. Inquiry was made of the Delphic oracle, which, according to Herodotus, at first urged the Athenians to "flee to the ends of the earth," but then softened its tone somewhat when asked for a more comforting reply. This second oracular response, while still dire, spoke of safety that could be found behind a "wooden wall" and of a disastrous battle that would take place off the nearby island of Salamis. Now the debate at Athens centered on the meaning of this oracle: Some interpreted the "wooden wall" to mean the wooden fence surrounding the acropolis, others the wooden ships of Athens's newly built navy; while the verse proclaiming that "Holy Salamis will destroy mothers' sons" raised the question of whether Greek or Persian "sons" would be destroyed. In the gloomy atmosphere of a city awaiting a massive assault, most Athenians assumed that they themselves would be the casualties at Salamis. Into this debate stepped the emerging leader of the democracy, Themistocles.

---

* Many cities consulted the Delphic oracle as to whether they should submit to Xerxes or fight for their freedom; usually they were advised to submit. The oracular response given to the Athenians, as will be seen in the next section, was terrifying but ambiguous.

[7.143] There was someone among the Athenians, a man newly risen to prominence, Themistocles by name, said to be son of Neocles.* This fellow said that the oracles had been entirely misunderstood; if the Athenians' interpretation were right and they were destined to die in a sea-battle at Salamis, he said, the oracle would surely have referred to Salamis as "cursed" rather than "holy." If one interpreted correctly, he told them, then the oracle had been speaking of the enemy and not the Athenians when it said "Holy Salamis will destroy mothers' sons." Themistocles therefore advised them to prepare to encounter the enemy by sea, their ships being the wooden wall indicated by the oracle. When he had made this clear, the Athenians embraced this view in preference to that of the official interpreters, who were against fighting at sea or lifting a hand against the enemy, who instead urged them to abandon Attica and settle in another country.

[7.144] There had been a previous occasion† when the advice given by Themistocles had proved its worth. The Athenians had acquired a large sum of money for the treasury, the revenue of the mines at Laurium, and there was a proposal that they should share this out between all citizens, ten drachmas apiece. But Themistocles persuaded them to renounce this distribution and to use the money to build two hundred ships for "the war," meaning the war against Aegina. It was the outbreak of this war that saved Greece, compelling the Athenians to become a sea power. In actual fact, the ships were not used for the original purpose but served Greece in the time of crisis.‡ These ships, already built, were ready for use, and more had to be built to add to their number. In the debate they held after receiving the oracle's reply, they resolved, in obedience to the god, to

---

* This introduction of Themistocles is peculiar in two ways, first because the man was not newly prominent but had in fact held various offices for years, and second because the phrase "said to be son of Neocles" seems to cast doubt on his parentage. Like the democratic regime that produced him, Themistocles is characterized by Herodotus as innovative, self-fashioning, and somewhat irregular.

† Herodotus here jumps backward in time a few years, to 483 or 482, to trace the origin of the naval forces on which Themistocles now proposes to rely. The brief notice he gives to this episode understates its historical importance: Themistocles had early on committed Athens to a navy-based military posture, which was to be the foundation of her power for more than a century to come.

‡ That is, though built for service against Aegina, the ships actually saved Greece from the Persians. It is possible that Themistocles had been targeting Persia from the start of the naval buildup but used Aegina as a politically convenient pretext.

meet the invaders in their ships in full force, along with such Greeks as would join with them.

———

In the fall of 481, before the Persians had crossed into Europe, the Greek states that had decided to resist the Persians (now including Athens) had sent representatives to a kind of multistate congress at the Isthmus of Corinth. The first steps in organizing a joint defense of Greece were to send out a reconnaissance party to spy on Xerxes' forces and to use diplomacy to resolve long-standing quarrels within the Greek world. Athens and Aegina easily patched up their feud, but Argos remained steadfast in its hatred of Sparta, refusing to serve in any joint force led by its old enemy. Efforts to bring in Greek allies from outside the mainland, principally from Sicily and Crete, also failed.

A second congress of the allied Greek states was held in the spring of 480, under more urgent circumstances. A preliminary line of defense in Thessaly had been abandoned for strategic reasons, causing the Thessalians, who now lay exposed to Persian assault, to go over to the enemy. To prevent the Boeotians and the vital city of Thebes from doing the same, the Greeks had to find a new defensive position that would safeguard these places. The decision was made to take a stand at Thermopylae, where steep mountains running down to the sea would force the Persians to march through a narrow pass; meanwhile the Greek fleet could defend the nearby strait off Artemisium, where again the enemy would be forced into a bottleneck. By defending these spots, the Greeks hoped to offset the great numerical advantage of their enemy, since the narrow passageways would admit only a small portion of the Persian forces at any one time. The Greeks considered it essential to stop the Persian army and navy together; either force could do great damage to their territory even without the help of the other.

As the Persians neared Thermopylae and Artemisium, major confrontations both on land and at sea began to take shape. Herodotus pauses before the outbreak of combat to count up, once again, the immensity of Xerxes' forces. Though precise, his figures are impossibly large. Some scholars have suggested that through a misunderstanding of the Persian regimental system, he accidentally multiplied everything by ten.

———

[7.184] The Persian fleet had got to Sepias in Magnesia and the Persian army had advanced as far as Thermopylae, as yet without loss, and their numbers were still, by my reckoning, as follows: The fleet that sailed from Asia numbered 1,207 ships of various nations, with their original complement of 241,400, allowing 200 men to a ship. Each of these vessels carried on board, apart from their native soldiers, 30 fighting men, who were either Persians, Medes, or Sacae. This amounted to an additional 36,210 men. To this and the previous figure must be added the crews of the penteconters that each carried an average of 80 men. As I have already said, there were 3,000 penteconters, making an addition of 240,000 men. This was the naval force brought from Asia, amounting to 517,610 men.

As to the army, the infantry were 1,700,000 strong, and the cavalry 80,000. To this must be added the Arabian camel corps and the Libyan charioteers, a total of 20,000 men. Adding together the naval and land forces we get a total of 2,317,610. This is the sum of the forces brought from Asia, excluding camp followers and food transport ships with their crews.

[7.185] To this account we have still to add the forces gathered in Europe, regarding which I can only make a rough estimate. The Greeks of Thrace and the offshore islands provided 120 ships, which would total 24,000 men. The infantry furnished by the Thracians, Paeonians, Eordi, Bottiaei, Chalcidians, Brygi, Pierians, Macedonians, Dolopes, Magnetes, Achaeans, and those who dwell on the Thracian coastlands I would put at 300,000. These figures added to the force from Asia make a total of 2,641,610 fighting men.

[7.186–87] Such being the number of the fighting men, I am of the opinion that the camp followers and the crews of the provision vessels and other transports accompanying the expedition amounted to a number not less but more than that of the fighting men. Still, taking them as equal in number, I arrive at the final estimate, which is that Xerxes, son of Darius, brought as far as Sepias and Thermopylae a total of 5,283,220 men. Thus it does not at all surprise me that the streams of rivers sometimes dried up as the army drank from them, but I *do* wonder that the food never gave out for so many millions. For by my reckoning, counting only one quart of grain per person per day, they consumed over 10,000 gallons daily—and I don't include portions for the women, eunuchs, pack-animals, and dogs. Among so many millions of men, no one save Xerxes was so worthy of command, on account of his great height and beauty.*

The first contact between the opposing forces (mid-August 480) came in the form of a small naval skirmish: Three Greek ships out on reconnaissance were spotted by

---

* An oddly laudatory remark, given the context. Herodotus constructs a truly complex portrait of Xerxes, colored in different places by both vengeful anger and affection or admiration.

the advancing Persian vessels, which gave chase and captured all three; however, the
crew of the Athenian vessel had enough time to beach their craft and flee to safety.
Already in this first engagement the Athenians demonstrated the superior naval
skills that made them so essential to the Greek defense.

Now that they had actually encountered the enemy, the Greek fleet withdrew to
Chalcis, about ninety miles south of their original position, "in a panic," as Herodo-
tus says; but their new anchorage also put them in the lee of the island Euboea in
case of bad weather. The Persians, by contrast, were sailing down the exposed and
harborless coast of Magnesia.

———

[7.188] The Persian fleet weighed anchor and made for the Magnesian
coast between Castanea and Cape Sepias. The leading ships were moored
to the land, while the others, there being little room on the beach, came
to anchor offshore in lines eight deep. In this way they passed the night,
but when dawn broke, the clear skies and stillness gave place to a raging
sea, and a violent storm came upon them with a strong easterly gale,
which the natives call a Hellespontine. Those of them who had marked
the wind rising and were conveniently moored anticipated the storm by
beaching their ships, thus saving themselves and their vessels. But of
those that were caught at sea, some were driven onto a place called Ipni
at the foot of Pelion; others were driven onto the coast; others were
wrecked on Sepias; while others were thrown onto the shore off Melboea
and Castanea. It was a monstrous storm, impossible to weather.

[7.189] The story goes that the Athenians had called on Boreas* to assist them in consequence of an oracle that had come to them, bidding
them seek help from their son-in-law. For according to Greek tradition,
Boreas took to wife a woman of Attica, Oreithyia, daughter of Erechtheus.[†] So the Athenians, as the tale is told, taking Boreas to be their son-
in-law through this marriage, when they perceived from their station off
Chalcis in Euboea that a storm was rising, then—or even before—they
offered sacrifice to Boreas and Oreithyia and called on them to come to
their assistance by destroying the Persian ships, as they had done off
Athos.[‡] Whether this was the reason that Boreas fell upon the Persians as
they lay at anchor I cannot say, but the Athenians claim that Boreas had

---

* Boreas is the Greek name for the North Wind, personified as a god.

[†] Erechtheus, according to mythology, was the first king of Athens.

[‡] In 492; see p. 63.

helped them before and was responsible for what now happened. On their return, they built him a shrine on the river Ilissus.

[7.190] At the lowest estimate, four hundred ships are said to have been destroyed in this disaster, together with countless men and an enormous amount of treasure. But for Ameinocles, son of Cretines, a landowner near Cape Sepias, the shipwreck turned out to be a great boon. Many were the gold and silver drinking cups that he gathered, after they washed ashore some time later, and among the finds that came into his possession were Persian treasure chests and other valuable articles beyond count. Thus he became a rich man, but he did not fare well in other ways: For he ended up as the murderer of his children and thus bore a tormenting grief.

—

With things at sea having taken this turn, Herodotus returns to the land, where the Persian army was preparing to force the pass at Thermopylae.

—

[7.201] Xerxes had taken up position at Trachis in Malian territory, while the Greeks occupied the pass generally called Thermopylae, though known by the natives as Pylae. This was the situation of the two armies, the one in control of all the region from Trachis northward, the other of all the country extending south.

[7.202] The Greeks who awaited the Persians at this place were as follows. From Sparta, 300 hoplites;* from Tegea and Mantinea, 500 from each; from Orchomenus in Arcadia, 120; 1,000 from the rest of the Arcadia; from Corinth, 400; from Phlius, 200; and from Mycenae, 80 hoplites. Such were the contingents from the Peloponnese. From Boeotia there were 700 from Thespiae and 400 from Thebes.

[7.203] In addition to these, the Locrians of Opus answered in full force, and the Phocians sent 1,000. For the Greeks had summoned these through messengers, saying that they were themselves an advance force, that the rest of the allied force was daily expected, and that the sea was under good guard, watched over by the Athenians and Aeginetans and

---

* A hoplite is an armed infantry soldier, wearing metal armor and helmet and carrying a spear and shield. It may seem odd that the Spartans, who were leaders of the joint defense forces, sent so few hoplites. Herodotus explains below (7.206) that the three hundred were an advance force and that more were to be sent soon. It also bears mentioning that the highly trained Spartan soldier was considered the equal of several of the soldier-farmers enlisted by other Greek states, and that, for Sparta, with her tiny citizen population, three hundred was not a small number.

other naval contingents. There was no cause for fear; it was not a god that was threatening Greece but a man. There never was, nor ever would be, a mortal who was not liable to misfortune from the day of birth, and the greater the mortal, the greater the misfortune. So their enemy, too, being but a mortal, would be bound to fall from the height of glory. Thus persuaded, the Locrians and the Phocians sent troops to Trachis.

[7.204–205] The troops from the various cities were commanded by their own officers, but the one who was held in the greatest respect and who held command over the entire force was the Spartan Leonidas, son of Anaxandrides, who in turn was son of Leon, son of Eurycratides, son of Anaxandrus, son of Eurycrates, son of Polydorus, son of Alcamenes, son of Telecles, son of Archelaus, son of Hegesilaus, son of Doryssus, son of Leobotas, son of Echestratus, son of Agis, son of Eurysthenes, son of Aristodemus, son of Aristomachus, son of Cleodaeus, son of Hyllus, son of Heracles.* Leonidas had become king of Sparta quite unexpectedly. With two elder brothers, Cleomenes and Dorieus, he had no expectation of succeeding to the throne. But when Cleomenes died without male issue, Dorieus having already perished in Sicily, he found himself next in succession, being older than Cleombrotus (Anaxandrides' youngest son), and moreover being married to Cleomenes' daughter. It was he who came to Thermopylae, accompanied by three hundred men whom he had chosen and who all had sons living.† He also brought with him the Theban troops as I have listed, who were commanded by Leontiades, son of Eurymachus. The reason why he was concerned to take troops from Thebes, and only Thebes, was the strong suspicion that their sympathies were with the Persians, so his request for troops was intended to find out whether they would answer the call or openly refuse to join the Greek alliance. They did in fact send troops, but their intentions were otherwise.‡

[7.206] The force accompanying Leonidas was sent by the Spartans in order that their appearance in the field might encourage their allies to fight and not defect to the Persians, as they might have done if they saw

* This magnificent fanfare of an introduction should be compared with the understated introduction of Themistocles above (7.143). In contrast to the arriviste leading the Athenians, Leonidas carried with him the full legacy of ancient Spartan tradition.

† The Spartans considered men with living sons to be the best-motivated soldiers.

‡ Since ancient times Herodotus has been accused of anti-Theban bias, and the charge seems justified here. It is unlikely Leonidas would have taken along troops of uncertain loyalty. Probably the Thebans at this point fully intended to resist the Persians; only after the Greek defeat at Thermopylae were they forced to medize, i.e., side with the Persians.

the Spartans delaying. It was the intention of the Spartans when the Carneian festival was over—it was this that hindered them—to leave a garrison in Sparta and take the field with all speed with their entire force. The rest of the allies intended to act similarly, for it so happened that the Olympic festival fell just at the same period. None of them expected the action at Thermopylae to be decided so soon, and so they merely sent advance parties.

[7.207] The Greek forces at Thermopylae, as the Persians drew near to the pass, were seized with fear and held a council to consider the question of retreat.* It was the general view of the Peloponnesians that the army should retire to the Peloponnese and guard the Isthmus. But, with the Phocians and Locrians expressing their indignation at this proposal, Leonidas gave his vote for remaining where they were, while sending envoys to the various cities to ask for help, since they were too few in number to make a stand against the army of the Medes.

[7.208] As they so deliberated, Xerxes sent a spy on horseback to see how many they were and what they were doing. While he was still in Thessaly, news was brought to Xerxes that a small force had assembled here, led by the Spartans under Leonidas of the house of Heracles. The rider approached the camp and made his survey, but he was unable to see the entire force, for there were troops on the farther side of the wall that had been rebuilt and was under guard. He saw only the troops in front of the wall, who happened at this time to be Spartans. Some of those were engaged in gymnastic exercises, others were combing their hair. The Persian observed them with astonishment, marked their number carefully, and with all this information rode quietly back. No one pursued him; no one took any notice of him. So he returned and told Xerxes all he had seen.

[7.209] Xerxes was quite unable to grasp the truth, which was that these men were getting ready, as best they could, to kill and be killed, and their actions seemed to him simply ridiculous. Sending for Demaratus, who happened to be there with the Persian army, he questioned him about all this, for he wanted to know the meaning of the behavior of the Spartans. "Once before," said Demaratus, "at the beginning of our march against Greece, you heard what I had to say about these men and you laughed at me when I told you how things were likely to be.[†] It is my

---

* Retreat was now an option because the expected reinforcements had not yet arrived.

[†] See 7.101–104.

most earnest endeavor, O king, to speak the truth before you, so hearken to me once again. These men have come to fight us for the pass, and it is for this they are preparing. It is their custom, when they are about to fight to the death, to beautify their hair. But mark this: If you can conquer these men and the others left behind at Sparta, there is no other people in the world who will venture to oppose you. You are now face-to-face with the finest kingdom in Greece and with the bravest men." But Xerxes found his words unbelievable, and once again he asked how so small a force could fight against his army. "O king," said Demaratus, "let me be treated as a liar if things do not turn out as I say."

[7.210] Xerxes was still not convinced and allowed four days to pass, all the while expecting the Greeks to run away. On the fifth day, when they made no move and their continued stand seemed to him sheer impudence and folly, he grew angry and sent against them the Medes and the Cissians, with orders to take them alive and bring them before him. The Medes charged the Greeks and fell in great numbers. But others took their place and would not be beaten off, although they suffered terrible losses. Thus was it made clear to all, and especially to the king, that he had much manpower but few real men.

[7.211] All day long the struggle continued. The Medes, after this rough handling, withdrew from the battle, and their place was taken by the band of Persians whom the King called the Immortals, commanded by Hydarnes. These men, it was thought, would soon settle the matter; but when they engaged, they met with no more success than the detachment of Medes. All went on as before; they fought in a narrow defile, having shorter spears than the Greeks and deriving no advantage from their numbers. The Spartans fought most memorably and showed themselves far more skillful in battle. They would turn their backs in unison as if they were in flight, whereupon the enemy would pursue them with much noise and shouting; then the Spartans, just when the Persians were upon them, they would wheel around, face the enemy, and inflict heavy losses on them.* Some Spartans also fell, but not many. At last the Persians, finding that all their attempts to gain the pass, whether they attacked by divisions or in any other way, were of no effect, withdrew from the pass. During these assaults, Xerxes, who was

---

* An excellent illustration of the superiority of Spartan warcraft. Only after constant drill and training could a body of soldiers execute such coordinated movements while under attack, and only the Spartan system provided for, and indeed required, such training.

watching the battle, is said to have leapt from his seat three times in fear for his army.

[7.212] Next day, the fighting was renewed with no better success for the Persians, who had engaged the enemy in the hope that the Greeks, being few in number and disabled by wounds, would not be able to offer further resistance. But the Greeks had been drawn up in divisions according to their cities, and each division took its share of the fighting, except for the Phocians, who had been stationed to guard the track over the mountains. So when the Persians found that they fared no better than on the previous day, they withdrew.

[7.213–17] While the King was wondering what to do in this difficult situation, Ephialtes, a man from Malis, was admitted to his presence. In the hope of receiving a rich reward from the king, he told him of the path that led over the mountains to Thermopylae, and by so doing he brought destruction on the Greeks, who were holding the pass. (Some time later this man, in fear of the Spartans, fled to Thessaly, and during his exile a price was put on his head at an assembly of the Amphictyons at Pylae. After some time he returned to Anticyra, where he was killed by Athenades of Trachis. It was actually for a different reason that Athenades killed him, as I shall explain later on,* but Athenades was nonetheless honored by the Spartans. Thus did Ephialtes perish some time after these events.) ... Xerxes was overjoyed; he gave his approval to Ephialtes' proposal and immediately sent forth Hydarnes with the troops under his command, who left camp around the time of lighting of lamps. They reached the summit of the mountain by dawn. This part of the mountain was guarded, as I said earlier, by a thousand Phocian men at arms, stationed here to defend their own country and to guard the path, while the pass below was defended as I have described. The Phocians had voluntarily undertaken to Leonidas to guard the track over the mountains.

[7.218] As the whole mountain was covered with oakwoods, the ascent of the Persians was for a time concealed from the Phocians, who finally became aware of it in the following way: there was a complete stillness, and so the Phocians could hear a lot of rustling, as one hears from leaves trodden beneath trampling feet; they jumped up and seized their arms, and in a moment the enemy came in sight. Seeing armed men before them, the Persians were taken by surprise, coming upon an enemy where they had expected no resistance. Alarmed, lest the Phocians might turn

---

* The promised explanation is not found in the preserved text of the *Histories*.

out to be Spartans, Hydarnes inquired of Ephialtes of what nation were these men, and, learning the truth, he drew up the Persians for battle. The Phocians, having to endure a heavy shower of arrows, fled to the crest of the mountain and, supposing themselves to be the main object of attack, prepared to perish. But the Persians with Ephialtes and Hydarnes paid no further attention to them and descended the mountain with all possible speed.

[7.219] The Greeks in the pass at Thermopylae received their first warning from the seer Megistias, who saw in the sacrificial victims the doom that would overtake them with the dawn. Deserters too came in the night, bringing news of the Persians' encircling movement, and finally at daybreak scouts came running down from the hills with the same news. Then the Greeks held a council, and opinion was divided, some urging that they must not abandon their post, others holding a contrary view. So the force split up; some departed and made their way in scattered bands to their several cities, while others resolved to remain and stand by Leonidas.*

[7.220] There is a story that Leonidas himself sent away the troops that departed, being concerned for their lives, but he thought it ignoble that he and his company of Spartans should quit a post they had come to guard. I myself am inclined to think that Leonidas, seeing that the allies were dispirited and reluctant to share the danger, ordered them to retire, while regarding it as dishonorable that he himself should retreat. And by remaining at this post he left behind a glorious name and avoided the obliteration of Sparta's prosperity. For when, right at the beginning of war, the Spartans sent to consult the oracle regarding its outcome, the answer they received from the Priestess was this: that either Sparta would be overthrown by the foreign invaders, or that one of their kings would perish. It was with this answer in mind, I think, and wishing to secure all the glory for the Spartans alone that Leonidas sent away the allies. This is more probable, I think, than that those who departed did so in an undisciplined fashion because of a difference of opinion.

[7.222] So the allies, thus dismissed, obeyed Leonidas and departed,

---

* There has been much debate regarding Leonidas' motives in holding to a now indefensible position. Some have seen in this episode a delaying action designed to permit the other Greek forces to get away unscathed; others see a public-relations move to prevent massive defections from the fragile Greek alliance; others, more cynically, saw an accident in which the Persians had closed the trap before Leonidas could effect his planned escape. Herodotus, typically, finds a religious explanation for Leonidas' seemingly superhuman courage.

except for the Thespians and the Thebans, who alone remained with the Spartans. But whereas the Thebans remained reluctantly and with ill grace, being retained by Leonidas as hostages, the Thespians stayed entirely of their own accord, refusing to desert Leonidas and his men. They remained and died with them. Their leader was Demophilus.

[7.223–24] At sunrise, Xerxes made his libations and, having waited until the time of the filling of the marketplace, moved forward. This was in accordance with Ephialtes' instructions, because the descent from the ridge is much more direct and shorter than the circuitous ascent. As the army of Xerxes drew nearer, the Greeks with Leonidas, knowing that they were going forth to die, pressed forward to the wider part of the pass to a greater degree than previously. Until then, they had been holding the wall and making sorties into the narrower section; but now the battle raged beyond the confined space, and the Persians fell in great numbers, for behind them their company commanders whipped on every single man, urging them forward. Many of them tumbled into the sea and perished, and many more were trampled to death by others. No attention was paid to the dying. For their part the Greeks, knowing that their fate was sealed by those who were coming over the mountain, fought with reckless fury, exerting every ounce of their strength against the enemy. By this time, most of them had had their spears broken and were hewing down the Persians with their swords. It was at this crisis that Leonidas fell, after showing exceptional courage, and with him many notable Spartans whose names, together with the names of all three hundred, I have taken care to learn, they being men of great worth. Among the Persian losses were men of note, among them two sons of Darius, Abrocomes and Hyperanthes, both of them born to Darius by Artanes' daughter Phratagune.

[7.225] There now arose a fierce struggle between Persians and Spartans over the body of Leonidas.* Four times the Greeks drove off the enemy and at last by their bravery succeeded in bearing the body away. Thus did the fighting continue until the troops with Ephialtes were close at hand, when the Greeks, informed of their approach, changed the manner of their fighting. They withdrew again to the narrow section of the

---

* The image of the Greeks fighting to reclaim the body of a fallen hero suits the larger-than-life dimensions of the whole Thermopylae narrative, for this is what Homeric heroes commonly do in the *Iliad*.

pass and behind the wall and took up a position in close formation on a hillock, all except the Thebans. This hillock is at the entrance to the pass, where now stands a stone lion in honor of Leonidas.* Here they resisted to the last, with their swords if they had them, if not, with their hands and teeth, until they were overwhelmed by the encircling Persians, of whom some came on from the front after demolishing the wall, while others closed in from behind.

[7.226] Thus valiantly did the Spartans and the Thespians behave; but one man, Dieneces the Spartan, is said to have distinguished himself above all others. They say that before the battle, a man of Trachis told him that when the Persians discharged their arrows, they made such a dense multitude that they hid the sun. Dieneces, not at all dismayed by these words, made light of the numbers of the Medes and replied: "Our Trachinian friend brings us very good news. If the Medes hide the sun, we shall be fighting in the shade instead of the sunshine." He is said to have left behind him many sayings of this kind in popular memory.

[7.228] The dead were buried where they fell,† and in their honor, and likewise in honor of those who fell before Leonidas dismissed the allies, an inscription was set up as follows:

Against three million on this very spot
There fought four thousand—but these were Dorian Greeks.

This was in honor of the entire force. For the Spartans alone there was this:

Go tell the Spartans, thou that passest by,
That here, obedient to their words, we lie.

[7.229] It is said that two men of the three hundred, Eurytus and Aristodemus, suffering from a severe disease of the eyes, had been dismissed by Leonidas before the battle and were recuperating at Alpeni. These two men might have agreed together to return safely to Sparta, or, if they did not wish to do so, to die with their countrymen. While either course was open to them, they could not agree but were of different minds. Eu-

* The name Leonidas carries within it the Greek word for "lion."
† An unusual mark of respect in the Greek world.

rytus, learning of the encircling movement of the Persians, called for his armor, buckled it on, and ordered his helot* to lead him to the scene of battle. When they arrived, the helot fled, and Eurytus rushed into the thick of the fray and perished. But Aristodemus, faint of heart, remained behind. Now if Aristodemus alone had been sick and had returned to Sparta, or if both had returned together, I do not think the Spartans would have been angry. But with the same excuse open to both, and one giving his life while the other declined to do so, the Spartans could not but be very angry with Aristodemus. [7.230] This is one account to explain how Aristodemus returned safely to Sparta; but there is another story that he in company with another had been sent from the camp with a message, and though he might have returned in time for the battle, he lingered on the road and so survived, whereas his fellow messenger came back in time and perished.

[7.231] When Aristodemus returned to Sparta, he was met with reproach and disgrace. His disgrace took this form that no Spartan would provide him with a light to kindle his fire or speak to him, and his reproach was to be called Shaky Aristodemus. However, in the Battle of Plataea he would later cleanse himself of all the shame that had been heaped on him.

[7.232] There is a story that one more of the three hundred, a man named Pantites, survived. He had been sent with a message to Thessaly, and on returning to Sparta he found himself in such dishonor that he hanged himself.

[7.233] The Thebans under Leontiades stayed together for a while with the Greek force and were compelled to make some show of fighting against the Persian army. But when they saw the Persians gaining the upper hand, they took advantage of Leonidas' retreat to the hillock to detach themselves from the main body. With outstretched hands they approached the Persians, saying (as was quite true) that they favored the Persian cause and had been among the first to give the King earth and water; they had come to Thermopylae under compulsion and were guiltless of any injury done to the king. By so saying they saved their lives, for the Thessalians bore witness to the truth of their claim. Nevertheless, they did not get off entirely without misfortune. Some of them were slain by the Persians at their first approach, while the greater number, at Xer-

---

* Each Spartan warrior went to battle accompanied by several helots, essentially slaves who carried his weapons and tended to his needs.

xes' command, were branded with the royal mark, beginning with their commander, Leontiades. (Much later, this man's son, Eurymachus, was killed by the Plataeans as he led a contingent of four hundred Thebans attempting to seize Plataea.)*

[7.234] So went the battle mounted by the Greeks at Thermopylae. Xerxes went over the battlefield to view the bodies, and, learning that Leonidas was the king and commander of the Spartans, he ordered his head to be cut off and impaled on a stake. This is one piece of evidence among many others that convinces me that King Xerxes was more angry with Leonidas, while the Spartan yet lived, than with any other man. Otherwise he would not have committed this outrage against his body, since the Persians more than any other nation are accustomed to honor men who have distinguished themselves in battle. But the king's orders were carried out.

———

At nearly the same time as the Battle of Thermopylae (mid-August 480), the collective Greek fleet was engaging the Persian navy in the waters off Artemisium. In contrast to the land battle, these first naval confrontations went rather well for the Greeks, and in addition the Persian forces were again weakened by a terrible storm at sea. A contingent of Persian vessels that had been sent around Euboea to outflank the Greeks—just as the detachment under Hydarnes had outflanked them on land—was caught by the storm in open water and destroyed. Herodotus comments, in one of his most pious pronouncements, that "the god was doing his utmost to make the Persian forces equal to the Greek, instead of more numerous."

The successes at Artemisium dwindled in importance, however, once the sailors learned that the defense of Thermopylae had failed. It would do little good now to hold the Persians' ships at bay while their army marched unimpeded into the Greek heartland. So the Greek navy now withdrew at once, slipping away under cover of darkness, to find a safer, more southerly base. Themistocles, commander of the large Athenian contingent, tried a form of psychological warfare during the retreat: He stopped at water sources along the way to leave rock-carved messages urging the Ionian sailors serving in Xerxes' fleet to desert or at least to fight weakly in the next engagement against their countrymen. He hoped that even if no desertions resulted, he might at least trouble Xerxes' mind with the fear that they might.

———

* This is one of several fascinating passages in which Herodotus draws a link between the two great wars of his day, the Greco-Persian conflict and the Peloponnesian War between Athens and Sparta, which was just beginning at the time he finished writing the *Histories*. Readers of Thucydides' history of that later war will vividly recollect the Theban attack on Plataea in 431.

Stripped now of both land and sea defenses, the entire region of Boeotia, with the sole exception of Phocis, went over to the Persian side, including the all-important city of Thebes. Even the sacred oracle at Delphi, with its vast store of riches and precious art objects, lay open to a Persian plundering raid; but Herodotus reports that a series of miraculous portents put the Persians into a panic and drove them from the site. The Delphians even witnessed two gigantic soldiers helping to cut down the fleeing invaders—seemingly gods fighting in human form, an apparition straight out of the poetry of Homer.

The leaders of the city of Athens, meanwhile, knew better than to expect help from miracles and soon learned that they could also expect none from the Spartan-led Greek army. There were no readily defensible barriers between Boeotia and Attica, and in any case the Spartans were disinclined to run risks now that they had lost Leonidas and the three hundred at Thermopylae. They led the joint Greek army straight to the Isthmus of Corinth, where there was a fair chance of defending the Peloponnese (Sparta's own backyard), but none at all of protecting Attica. Athens knew now that it could not avoid a full Persian assault and at this point, according to Herodotus, began evacuating its people and property to the islands of Salamis and Aegina and the town of Troezen in the Peloponnese. (A recently discovered inscription called the Troezen Decree gives evidence that the evacuation had in fact begun well before this, but no one knows whether it is genuine.) A few thousand stalwarts remained in the city, perhaps trusting that the "wooden wall" oracle referred to the acropolis and not the navy after all. When the Persians arrived (early September 480), they quickly smashed this desperate band of holdouts and put the now empty acropolis to the torch.

Athens itself had fallen into Persian hands, but its people had become "a city on the sea." The refugees at Salamis were soon joined by the retreating Greek navy, which itself had roughly two hundred Athenian ships and therefore forty thousand Athenians. Themistocles had engineered this retreat to Salamis so that the navy could be used to defend the refugees and, if possible, fight to reclaim the city of Athens itself. But command of the allied fleet was not in his hands; Athens had agreed at the start of the war to allow Sparta to lead both land and sea forces. And the Spartan admiral, Eurybiades, inclined toward the Peloponnesian defense strategy, which meant abandoning Attica as well as Salamis and taking the navy to the Isthmus of Corinth. The conflict between Peloponnesian and Athenian war goals broke out into the open in a series of urgent meetings of the Greek naval commanders at Salamis, superbly dramatized by Herodotus as part of his inquiry into how the Greek "nation" had united under one banner:

—

Satellite photo of the island of Salamis. The sea battle was fought in the narrow strait between the northeastern part of the island and the mainland of Attica. WIKIMEDIA COMMONS

[8.49]* The commanders of the various allied naval contingents met to make plans, and Eurybiades asked for recommendations as to where would be the most suitable place for a sea-fight in all the territory still under Greek control (Attica he excluded as being already lost to the enemy). The majority opinion was for sailing to the Isthmus and fighting to save the Peloponnese; the reasoning was that if they were defeated at Salamis they would be bottled up on an island with no possibility of rescue, whereas at the Isthmus they could always find safety by fleeing to their own cities. While the Peloponnesian commanders were advocating this course, an Athenian messenger arrived and reported that the barbarians had arrived in Attica and were burning the whole region.

[8.56] When the Greeks heard the report that the Persians had seized the Athenian Acropolis, they were thrown into confusion, and some did not wait for a vote on their proposed strategy but dashed for their ships and hoisted sail as if to start out at once. But the others, who stayed at the council meeting, passed the proposal to stage their sea-battle at the Isth-

---

* The passages from here through chapter 58 were translated by the editor.

mus. Then night fell, and they broke up the council meeting and returned to their ships.

[8.57] When Themistocles arrived at his ship, a certain Athenian named Mnesiphilus asked him what strategy had been adopted. When he learned that the course was set for the Isthmus and a defense of the Peloponnese, Mnesiphilus said: "But once you sail away from Salamis, you will no longer be fighting for a united homeland; each contingent will peel off and return to its own city, and not even Eurybiades—not anyone!—will stop the fleet from splitting apart. Greece will be wrecked by bad strategy. If in any way you can, go try to reverse this decision; perhaps you can persuade Eurybiades to change plans and stay right here." This idea greatly pleased Themistocles, and without even making a reply he went off to Eurybiades' ship.

[8.58] When he got there, he told Eurybiades he wanted to discuss something of common concern, and Eurybiades invited him to come on board. There Themistocles sat down and repeated everything he had heard Mnesiphilus say (though pretending the arguments were his own) and added much more besides. Finally he persuaded Eurybiades to disembark and summon all the commanders, once again, to a council.

[8.59] The council met, and before Eurybiades even had time to explain why he had recalled them, Themistocles broke into a long and passionate speech. As he was speaking, he was interrupted by Adeimantus, the Corinthian commander. "Themistocles," he said, "at the games, those who start the race before the signal are whipped." "Yes," said the other, defending himself, "but those who are left behind do not win the crown."

[8.60] Thus he gave the Corinthian a mild answer—for the moment.* Turning then to Eurybiades, he used none of his previous arguments—that if they left Salamis their force was likely to disperse—for he deemed it unseemly to accuse any of the allies to their faces. Instead, he adopted another line and said: "It now lies with you to save Greece, if you will hearken to me and engage the enemy here and disregard the suggestions that we should withdraw to the Isthmus. Compare the two situations: At the Isthmus you will be fighting in the open sea, very much to our disadvantage with our heavier ships and smaller numbers. Then again, even if we are victorious, you will have lost Salamis, Megara, and Aegina. Fur-

* Later (see 8.61) the polemics between these two will grow harsher. As a Peloponnesian state, an oligarchy, and a long-standing commercial rival of Athens, Corinth had little love for democratic upstarts like Themistocles.

thermore, if their fleet advances south, so will their army, and you will be drawing them to the Peloponnese, thus imperiling the whole of Greece.

"Now, if you do as I suggest, you will secure the following advantages: In the first place, we shall be fighting in narrow waters with fewer ships against many, with a good chance of coming off best. Fighting in narrow waters favors us, as fighting in the open sea favors them. Secondly, Salamis, where we have lodged our wives and children, will be preserved. And then there is this further consideration—for you a consideration of the greatest importance—that by fighting here you will be defending the Peloponnese just as well as by fighting at the Isthmus; and, if you act thus wisely, you will not be drawing the enemy on to the Peloponnese. If things turn out as I expect and we beat them at sea, they will not attack you at the Isthmus nor will they advance beyond Attica; they will retreat in disorder, and we shall gain by retaining Megara, Aegina, and Salamis, where the oracle foretold victory for us. When men take counsel reasonably, they generally meet with success; but if they reject reason, the god is unlikely to foster human designs."

[8.61] When Themistocles had thus spoken, Adeimantus again insulted him, bidding him be silent since he was a man without a country and calling on Eurybiades not to allow a vote to be taken on a proposal by a man without a city. Themistocles, he said, should indicate which city he represented before adding his voice to their counsel. The point of this gibe was that Athens had been captured and was in enemy hands. Thereupon Themistocles launched into a long and bitter attack on him and the Corinthians, making it quite clear that the Athenians had a city and a country greater than theirs, as long as they had two hundred ships fully manned; for none of the Greeks were capable of resisting these, should the Athenians attack.*

[8.62] After this, he turned to Eurybiades, speaking with even greater urgency. "If you remain here," he said, "you will be playing a man's part; if not, you will be the ruin of Greece. In this war everything depends on our ships. Be persuaded by me. If not, we will take our families on board and make for Siris in Italy.† It has long been ours, and oracles foretell that we must colonize it someday. When you are deprived of allies such as we are, you will remember my words."

---

* A pregnant observation, in light of the strong-arm tactics Athens would later use to maintain its naval empire.

† A desperate threat, though probably not a hollow one.

[8.63] At these words of Themistocles, Eurybiades changed his mind, mainly, in my opinion, through fear that the Athenians would desert the fleet if he withdrew to the Isthmus; for without the Athenians the remainder of the fleet would be no match for the enemy. So he came to the decision to remain where they were and fight it out.

[8.74] Meanwhile, the Greeks at the Isthmus toiled away as if they had no confidence in success at sea and realized that everything was at stake. The news of their activities caused great alarm at Salamis; they feared not so much for themselves as for the Peloponnese. At first they talked among themselves secretly, expressing amazement at Eurybiades' folly. Then this undercurrent broke out into the open, and another council was called. They went over the old ground again: Some maintained that they should withdraw to the Peloponnese and fight for that, rather than stay to fight for land already lost, whereas the Athenians, Aeginetans, and Megarians urged that they should stay and to fight where they were.

[8.75] Then Themistocles, seeing that the Peloponnesians would carry the vote against him, quietly left the meeting and sent a man in a boat to the Persian fleet, instructing him what to say. This man was Sicinnus, one of Themistocles' household slaves and tutor to his children. (Some time later, when the Thespians were admitting others to citizenship, Themistocles made him a Thespian and a rich man.) Arriving in his boat, Sicinnus addressed the Persian generals as follows: "The Athenian commander has sent me to you secretly, unknown to the other Greeks. He wishes well to the King and hopes for a Persian victory. He bids me tell you that the Greeks are in a panic and contemplate flight, and that you have the opportunity to achieve a brilliant success by not allowing them to get away. They have lost all concord and unity and will not oppose you. Indeed, you will see them fighting among themselves, those who are on your side against those who are not." Having delivered this message, he went off.

[8.76] The Persians, believing what he said, proceeded to put ashore a considerable number of troops on the islet of Psyttaleia, which lies between Salamis and the mainland. Then, about midnight, they advanced their western wing toward Salamis in an encircling movement, while those stationed at Ceos and Cynosura advanced to block the whole channel as far as Munychia with their ships. Their purpose was to prevent the escape of the Greeks, to hem them in at Salamis, and to exact revenge for the battles fought off Artemisium. Troops were landed on the islet of Psyttaleia because it lay directly in the path of the coming action, and when the battle began, most of the men and wrecks were likely to be carried there, so then they could rescue their own men and destroy the enemy. All this was done in silence, so that the Greeks would not know, and the men had no sleep that night as they prepared for action.

[8.78] Meanwhile, among the commanders at Salamis the battle of speeches continued. As yet they did not know that they were surrounded, thinking the enemy occupied the same position as on the previous day. While they were arguing, Aristides, son of Lysimachus, crossed over to them from Aegina. He was an Athenian who had been ostracized by a vote of the citizenry;* yet I gather from what I have learned of his character that he was the best and most upright man among the Athenians. Standing outside the conference, he called for Themistocles, who was by no means his friend but his bitter enemy. But putting all that aside in the face of the impending danger, he called him out to talk to him. He had already heard that the Peloponnesians were anxious to withdraw the fleet to the Isthmus. As soon as Themistocles came out, Aristides spoke as follows: "You and I have been rivals before, but now more than ever we should compete to see which of us can do most good to our country. First let me say that however much the Peloponnesians may talk about withdrawal from here, it will make no difference. With my own eyes I have seen what I now report; even if the Corinthians and Eurybiades himself want to get away, they will not be able to do so. For we are completely cut off and surrounded by the enemy."

[8.80] "Excellent advice and good news," replied Themistocles. "That which I wanted to happen, you tell me you have seen with your own eyes. Know that I am responsible for what the Medes have done. Since the Greeks were not willing to fight here, it was necessary to *make* them fight. But as you have brought the good news, go tell them yourself; if I tell them, they will think I have invented it and will not believe that the Persians have acted so. Go in and report the facts yourself. If they believe you, well and good; if not, it will make no difference, for they won't go anywhere if we are surrounded on all sides, as you say."

[8.81] So Aristides went in and made his report, saying that he had come from Aegina and had with difficulty slipped through the blockading fleet, and that the entire Greek force was encircled by Xerxes' ships. He urged them to prepare to defend themselves. Having said so much,

* The Athenian constitution allowed the citizen body to "ostracize," or exile for ten years, anyone it wished. The provision was designed to prevent stalemates between two rivals for power, and in fact Aristides had been ostracized in a standoff against Themistocles (483).

he withdrew. And now there began another contest of speeches, for most of the commanders refused to believe his report.

[8.82] But while they still doubted, a Tenian trireme commanded by Panaetius deserted from the Persians and arrived with a full account of the truth. For this service the name of the Tenians was later inscribed on a tripod at Delphi among those who helped to defeat the invader. With the accession of this ship that deserted to the Greeks at Salamis, and with the Lemnian ship that had previously joined them at Artemisium, the Greek fleet was brought to the full number of 380 vessels. Previously they had fallen short of this figure by two.

[8.83] Now the Greeks, convinced by what the Tenians had told them, prepared for battle. At dawn the men at arms were assembled, and Themistocles delivered the finest speech of the hour, contrasting the better and the worse in man's nature and condition and urging them to choose the nobler course. Then, finishing off his speech, he gave the order to embark, and they went on board their ships.

[8.84] The Greek fleet now got under way and was immediately attacked by the Persians. Most of the Greek ships backed astern and were close to running aground when Ameinias of Pallene, an Athenian, drove forward and rammed an enemy ship. The two ships became entangled and could not disengage, whereupon the others came to Ameinias' assistance and engaged the enemy. This is how the Athenians describe the beginning of the battle, but the Aeginetans claim that the first to go into action was the ship that had been sent to Aegina to bring the Aeacids.* There is also a story that there appeared a phantom in the form of a woman, and in a voice that could be heard from one end of the fleet to the other cheering them on, after first rebuking them with these words: "Incredible! How long are you going to keep on backing water?"†

[8.85] The Athenian contingent, which formed the western wing toward Eleusis, was facing the Phoenicians; the Spartans, who formed the eastern wing toward the port of Piraeus, faced the Ionians. Of these last, a few, but not the majority, heeded Themistocles' appeals‡ and held back

---

* The Aeacids were mythical heroes. A few days earlier a ship had been sent to Aegina to fetch their cult statues, in the hope that these would aid the fleet with divine power.

† The playwright Aeschylus, who fought at Salamis and later described the battle in his play *The Persians,* similarly reported a divine voice urging the Greeks on (though with different words) just as the fighting commenced.

‡ That is, the rock-carved messages he had left near springs around Artemisium (see p. 109 above).

from the fighting. I could here mention the names of many captains serving in the enemy's fleet who captured Greek vessels, but I shall confine myself to two, Theomestor and Phylacus, both Samians. I mention only these two because Theomestor, in reward for this service, was made ruler of Samos by the Persians, while Phylacus was enrolled among the King's Benefactors and presented with a large estate. The King's Benefactors are called Orosangae in the Persian tongue.

[8.86] But by far the greater number of Persian ships at Salamis were severely disabled, some at the hands of the Athenians, others at the hands of the Aeginetans. For whereas the Greek ships fought in good order and in line, the Persians were not in good array and had no plan in what they did, so that the final issue was bound to be as it was. Nevertheless they fought well that day, far better than in the actions at Euboea. Every man exerted himself to the full in fear of Xerxes, each imagining that the king's eye was on him.

[8.87–88] I cannot give exact details as to the part played in this battle by the various foreign and Greek contingents on the Persian side, but I know that Artemisia* distinguished herself in a way that raised her even further in the king's esteem. When there was utter confusion on the Persian side, at this juncture Artemisia's ship was being pursued by an Athenian vessel. Having nowhere to flee because directly in her path were other friendly vessels and her own ship was nearest to the enemy, she resorted to a measure that turned out to be to her advantage. Pressed by her Athenian pursuer, she rammed a ship of her own side, a ship of Calynda, which happened to have aboard Damasythimus, the Calyndian king. I cannot say whether she had any quarrel with this man dating from the time when they were at the Hellespont, nor can I say whether she did this of set purpose or whether the Calyndian ship just happened to be in the way. But by ramming and sinking it, she derived a double advantage for herself. In the first place, the captain of the Athenian vessel, seeing her ramming an enemy ship, thought that either Artemisia's ship was a Greek or that it had deserted from the Persians and was fighting on their side; and so he turned away to attack others. Thus it came about that Artemisia escaped with her life. Secondly, by causing injury to her own side she raised herself higher than ever in the esteem of King Xerxes. It

---

* A non-Greek woman who had become ruler of the Greek city of Halicarnassus on the Turkish coast (Herodotus' hometown). In an earlier passage, not included in this volume, she had urged Xerxes not to fight the sea battle at Salamis but to simply wait for the Greek fleet to fall apart.

is said that as the King watched the battle, he observed this incident of the ramming, and one of his attendants remarked: "Do you see, master, how well Artemisia fights and how she has sunk an enemy ship?" The King asked if this was really Artemisia's doing and they assured him it was so, for they knew her ensign. (Of course, they supposed that it was an enemy ship that had been sunk. She was indeed fortunate, especially in there being no survivors from the Calyndian ship to accuse her.) The story is that Xerxes said in reply: "My men have become women, my women, men."

[8.89] There fell in this struggle Ariabignes, a commander in the fleet, son of Darius and brother of Xerxes, and with him many other men of note among the Persians, Medes, and their allies. Of the Greeks there perished not many, for, knowing how to swim, those who lost their ships but were not actually slain in combat swam over to Salamis, whereas most of the enemy, unable to swim, were drowned. It was when the enemy's leading ships turned to flee that the greatest destruction took place. For those behind them, being eager to display their valor to the king, pressed forward to the front and became entangled with the ships of their retreating comrades.

[8.90] In the confusion that followed, some of the Phoenicians whose ships had been destroyed came to Xerxes and alleged that the Ionians were responsible for the loss of their ships, accusing them as traitors. But as a result, the Ionian captains escaped death while their Phoenician accusers died instead. For it so happened that while they were still speaking to Xerxes, a Samothracian ship rammed an Athenian ship, and while this was sinking, an Aeginetan vessel attacked and sank the Samothracian ship. But the Samothracians, being skilled javelin throwers, cleared the decks of the vessel that had disabled them, leapt aboard, and captured it. This proved to be the salvation of the Ionians, for when Xerxes saw this remarkable exploit, being already very vexed and ready to blame anyone, he turned on the Phoenicians and ordered their heads to be cut off, so that they could nevermore blame braver men for their own cowardice.

[8.93] In this sea-battle the greatest glory on the Greek side went to the Aeginetans, and after them to the Athenians; and of individuals, to Polycritus the Aeginetan and to the Athenians Eumenes of Anagyrus and Ameinias of Pallene. It was the latter who had given chase to Artemisia, and had he known that Artemisia was on board he would never have desisted from the chase until either he had captured her or else been captured himself. For the Athenians, indignant that a woman should make war on them, had given the captains special orders regarding the queen, and a reward of ten thousand drachmas was proclaimed for whomever would take her alive. However, as I have said, she succeeded in escaping. Her ship and the others that got away now lay at Phalerum.*

[8.94] The Athenians say that right at the beginning of the action, the Corinthian commander Adeimantus was seized with panic and, hoisting sail, ran away, whereupon the rest of the Corinthian contingent, seeing their commander in flight, followed his example. But when they were off that part of the coast of Salamis where stands the temple of Athene Sciras, they encountered a small boat, sent by some divine force—since it was never discovered that anyone had sent it to them. Until its appearance, the Corinthians knew nothing of how the battle was going, but from what ensued they concluded that the will of the god was there manifested. When the bark came close to them, those on board cried out: "Adeimantus, by turning away in flight you are betraying the Greeks, while they are gaining as great a victory over their enemies as ever they prayed for." When Adeimantus refused to believe these words, they went on to say that he might take them along as hostages and put them to death if he did not find the Greeks having the upper hand. So he and the rest of his ships turned around and rejoined the fleet, but when they arrived, the fighting was already over. Such is the story told by the Athenians, but the Corinthians deny this. On the contrary, they claim that they were among the foremost in the fight, and the rest of Greece bears witness in their favor.[†]

[8.97] When Xerxes realized what a disaster he had suffered, he feared that the Greeks, either on their own initiative or prompted by the Ionians, might sail to the Hellespont to destroy the bridges. He would then be cut off in Europe and in danger of his life. So he made up his mind to take flight, but lest this should become apparent to the Greeks and to his own people, he set to work to construct a causeway across the channel to Salamis, lashing together some Phoenician merchant ships to serve as a floating bridge and a wall. At the same time, he made preparations as if to

* Phalerum was at this time the harbor of Athens.

† The dispute Herodotus records here reflects the political alignments of his own day. Athens and Corinth had become bitter enemies by the 430s, so the Athenians had ample motive to bad-mouth the Corinthians for not assisting "their" great effort at Salamis.

renew the sea-battle. Seeing him thus engaged, all were persuaded to remain and pursue the war as vigorously as possible. But he did not deceive Mardonius, who well knew Xerxes' mind.

[8.98]* Xerxes also sent off messengers to Persia to bring them news of his misfortune. (There is nothing in this world faster than these Persian messengers. The Persians run them by the following system: However many days a journey will take, they station that number of men and horses along the way, assigning one horse and rider to each stage of the trip. The riders stop neither for snow, nor rain, nor heat, nor nightfall as they make all haste to complete their stages.† The first rider hands off his orders to the second, and the second to the third, and so the messages pass from one to the next just as the Greeks pass torches to each other in the Festival of Hephaestus. This horse-relay system the Persians call the *angareion*.)

[8.99] Now Xerxes' first message to Susa, with news of the capture of Athens, had evoked such joy among the Persians who had remained behind that they strewed all the roads with myrtle boughs and burned incense and gave themselves up to celebration and merrymaking. The second message caused so much distress that they all rent their garments, weeping and wailing without cease and laying the blame on Mardonius. Their grief arose not so much from the loss of the ships as from their fear for Xerxes' safety. And in this state they continued without a break until Xerxes' safe return.

[8.107] Xerxes summoned Mardonius and ordered him to select those of the land forces that he wished and to see to it that his deeds should be as good as his words. That day nothing more was done, but at nightfall, at the King's orders, the fleet quit Phalerum, each vessel making the best speed it could toward the Hellespont to guard the bridges for the King's return journey. Off Zoster, they saw some rocky headlands projected into the sea and mistook these for ships and took flight;‡ then, realizing their error, they joined company again and continued their voyage.

[8.108] The next day, the Greeks, seeing the Persians' land forces still

---

* This chapter was translated by the editor.

† If one substitutes "gloom of night" for "nightfall," this sentence becomes more familiar. Since being inscribed above the U.S. Postal Service building on Eighth Avenue in New York City (now part of Pennsylvania Station), it has become an unofficial motto.

‡ An interesting detail, revealing the fearful state of mind of sailors who have endured a bloody defeat.

occupying the same position, expected that their fleet would also be at Phalerum and made preparations to encounter the enemy in another sea-battle. When they saw that the fleet had departed, they resolved to pursue them, and they did get as far as the Andros without sighting the Persian fleet. They stopped at Andros and held a council. Themistocles proposed that they should carry on through the islands direct to the Hellespont to destroy the bridges. But Eurybiades put forward an opposing view, declaring that if they destroyed the bridges they would be doing Greece a grave disservice. If Xerxes were cut off and forced to remain in Europe, he was not likely to remain inactive, since this would not improve his chances of success and would deprive him of a return home, while his army was being destroyed by lack of provisions; if he took the offensive and acted with vigor, the whole of Europe might fall to him, city by city and people by people, either by subjugation or by prior agreement, while the annual harvest would allow his troops to live off the land. But, he said, as things stood now, the Persian king, defeated at Salamis, did not intend to remain in Europe, and so he should be allowed to escape back to his own country. Thereafter the war should be transferred to the king's own country, Eurybiades said.

[8.109] Finding that he could not persuade the majority of the allies to advance to the Hellespont, Themistocles changed his ground, and addressing himself to the Athenians—who of all the allies were most vexed at the enemy's escape and were eager to sail on to the Hellespont even by themselves if the others would not accompany them—he spoke as follows: "I have myself seen many instances, and heard of many more from others, where men who have been beaten and driven to desperation have recovered their fighting spirit and made amends for earlier disaster. Now we have had the good fortune to save ourselves and Greece by repelling such a vast horde of men. Let us not pursue those who are in flight. It is not we who have wrought this deed, it is our gods and our divine guardians who begrudged that one man should rule over both Asia and Europe, an unholy and presumptuous man who treats alike things sacred and profane, who burns and casts down the statues of the gods, who scourged the sea and cast fetters into it. For the present, all is well with us; so let us remain in Greece and see to ourselves and our families. Now that the enemy has been completely driven off, let each man repair his own house and sow his land diligently. And in the spring we can sail to the Hellespont and Ionia." All this he said with the intention of establish-

ing a claim on the Persian king, so as to have a place of refuge if ever he
got into trouble with the Athenians—which did in fact come about.*

[8.110] Thus did Themistocles speak with ulterior purpose, and the
Athenians were persuaded. Since his previous reputation for wisdom and
good counsel had been thoroughly vindicated by recent events, they
were quite willing to hearken to what he said. Themistocles lost no time
in sending a boat carrying Sicinnus, his house slave, together with other
men who could be trusted to keep silent even under torture, to take a
message to the king. When they reached Attica, Sicinnus left the others
in the boat, obtained an audience with Xerxes, and spoke thus: "I have
been sent by Themistocles, son of Neocles, the Athenian commander,
the most outstanding and wisest of the allies, to convey this message:
Themistocles the Athenian, desiring to serve you, has held back the
Greeks from pursuing your fleet and destroying the bridges at the Hellespont. Now return at your leisure." Having delivered this message, they
sailed away.

[8.111] The Greeks, having decided neither to continue their pursuit of
the enemy nor to sail to the Hellespont to destroy the crossing, laid siege
to Andros, intending to capture it.† For the Andrians were the first of the
islanders to refuse money demanded by Themistocles. Themistocles had
put before them the proposition that the money had to be paid because
the Athenians came supported by two mighty gods, Persuasion and Necessity. To this the Andrians replied that Athens might well be a great
and glorious city, being blessed with such useful gods; but the Andrians
were wretchedly poor, stinted for land and plagued by two unprofitable
gods who never quit their island but always dwelt with them, Poverty and
Hardship. Saddled with these gods, the Andrians said, they would not

* The story of Themistocles' medism is told not by Herodotus but Thucydides. Ostracized from Athens and under suspicion of treachery, Themistocles appealed to the Persian
king (Artaxerxes at that time) for refuge to escape prosecution by his political enemies. In a
letter quoted by Thucydides, Themistocles did in fact claim to have saved Xerxes' life by
preventing the breakup of the Hellespont bridge. His machinations succeeded, and he
ended his life as a distinguished governor of a Persian province.

† Themistocles' actions here parallel those of an earlier Athenian war hero, Miltiades:
Both men tried to capitalize on a great military success by turning to the extortion of money
from Greek islanders. In both cases, the pretext was given that reparations were owed by
states that had helped the Persians, but mercantile motives were obviously at work too. The
tactics employed by Themistocles here prefigure those of the mature Athenian Empire, and
his exchange of words with the Andrians contains the germ of Thucydides' Melian Dialogue (see 5.85–112).

pay the money; for Athenian power could never be mightier than Andrian inability to pay. Having spoken these words and refused to pay the money, they were put under siege.

[8.112] Meanwhile, Themistocles, ever eager for gain, sent threatening demands for money to the other islands, using the same messengers as he had sent to the Persian king. If they did not meet his demand, he said, he would bring the Greek fleet upon them and besiege them until they surrendered. By such threats he collected large sums of money from the Carystians and the Parians, who, learning that Andros was besieged because of its support of Persia, and that Themistocles was the most highly esteemed of the commanders, complied with the demands through fear. I cannot say if any of the other islanders gave money, but I rather think there were some. The Carystians, despite their compliance, were not spared, but the Parians, by appearing before Themistocles with money, escaped a visit from his force. Thus it was that Themistocles, while at Andros, extorted money from the islanders unbeknownst to the other commanders.

THUCYDIDES

THUCYDIDES

(C. 460–C. 400 BC)

TRANSLATED BY RICHARD CRAWLEY, WITH REVISIONS BY
MARY LEFKOWITZ AND JAMES ROMM

The ancient Greeks understood that, of all human activities, war is the most trans-formative. Like plague, war is not only deadly, but disruptive and indiscriminate. No one, not even those who manage to emerge from it alive, can remain untouched by it. Even worse, war has been a constant feature of human existence. The ancient Mediterranean world was no exception. So it is not coincidental that the first long narratives produced by ancient Greeks described the causes and consequences of human conflict. The subject of the Iliad, *the best-known work of literature in the ancient Greek world, is an account of a short but decisive period in the ten-year war between the Greeks and the Trojans. Herodotus in his Inquiry (*historiē*) wrote about the events that culminated in the wars between Greeks and Persians. Thucydides, a younger contemporary of Herodotus, wrote about the course of the long and terrible conflict that followed the Persian wars, the long conflict between Athens and Sparta and their allies, known to us now as the Peloponnesian War.**

Writing the history of a war was a task for which Thucydides was well quali-fied. He was a member of a wealthy family whose income derived from gold mines in Thrace. His wealth enabled him to become a general in the Athenian army, where rank was determined by wealth as well as by ability. But (as he tells us), in 424–423 BC he and the soldiers under his command arrived too late at the northern Hellenic city of Amphipolis (an ally of Athens) to save it from being conquered by the Spar-tan troops. As a result, the Athenians voted to send him into exile. Fortunately for posterity, that misfortune gave him time to write an account of the war in which he had been directly involved. His financial resources made it possible for him to travel around Greece, to consult with both the allies of Athens and her enemies (see 5.26.5, p. 171). As he tells us, he lived through the whole of the war, until Athens was defeated

---

* In the first sentence of his narrative, Thucydides himself calls it "the war between the Peloponnesians and the Athenians." The term "Peloponnesian War" (which looks at events from the perspective of Athens) dates from the first century BC.

in 405–404 BC. But his narrative ends with the summer of 411. We do not know why he failed to complete it.

Thucydides explains that he chose to write about this war because "it was the greatest upheaval yet known in history, not only of the Greeks, but a large part of the foreign world—I had almost said of mankind." In the East, Persians sided with the Spartans because the Athenians had been instrumental in defeating their invasions of 490 and 480–479 BC. In Sicily, non-Hellenic people encouraged the Athenians to protect them against Syracuse, a colony of Sparta. In other words, it was a war that involved many peoples in the world that was known to the Greeks at that time, and that lasted for a much longer period than any other war at that time, starting in 430 BC and ending only in 404.

Like Herodotus, whose work he may have heard in Athens and certainly knew about, Thucydides wrote to ensure that the significant deeds and the reasons for conflict among nations might not be forgotten over time. But what gives his account of the war its continuing relevance is his analysis of the motives of the politicians and generals who were involved in the conflict. Like the great tragedians who were his contemporaries in Athens, Thucydides was keenly aware of the fallibility of judgment that is inherent in human nature, our tendency to suppose that our self-interest is synonymous with the common good, and our willingness to suppose that we have been able fully to understand things that in fact we know very little about. The great tragic poets had words for these universal human tendencies: atē (delusion) and hybris (self-confident arrogance), weaknesses that cause humans to make errors in judgment (the tendency that Aristotle called hamartia).

Thucydides does not use these words, nor does he imply that it is because of the gods that it seems impossible for humans to escape the malignant effects of atē and hybris. Nonetheless he arranged his narrative to emphasize these themes, which have been familiar to his Athenian audience from the tragic dramas that were performed every year throughout the course of the war. He relates events in chronological order, year by year, but within that general framework he describes only those events and speeches that he deems significant, and sometimes juxtaposes them so that his audience can see more clearly the difference between human aspiration and reality. After describing a fine oration in which Pericles praises Athenian culture, Thucydides quickly introduces a graphic description of the devastating plague that killed many Athenian citizens, a disease that he himself caught and managed to survive. Later in his narrative he relates how in 415 BC the Athenians refused to allow the inhabitants of the island of Melos to side with Sparta, insisting that Athenian military power gave them the right to treat the Melians as they saw fit. But he follows the account of their defeat of the Melians with a description of the Athenians' disastrous attempt to conquer Syracuse and the entire island of Sicily.

The expedition ended in total defeat and ultimately led to the Athenians' losing their long war with Sparta and her allies. His account of the Athenian debacle in Sicily seems even more tragic because he places it immediately after his narrative of their confident triumph in Melos.

Unlike Herodotus, who in his narrative calls attention to human behavior that tempted the gods to intervene, Thucydides does not refer specifically to divine action in his narrative. But his silence on that topic should not be taken as an indication that he himself did not believe in the existence of the traditional gods. In fact, he does call attention to the kinds of events that ordinarily were regarded as indications of divine disfavor, such as unusually violent earthquakes, eclipses of the sun, droughts, and famines that occurred during the long war. In his account of the terrible plague that struck Athens at the start of the war in 431 BC (1.23.3), he observes that old men remembered a prophecy that predicted a Dorian war that would come and with it a pestilence, noting that the plague did not have an observable effect on the Peloponnese (see 2.54.2, 5), which was populated primarily by Dorians. But unlike an epic poet, who was free to imagine and describe the roles the gods might have played in the traditional story that he was narrating, Thucydides did not try to imagine what the gods might have thought or done to make the war turn out as it did.

*What he could do, and says he did, was relate what he could learn by inquiry (*historiē*) from the human participants in the story, including himself (see above, p. 3). In addition to his record of significant events, he also brought to his account of the war a general's understanding of human capability and military strategy. He was able to explain (which Homer does not) that it took the Greeks ten years to conquer Troy because they did not have a means of provisioning their troops and thus needed to take time away from their siege to scavenge the area for food. Thucydides is able to call attention to the strategic mistakes that the Athenian generals made in their unsuccessful siege of the city of Syracuse in Sicily, where they camped in a swamp and spent so much time building fortification walls to protect themselves that they allowed the Syracusans time to summon help from the Spartans. He records when, where, and from whom Athenians on campaign were able to purchase or seize their food, details that Herodotus (who was not a military man) does not include.*

Thucydides also tells us how he went about learning what he could not already know from his own experiences. He explains how he composed the speeches in his narrative: "Some I heard myself, others I got from various quarters; it was in all cases difficult to carry all of them word for word in one's memory, so my habit has been to make the speakers say what was in my opinion demanded of them by the various occasions, of course adhering as closely as possible to the general sense of what they really said" (see 1.22.1). Herodotus made no such disclaimer, perhaps

because he knew that his audiences understood that it would have been impossible for him to know exactly what Croesus or Xerxes had said to his troops or to record a speech verbatim. Words and facts needed to be memorized, or notes etched onto wax-coated wooden tablets. There were no formal records, no archives nor libraries. Historians were compelled to reconstruct what people had, or were thought to have, said.

Thucydides, by contrast, explicitly states that he was writing not just for his contemporaries, but also for posterity. He understood that human nature was not likely to change, and so he believed that humans would continue to make the same kinds of errors of judgment that the Athenians had made in their war with Sparta and her allies. That is why we continue to read Thucydides today—not only to understand what happened in the past but also to see reflected in his narrative the overconfident, costly, and unsuccessful American decisions to invade Vietnam, Iraq, and Afghanistan. Even though the events Thucydides describes are far from us in time and space, his history has become, as he intended it to be, a work that readers will always find useful.

———

[1.1] Thucydides the Athenian* wrote the history of the war between the Peloponnesians and the Athenians, beginning from the time when it began. He expected that it would be an important war and more worthy of recording than any that had come before. He had observed that both sides had perfected their preparations, and he saw that the rest of the population of Greece was taking sides in the conflict, some doing so right away, some considering doing so. Indeed, this was the greatest upheaval known in history, not only among the Greeks, but also in a large part of the foreign† world, and I might even say of all humankind.

———

Drawing on his knowledge of the Peloponnese in his time, as well as mythological tradition, Thucydides now explains why up to the time when the war began, the inhabitants of Greece had not regarded themselves as a united nation.

———

[1.2] It seems in ancient times that the country now called Greece had no settled population. On the contrary, there were frequent migrations with different tribes being driven out by ever greater numbers. Without commerce, without frequent contact with one another either by land or

---

* Thucydides refers to himself in the third person in this narrative.

† The Greek word for "foreign" is *barbaros*, a term that originally referred to the sound of an unfamiliar language.

sea, they cultivated no more of their territory than they needed to live on. Because they did not have a surplus of goods, they did not cultivate their land, because they could not tell when someone might come and take it away, since they had no walls to stop them. They thought that what they needed for daily sustenance could be supplied in one place equally as well as another, so it was not hard for them to leave their homes, and for that reason they did not have the security of large cities or any other resources. The most fertile land was always most subject to changes of settlers, such as the district now called Thessaly, Boeotia, most of the Peloponnese (except for Arcadia),* and the best areas of the rest of Greece.

The excellence of the land allowed certain individuals to grow in power.† That created factions‡ that caused their destruction and at the same time made them more vulnerable to outside attack. Thus Attica,§ because of the poor quality of its soil, enjoyed from an early period freedom from factional strife and never changed its inhabitants. And this is a clear illustration of my claim that migrations were the reason why there was no corresponding growth in other locations. The most powerful victims of war or faction from elsewhere in Greece took refuge with the Athenians because it was a safe retreat. They became citizens from an early period and immediately made the city greater because of its large population. Later it became necessary to send these people to Ionia because the settlement in Attica was not large enough for them.¶

[1.3] The following is also the best indication of unity** in ancient times. There appears to have been no evidence of any common undertaking in Greece before the Trojan War, nor indeed any sign of the universal use of the name Greece. On the contrary, before the time of Hellēn, son of Deucalion,†† the appellation did not exist, but the tribes were known by different names and for the most part called Pelasgian.‡‡

* Arcadia is a mountainous district in the central Peloponnese.

† That is, wealthy landowners.

‡ By "faction" (*stasis*), Thucydides means the creation of political groups that attempt to take control of government and property.

§ The region surrounding Athens.

¶ Ironically, because Attica was believed to have been first settled by people from Ionia (i.e. the west coast of what is now Turkey, which until AD 1922 was occupied by Hellenes).

** That is, in respect to military strength.

†† Hellēn was believed to have been the ancestor of all the Hellenes.

‡‡ A name used by Hellenes to designate pre-Hellenic populations.

It was not until Hellēn and his sons became powerful in Phthiotis* and were invited into the other cities as allies that they gradually acquired, from association, the name Hellenes, though it did not take long before that name was applied to all of them.[†]

The best proof is furnished by Homer.[‡] Although he was born long after the Trojan War, Homer nowhere calls all of them Hellenes—nor indeed any of them except for the followers of Achilles from Phthiotis, who were the original Hellenes. In his poems they are called Danaans, Argives, and Achaeans. Homer does not even use the term "barbarian," probably because the Hellenes had not yet been distinguished from the rest of the world by a single name. So it seems that the several Hellenic communities, comprising not only those who first acquired the name, city by city, as they came to understand one another, but also those who assumed it afterward as the name of the whole people, were before the Trojan War prevented from undertaking any collective action by their lack of strength and lack of contact with one another. Indeed, they were only able to come together for the expedition[§] after they had become more familiar with the sea.

[1.4] The first person known to us by tradition as having established a navy is Minos.[¶] He made himself master of what is now known as the Hellenic sea and ruled over the Cyclades.[**] He was the first colonist of most of the islands. He expelled the Carians[††] and set up his own sons as rulers. It seems he also eliminated piracy as best he could, so the revenue from the islands would come to him.... [1.8] As soon as Minos had formed his navy, communication by sea became easier (the pirates had left the islands because of him, after he had colonized most of the islands). The coastal population now began to apply themselves more to the acquisition of wealth, and their lives became more settled. Some even began to

---

* The area of Greece from which Achilles came (see below).

[†] Hellenes are known as Greeks in English, because they first became known to speakers of English from Roman literature, where they were called Graeci.

[‡] The legendary author of the *Iliad,* the epic with which all ancient Greeks were familiar. The *Iliad* is now believed to have been composed in the late eighth century BC.

[§] That is, to Troy, to bring Helen back to Hellas.

[¶] A legendary king of the island of Crete. In recent times his name has been used as a general title for prehistoric Cretan civilization.

[**] A group of thirty islands often used as stopping places for ships traveling across the Aegean (here called the Hellenic Sea).

[††] The inhabitants of a mountainous region in southwest Asia Minor.

build walls for their cities because they had become even more wealthy. The love of wealth encouraged the weaker to serve the stronger, and the possession of wealth enabled the more powerful to make the smaller towns their subjects. And it was at a somewhat later stage of this development that they went on the expedition against Troy.

[1.9] What made it possible for Agamemnon* to muster his army was not, in my opinion, the oaths that the suitors had given to Tyndareus.[†] . . . Agamemnon's power was continental, and he could not have been ruler of any islands except those adjacent to his territory (and these could not have been numerous) if he had not possessed a fleet of ships.[‡]

[1.10] Mycenae was a small town,[§] and the settlements at that time do not appear to have been significant. But no one would use that as an indication that Agamemnon's army was as large as the poets say it was and as tradition has it. For if Sparta were to become depopulated, and only the temples and the foundations of the public buildings were left, as time went on posterity would be likely to decline to accept the city's reputation as an actual measure of her power. And yet the Spartans occupy two-fifths of the Peloponnese and are leaders of all of it, as well as many allies outside of it. Still, because the city is not densely built nor adorned with magnificent temples and public buildings, but rather composed of villages after the old fashion of towns in Greece, their city would appear to be inferior.

But I think that if Athens were similarly depopulated, any inference based on its appearance would make its power seem to have been twice as great as it is. So it is not a good idea to doubt or only consider a city's appearance without considering its power. But we may safely conclude that the strength of Agamemnon's army was greater in size than any that came before it, leaving aside the armies of the present day, if we can trust Homer's poems here as well (allowing for poetic elaboration).

[1.13] But as the power of Greece grew, and they had acquired more

* The legendary ruler of a large section of the Peloponnese, and in the *Iliad* the leader of the Greek army in the Trojan War.

[†] According to legend, all the suitors who wished to marry Helen swore an oath to Tyndareus, king of Sparta, to defend the rights of the one who married her. That turned out to be Menelaus, and the oaths were then invoked when Helen was taken off to Troy.

[‡] Information derived from *Iliad* 2.108.

[§] Thucydides now explains why he bases his estimate of the size of Agamemnon's army on the *Iliad* rather than on the physical appearance in his own lifetime of the cities that sent ships to Troy.

wealth than they had before, in general more tyrannies were established in the cities (the old form of government was hereditary monarchy with definite prerogatives), Greece began to fit out fleets and apply herself more closely to the sea....

A modern reconstruction of an ancient Greek trireme, the foundation of Athenian naval power. The ram at the front was cast from bronze and was used to stave in the hulls of opposing ships. Armed soldiers stood on the decks. The sails would be furled in a sea battle and the ship powered solely by its 170 rowers. WIKIMEDIA COMMONS

The earliest naval battle was between the Corinthians and Corcyrae-ans.* This was about two hundred and sixty years ago.† ... Situated on the Isthmus, Corinth had always been a center of commerce, because formerly almost all communication between the Greeks within and outside the Peloponnese was carried by land rather than by sea, and the Corinthian territory was the highway through which it traveled.‡ Consequently, Corinth had great financial resources, as is shown by the epithet "wealthy" bestowed on her by the old poets. After seafaring became more common,

* The island of Corcyra (modern Corfu) on the northwest side of Greece was at the time an independent state.

† That is, around 675 BC.

‡ All land traffic, then as now, had to travel across the narrow isthmus between the mainland and the Peloponnese. The city also collected fees from the ships that were dragged across the isthmus from the gulf of Corinth to the Aegean Sea and vice versa.

Corinth acquired her own navy and put down piracy, and because she could offer a market for trade in both directions, she acquired for herself all the power afforded by a large income.... [1.14] For after this there were no navies of any importance in Greece until the expedition of Xerxes. Aegina, Athens, and others may have possessed a few vessels, but they were mostly fifty-oared ships.* It was not until the end of this period that the war with Aegina† and the prospect of the Persian invasion allowed Themistocles to persuade the Athenians to build the fleet with which they fought at Salamis,‡ and even these vessels did not have complete decks.§

[1.15] Such were the Greeks' navies during the period we have surveyed. They brought significant benefit to those who developed them through increased revenue and dominion over others, especially for those who did not have enough land and who sailed to the islands and conquered them. There were no land wars that brought an increase in power. What wars there were, for whatever reason they arose, were against their neighbors, but the Greeks did not go out on expeditions far beyond their own boundaries to attack others. There was no union of subject cities around a great state, no spontaneous combination of equals for joint expeditions; what fighting there was consisted merely of local warfare between rival neighbors.

[1.16] The obstacles to national growth varied in different places. The power of the Ionians¶ was advancing rapidly, when it came into collision with Persia under King Cyrus, who after dethroning Croesus and overrunning everything between the river Halys** and the sea, did not stop until he had conquered the cities of the Ionian coast; only the islands were left to be subdued by Darius and the Phoenician navy.††

---

* Later warships, called triremes, were larger and had 170 oars (for greater speed and ramming power).

† An island city-state in the Saronic Gulf south of Athens.

‡ The reference is to the Persian invasion of 480 and the naval policy of Themistocles, leader of Athens at that time (see above, pp. 96–97).

§ In subsequent sea battles, soldiers fought one another on the decks of ships.

¶ The term Ionians often refers, as it does here, to the Greeks who had colonized the west coast of Asia Minor (modern Turkey).

** Cyrus the great, the sixth-century emperor of Persia (see Herodotus 1.75, p. 21 above).

†† The moves by Darius (Great King of Persia after 522 BC) into the Aegean, further encroaching on Greek lands, is documented by Herodotus (see above, p. 55).

[1.17] The tyrants* in Athens and the rest of Greece mostly provided for themselves, and their personal comfort and their own households. They made safety the great aim of their policy, and undertook no significant expeditions, even though they each had disputes with their neighbors. In Sicily the tyrants acquired very great power. So for a long time in Greece there were no significant projects undertaken in common and no adventurous actions in the cities.

[1.18] But at last a time came when the tyrants of Athens and the far older tyrannies of the rest of Greece were, except for those in Sicily, once and for all put down by Sparta. Although after the settlement of the Dorians (its present inhabitants)† Sparta suffered from civil unrest for an unparalleled length of time. Nonetheless from early times on it was well governed and enjoyed an unbroken freedom from tyrants. Sparta has possessed the same form of government for more than four hundred years, down to the end of the Peloponnesian War, and has thus had the freedom to arrange the affairs of other states.‡

Not many years after the ouster of the Athenian tyrants,§ the Battle of Marathon was fought between the Persians and the Athenians.¶ Ten years afterward, the Persians came back with their fleet to enslave Greece. Against this great danger, the command of the allied Greeks was assumed by the Spartans because of their superior power. The Athenians, after deciding to abandon their city, broke up their homes, threw themselves into their ships, and became a naval people. The coalition of Athens and Sparta, after repulsing the Persians, soon afterward split into two parts. One included the Greeks who had revolted from the king of Persia, as well as those who had aided him in the war. At the head of the one stood Athens, at the head of the other was Sparta; the first was naval, the other the foremost military power in Greece.

For a short time the league held together. But then the Spartans and

* The term "tyrants" in Greek denotes rulers who did not inherit power, as kings did, but seized it. The Greek cities were often dominated by tyrants in the sixth century BC.

† The term "Dorian" describes a population of Greeks that arrived later than, and spoke a different dialect from, the Ionians and other Greek peoples. The Peloponnese generally, and especially Sparta, were considered Dorian.

‡ Sparta was free to intervene elsewhere because of its stable government at home.

§ Specifically, the Athenian tyrant Pisistratus and his sons (see Herodotus 6.102ff., p. 65 above).

¶ 490 BC. This and all the events described in this paragraph are the subject of Herodotus' *Histories* (books 6 through 9), excerpted in the previous section of this volume.

Athenians quarreled and went to war against each other with their allies. It was a duel into which all the Greeks sooner or later were first drawn, though some wanted at first to remain neutral. As a result, the whole period from the [second] Persian War to the present war, with some peaceful intervals, was spent by each power in war, either with its rival or with its own allies who had revolted against it. That gave them the opportunity to have constant practice in military matters and experience in danger.

[1.19] The policy of Sparta was not to exact tribute from her allies, but merely to secure their subservience to her interests by establishing oligarchies among them.* Athens instead had by degrees deprived its allies of their ships,† and instead required contributions in money from all except Chios and Lesbos. The power of Athens for this war was greater than the combined power of Sparta and Athens that had hastily been assembled against the Persians.

[1.20] Such is the result of my inquiries into early Greece, even though it has been hard to have confidence in every detail. [1.21] Nonetheless, those who consider what I have discussed would not be misled. Assuredly they will not be disturbed either by the exaggerations of a poet or by the compositions of the chroniclers that are attractive at the expense of truth, because the subjects they write about are beyond the reach of evidence and time has robbed most of them of historical value. Turning from these, we can be satisfied that I have proceeded upon the clearest data and have arrived at conclusions as exact as can be expected in matters of such antiquity. As far as the present war is concerned, despite the known tendency of the participants in a struggle to exaggerate its importance (and when it is over to return to their admiration of earlier events), an examination of the facts will nonetheless show that this war was greater than the wars that preceded it.

[1.22] About the speeches that were made, both the ones before the war began and the ones delivered while it was going on, it was in all cases difficult to keep them word for word in my memory, both the ones I heard myself and those that I heard from various people. So my practice has been to make the speakers say what was in my opinion demanded of

---

* The government of Sparta was run by an elite clan, the Spartiates. As a result, Sparta supported narrow oligarchies elsewhere in Greece.

† Initially the states in the Athenian Empire had the choice of contributing ships or money to the common defense of the Aegean from Persian aggression. Over time, most had opted to contribute money and allow their navies to lapse.

them by the various occasions, keeping as close as possible to the general sense of what they actually said. As for my account of what occurred, I did not think it appropriate to write down what I heard from just anyone who came along, or on what I thought might have happened. Instead, I have written down what I saw myself, and I have recorded as accurately as possible in every detail what I learned from others. It took some effort to do this, because the witnesses to each of these events did not say the same things but recounted the events as each wanted them to be or remembered them as such. My history will, I fear, seem less enjoyable to listen to because it does not tell stories.* But those who wish to have an accurate knowledge of what happened and, because of human nature, will likely happen to be the same as or similar to these events, it will be enough if they consider my work to have been helpful. In short, my work is a lasting possession, rather than a prize competition meant to be heard for a moment.†

[1.23] The Persian War, the greatest achievement of past times, was concluded quickly by two battles by sea and two battles by land.‡ The Peloponnesian War went on for a long amount of time, and with correspondingly large suffering in Greece herself, unlike any other suffering in the same length of time. Never had so many cities been taken and laid desolate, some by foreigners, others by the antagonists themselves (some cities after being captured changed their inhabitants). Never was there so much banishment and bloodshed, now on the field of battle, now in the conflicts between opposing political parties. Old stories handed down by tradition, but barely confirmed by experience, suddenly ceased to be incredible. There were earthquakes of unparalleled extent and violence. Eclipses of the sun occurred with a frequency unrecorded in previous history.§ There were great droughts in different places and subsequent famines, and there was that terrible and often fatal disease, the plague.¶ All this came upon them along with this war, which was begun by the

---

* Here Thucydides may be contrasting his history to that of Herodotus, who included many stories that do not seem to have been strictly historical.

† Thucydides explains that his work is not meant primarily to be an entertainment, but to be read again and again because of its continuing relevance.

‡ The sea battles were Salamis and either Artemisium or Mycale; the land battles were Thermopylae and Plataea (see the Herodotus selections above, pp. 99ff).

§ Many ancient peoples believed that such natural phenomena were sent by the gods as evidence of their displeasure.

¶ The plague is described in detail in 2.47–53 (see pp. 153–58).

Athenians and Peloponnesians because of the dissolution of the thirty years' truce made after the conquest of Euboea.*...I believe that the true cause of the war was the one that remained unspoken: the growth of the power of Athens, and the alarm that it inspired in Sparta, which made war inevitable.

———

Having laid out his thesis that the coming war was the greatest up to his time, Thucydides begins his narrative of events, proceeding chronologically from 432 BC. In that year Athens became embroiled in a dispute between Corcyra and Corinth, taking the side of the Corcyraeans against the Corinthians. Athenian ships went to aid Corcyra, but their captains were told to avoid fighting with Corinthinan vessels if possible; Athens was mindful of Corinth's alliance with Sparta and of the provisions of the Thirty Years' Peace (446 BC), under which Athens swore not to harm Spartan allies. In the event, however, the Athenian ships did come to blows with those of Corinth, to prevent the Corinthians from defeating the Corcyraeans.

Sparta now had to decide whether the Thirty Years' Peace had been broken and, if so, whether to declare war on Athens. A conference was held at Sparta to debate this question. Thucydides records (or perhaps invents) a speech that a Corinthian envoy delivered at that conference.

———

[1.68] "Spartans: The confidence you feel in your constitution and social order makes you inclined to receive our thoughts about other powers with a certain skepticism. This gives rise to your moderation, but also to the rather limited knowledge you display in dealing with foreign policy. Time after time our voice was raised to warn you of the blows about to be dealt us by Athens, and time after time, instead of taking the trouble to ascertain the value of what we told you, you were content to suspect the speakers of being motivated by private interest. And so, instead of calling these allies together before the blow fell, you have delayed till we are smarting under it—allies among whom we have not the least right to speak, as having the greatest complaints to make, complaints of Athenian outrage and Spartan neglect.

"Now if these assaults on the rights of Greece had been made secretly, you might be unacquainted with the facts and it would be our duty to enlighten you. As it is, long speeches are not needed where you see slavery thrust on some of us and planned for others—in particular for our

---

* The Thirty Years' Peace of 446 BC ended after Athens put down a revolt on the island of Euboea.

l prolonged preparations by the aggressor for the hour of war.

se is the meaning of their deceitfully receiving Corcyra and

ⁿ ⁻ ⁻ against us by force? What of the siege of Potidaea? The latter place is most convenient for any action against the Thracian region, while the former would have contributed a very large navy to the Peloponnesians.

[1.69] "For all this you are responsible. You it was who first allowed the Athenians to fortify their city after the Persian War, and afterward to build the Long Walls—you who, then and now, are always depriving of freedom not only those whom *they* have enslaved, but also those who have thus far been *your* allies. For the true author of a people's subjugation is not so much the one who acts upon it as the power that permits it even though it has the means to prevent it, particularly if that power aspires to the glory of being the liberator of Greece.

"We have at last assembled. It has not been easy to assemble, and even now our goals are not defined. We should not still be inquiring into whether we have been wronged but into the means of our defense. For the aggressors, with their well-formed plans to oppose to our indecision, have cast threats aside and have taken action. And we know the paths by which Athenian aggression travels and how insidious is its progress. Athens may feel a degree of confidence from the idea that your bluntness of perception prevents your noticing her. But that confidence is nothing compared to the strength her advance will gain from the knowledge that you see it but do not care to interfere.

"You, Spartans, of all the Greeks are alone inactive and defend yourselves not by doing anything but by looking as if you were going to do something. You alone wait till the power of an enemy is growing to twice its original size instead of crushing it in its infancy. And yet the world used to say that you were to be depended on; but in your case, we fear, what is said goes beyond the truth. The Persians, we ourselves know, had time to come from the ends of the earth to the Peloponnese without any force of yours worthy of the name advancing to meet them.

"But this was a distant enemy. Athens is a near neighbor, and yet you utterly disregard her; against Athens you prefer to stay on the defensive instead of seizing the offensive, and to take your chances by deferring the struggle until she has grown far stronger than at first. And yet you know that the Persians brought about their own defeat, and that if we have survived against Athens, our present enemy, we owe our survival more to her blunders than to your protection. Indeed, some have already been ruined by the expectations they had of you, because their faith in you kept them from making adequate preparation.

"We hope that none of you will consider these words of reproach to be words of hostility. Men reproach friends who are in error but save accusations for enemies who have wronged them.

[1.70] "Besides, we think we have as good a right as anyone to point out a neighbor's faults, particularly when we contemplate the great contrast between two national characters, a contrast of which, as far as we can see, you have little perception. You have never yet considered what sort of antagonists you will encounter in the Athenians, how widely, how absolutely different from yourselves. The Athenians are addicted to innovation, and their plans are characterized by swiftness in conception and execution; *you* have a genius for keeping what you have got, accompanied by a total want of invention. When forced to act you never go far enough. What's more, *they* are adventurous beyond their power and daring beyond their judgment; in danger they remain steady of nerve. *Your* way is to try for less than what lies in your power, to mistrust even what's approved by your judgment, and to imagine that there is no release from danger. In addition, *they* have quickness to act on their side against procrastination on yours. *They* are never at home, *you* are never away from it; for they hope by their absence to extend their acquisitions, while *you* fear that by advancing you will endanger what you have left behind. *They* are swift to follow up a success and slow to recoil from a reverse. . . . To describe their character in a word, it would be right to say that they were born into the world to take no rest themselves and to give none to others.

[1.71] "Such is Athens, your antagonist. And yet, Spartans, you still delay, and fail to see that peace stays longest with those who take less care to use their power justly than to show their determination not to submit to injustice. On the contrary, your ideal of fair dealing is based on the principle that if you do not injure others you need not risk your own fortunes in preventing others from injuring you. You could scarcely have succeeded in such a policy even with a neighbor like yourselves; but in the present instance, as we have just shown, your habits are old-fashioned as compared with *theirs*. It is the law that, just as in art so it is in politics, improvements always prevail; and though fixed usages may be best for undisturbed communities, a constant need for action must be accompanied by constant improvement of methods. So it has been that the vast experience of Athens has carried her further than you on the path of innovation.

"Your procrastination must now end. Assist your allies, and Potidaea in particular, as you promised, by a speedy invasion of Attica. Do not sacrifice friends and kindred to their bitterest enemies and drive the rest of us in despair to some other alliance. Such a step would not be condemned either by the gods who received our oaths, or by the men who witnessed them. The breaking of a treaty cannot be blamed on the people who are deserted and compelled to seek new alliances, but on the power that fails to assist its partner. But if you will only choose to act, we will stand by you. It would be unnatural for us to change, and we would never meet with such a congenial ally. For these reasons choose the right course, and do not seek to let the Peloponnese, under your supremacy, decline from what it was when your ancestors bequeathed it to you."

———

Sparta was divided in its opinions. One of its two kings, Archidamus, argued before the conference (according to Thucydides) that Sparta did not have enough money or resources for the war ahead, which he forecast would be a long and difficult one. He advocated a delay to prepare more fully. But an impatient Spartan magistrate demanded a vote for war there and then and got it. The Spartans then convened a larger meeting of its allies and got them to affirm this decision. At that point the Thirty Years' Peace was suspended, having endured, as Thucydides says, for a bit less than half its allotted span.

At the moment the Peace is voided, Thucydides takes occasion to declare, once again, that the true reason Sparta went to war, in his view, was their fear of Athenian power. Later he adds the following observations:

———

[1.118] The Spartans felt that the situation was no longer tolerable and that they should take active hold of it and, if they could, destroy the Athenians' power completely by taking on the present war.

Once the Spartans had decided that the treaty had been broken and the Athenians were in the wrong, they sent to Delphi and asked the god* whether it would be better for them if they went to war; and, as it is reported, the god gave the answer that if they put their whole strength into the war, victory would be theirs, and he himself would be with them, both when they called on him and when they did not.

[1.119] Again they summoned their allies and asked them to take a vote

---

* The oracle of Apollo at Delphi, often consulted by individuals and nations before attempting any great undertaking, as (for example) when Croesus learned from that oracle (and misinterpreted what he heard) that if he were to wage war against the Persians, he would destroy a great empire.

on whether they should go to war. After the ambassadors from the allies had arrived and a congress had been convened, some said that they wanted to, and the majority denounced the Athenians and said that they thought there should be a war.

———

The Spartans sent envoys to Athens, making various demands under threat of impending war. Their final message insisted that Sparta wanted peace and that war could be avoided "if you Athenians give the Greeks their freedom"—in other words, disband the naval empire. They could not have expected a positive reply, but they clearly wanted blame for the start of the war to lie with Athens.

Pericles, son of Xanthippus, was the leader Athenians most trusted at this moment. He had served many times in the office of stratēgos, *one of a board of ten annually elected generals, and was admired for his sobriety and wisdom. In a speech before the Athenian Assembly, the sovereign body of the democracy, Pericles urged that the Spartan demands be rejected, and he enumerated the advantages Athens would have in the war: plenty of money, control of the seas, and a large corps of experienced oarsmen to row its huge fleet of warships. Like Themistocles before him (see pp. 96–97), Pericles urged the city to place its trust in the sea.*

In a small concession to the Thirty Years' Peace, the treaty by which Athens and Sparta had for nearly fourteen years avoided hostilities, Pericles got a motion passed by which Athens offered to submit the dispute with Sparta to arbitration. The envoys from Sparta were told of this offer, after which, Thucydides says ominously, "they went back home and never came again on a diplomatic mission." Even so, true warfare had not yet begun.

———

[2.1] The war between the Athenians and Peloponnesians and the allies on either side now really begins. As of this time all communication stopped except through the medium of heralds,* and they began to fight against one another continuously. This history follows the chronological order of events† by summers and winters.

———

Hostilities commenced not with any clash between Sparta and Athens, but with a proxy fight between two of their allies. Thebes, an ally of Sparta, attempted an overthrow of the government at Plataea, an ally of Athens. Things went awry and the Thebans were captured and executed; Sparta then helped Thebes put Plataea

———

* That is, since war was officially begun, citizens of either side were not safe in the other's territory unless they carried the insignia that marked them as heralds (official messengers).

† A practice that often makes the narrative hard to follow.

_iege. With that, the war was finally begun, and Sparta summoned its allies and prepared to invade the Athenian countryside.

In response to this invasion, the rural population of Attica moved inside the walls of Athens, bringing with them whatever property they could. Pericles' strategy called on Athenians to allow the Spartans to ravage their fields and farms without offering battle. Only a few troops ventured outside Athens to skirmish with the Spartans; the soldiers killed in these fights were buried in a solemn ceremony recorded by Thucydides.

———

[2.34] During that same winter* the Athenians held a funeral at public expense for those who were the first to have fallen in this war. The funeral was an ancestral custom, and it is conducted as follows: Three days before the ceremony, the bones of the dead are laid out in a tent that has been set up, and the kin bring to their dead relatives such offering as they please. In the funeral procession cypress chests are carried in on carts, one for each tribe.† After the bones of the dead have been placed in the chest of their tribe, one empty bier is spread out for the missing, that is, for those whose bodies could not be recovered. Any citizen or stranger who pleases joins in the procession, and female relatives are there to wail at the burial. The dead are laid in the public sepulcher in the most beautiful suburb of the city.‡ Those who fall in war are always buried there, except for those who were killed in the Battle of Marathon. Because of their singular and extraordinary courage, the Athenians buried them on the spot where they fell.§

In Athens, after the bodies have been laid in the earth, a man chosen by the state for his wisdom and reputation delivers an appropriate eulogy. After that they all depart. Such is the manner of the burial. Throughout the whole of the war, whenever the occasion arose, they performed this ritual. But these were the first that had fallen, and Pericles, son of Xanthippus,¶ was chosen to pronounce their eulogy. When the right mo-

---

* Of 431–430 BC. The term "winter" for Thucydides denotes the rainy half of the year, starting roughly in October, when Greek armies returned home and ceased campaigning.

† The citizens of Athens were subdivided into kinship groups.

‡ That is, in a cemetery outside the city walls on the road where in later times Plato's Academy was located.

§ The burial mound can still be seen near the site of the battle.

¶ Pericles was the most important statesman and general in Athens (see 6.16 below), who not long after died from the plague that Thucydides describes starting at 2.47.

ment arrived, he came away from the sepulcher to an elevated platform so that he could be heard by as many of the crowd as possible, and spoke as follows:

[2.35] "Most of my predecessors here have praised the man who added this oration to our customs and have said that it is good for it to be delivered when those who have fallen in battle are being buried. But it seems to me that the worth displayed in their actions would have been adequately rewarded by actions, like the ones you now see in this funeral prepared at public expense, and that the reputations of many brave men ought not to be put at risk by relying on whether one man has spoken well or badly. For it is hard to speak properly on a subject when it is even difficult to convince your audience that you are speaking the truth. The friend who is familiar with every fact of the story may think that some point has not been set forth as well as he wishes and as well as he knows it deserves. The person unfamiliar with the subject may out of envy suspect exaggeration if he hears anything that surpasses his own nature. Praise of others is endurable only up to the point that people think themselves capable of doing whatever they have heard about. Men are envious of anyone superior to themselves and do not trust that person. But since our ancestors believed that this custom was good, I must observe the custom and try to fulfill your wishes and win your approval as best I can.

[2.36] "I shall begin with our ancestors: It is both right and proper that they should have the honor of first mention on an occasion like the present. They dwelt in the country without break in succession from generation to generation and handed it down, free to the present day by their valor. And if our ancestors deserve praise, still more do our own fathers. They added to their inheritance the empire which we now possess and worked hard to leave it to us. But we who are for the most part in the prime of life have augmented our dominions and have furnished our country with everything that can allow her to be self-sufficient, whether for war or for peace. I shall not talk at length about that part of our history that tells of the military achievements that gave us our many possessions, or of the ready valor with which either we or our fathers vigorously defended our country from Greek or foreign aggression, I shall not go on about it, because you know it well. But what road allowed us to reach our position, what form of government allowed our greatness to grow, what were the national habits which it sprang from—these are questions I shall try to answer before I proceed to my eulogy for the dead. For I believe those are subjects about which a speaker may properly dwell on the present occasion, and which the whole assemblage, whether citizens or foreigners, may profit from hearing.

[2.37] "Our system of governance does not copy the laws of neighboring states; rather, we are an example for others rather than imitators. This system's name comes from favoring the many rather than the few; that is why it is called democracy.* Our laws offer equal justice to all in private disputes. Advancement in public life depends not on social standing, but rather on each man's reputation, and a man is not honored more for his share in public service than for his achievements. No one who can do something good for the city is hindered because his poverty prevents him from being recognized for his worth.†

"The liberality we enjoy in our government extends also to our ordinary life. There, far from being suspicious of one another, we do not feel called on to be angry with our neighbor for doing what he likes, ‡ or even to indulge in those injurious looks that cannot fail to be offensive, although they do not do any harm. But all this ease in our private relations does not make us lawless as citizens. We are prevented from doing wrong by fear of the magistrates and the laws, particularly those that work for the benefit of those who have been wronged, as well as those laws that, though unwritten, cannot be broken without acknowledged disgrace.

[2.38] "And we also have provided many ways for the mind to have respite from sorrow. We celebrate games and sacrifices throughout the year and enjoy splendid private houses and furnishings that provide pleasure every day and drive out sorrow. Because of the greatness of our city every kind of thing comes to us from the whole earth, so that we profit from our local goods with no greater personal expense than from those that come from other countries.

[2.39] "If we turn to our military policy, there also we differ from our antagonists. We throw open our city to the world, and do not have legislation to expel foreigners to keep them from learning or observing. Al-

---

* *Dēmokratia* literally means the power (*kratos*) of the people (*dēmos*).

† These statements apply only to native free male citizens. Women, foreigners, and slaves could not vote or hold public office.

‡ This claim clearly did not apply to extravagant aristocrats like Alcibiades; see 6.16 below.

though an enemy may occasionally profit from seeing what is not hidden from him, we do not place more trust in preparations and trickery than in our own enthusiasm for our projects. In education also, while our enemies even from the start of youth pursue manliness through painful discipline,* we spend that time without restrictions and still go no less bravely toward similar dangers. In proof of this it may be noted that the Spartans do not invade our country alone but bring along with them all their allies. But we Athenians advance unsupported into the territory of a neighbor, and when fighting on foreign soil usually vanquish with ease those who are defending their homes. Our united force was never yet encountered by any enemy because we have both attended to our navy and sent our citizens by land on many different missions. As a result, wherever our enemies engage with some fraction of our strength, success against one detachment is magnified into victory over the nation, and a defeat is magnified into defeat suffered by our entire people. Yet with habits not of ease but of labor, and with courage enforced not so much by law as by manly character, we are still willing to encounter danger. We have the advantage of not being exhausted by hardships before they happen, and of facing them in the hour of need no less fearlessly than those who are constantly struggling against them. For these reasons, as well as for others, our city is worthy of admiration.

[2.40] "Without extravagance we love what is noble, and we love knowledge without becoming soft. Wealth we employ more for use than for show, and we place the real disgrace of poverty not in admitting it but in refusing to struggle against it. Our public men have both politics and private business to attend to. Our ordinary citizens and others concerned with their work do not lack interest in politics.[†] For we consider the man who plays no role in politics to be not just uninvolved but useless. We ourselves are good judges of policies even when we are not the ones who create them. We do not think of words as an obstacle to actions, but rather as a necessary preliminary to whatever needs to be done. Indeed we are different also in this, that we dare to think about what we are doing before we act, whereas for others ignorance is daring and due consideration is hesitation.

---

* The reference is to aristocratic Spartan men, known as Spartiates, who were trained from boyhood to be soldiers and lived apart from their families.

† Meaning only property-owning males with Athenian parents.

A scale model of the Athenian Acropolis in the late fifth century BC, *with the Theater of Dionysus at lower right. Pericles initiated the building program in midcentury, drawing on the revenues from the naval empire, and construction went on all through the Peloponnesian War.* ALAMY

"But those who are rightly considered the best judges about life are the ones who clearly know the difference between hardship and pleasure and for that reason do not turn their backs on danger.

"In generosity we are unlike other peoples. We make friends not because they treat us well, but because we do favors for *them*. Those who grant favors are the firmer friends, because by their kindness they keep the recipients in their debt. But the recipients are less determined, because they know that repayment is not given for the purpose of doing good. And it is only we Athenians, who, without considering the advantages for ourselves, fearlessly help others with confidence in our independence.

[2.41] "To sum up, I say that Athens as a whole is a model for Hellas, and in every aspect I believe that every man among us can most easily make himself ready for many forms of action with grace and versatility. And this is not a boast thrown out for the present occasion, but rather a plain statement of fact. This is the power of the city, acquired by our way of life. For Athens alone is greater than her reputation, and only Athens does not provide any reason for an enemy attacker to object that he has been defeated by such people.

"There are many strong indications that our power is not unknown

now and that we shall be admired by people in the future. We have no
need of a Homer to praise us, or of other poets, whose verses might bring
us momentary pleasure but only until reality destroys the impression
that there was truth in their praise. We have forced every sea and land to
be a path for our daring, and everywhere, whether for evil or for good, we
have left monuments behind us that will not be forgotten. Such is the
Athens which these men judged should not be destroyed and for which
they nobly fought and died. And every one of their survivors should be
ready to lay down their lives on her behalf.

[2.42] "The reason I have spent so much time describing our country
has been to explain that the contest is not the same for us as for those who
have nothing of such value to lose. Also, I sought to base on established
facts the eulogy for the men for whom I am now speaking. The greater
part of that eulogy is now complete. I have sung the praises of Athens in
my speech, but these men and their like have honored her with their
heroism. Only for a few of the Greeks could words live up to their deeds
as well as it does for these men.

"I believe that a man's death is both the first indication of his merit and
its final confirmation. For it is right that even those who are deficient in
other respects should display courage in defense of their country. These
men make their wrongdoing disappear because of their courage and pro-
mote the common good instead of harming their country because of private interests.

"As for these men: Not one postponed the dreadful moment. Those
who had wealth did not turn cowardly because they still wished to enjoy
it. Neither did those who were poor because they hoped to become rich.
Instead, they considered vengeance on their enemies to be more glorious
than their desire for wealth. They turned with hope toward the uncertain
future. Because of what they had already seen, they knew that they could
trust themselves in action. In the business before them they thought fit to
act boldly and trust in themselves. In believing that they would rather
resist and die, than submit and be saved, they escaped the reputation of
dishonor, faced action with their bodies, and departed from us, in the
briefest of moments, at the summit of their glory rather than of their fear.

[2.43] "Such were these men who died, worthy of their city. The rest
of us must pray to have a firmer resolve, and one that is in no way less
courageous toward the enemy. We must consider our city's welfare, but
not just in words that anyone can lecture you about at length (even
though you already know them), saying how good it is to defend her

against the enemy. Instead, you must yourselves consider the power of Athens every day and become her lovers. When she seems to you to be great, remember it was these men who by their courage, their sense of duty, and a sense of honor in their actions, were able to win all this. They did not think it right to deprive their country of their valor, but they bestowed it on her as the most glorious contribution they could offer.

"For this offering of their lives, made in common by them all, each of them received the renown that never grows old and a most glorious tomb—not the one in which they have been laid to rest but the one in which their glory is laid up, to be eternally remembered on every occasion whenever speech or action is required. For heroes have the whole earth for their tomb, not just the inscriptions on the gravestones in their own country. In lands far from their own an unwritten memorial endures in the minds of all, even without stone tablets. Emulate these men and consider freedom to be happiness and courage to be freedom, and do not decline the dangers of war. For it is not more just that the unfortunate should be willing to give up their lives, even though they have nothing to hope for. Rather, it should be those who are at risk for a reversal in their lives, which for them would be great and decisive if they should fail. For the intelligent, the disgrace of cowardice is more grievous than a painless death that strikes amid strength and patriotism.

[2.44] "For that reason I do not pity those parents of the men who have died who may be here; instead I offer comfort. They understand because they grew up in dangerous times. It is good fortune to win a glorious death as these have done, though that death has brought you grief. Life has been measured out for them similarly to have prospered in and to have died in. I know it is hard to believe this is so because you will also be reminded of them when you see other people's happiness, a happiness you had enjoyed in the past. We grieve not so much because we have been deprived of what we never had, but because of what we had become used to and has been taken away.

"Still, you must carry on in the hope of having other sons, you who still are of an age to have them. For some of you the new sons will help you forget the ones that you've lost. They will bring a double benefit to the city because they will keep her from being underpopulated and will protect her. For men cannot offer fair or just advice if they do not make their sons confront the same dangers as themselves.

"Those of you who have passed your prime must consider that the best part of your life was fortunate and that the remainder will be short, and the weight of your grief will be lightened by the fame of those who died. It is only love of honor that never grows old, rather than wealth (as some say), and that brings joy to the heart in the helplessness of old age.

[2.45] "As for the sons or brothers of the dead, I see a hard struggle before you, because when a man is dead, everyone likes to praise him. You will not be equal to them in their exaggerated virtue, but will be judged a little worse. The living are envious of their competitors, while those who are no longer in our way are honored with a goodwill that includes no rivalry. But if I need to say something about the virtues of womanhood to those of you who will now be widowed, I shall convey it in this brief admonition: If your nature does not grow worse, your reputation will be great, and greatest will be hers who is least talked about among men, whether for virtue or for blame.*

[2.46] "My oration is now finished and has been suitably performed and in words, at least, the requirements of the law are now satisfied. As for actions,† those who are interred here have received part of their honors already, and from now on their sons will be brought up to adulthood at public expense. The state offers this valuable prize, a garland of victory in this race, for them and for those who survive them. And where the rewards for merit are greatest, there are found the best citizens.

"Now once you have finished lamenting your own dead, you are free to go."

[2.47] Such was the funeral that took place during this winter, with which the first year of the war came to an end.

———

The war went on, without a major confrontation between the combatants. Sparta invaded Attica year after year, and Athenian farmers went inside the city for protection. That increased the density of the urban population, leading to unforeseen consequences. The passage below directly follows the one just completed—a harrowing juxtaposition of the heights and the depths of Athenian morality.

———

In the first days of summer‡ the Spartans and their allies, with two-thirds of their forces as before, invaded Attica, under the command of Archida-

---

* In other words, women should not display excessive grief; they should also behave appropriately, abiding by the norms of Athenian society and not attracting attention.

† Thucydides represents Pericles as making a traditional contrast between words (*logoi*) and actions (*erga*).

‡ 430 BC.

mus, son of Zeuxidamus, king of Sparta. They occupied the country and laid waste to it.* Not many days after their arrival in Attica the plague first began to show itself among the Athenians. It was said that it had broken out before in many places, both around Lemnos† and elsewhere. But a pestilence so destructive was not remembered anywhere. Neither were the physicians at first of any use, because they did not know how to treat it. But they were the ones who died most often, because they visited the sick, and no other human art worked any better. No matter how many prayers were offered in the temples, or inquiries made at oracles, all such were useless, and in the end people gave up using them because they were overcome by the disease.

[2.48] The disease first began, it is said, in the parts of Ethiopia beyond Egypt, and from there descended into Egypt and Libya and into most of the lands of the Great King.‡ Suddenly it fell upon Athens. At first it attacked the population in Piraeus§—that was the reason for the rumor that the Peloponnesians had poisoned the cisterns,¶ because there were no springs in that area. Afterward the disease appeared in the upper city,** where the deaths became much more frequent. All speculation about its origin and causes—if any causes can be thought adequate to produce so great a disturbance—I leave to other writers, whether amateur or professional. I shall describe what it was, and how one might recognize it if it should ever happen again, so that one might not be incapable of recognizing it.†† I shall explain the symptoms clearly, because I had the disease myself and saw others suffering from it.

[2.49] That year—as everyone agreed—more than any other year happened to be free from other illnesses. If anyone had been sick from something before, all illnesses were thought to have ended in this one. In all other cases, there was no ostensible cause; but suddenly people in

---

* Following the pattern in which the Spartans attempted to draw the Athenians into battle by destroying their crops. Pericles insisted on not offering battle despite the hue and cry raised by displaced farmers.

† An island in the Aegean, west of Troy.

‡ That is, the Persian Empire, comprising most of Asia as far east as modern Pakistan.

§ The port of Athens. Communication and trade with the Persians continued after the Persian wars.

¶ Water was collected in cisterns during the winter and early spring.

** Meaning Athens itself.

†† In fact, nothing quite like the plague described here has ever been seen again, and efforts to identify the illness have mostly been futile.

good health were seized by violent feverishness of the head and redness and inflammation of the eyes. Their internal parts, such as the throat or tongue, became bloody and emitted an unnatural and fetid breath. These symptoms were followed by sneezing and hoarseness.

Soon after that, pain entered the chest along with a hard cough. When the disease settled in the heart, it caused turmoil there, and discharges of bile, of every kind named by physicians,* then followed, accompanied by very great distress. In most cases also dry heaves followed, which produced violent spasms. In some cases, these stopped soon afterward, but in others much later. Externally the body was not excessively hot to the touch, nor pale in appearance, but reddish, livid, and broken out into small pimples and lesions. But internally it burned so that patients could not bear to have clothing on them or linen even of the very lightest sort, or indeed to be other than stark naked. What they would have liked best was to throw themselves into cold water, as some of the sick did in fact do when no one was paying attention. They plunged into cisterns in their agonies of unquenchable thirst, though it made no difference whether they drank a lot or a little.

Besides this, the miserable feeling of not being able to rest or sleep always tormented them. The body meanwhile did not waste away so long as the disease was at its height, but held out to a remarkable degree, so that when people died from internal inflammation, in most cases on the eighth or sixth day, they had still some strength left in them. But if they survived, the disease descended further into the bowels, inducing a violent ulceration there along with uncontrolled diarrhea; most people later died from weakness on account of that. For the disease first began in the head, then proceeded from there through the whole of the body, and even when someone survived the worst of it, it still left its mark on the extremities. It struck the genitalia, fingers, and toes, and many escaped by having these removed, some too by losing their eyes. Others again were seized with a complete loss of memory as soon as they recovered and did not recognize either themselves or their friends and family.

[2.50] Just as the form of the plague was beyond all explanation, so it also attacked each person with a severity beyond human standards. In this respect it revealed itself to be something different from any other diseases. All birds and beasts that prey on human bodies (there were

---

* Contemporary medical texts show that Greek doctors paid close attention to the excreta of their patients and had elaborate labels for different types.

many of these still lying unburied) either did not approach them or died after eating them. My proof is that such birds were not seen near the bodies, or indeed at all. Dogs provided a better sense of what could happen.

Such was the general nature of the disease (to leave aside its many and varied forms, because it affected people in different ways). Also, none of the customary diseases troubled them at that time. Any that did occur ended with the plague. Some people died from lack of care; others received every attention. No remedy was found that could be called a treatment, because what helped one person harmed another. No one's body, either weak or strong, proved capable of resisting the disease, but all alike were swept away, even though they had been treated with every regimen.

By far the most terrible feature of the disease was the depression that people felt once they realized they were becoming sick; as soon as they decided there was no hope, they threw themselves further into the disease and did not resist it. Besides, they saw one person after another dying like sheep, because they caught it while caring for one another. That caused the greatest mortality. Because they were afraid to visit one another they perished from neglect, and many houses were emptied of their residents for want of someone to care for them. The people who tried to help also died, particularly those who made some claim to virtue. Conscience compelled them not to hold back from going to friends' houses, because the members of the family also were overcome by the moans of the dying and the extent of the disaster.

But it was mostly the people who had had the disease who took pity on the dying and the sick, because they knew what it was and now were no longer afraid of it. The same person was never attacked twice—at least never fatally. And not only did such persons receive the congratulations of others, they themselves, in the elation of the moment, entertained the vain hope that in future they would never be killed by any other disease.

[2.52] The influx from the country into the city had aggravated their existing troubles, particularly for all the people who had recently arrived. Because there were no houses for them, they had to be lodged during the hot season of the year in stifling cabins, where mortality raged without restraint. So the bodies of the dying lay on top of one another and the half-dead rolled about in the streets and gathered around all the fountains in their desire for water. Also the temple grounds in which they were camping were full of the corpses of persons who had died there.* Because people were overwhelmed by disaster and did not know what was to become of them, they became completely careless about both the sacred and profane. All the burial customs that they had used in the past were entirely upset, so they buried bodies as best they could. Many lacked the necessary equipment, because so many others had died before. Some threw the bodies of their own dead on a stranger's pyre and set it on fire; sometimes they tossed the corpse they were carrying on top of another pyre that was burning, and they went away.†

[2.53] At first the plague began to encourage lawlessness in other areas as well. Men now openly dared to do what they had formerly kept hidden because people did not approve. They could see the rapid reversals of prosperous men who died suddenly, and of those who previously had nothing but immediately acquired another's property. So they decided to spend money quickly and enjoy themselves, regarding their lives and riches alike as ephemeral. People were not eager to wait around for whatever seemed right because they thought it unclear that they could attain it before they died. It was universally agreed that what was pleasurable and profitable was honorable and useful.

Neither fear of the gods nor law of man restrained them. They judged it was just the same if they worshipped the gods or not since they saw everyone perishing. No one expected to live to be brought to trial for their offenses. Rather, they each felt a far more severe sentence had been already passed on them and was hanging ever over their heads, and before that happened it was reasonable to enjoy their lives.

[2.54] Such was the disaster the Athenians had fallen into and been weighed down by, with people dying inside the city while their land outside was being destroyed. Among other things that they likely remembered in their distress was the following verse, which the old men said had been recited long ago: "A Dorian‡ war shall come and with it a plague." People argued over whether "famine" (*limos*) rather than "plague" (*loimos*) had been the word in the old men's verse. But at the

---

* A significant detail, since the presence of a dead body in a temple was considered sacrilege. Earlier, Thucydides reported (in a passage not included here) that an oracle had warned Athenians against using the temples for housing.

† The chaos described here seems more horrifying because it follows so closely on the solemn and orderly burial of the war dead described in book 2.34.

‡ The Spartans and Corinthians were Dorians, so the current invasions of Attica constituted a "Dorian war."

present juncture, the winning word of course was "plague" (*loimos*), because people made their recollection match their sufferings. I believe, however, that if another Dorian war should ever afterward come upon us, and a famine (*limos*) should happen to accompany it, the interpreters of oracles likely will recite the verse in *that* way.

Also, an oracle that had been given to the Spartans was now remembered by those who had known about it. When the god* was asked whether the Spartans should go to war, he answered that if they put their might into it, victory would be theirs, and that he would help them. Events appeared to match this oracle. For the plague broke out as soon as the Peloponnesians invaded Attica, and it never entered the Peloponnese (not to an extent worth noticing); it fell hardest on Athens, and then on the most populous of the other towns. Such was the history of the plague.

———

During the summers of 431 and 430, Pericles continued to refuse to let the Athenians leave the city to confront the Spartans. He even at one point prevented the Assembly from convening, lest they vote on intemperate action. After the second Spartan invasion, the Athenians wanted to negotiate a peace, but Pericles refused to do so, advising them instead to concentrate on retaining their naval supremacy and reminding them to fight for their independence. But he too soon contracted the plague and would not survive long.

The Athenians remained in the war, but as Thucydides explains, they ultimately were not able to carry out Pericles' plans for victory.

———

[2.65] [The Athenians] applied themselves with increased energy to the war. But as private individuals, they were depressed by their sufferings. The common people had been deprived of what little they possessed, while the powerful had lost fine properties in the country with buildings and costly furnishings. But worst of all, the Athenians had war instead of peace.

In fact, the public's animosity toward Pericles did not subside until they had fined him.[†] But not long afterward, as the multitude are accustomed to do, they again elected him general and committed all their affairs to his hands. They were now less sensitive about their personal

---

* "The god" refers to Delphic Apollo. For this oracle, see above, 1.118.3.

[†] Punishment either by fines or banishment was a common way for the Assembly to express its displeasure with its leaders.

losses, and they thought that he was the man best suited for what the city needed. For as long as he was the head of the state during peacetime, he led and guarded it cautiously and safely; the city was at its height during his day. And when the war broke out, here as well he seems to have rightly understood the potential of his country.

Pericles outlived the start of the war by two years and six months.* After he died, his foresight about the war was better understood. He told them to wait quietly, to pay attention to their navy, and that they would win if they did not expand their empire during the war and put the city at risk. But they did the opposite of everything he recommended. Instead, they governed by allowing private ambitions and private interests and matters that seemed unrelated to the war to lead them into projects harmful both to themselves and to their allies. These were policies that, if successful, would bring honor and success only to individuals, but if they failed resulted in certain disaster for the city in the war.

The reason for this was that Pericles owed his influence to his personal distinction and his knowledge of finance and his transparent integrity. He could keep the common people under control without difficulty. In short, he led them instead of being led by them. Because he had not acquired his power from the wrong sources, he never needed to flatter. On the contrary, he was so highly regarded that he could anger the people by contradicting them. Whenever he saw that they were unreasonably elated and arrogant, he would confound them and frighten them, but if they were terrified for no good reason, he could at once restore them to confidence. In short, what was nominally a democracy became in practice government by the first citizen.†

Since none of the leaders who came after him were better than the others, each of them grasped at becoming first citizen by turning over government affairs to the wishes of the people. For that reason, many other mistakes were made, as might have been expected in a great city that also had an empire, including the Sicilian expedition.‡ But that failed not so much through a miscalculation about the enemy against whom the expedition was sent, as because of bad decisions by the people who sent

* That is, he died in 429 BC, of the effects of the plague.

† Thucydides, like many members of his wealthy class, was instinctively mistrustful of radical democracy. Later in the *History* he asserts that Athens was governed best by a broad oligarchy, instituted in 411, in which only those with some property held full voting rights.

‡ The Sicilian expedition is recounted in Books 6 and 7 below.

the expedition out.* They did not know what those on the expedition needed or what was required afterward to assist them once they were there. Instead, they chose to concentrate on plotting for the leadership of the common people of Athens. As a result, they paralyzed operations in the battlefield and introduced civil strife at home.

Yet after losing most of their fleet as well as other forces in Sicily, and with most of their allies in revolt, the Athenians could still for eight years make headway against their original enemies, who had been joined also by their enemies in Sicily.† At the same time nearly all their own allies were in revolt against them, and later these were joined by Cyrus, son of the king of Persia, who provided the funds for the Peloponnesian navy.‡ The Athenians did not give up until they fell victim to their own internal differences, so abundant were the resources from which Pericles foresaw that they could easily triumph over the Peloponnesians in the war.

———

While their fight against Sparta continued, the Athenians also needed to keep the cities in their empire under control, by force if necessary. A crisis soon developed on the island of Lesbos. Along with most of the other settlements on the island, the citizens of Mytilene, its chief city, had wanted to ally with Sparta rather than Athens, but the Spartans did not seem to be interested. In 428 the Mytileneans declared themselves Spartan allies and attempted to conquer other cities on the island. When the Athenians learned what was happening on Lesbos, they sent their general Paches with a thousand Athenian hoplites to subdue the rebellion and besiege Mytilene. The Mytileneans surrendered to Paches in the spring of 427 after he agreed not to allow the Athenians to harm them. Paches then went off to deal with other rebellions and returned to Lesbos later that summer.

The question of how Athens should deal with Mytilene prompts one of Thucydides' most intense Assembly debates. Hanging over the decision were larger questions of how empire should be sustained and how a democratic society should carry on debate.

---

* For example, the decision to recall Alcibiades from Sicily because he allegedly had profaned the Eleusinian Mysteries (see below, pp. 200–202).

† Thucydides here looks ahead to the last phase of the war, from 412 to 404 BC, in which Athens recovered some of its strength and won important battles before its ultimate defeat. Though he lived to see the war through to its end, his *History* ends abruptly in 410.

‡ In 407 BC the Persian prince Cyrus, then stationed in western Turkey, began funding the Spartan war effort in earnest; his subsidies proved decisive. For Cyrus' later story, see the selections from Xenophon's *Anabasis* later in this volume.

[3.35] After Paches arrived at Mytilene,... he found the Spartan Salae-thus* in hiding in the town and sent him off to Athens, along with the Mytileneans he had placed in Tenedos and any other persons he thought had been involved in the revolt. He also sent back the greater part of his forces, remaining with the rest of them to settle affairs in Mytilene and elsewhere in Lesbos as he thought best.

[3.36] When the Mytilenean prisoners arrived with Salaethus, the Athenians executed Salaethus immediately, even though he offered, among other things, to arrange for the withdrawal of the Peloponnesians from Plataea (which they were still besieging). Then, after deliberating what to do with their Mytilenean prisoners, in their anger they decided to execute not only the prisoners at Athens but the whole adult male population of Mytilene, and to enslave the women and children.[†] It was pointed out that Mytilene had revolted even though it had not been sub-jected to Athenian dominion, like other cities.[‡] What above all increased the Athenians' anger was that the Peloponnesian fleet had risked coming to Ionia to support Mytilene.[§] So the Mytileneans did not appear to have undertaken their revolt from Athens on short notice.[¶]

The Athenians sent a trireme to communicate their resolution to Paches, ordering him to deal with the Mytileneans immediately. But the next day brought repentance and reflection on the cruelty of a decree that condemned a whole city to the fate deserved only by the guilty. As soon as the Mytilenean ambassadors at Athens and their Athenian sup-porters heard about this change of heart, they urged the authorities to put the question to a vote again. This they more easily consented to do because they themselves plainly saw that most of the citizens wished some of them to reconsider. So immediately an Assembly was called, and after many speeches on each side, Cleon, son of Cleaenetus, came for-

* Salaethus was a general sent by Sparta to help organize the revolt. Similarly, in 415 BC the Spartans sent their general Gylippus to help the city of Syracuse repel an attack by Athens (see book 6).

† It was a harsh but not unheard-of practice among the Greeks for victors in war to kill the male population of a conquered Greek city and to enslave the women and children.

‡ Most islands in the Athenian Empire did not maintain their own navy; Lesbos was one of the last that did.

§ Since the Aegean had long been an "Athenian lake," this intrusion by a Spartan navy was threatening and humiliating.

¶ That is, they had plotted with Sparta.

ward a second time (he was the speaker who had won the previous motion to execute the Mytileneans). He was the most violent man in Athens, and at that time had by far the greatest influence on the citizens.* He spoke as follows:

[3.37] "In the past I have often thought that a democracy is incapable of maintaining an empire, but never more so than now because of your present change of mind about Mytilene. Because fears or plots are unknown to you in your daily relations with one another, you suppose your allies will behave the same way. So when you make the mistake of listening to their speeches, or take pity on them, you do not think that it's dangerous for you and that you are weakening yourselves to your allies' benefit. You are not keeping in mind that your empire is a tyranny and that your allies are plotting against you and are being ruled against their will. They will obey you not because you try to please them, but because you are stronger, and not on account of loyalty to you.

"The most terrifying thing of all is that there will be a constant change of decisions for us to consider. We will not know if a city is better off using worse laws that are not perfect than good laws that are not enforced, or whether unsophisticated common sense is more useful than cleverness based on immorality, or whether ignorant men usually manage public affairs better than their more knowledgeable fellows. Knowledgeable men always want to be thought wiser than the laws and to overrule every proposition brought forward. They suppose they cannot show their knowledge in more important matters, and so usually undermine our cities. But the men who mistrust their own cleverness consider themselves less learned than the laws and less able to criticize the argument of a good speaker. Because they are impartial judges rather than contestants, usually they manage public affairs more successfully. So I too ought to advise all of you not to go against your judgment by relying on cleverness and a display of learning.

[3.38] "As for myself, I think the same as I did before, and I am amazed by the men who again want to discuss the Mytileneans and impose a delay. That works in favor of the guilty party because the injured party proceeds with his anger diminished but defending oneself as close as possible to the time most effectively offsets the wrongdoing. I wonder

---

* In the wake of Pericles' death it was Cleon who exercised the most influence over Athenian policy. Unlike previous politicians who had steered Assembly votes, Cleon did not hold office but held sway simply by his eloquence and his ability to evoke emotions.

also who is prepared to argue against such a delay and who thinks it appropriate to show that the Mytileneans' wrongdoing was helpful to us or that our misfortunes were harmful to our allies. Such a man must plainly either have such confidence in his rhetoric that he dares to prove that what has been decided should still be under discussion; or he has been bribed to try to delude us by the elegance of his argument. In such contests the city gives the prizes to others and takes home the risks.

"You are the ones to blame, you who do a bad job of setting up these contests. You like to be observers at speeches and listeners when it is action that's required. You consider that a project is worth doing because its advocates are good speakers. When it comes to past actions, you believe less in what you can see has occurred than in what you have heard its supporters tell you. You are easily taken in by any new argument and are not willing to follow received wisdom. You are slaves to every new wonder, and despisers of the commonplace.

"The first wish of every one of you is yourselves to be good at speaking; your next wish is to rival those who make new arguments by seeming to be quite up to date on their ideas, and you applaud every clever remark before it is made. You are as eager to anticipate what is said as you are slow in foreseeing its consequences. One could say you are looking for something other than the circumstances in which we are living, but without sufficiently understanding those circumstances. In general, you are overwhelmed by what brings pleasure to your ears, and more like spectators of performing sophists than councilors making decisions about their city.

[3.39] "To dissuade you, I can show you that no one city has ever injured you so much as Mytilene. Subjects who revolt because they cannot endure our empire, or who have been forced to do so by our enemies—these I can forgive. But the Mytileneans are islanders and have walls and need only fear our enemies by sea. They had their own fleet of triremes to protect them. They were independent* and held in the highest honor by you, and they did this to you! What is this other than a betrayal? It is not a revolution—a revolution implies they had been suffering from oppression. They tried to destroy us by siding with our enemies. That is worse than if they had fought a war against us independently.

"They learned nothing from misfortunes of their neighbors who had

---

* In the sense that they maintained their own navy. They still made tribute payments to Athens.

already rebelled against us and had been subdued. The happiness they enjoyed did not prevent them from taking a dangerous step. They approached the future boldly and had ambitions greater than their powers but weaker than their planning. They declared war and decided to put might ahead of right. When they thought they could win they attacked us, even though we had done them no wrong. It seems that when great good fortune comes suddenly and unexpectedly to cities that least expect it, it makes them arrogant. Usually it is safer for men to have expected success rather than unexpected. One might say that it's easier for them to rid themselves of adversity than to sustain prosperity.

"We should not have given preference to the Mytileneans as we have done. If in the past we had treated them like our other allies, they would never had offended us. But people look down on those who treat them well and have respect for those who do not cater to them. So now we should punish the Mytileneans as their crime deserves. You should not only punish the oligarchs, but also you should not let the common people get away with it.* All of them alike attacked you, though they might have come over to us and now been back again in their city.† But no, they thought it safer to take a chance and join with the oligarchs in their rebellion.

"And consider your allies. Suppose that you impose the same punishment on an ally who is forced to revolt against you by an enemy and on one who rebels against you voluntarily? Which of them, do you think, will not revolt on the slightest pretext, if the reward for success is freedom and the penalty for failure is to suffer nothing that cannot be repaired? We meanwhile shall risk our money and our lives against one city after another. If we win, we shall receive a city that has been ruined and from which you can no longer draw the revenue upon which our strength depends. If we lose, we shall have their citizens as enemies in addition to our existing ones, and while we are fighting those existing enemies we will be fighting our own allies.

[3.40] "Therefore we should not offer them any hope that can be secured by speeches or bought with money, the hope that they can be forgiven because it's human nature to make mistakes. They did not harm us

---

* The Athenians tended to support cities that were governed by ordinary citizens, like themselves, rather than a small group of aristocrats who possessed vast tracts of land. In Mytilene the oligarchs had led the pro-Spartan revolt.

† Paches had removed some of the Mytileneans to keep them under guard elsewhere.

because they were forced to. No, they knew what they were doing when they plotted against us. Only involuntary action is pardonable. Therefore, I remain, now as before, opposed to your reversing your previous decision. You must not give in to the three faults most fatal to empire: pity, persuasive speeches, and the desire to be fair. It is right to feel pity for our equals, but not toward those who will never pity us in return and who will continue to be our established enemies. The orators who enchant us with their speeches will need to work hard even among less important people than yourselves. But they should not need to struggle to persuade you in a matter like this. In this case the city will pay a heavy penalty in return for momentary pleasure, even when the orators receive fine treatment for their fine phrases. Appreciation should rather be shown toward those who will be our friends in future, rather than men who will remain as they were, no less our enemies than before.

"In conclusion I have this one request. If you listen to me and do what is right concerning the Mytileneans, at the same time you will be doing what is beneficial for yourselves. But if you think otherwise, you will not be doing them a favor so much as punishing yourselves. For if it's right for them to revolt, then you are in the wrong for having an empire. But even if you do not think it is appropriate to have an empire, it is appropriate and necessary for you to punish them. Otherwise, stop having an empire, and be courageous and behave nobly once you are out of danger.

"Decide, therefore, to defend yourselves with the same punishment as they gave you; and do not let the men who got away suffer less than the conspirators who planned the revolt. Keep in mind what they would have done if they had won out over you, especially since they were the ones who plotted the crime. It is the people who attack others without cause who keep after their foe and destroy him, because they expect to be in danger if that enemy survives. They know that when a man is wronged for no reason, he is more dangerous, if he escapes, than an enemy who has suffered only after inflicting suffering.

"So do not betray your own interests but recall as nearly as possible what you have suffered and above all how important you thought it was to defeat them. Now pay them back in their turn, and do not lose your resolve in the present situation or forget the danger that once hung over you. Punish them as they deserve and offer your other allies a clear proof that if *they* rebel, the penalty is death. For if they understand *that*, you will spend less time neglecting your enemies and fighting your own allies."

[3.41] Such were the words of Cleon. After him Diodotus, son of

Eucrates,* who in the previous Assembly had spoken most strongly against executing the Mytileneans, came forward and spoke as follows:

[3.42] "I do not blame those who have proposed a review of the case of the Mytileneans, and I do not praise those who complain that too much time is spent discussing important matters. I think the two things most contrary to good decision-making are haste and passion. Haste usually goes hand in hand with folly, passion with ignorance and closed-mindedness. Anyone who says that speech should not guide action is either ignorant or self-contradictory. A man is ignorant if he believes it possible to consider an uncertain future in any way other than discussing it openly. He is self-contradictory if he wishes to persuade you to do something discreditable and doubts his ability to speak well about a bad cause, and in the meantime frightens his opponents and his audience by effectively slandering them.

"The most unbearable speakers are those who accuse another speaker of showing off so he can be paid for it. If they had accused him of ignorance, an unpersuasive speaker could step down with a reputation for honesty. But the charge of dishonesty leaves him under suspicion: Whether he succeeds or is defeated, he is nonetheless thought ignorant as well as dishonest. The city is not helped in such a situation, because her advisers are deterred from speaking. The city might be better governed if the slanderers were barred from speaking among her citizens. That way the citizens might be persuaded to make the fewest mistakes.

"The good citizen ought to win arguments not by frightening his opponents but rather by showing fair and square that his advice is better. Also, a wise city, without over-rewarding its best advisers, will nevertheless not deprive them of their due. Rather than punishing a counselor who gives bad advice, the city should not even regard him as disgraced. In this way a successful orator would be less tempted to sacrifice his convictions to please his audience in hope of winning still greater respect; the unsuccessful speaker might reach out to the common people and bring them along by pleasing them in some way.

[3.43] "But we do the opposite, and besides, whenever someone is suspected of giving advice—even if good—from corrupt motives, we deprive the city of the clear benefit of his ideas and resent him because we suspect him of wanting to profit. So straightforward good advice has come to be no less suspected than advice that is bad; the advocate of the

* Almost nothing is known of this man other than this speech.

most destructive advice must use deceit to persuade the people; and a man offering better advice must lie so he can be believed. It is only in this city and this city only because of this excessive cleverness that a man can do what is obviously right without deception. The man who does serve the city openly is always suspected of serving himself in some secret way in return. But because of the significance of the interests involved, and in the present matter, we orators ought to consider it our business to look a little farther than you who judge in a short amount of time, especially since we, your advisers, are accountable for the advice we give, while you, our audience, are not accountable for our advice. If those who gave the advice, and those who followed it, suffered equally, you might judge more responsibly. As it is, whatever mood you happen to be in when you've made a mistake, you punish only the judgment of the person who persuaded you rather than your own mistake, for which you were collectively responsible.

[3.44] "I have, however, not come forward to advocate either for or against the Mytileneans. In fact, the question before us—if we think responsibly about it—is not their guilt, but what are our best interests? For if I also show that they are indeed guilty, I shall not advise you to execute them for that reason, unless it is to our advantage. Not even if they had some claim to mercy would I recommend it, unless it appeared to be for the good of our city. I believe we are deliberating about the future rather than the present. As for expediency: This is the issue Cleon considers important, saying that in future it will be to our advantage if we impose the death penalty, because revolts will be less likely. Even though I also think about our future just as much as he does, I know that the opposite is true. I do not think you will prefer the righteousness of his argument to the practicality of mine. His arguments seem appealing to you because of your present anger against the Mytileneans. But we are not prosecuting them in a court of law, where we would need to decide about justice. Rather, we are making a political decision about how they can be more useful to us.

[3.45] "Now of course there are cities in which there have been penalties of death for offenses not like this one, but for crimes less serious. Nonetheless hope still leads men to take risks, and no one ever yet undertook a dangerous enterprise without the inward conviction that he would succeed. Again, what city ever was there that did not believe it possessed the resources for such an enterprise, either by herself or in alliance with others? Everyone, whether in private affairs or in public, naturally makes errors in judgment, and there is no law that will prevent them from doing so; men have exhausted the list of punishments that they have enacted in hope that somehow they would be less frequently wronged by evildoers. It seems likely that in early times the penalties for the greatest offenses were less severe, but that after those penalties were disregarded, they arrived at the penalty of death—and nonetheless that too is disregarded. Either then some means of terror more dreadful than this must be discovered, or it must be admitted that the death penalty is useless.

"So long as poverty makes men daring because of necessity, or because wealth gives them the ambition that comes with insolence and pride, and other conditions of life, they remain enslaved to some fatal and master passion, the impulse that drives men into danger will never be absent. In every case hope and desire cause the greatest harm,* one leading and the other following: one planning the plot, the other suggesting that luck will make it easy; and, because they are invisible, these forces are far more powerful than dangers that men can see. Good fortune too encourages delusion and, by the unexpected aid that fortune sometimes lends, tempts a man without sufficient resources into danger. This is no less true for cities than for individuals because the stakes are highest: freedom or subjection.

"When all these forces act together, each man irrationally magnifies his own capacity. In short, it is impossible and very foolish to prevent, by the power of law or by any other deterrent, human nature from doing what it has once set its mind upon.

[3.46] "So we should not make the wrong decision in the belief that a death penalty will bring us security, or that there is no reason to allow the rebels to expect no forgiveness nor amnesty in the short term for their error in judgment. Consider that now, if a city in revolt realizes it will not survive, would it not reach a settlement while it was still able to do so, and refund expenses, and pay tribute in the future? Or what city do you think, if we exact the death penalty, would not make better preparations than they now have and hold out to the last against its besiegers, if it does not matter whether they surrender at their leisure or immediately? And how can it be other than hurtful to us to be put to the expense of a siege†

---

* Here Diodotus expresses traditional views about the forces that lead men to make disastrous decisions; see, e.g., Sophocles, *Antigone* 615–26.

† Since sieges of walled cities require large forces to stay in the field for months or years, they consume huge amounts of money.

if surrender is out of the question? And if we take the place, we shall receive a ruined city from which we can no longer draw revenue. For it is revenue that forms our real strength against the enemy.*

"Therefore we must not serve as harsh judges of those who have done us wrong and do harm to ourselves, but rather we should see how, by *moderate* punishments, we can benefit in future from their power to produce revenue. And we must make up our minds to protect ourselves not by a rule of terror, but rather by careful supervision. At present we do the opposite. When a free community revolts after being held in subjection by force, and (as is only natural) asserts its independence, we conquer it, and we think that we must punish it severely. But the right course is not to punish free men harshly when they revolt, but to keep close watch on them before they revolt and prevent them from even contemplating the idea, and, once we have established control, to impose on them the least blame possible.

[3.47] "You must consider how big a mistake you would make if you listen to Cleon. As things are at present, in all the cities the common people are your friend, and either do not revolt with the oligarchs, or, if they are forced to do so, immediately become the oligarchs' enemies. So that when a city *is* in revolt, you will go to war with the common people on your side. But if you kill the common people of Mytilene, who did not participate in the revolt, and who, once they took possession of the enemies' weapons, willingly surrendered the town to you—if you kill them, first you will be committing the crime of killing your benefactors. Next, you will be giving the people in power what they want the most. As soon as they persuade their cities to revolt, they will immediately have the common people on their side, because you showed in advance that you would impose the same punishment on those who revolted and those who did not.

"Even if the common people are guilty, you ought to pretend not to notice it, so that our only ally does not become our enemy. I believe it will be more advantageous for the preservation of our empire voluntarily to allow wrongdoing rather than justifiably put the people to death. Cleon's idea that we shall find it both just and in our best interest to execute them cannot be shown simultaneously to be possible.

---

* This point had been made earlier by the Spartan king Archidamus and in the opening speech of Pericles (neither passage included here): The great wealth of Athens gave it a strength that Sparta, with its nonmonetary economy, was hard put to match.

[3.48] "You are aware that this is the better course of action, and without conceding too much either to pity or to clemency—by neither of which I allow you to be influenced*—but trusting in the advice I have given you, be persuaded by me not to judge harshly the Mytileneans whom Paches sent off as guilty, and to let the rest live where they are. These actions will prove best for the future, and most terrible to your enemies at the present time. A man who has effective policies against his adversaries is more formidable than someone who attacks with the severity of unreasoning violence."

[3.49] That was what Diodotus said. After these two opinions were expressed—and they were the ones most contradictory to each other—the Athenians argued with one another along the same lines. The votes by show of hand turned out to be almost equal, but Diodotus' argument won.

Another trireme was immediately sent off in haste lest the first ship get to Lesbos before them and they arrive to find Mytilene destroyed. The first ship had about a day and a night's head start. Wine and barley cakes were provided for the ship by the Mytilenean ambassadors, and great promises made if it arrived ahead of the first ship. So while the men were rowing they ate their meals of barley cakes kneaded with oil and wine and only slept by turns while others were rowing.[†] Fortunately they met with no adverse wind. Meanwhile, the first ship had not been eager to proceed on such an extreme errand, but the second ship rushed ahead as described. So Paches had only just had time to read the decree and prepare to carry out the sentence when the second ship came into port and prevented the destruction of the city. Mytilene had escaped danger only by that much.

[3.50] The other men, who Paches had sent away because they were primarily responsible for the rebellion, were executed by the Athenians on a motion by Cleon (there were slightly more than a thousand of them).[‡] The Athenians also demolished the Mytileneans' walls and took possession of their ships. Afterward they did not impose tribute on the

---

* It's noteworthy that Diodotus has scrupulously made all efforts to evoke sympathy for the Mytileneans. In an Athenian court of law, defendants were expected to bring forward parents, wives, and children to pluck at the heartstrings of the jury.

† Normally a trireme would put to shore to allow its crew to eat and sleep.

‡ The Athenian settlement at Mytilene still involved a huge loss of life despite its comparative leniency. The economic enslavement of the island (described below) also left its surviving population greatly impoverished.

people of Lesbos, but they divided up the whole island (except for the land belonging to the Methymnians) into three thousand plots, three hundred of which were dedicated to the gods. The rest were assigned by lottery to Athenian landlords, who they sent out to the island. The Lesbians paid a rent of two minae* a year for each plot to these landlords and cultivated the land themselves. The Athenians also took possession of the towns on the mainland† that the Mytileneans had controlled, and afterward these were subject to Athens. That is what happened in Lesbos.

———

The war continued. Both sides incurred losses that neither could have predicted. A company of Spartans became trapped on the island of Sphacteria, off Pylos, and after a long blockade by Athenian ships, nearly two hundred were taken prisoner. Meanwhile the Athenians found their empire growing increasingly hard to defend. The Spartans sent a commando force into Thrace and persuaded several Athenian allies there to revolt and join with Sparta. One of these rebel cities, Amphipolis, was of huge economic benefit to Athens; Thucydides, serving as general that year, was exiled from Athens for his failure to prevent the defection.

    Setbacks on both sides induced the Athenians and the Spartans to sign a truce, the Peace of Nicias—named for its principal Athenian supporter—in 421. The peace lasted for six years, during which time both sides pursued their goals in cautious or indirect ways. No one was convinced that the war was truly over, since nothing had been resolved. Hostilities began anew in 415.

    Thucydides wrote the following introduction to his narrative of the second period of the war, to clarify that the two spans were really part of one continuous conflict.

———

[5.26] The history of this period has been also written by the same man, Thucydides the Athenian, in the order that each event took place, by summers and winters, up to the time when the Spartans and their allies put an end to the Athenian Empire and had captured the Long Walls and Piraeus. By then the war had lasted twenty-seven years in all.‡ If anyone supposes that this interval§ was not part of the war, his judgment will be incorrect. If he considers the events as they occurred, he will find that this period should not be considered a state of peace, because during that

---

* Two minae is two hundred drachmas.

† That is, on the continent of Asia Minor east of Lesbos.

‡ From 430 to 404 BC.

§ The Peace of Nicias, 421–415 BC.

time neither party gave nor received all they had agreed upon.... The allies in the region of Thrace were in as open hostility as ever, while the Boeotians only had a truce that was renewed every ten days. So he will find that the first ten years' war and the treacherous armistice that followed it, as well as the subsequent war, if he calculates by the seasons, will make up the number of years I have mentioned, with the difference of a few days.

Also, it is only this number that corresponds closely with those who have some confidence in oracles. For I always remember that from the beginning to the end of the war it was declared by many that it would last three times nine years. I lived through the whole of it, and was old enough to understand it, and I paid attention to it, so that I would have an accurate understanding of it. It also happened that I was exiled from my country for twenty years after my command at Amphipolis. I was familiar with matters on both sides, and not least with the actions of the Peloponnesians, because I was in exile, which gave me the opportunity to understand something about them. So I shall now describe the disputes that arose after the ten years' war, the breach of the treaty, and later events as the war continued.

———

Although it's clear from the preceding passage that Thucydides lived to witness the Athenians' defeat in 404 BC, his history of the war breaks off abruptly with events in the summer of 411.

In the second period of the war, the Athenians became more ruthless in expanding their empire. In 416 BC the Athenians sailed to the island of Melos, in the central Aegean, to force the Melians to join their empire rather than stay neutral or ally with Sparta. Before besieging the island's main town, the Athenians attempted to negotiate with the Melian leaders. As Thucydides portrays the negotiations, the Athenians' main justification for using force on the Melians was that they were entitled to expand their empire as they chose, or (in effect) that might equals right. In a striking departure from his normal narrative style, Thucydides presents the negotiations between the two sides as a dialogue, as if they were characters in a drama.

———

[5.84] The Athenians also made an expedition against the isle of Melos with thirty ships of their own, six vessels from Chios, and two from Lesbos, sixteen hundred hoplites, three hundred archers, and twenty mounted archers from Athens, and about fifteen hundred hoplites from the allies and the islanders. The Melians are a colony of Sparta that would not submit to the Athenians as the other islanders had done. At

[handwritten marginalia: why is he proving his credibility? (to justify his work)]

first, they remained neutral and took no part in the struggle, but afterward, when the Athenians used force and devastated their land, the Melians turned to open war. Cleomedes, son of Lycomedes, and Tisias, son of Tisimachus, both Athenian generals, camped in Melian territory with the forces described above. Before doing any damage to the Melians' land, they sent envoys to negotiate.

The Melians did not bring the Athenian envoys before the common people.* Instead, they asked them to state the purpose of their mission to the magistrates and the oligarchs.† The Athenian envoys spoke as follows:

[5.85] "Since these negotiations are not taking place before the people, to keep them from being deceived by hearing us make seductive and unchallenged arguments without interruption—we know this is the reason we were brought before the oligarchs—you sitting there should take an even more cautious approach. You should not make a single speech about each issue, but instead respond immediately to whatever you disapprove of in our speeches and deliver your judgment.‡ So first tell us if this proposal of ours suits you."

[5.86] The Melian commissioners answered: "We have no complaint about the fairness of quietly instructing one another as you propose. But the fact that your preparations for war are here in the present and not just in the future—that seems not to fit with your proposal. We see that you have come to be our judges in the discussion, and we see that the conclusion of it most likely will bring us war if we win the case and do not agree to your terms, or slavery if we do accept them."

[5.87] *Athenians.* If you have met to debate about the future or have anything in mind other than the present and the facts before you, and are considering anything other than the safety of your state, then we should stop. But if that is not the case, we will continue speaking.

[5.88] *Melians.* It is natural and excusable for men in our position to turn in many directions in both what we think and what we say. However, the question in this conference is the safety of our country, and if you approve, the discussion can proceed in the way you propose.

[5.89] *Athenians.* For ourselves, we shall not trouble you with noble speeches, such as how we have a right to our empire because we defeated

---

* In Athens, such a discussion would have been held in the Assembly, before all the male citizens who chose to attend on that day.

† The governing council, as opposed to the citizens in general (the *demos*).

‡ This procedural note effectively gives Thucydides license to write in dialogue form.

the Persians or that we are attacking you now because of wrong you have done us. We will not make a long speech that would not be believed.* Nor do we suppose you will think you can persuade us by saying that although you are a Spartan colony, you did not join the Spartans, or that you have done us no wrong. But we will aim at what is feasible, holding in view what we both really think. You know as well as we do that in the discussion of human affairs, justice is decided between equals in power, and the strong do what they can and the weak yield to them.

[5.90] *Melians.* Here indeed we think it is expedient (we need to do so, since you insist that we talk about self-interest rather than justice) that you should not destroy what is our common good, which in times of danger is the privilege of being allowed to invoke what is fair and right, and even to profit by reasonably valid arguments if they can be helpful to us. And this principle is also useful for you, because if you should fail, you will encounter the greatest vengeance and would become an example to others.†

[5.91] *Athenians.* The end of our empire, should it come to an end, does not discourage us. For we do not rule over others, like the Spartans, nor are we so terrible to the people we have conquered—and the present issue is not about the Spartans. Rather, it is about whether those who are subject to our rule can attack us and win. About this you must permit us to risk our lives. We will now proceed to show you that we are come here in the interest of our empire, and that we are here to talk about the welfare of your city, because we want to rule over you without trouble and see you protected for the good of us both.

[5.92] *Melians.* And how could it turn out as good for us to be your slaves as it would be for you to rule over us?

[5.93] *Athenians.* Because it would be better for you to submit to us, instead of suffering the worst; and we would profit by not destroying you.

[5.94] *Melians.* So you would not accept the idea of our being neutral, friends instead of enemies but allies of neither side?

[5.95] *Athenians.* No, because your hostility cannot hurt us as much as your friendship, which would be proof of our weakness, and your contempt for our power would set a bad example for our subjects.

---

* The Athenians had made a speech of just this kind, at Sparta, in book 1 of Thucydides' work.

† Perhaps Thucydides wrote this passage after the catastrophic failure of the Athenian expedition to Sicily, which he describes in books 6 and 7 of his history (see below).

[5.96] *Melians.* Are your subjects likely to consider it fair to put those not connected to you in the same category as those who are mostly your own colonists, along with some conquered rebels?

[5.97] *Athenians.* As far as justice is concerned, none of our subjects think they are deprived of it. They think that they prevail when they are strong and that we do not attack them when we are afraid. So your destruction, beyond letting us rule over more people, would give us security—should you submit—particularly because you are islanders and we are masters of the sea, and because you are weaker than the others.

[5.98] *Melians.* Do you think there is security in that policy? Here again, because you keep us from talking about justice and persuade us to conform to your interest, we also must explain what is in our interest, and try to persuade you, in case it might coincide with yours. As for those who are allies of neither of us—how can you avoid making enemies of *them,* if they see what is happening to us and suppose that someday you will attack them? And what is this but to increase the enemies you already have and to force others to become enemies who otherwise may have been reluctant to do so?

[5.99] *Athenians.* No, we believe that the mainlanders are more loyal to us because of the liberty which they enjoy and that they will be hesitant to leave our protection. It is rather disobedient islanders like yourselves, and those already annoyed by the demands of our empire—they are the ones who would be the most likely to take a rash step and put themselves and us into obvious danger.

[5.100] *Melians.* Well then, if you risk so much to retain your empire, and your subjects to get rid of it, it would surely be great weakness and cowardice in those of us who are still free if we don't try everything before submitting to slavery.

[5.101] *Athenians.* No, not if you consider the matter carefully. For you, this is not a contest about manliness, nor is it an equal one or one fought to avoid the penalty of disgrace. It is rather a question of self-preservation and not opposing those far stronger than you are.

[5.102] *Melians.* But we know that the fortune of war is sometimes more impartial and does not consider the difference in size of the forces involved. For us, submission offers no hope, but if we act, there is hope that we may remain standing.

[5.103] *Athenians.* Hope is a solace in danger for those who have the power to make use of it. Even if it harms them, it does not destroy them.

But people who risk all their resources on a venture (because hope* is naturally generous) recognize hope for what she is only after they are ruined.† But during the time in which a man can still guard against hope and recognize it for what it is, he will not fail. You are weak and hang on a single turn of the scale. Do not wish to have that experience. Do not be like most people, who, though it is still humanly possible to save themselves, turn to invisible hopes when in times of extremity the hopes they can see fail them, and to prophecies and oracles, and other such inventions that destroy them, along with their hopes.‡

[5.104] *Melians.* We also think, as you must know, that it will be hard to fight against your power and against fortune, unless fortune can be a fair judge. But we trust in divine justice that we will not be defeated, because we are righteous men fighting those who do not have justice on their side, and because our weakness will be balanced by our alliance with the Spartans. They are bound to come for the sake of our kinship if for no other reason, and they would be ashamed not to help us.§ So our confidence is after all not so irrational.

[5.105] *Athenians.* As for the divine favor you speak of, we think we also are entitled to it. Nothing we are doing goes against what humans believe about the gods, or beyond what men think right to do or plan among themselves. We believe that it seems true of the gods, and we know it is true of men, that in accord with a fixed law of nature they rule whenever they can. We were not the first to make this law; we took hold of it and used it because it exists and will exist forever. We know that you and everyone else, if you had the same power as we have, would do the same. So as far as the gods are concerned, we are not afraid that it is likely that we shall be defeated. As for your idea about the Spartans—your belief that shame will make them come to your rescue—we bless your innocence, but do not envy your lack of sense. The Spartans, when their own interests or their country's laws are in question, are usually excellent. As for their conduct toward others much might be said, but in general one

---

* In early poetry, hope is characterized as a deceptive female.

† Thucydides will emphasize this theme in his account of the vote by the Athenian Assembly to invade Sicily, 6.24 (below, p. 192), and in the hour of their defeat, 7.77 (below, p. 235).

‡ This statement should not be taken to mean that the Athenians (or Thucydides) do not believe in the gods. Hector makes a similar argument in *Iliad* 12.43.

§ The Melians were originally colonists sent out by Sparta, and hence had "kinship" ties. This was a false hope, as it turned out.

may say that of all those we know they most clearly think that what they like is noble and what is in their own interest is just. But *that* sort of attitude offers no hope of the salvation that now, contrary to reason, you count on.

[5.106] *Melians.* But it's for this very reason, and we believe it is to their advantage, that they will not want to betray their Melian colonists, and thereby establish themselves as unfaithful to their Greek supporters but helpful to their enemies.

[5.107] *Athenians.* Then you do not suppose that it is to their advantage to stay safe, when doing what's just and right involves danger? Which is what the Spartans least of all want to take on.

[5.108] *Melians.* But we believe that even they would be more likely to face danger for our sake, more confidently than they would for others, because we lie close to their activities in the Peloponnese;* and they can have more faith in our loyalty because we are their kinsmen.

[5.109] *Athenians.* But it is the strength of an ally, not their goodwill, that matters to the people who are summoned. *That* is what the Spartans are looking for, even more so than other cities. (Presumably, they have so little trust in their own resources that it is only with numerous allies that they attack their neighbors.) So it is not likely that they would undertake a journey to an island, when we are masters of the sea.

[5.110] *Melians.* But they would have other allies† they might send to help us. The Cretan Sea is broad, which makes it more difficult for those who command it to capture other ships than it is for ships who seek to elude them to do so safely. And should the Spartans fail to come to us, they could attack *your* territory, as well as the rest of your allies who Brasidas‡ did not attack. So instead of fighting for places that do not belong to you, you will need have to fight both for your allies and for your own country.

[5.111] *Athenians.* Something like that might happen to you; and you are not unaware that Athenians have never withdrawn from a siege because they were afraid of others. We recall that although you said you were planning for the safety of your city, you have said nothing in all this dis-

---

* The island of Melos was not close to the Spartan port of Gytheion, but Melos was a useful base for Spartan ships in the Eastern Mediterranean.

† That is, the Corinthians.

‡ The Spartan general who was particularly effective against the Athenians.

cussion that men might believe and suppose that they might be saved. Your strongest arguments are based on your hopes for the future, though your resources, compared to the forces arrayed against you, are too limited for you to survive.

You display considerable lack of logic in your argument if you do not change your minds and offer us more logical arguments than these. Do not turn to notions of honor, which often destroy men in circumstances they can already see will be dishonorable, but who, because of the seductive power of that word "honor," fall willingly into incurable disaster—and acquire a dishonor that's worse because it was foreseen and did not occur by chance. That is something you should guard against, once you take it into consideration. You will not think it dishonorable to submit to the greatest city in Greece, when it gives you the chance, on moderate terms,* of becoming her ally and keeping your city. Since you have been given the choice between war and security, do not choose the worse option. And it's certain that the most successful people hold their own with their equals, respect their superiors, and are moderate toward their inferiors. So think this over after we have left the meeting and continue to keep in mind that it's about your country that you are making your decision—the only country that you have—and that it will be on the basis of this one decision that your country will prosper and not be destroyed.

[5.112] The Athenians now left the conference.

The Melians, once they were left to themselves, reached a decision similar to the one they had maintained in the discussion. Their answer was: "Athenians,† our decision is the same as the one we made at first. We will not in a moment deprive of freedom a city that has been inhabited for seven hundred years.‡ Putting our trust in the fortune with which the gods have preserved it up till now, and in human help, namely that of the Spartans, we will try to save ourselves. Meanwhile we invite you to let us be friends to you and foes to neither side. We ask you to withdraw from our country after making such a treaty as shall seem appropriate to us both."

---

* "Moderate" refers to the requirement that allies of Athens must pay tribute.

† For the first time in this conference, with dramatic emphasis, the Melians call the Athenians by name.

‡ Seven hundred years apparently was believed to be the normal life span of cities.

↳ 10/24/24

[5.113] That is what the Melians answered.

The Athenians now brought the conference to an end and said: "So then you alone, as it seems to us, to judge from these resolutions, regard what is in the future as more certain than what is before your eyes, and what is out of sight as already taking place, simply by wishing it to be so. And because you placed your trust entirely on the Spartans, on your luck, and on your hopes, you will be disappointed."

[5.114] The Athenian envoys now returned to the army; and since the Melians had not yielded, the Athenian generals prepared themselves for war, and surrounded the Melians with a wall,* after dividing the work among themselves and their allies. Later the Athenians left some of their own citizens and allies to keep guard by land and sea and went home with most of their army. The force that was left behind remained and besieged the area....

[5.115] The Melians attacked by night and took the part of the Athenian wall down near the agora† and killed some of their men. They also brought in grain and whatever else they could find that they needed, and so returned and kept quiet. And the Athenians took measures to keep better guard in future.

[5.116] [During the winter] the Melians again took another part of the Athenian lines where not many guards were present. As a result, after reinforcements arrived from Athens under the command of Philocrates, son of Demeas, the Athenians now intensified their siege of the city. Then there was some treachery,‡ and some of the Melians surrendered to the Athenians so they could inform them about the others. The Athenians executed all the grown men and sold the women and children into slavery.

Afterward the Athenians sent out five hundred colonists and inhabited the area themselves.§

---

* The purpose of such a counter-wall was to prevent the Melians from escaping and from receiving outside help. In book 6 the Athenians start to build such a wall around Syracuse.

† The market area of the town.

‡ In any Greek city there were always men who did not agree with the policies of the current government, like the Argives or the Syracusans (see 7.48).

§ The standard practice in dealing with a rebellion, as in the case of Mytilene; see note on 3.36, above.

G10/26/24

THE ATHENIAN EXPEDITION TO SICILY

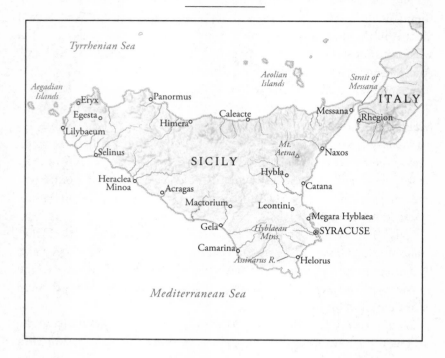

In books 6 and 7, Thucydides gives an intense account of the Athenians' invasion of Sicily. His focus stays on this one theater of war almost exclusively, and his emotional pitch rises as the situation becomes more critical and the stakes greater. These two books constitute a masterpiece of war reportage that has seldom been equaled.

Book 6 starts with the Assembly debate over the decision to invade, which occurred around the same time as the Athenian siege of Melos and follows it directly in Thucydides' text. The juxtaposition of these events is deliberate. In his account of the debate over Sicily, Thucydides shows how the Athenians were compromised by the same reliance on hope that had proved so disastrous for the Melians.

———

[6.1] In the same winter,* the Athenians again resolved to sail to Sicily, with a greater armament than those under Laches and Eurymedon,†

---

* 416–415 BC.

† Two generals who had previously commanded Athenian expeditions to Sicily, Laches in 427 BC, Eurymedon in 425. Both expeditions had far more limited goals than the present one.

aiming, if possible, to conquer the island. Most of them were ignorant of its size and of the number of its inhabitants, Greek and barbarian, and they did not realize that they were undertaking a war as large as that against the Peloponnesians, for the voyage around Sicily in a cargo ship is not far short of eight days. Also, as large as the island is, there are only two miles of sea that keep it apart from the mainland.*

———

Thucydides goes on to provide a concise history of the different peoples (natives and colonists, including other Greeks) who had settled in Sicily before the time of the Athenian expedition.

———

[6.6] Such is the list of the peoples, Greek and barbarian, inhabiting Sicily, and such the magnitude of the island the Athenians were now set on invading. In reality, they wanted to conquer all of it, although they also had the specious excuse of aiding their kindred[†] and other allies on the island. But they were especially encouraged by envoys from Egesta.[‡]

The Egestaeans had come to Athens and requested its help more urgently than ever. They had gone to war with their neighbors in Selinus[§] about questions of marriage and disputed territory. But those in Selinus had enlisted the help of the Syracusans and had surrounded Egesta by land and sea. The Egestaeans now reminded the Athenians of an alliance they had made in the time of Laches, during the former Leontine[¶] war, and begged them to send their ships to help them. Among many other considerations, the principal argument of the Egestaeans was that if the Syracusans were not punished for depopulating Leontini and destroying the allies Athens still had in Sicily, they would get the whole power of the island into their hands. Then one day there would be a danger of their coming with a large force, as Dorians, to the aid of their fellow Dorians,

---

* The Strait of Messina. Southern Italy was at this time largely settled by Greeks.

† Certain Sicilian cities were of Ionian Greek stock and thus "kindred" to Athens. Leontini and Catana were chief among these, and both had treaties of alliance with Athens. Syracuse, the principal city of Sicily, was of Dorian stock, originally populated by citizens of Corinth, and thus aligned with the Peloponnesian states.

‡ Modern Segesta in northwest Sicily. The Egestaeans were an indigenous Sicilian people who used Greek characters to write their language.

§ This war dates to 416 BC; it is one of several such wars between the Dorian Greek inhabitants of Selinus (modern Selinunte) and the Egestaeans.

¶ In 427 BC, Leontini (modern Lentini), an Ionian Greek city, had asked for Athenian help against Syracuse. Leontini was then conquered by Syracuse in 422.

whose colonists they were, and together destroy the Athenian Empire. The Athenians would therefore do well to unite with the allies they still had and make a stand against the Syracusans, especially since they, the Egestaeans, were prepared to provide enough money for the war.

The Athenians, after they had heard these arguments constantly repeated in their assemblies by the Egestaeans and their supporters, voted first to send envoys to Egesta, to see if the money they talked of really existed in their treasury and temples, and at the same time to find out about the state of Egesta's war with Selinus.

[6.7] The Athenian envoys were then dispatched to Sicily.

[6.8] Early in the spring of the following summer, the Athenian envoys came back from Sicily, and the Egestaeans came with them, bringing sixty talents of uncoined silver. That was a month's pay for the sixty ships they were going to ask to have sent to them. The Athenians held an Assembly, and after they had heard a report from the Egestaeans and their own envoys—as attractive as it was untrue—about the state of affairs generally, and in particular about the money (which was said to be in abundance in the temples and treasury),[*] they voted to send sixty ships to Sicily under the command of Alcibiades, son of Clinias; Nicias, son of Niceratus; and Lamachus, son of Xenophanes. These men were appointed with full powers;[†] they were to help the Egestaeans against the Selinuntines, to help recolonize Leontini as well (if it also could be of some advantage to them in the war), and to arrange all other matters in Sicily as they might think best for the interests of Athens.

Five days after this, a second Assembly was held, to consider the fastest ways to equip the ships and to vote on whatever else might be required by the generals for the expedition. And Nicias[‡] came forward. He had been chosen to take command against his will, and he thought that the city had not planned wisely, but that they were hoping to conquer all of Sicily, a huge undertaking, on a slight and specious pretext. He wanted to dissuade the Athenians from the enterprise, and he gave them the following advice:

---

[*] In fact, there were only thirty additional talents; see 6.46 below.

[†] That is, they were authorized to take action without consulting the home government at Athens.

[‡] Nicias had helped broker the Spartan-Athenian truce signed in 421 and still in effect at this moment (the so-called Peace of Nicias; see pp. 171–72). He was known for his cautious and conservative approach both to military commitments and to foreign policy.

[6.9] "This Assembly was convened in order to consider the preparations to be made for sailing to Sicily. I think, however, that we ought to examine this matter and consider whether it is to our advantage to send out these ships. I think we should not give so little consideration to a matter of such importance and should not be persuaded by foreigners into taking on a war that does not concern us. I say this even though I stand to win honor by such a course of action and fear less than other men for my own safety. It is not that I believe a man would be a worse citizen for thinking about himself and his property. On the contrary, such a man would for his own sake want his country to prosper more than others. Nevertheless, since I have never spoken contrary to my beliefs in order to gain honor, I shall not begin to do so now, but shall say what I think best. My words would have no force against your temperament,* if I were to advise you to keep what you have and not risk it for what is doubtful and in the future. But I shall teach you this: It is not the right time to rush into what you are planning, and it will not be easy to do it.

[6.10] "I say you are leaving many enemies behind you here so that you can go far away and bring more enemies back with you. You suppose, perhaps, that the treaty you have made† is secure. That treaty will continue to exist, though in name only, so long as you keep at peace (for some men here and some of our enemies would have it so).‡ But if you fail in any way, our enemies will respond swiftly with significant force. They will do so because the treaty was forced on them by disaster§ and was less honorable to them than to us. Then also there are many issues in that treaty that are still in dispute. In addition, some states have not accepted the treaty at all, and they are among the strongest. Some of these are openly at war with us; others (because the Spartans have not yet attacked them) are restrained by truces renewed every ten days.¶ So it is

---

* Nicias refer to the well-known Athenian qualities of expansiveness and acquisitiveness, described by the Corinthians earlier in Thucydides' *History* (see pp. 141–144).

† The Peace of Nicias, in force for the past six years, had stopped hostilities between Athens and Sparta.

‡ Nicias is referring to the war hawks at both Sparta and Athens who had undermined the Peace (keeping it "in name only").

§ The "disaster" was Athens's seizure of nearly two hundred Spartan prisoners at Sphacteria (see p. 171).

¶ In the first group were the Corinthians, in the second the Thebans. Neither city had signed on to the Peace.

only too probable that if they find we have divided our power, as we are rushing to do,* they would certainly attack us by joining with the Sicilian Greeks, whose alliance in the past they have valued more than that of many others.

"We ought, therefore, to consider these points, and not decide to run risks with our country hanging in the balance, nor to grasp at another empire before we have secured the one we have. The Chalcidians in Thrace have been all these years in revolt from us and still are not under control, and others on the mainland† are only occasionally loyal. We immediately rush to help our allies the Egestaeans on the grounds that they have been wronged, while we delay in mounting a defense against those who have been rebelling for a long time!

[6.11] "And if we conquer the Sicilians, they are too far away and too numerous for us to control them. It is foolish to go against men who could not be controlled even if conquered, and failure would leave us in a worse position than before. The Sicilians, it seems to me (to judge by the state of things now), would be even less of a danger to us than before if the Syracusans ruled them—just what the Egestaeans are afraid of. Now they might possibly come here as separate states out of loyalty to Sparta.‡ But in the other case,§ it is not likely that one empire would make war with another; for if they joined the Peloponnesians to overthrow our empire, they can expect to see the Peloponnesians overthrow them in the same way. The Greeks in Sicily would fear us most if we never went there at all, and next to this, if first we displayed our power and then quickly went away again.

"Most of all, we all know that anything that is far off, and whose reputation cannot easily be tested, is the object of admiration. If we slip up at all, those in Sicily would at once begin to look down on us and would join our enemies here against us. That is something, Athenians, you yourselves know from your experience with the Spartans and their allies. Your unexpected success, compared with what you first feared, has now made you disdainful of them and eager to attack Sicily. You should not be happy about your enemies' misfortunes but pleased that you have

---

* That is, by sending a large force to Sicily.

† Meaning cities in Thrace and Macedonia in the north and in Asia Minor in the east.

‡ That is, cities of native Sicilians (like Egesta) might be inclined, as allies of Sparta, to harm Athens.

§ The "other case" being their assimilation into the empire of Syracuse.

thwarted their plans. Do not think of anything other than how even now the Spartans will compensate, if they can, for their own dishonor by destroying us, because they care more than anything about their 'reputation for excellence.'* Our struggle, therefore, if we are wise, will not be for the benefit of the Egestaeans in Sicily, who are non-Greeks,† but about how to protect ourselves from an oligarchy that is intent on plotting against us.

[6.12] "We should also remember that we are only now enjoying some respite from the great plague and from war. That has helped both our finances and our health, and it's right to employ these resources here at home, on our own behalf, rather than on behalf of these needy exiles. It is to their advantage to tell us attractive lies. They do nothing but talk and leave the danger to those nearby; if they succeed they will not show proper gratitude, but if they fail they will destroy their friends along with themselves. And if there is any man here,‡ because he is pleased at being chosen to command, who urges you to make the expedition, and is thinking only of what is for his own benefit, particularly because he is still too young to command—a man who seeks to be admired for his stable of horses, and, because of his great extravagances, hopes for some profit from his appointment—do not allow such a person to maintain his private splendor at his country's expense. Keep in mind that such persons injure the public fortune while they squander their own, and that this expedition is a significant matter and not something that a young man should consider or rashly take control of.

[6.13] "When I see men now sitting here next to that man, urged on by him,§ I am frightened, and I urge the older men, if any are sitting near him, not to be shamed into voting for war if they do not think it right. No, whatever they have endured, they should not be enticed by what lies in the distance. They need to remember how rarely success is won by wishing but how often by forethought. Since his country is encountering the greatest danger, he should raise his hand against the war on her behalf.

---

* The last three words in this sentence are in dactylic hexameter, the meter of epic and elegiac verse, which suggests that it is a quotation from a lost poem.

† That is, the Egestaeans are Elymians, not Greeks; see below, 6.16.2.

‡ Nicias is referring to Alcibiades, who had been a ward of Pericles and was one of the young men who associated with Socrates. Alcibiades was at this time about thirty-five, Nicias a generation older.

§ In the Assembly, where displays of support were visible to all present, such groups of vocal partisans could help sway public opinion.

He should vote for the Sicilians to stay within the boundaries that now exist between us, which are not in dispute (for sailors, the Ionian Sea near the land and the Sicilian Sea, for a voyage across open water). They should enjoy their own possessions and settle their own quarrels. We should tell the Egestaeans privately to end the previous war they began against the Selinuntines without consulting the Athenians. In the future we should not make (as we used to do) an alliance to defend people when they are in trouble, unless we can get help from *them* when we need it.

[6.14] "And you, Prytanis,* if you think it your duty to care for our city, and want to be a good citizen, ask for the vote to be reconsidered,† and for a second time take the opinions of the Athenians. If you are afraid to move the question again, consider that in the presence of so many witnesses you will not be blamed for breaking the law, but rather that you will be a physician for your misguided city, and this is what governing means, to do for your country as much good as you can, or willingly to do no harm to it."

[6.15] That is what Nicias said. But most of the Athenians who came forward spoke in favor of the expedition and of not canceling what had been voted, although some spoke on the other side. The most eager support for the expedition was provided by Alcibiades, son of Clinias. He wished to oppose Nicias because he disagreed with him about affairs of state and because Nicias had made a personal attack on him. In particular, he was very eager to take command of the expedition and hoped to use it to conquer Sicily and Carthage,‡ and also personally to gain in wealth and reputation because of his success. He was highly regarded by the citizens and had ambitions greater than his means, in pursuit of which he raised horses§ and spent on other things. It was not least of all on account of these that later he destroyed the Athenian state.

Most people were afraid of the extent of his indulgences in his own life and habits and of the ambition he showed in whatever he undertook. They thought he aimed at becoming a tyrant, and so they became his enemies. Publicly his management of the war was as good as could be

* The president or chair of the Assembly, serving for that one day.

† A revote of this kind was taken in the question of Mytilene (see above, pp. 161–62) and was bitterly attacked by Cleon as a dangerous precedent.

‡ Carthage, on the shore of North Africa, had several colonies on Sicily and was a formidable naval rival for the Greeks.

§ The rearing of racehorses (then as now) was a mark of great wealth and competitiveness.

desired, but individually, everyone was distressed by his habits, and later turned to other leaders, and in a short time destroyed the city. But at that time Alcibiades came forward and gave the following advice to the Athenians:

[6.16] "Athenians, I have a better right to command than others—I must begin with this issue because Nicias has attacked me—and at the same time I believe myself worthy of this command. I am being criticized for things that bring fame to my ancestors and to myself and that are also profitable for this country. For the Greeks believe that the power of our city is even greater than it really is, because of the magnificence with which I represented it at the Olympic games, although they thought it had been destroyed by the war. At that time I sent in seven chariots, a number not previously entered by any private person, and won first prize, and came in second and fourth, and took care to have everything else in a style worthy of my victory.* It is customary to regard such displays as honorable, and people believe there is power behind such actions. Again, any splendor I may have exhibited at home in providing choruses,† or anything else, is naturally envied by my fellow citizens, but in the eyes of foreigners also gives the impression of strength. It's hardly a useless folly‡ when a man at his own private expense benefits not just himself but his city as well.

"It's not unfair for a man who prides himself on his position to refuse to be considered equal to the rest. A man who is badly off does not share his misfortunes with anyone, and in such a situation ought to accept his lot, though he is looked down on by the prosperous. Or he should treat all equally and expect similar treatment himself. I know that such people and all others that have attained any distinction, although they may be unpopular in their lifetimes in their dealings with their fellows and especially with their equals, leave to posterity the desire to claim connection with them even when there is no basis for it. They are boasted of by the country to which they belonged, not as strangers or wrongdoers, but as fellow countrymen and benefactors.

"That is what I hope to attain. Even if I am abused by them in private,

---

* Alcibiades won first, second, and third place in the chariot race at the Olympic games in 416 BC, a victory that was celebrated in an ode by the dramatist Euripides.

† Wealthy Athenians provided financial support for the public performances by choruses, including the tragic dramas.

‡ Alcibiades refers here to the charge his critics had made, that his lifestyle displayed a kind of madness.

you should consider whether anyone manages public affairs better than I do. I made an alliance with the most powerful states of Peloponnese,* without great danger or expense to you. I compelled the Spartans to stake their all on the outcome of a single day at Mantinea.† As a result, though they were victorious in the battle, they have never since regained their confidence.

[6.17] "And that is how my youth and apparently unnatural folly confronted the power of the Peloponnesians with appropriate arguments, and by its intensity won their confidence and persuaded them. Do not be afraid of my intensity now, but while I am still in my prime, and Nicias appears lucky,‡ make use of the services of us both. Do not reconsider your resolution to sail to Sicily, just because you think you would be attacking a great power. The cities in Sicily have large and diverse populations,§ and they have easy changes and influxes of citizens. On account of that no one is fighting as if for his own homeland or is equipped with armor for his body, and there the countryside has no proper farmsteads. Everyone thinks that he can obtain something at the public expense either by persuasion or by forming factions; then if things go wrong, they prepare to settle in another country. From a mob like this you need not look for either unanimity in planning or concert in action. Rather, they will probably surrender one by one if they get a fair offer, especially if (as we're told) they are torn by civil strife. Moreover, the Sicilians do not have as many hoplites as they boast of. The Greeks have falsified and greatly exaggerated their numbers in the present war.¶

"So that is what the cities in Sicily are like. From all that I can hear, they will be found even easier for us to conquer because we shall have the

---

* Principally Argos, a city opposed to Sparta but until recently neutral in the war. Alcibiades helped negotiate a treaty of alliance between Athens and Argos a few years before this.

† In book 5, Thucydides had used the phrase "in a single day" to characterize the strength of the alliance that helped the Spartans win the battle at Mantinea. By repeating the phrase in this passage, he reminds his audience that Alcibiades here is representing the Athenian defeat as a kind of victory.

‡ Nicias' string of military successes in his long career had given him a reputation for good luck.

§ By contrast, the Athenians thought of themselves as being descended from a common set of ancestors.

¶ This claim, like many others Alcibiades makes here, is based on vague reports rather than true knowledge.

help of many non-Greeks,* who from their hatred of the Syracusans will join us in attacking them.

"Enemy forces here† will not stand in your way if you make the right judgment. Our fathers had the same adversaries that, some say,‡ we shall leave behind us if we sail, and also had the Persians as their enemy, and yet were able to establish our empire, trusting solely to their superiority at sea. The Peloponnesians were never so much without hope against us as they are at present. Though they have the courage to invade our country even when we do *not* sail away, they still can never hurt us with their fleet, since the navy we shall leave behind is a match for them.

[6.18] "In this state of things what reason can we give to ourselves for holding back, or what excuse can we offer to our allies in Sicily for not helping them? They are our allies, and we have sworn to help them, without objecting that *they* have not assisted *us*. We did not take them into alliance to have them help us in Greece, but so that they might annoy our enemies in Sicily and prevent them from coming here and attacking us. That is how empires have been won, both by us and by all others that have had empires: by constant readiness to support all, whether barbarians or Greeks, who call upon them. If we were to remain at peace or pick and choose who to assist, we would make but few new conquests and imperil those we've already won. Men do not rest content with parrying the attacks of a superior, but often strike the first blow to prevent the attack being made. We cannot control the size of our empire like a household budget. No, it is essential, since we have come this far, to lay plans for the new while not letting go of the old, because of the danger that we shall be ruled by others unless *we* rule over *them*. Nor can you look at inaction from the same point of view as others do, unless you are prepared to change your practices and make them more like theirs.§

"So reckoning that things here will increase by our going there, let us make the voyage, to humble the pride of the Peloponnesians, since by sailing to Sicily we will seem to them to care little for the peace we have at present. At the same time, we shall either become masters, in all likeli-

---

* At this time, Egesta was the only barbarian city to have requested aid from Athens.

† Principally referring to the Spartans.

‡ Referring sneeringly to Nicias, who had just made the point that Athenian power in mainland Greece was still vulnerable.

§ A bold assertion of the idea that Athens had a superior way of life and therefore an obligation to maintain it by imperialism.

hood, of the whole of Greece through the acquisition of the Sicilian Greeks, or in any case destroy the Syracusans, to the advantage of ourselves and our allies. The ability to remain there if we succeed, or to return, will be provided by our navy. As masters of the sea, we shall be superior at sea to all Sicilians.

"Do not let Nicias dissuade you by advocating inactivity or by pitting the young against the old. But in the customary way, just as our fathers, as young men working with older men, together brought us to this point, now in the same way you must try to bring the city forward. You must also understand that neither youth nor old age can do anything without the other, and that the inferior and the ordinary and the very capable are most powerful when joined together. The city that rests, like anything else that does so, very quickly will become enfeebled, and its skill in everything will grow old. But when the city is active, it will always gain new experience and get used to defending itself in deeds, not just in words.

"In short, I think a city that's active by nature is destroyed by a sudden shift to inactivity, and that the safest way for men to live is to conduct the city's affairs in accord, as much as they can, with their character and institutions—even if it is for the worse."

[6.19] Such were the words of Alcibiades. After hearing him and the Egestaeans and some Leontine exiles, who came forward to remind them of their oaths and beg for assistance, the Athenians became more eager for the expedition than before. Nicias, realizing it would now be useless to try to deter them by his earlier arguments, thought he might perhaps dissuade them from their resolution by the number of men and amount of matériel needed. He came forward a second time and spoke as follows:

[6.20] "Because I see, Athenians, that you are thoroughly eager for the expedition—may it turn out as we hope it will—I will tell you what I know at present. From all I hear we are going against cities that are great and not subject to one another, nor are they in need of a change of government. They will not be relieved to pass from enforced servitude to a happier condition. They will not be at all likely to accept our rule in exchange for freedom. Also, the number of Greek towns is large for a single island. Aside from Naxos and Catana, which I expect to join us from their connection with Leontini,* there are seven others armed at all

---

* Leontini and Catana were colonies begun by settlers from Naxos; all three cities had been aligned with Athens in recent years. This Sicilian Naxos should be distinguished from the Aegean island of the same name.

points just like our own power. Not least of these are Selinus and Syracuse, the chief objects of our expedition. In these cities are many hoplites, archers, and javelin men. They have triremes in abundance and many to man them. They also have money, some belonging to individuals, some in the temples at Selinus.* The Syracusans receive tribute from some of the non-Greeks as well. But their chief advantage over us lies in the number of their horses, and in the fact that they grow their own grain at home instead of importing it.†

[6.21] "Against a power of this kind it will not do to have merely a weak naval force. We shall also need a large land army to sail with us, if we are to do anything worthy of our ambition and not be kept out of the country by a large cavalry, especially in case the cities are afraid of us and cooperate with one another‡ and we are left without friends, other than the Egestaeans, who might provide cavalry for our defense.§

"It would be disgraceful for us to be compelled to retreat or to send for reinforcements because our advance planning was careless. We must therefore set out from here with an adequate force because we will be sailing far from our country, on an expedition unlike any that you have yet undertaken. Up to now you have undertaken campaigns as allies among subject states, so that any supplies needed were easily drawn from friendly territory. But we are cutting ourselves off, and going to a completely strange land, from which, during the four winter months, it is not easy for a messenger to get to Athens.¶

[6.22] "So I think that we ought to take large numbers of hoplites, both from Athens and from our allies, and from our subjects, and also any from the Peloponnese who we can persuade or pay to join us, and great numbers also of archers and slingers,** so we can hold out against the Sicilian cavalry. We must have an overwhelming superiority at sea to enable us to more easily bring in what we need, and we must bring from here our own grain in cargo ships, specifically wheat and parched barley, and bakers

---

* Wealth deposited in temples, usually in the form of dedications to a god, could be drawn on by the state in cases of need.

† Cities in Greece, Italy, and Carthage imported wheat from Sicily.

‡ Exactly what later occurred.

§ In phalanx warfare, cavalry were used to protect the flanks of infantry formations and to drive off pursuers in case of a defeat.

¶ Sailing across the Adriatic was dangerous in winter.

** Slingers could hurl lead bullets or stones farther than men could throw them.

from the mills paid to distribute it in the proper proportions, which we can use in case of bad weather. That way the army will not lack provisions, because it is not every city that will be able to provide for numbers like ours. And so we will not be dependent upon others, we must also provide ourselves with everything else so far as we can. Above all we must take along with us from home as much money as possible, because the money said to be ready at Egesta, you must realize, is ready primarily in talk.*

[6.23] "Indeed, if we ourselves leave Athens with a force that is only equal to that of the enemy, except for the number of hoplites in the field,[†] even so we shall only with difficulty be able to win and get through safely. We must keep in mind that we are going in order to found a city among strangers and enemies,[‡] and that those who undertake such an enterprise should be prepared to become master of the country the first day they land, or else realize that if they fail to do so, they will find everything hostile to them. That is what I am afraid of, and I know we will have need of much good planning and of still more good fortune (a difficult thing for us mortals to count on). So I wish as far as possible to make myself independent of fortune before we sail, and when I do sail, to be as safe as a strong force can make me. This I believe to be most secure for the country and safest for us who are going to fight. If someone thinks differently, I resign my command to him."

[6.24] Nicias made this speech because he supposed the Athenians would be discouraged by the scale of the undertaking, or, if compelled to go on the expedition, they would do so in the safest way possible. But the Athenians, far from having their zeal for the voyage diminished by the burden of preparations, became more eager for it than ever. So the opposite of what Nicias wanted took place. They thought he had given them good advice and that now there would be great security.

All alike fell in love with the expedition.[§] The older men thought that

---

* An assertion that soon proves to be true (see 6.46, p. 197).

† Nicias takes for granted that the expeditionary force cannot equal the number of infantry it will encounter. The hope of the Athenians was that sea and not land power would decide the outcome.

‡ Nicias compares the expedition to a colonizing mission. Many Greek cities in Sicily had been founded in just this way, that is, inserted by force against the opposition of indigenous peoples.

§ As a tragic poet might have done, Thucydides represents the Athenians as basing their decision on hope and desire rather than on accurate information. The word he uses for "love" here connotes, in Greek, a controlling passion.

either they would subdue the places against which they were to sail, or in any case that so large a force could not come to a bad end. The young men were encouraged by a desire to see foreign sights and were certain they would come home safely. The main body of troops wanted to earn money and make conquests that would supply a never-ending source of pay in the future. And so because most people were enthusiastic, anyone who did not like the idea held his peace, afraid to appear unpatriotic by holding up his hand against it.

[6.25] Finally one of the Athenians came forward and called on Nicias, saying that he ought not to make excuses or delay but state at once before them all how large a force the Athenians should assign him by vote. In response Nicias said reluctantly that he would need time to consider that matter with his colleagues. But so far as he could see at the moment, they would need to sail with at least one hundred triremes—the Athenians to provide as many transport ships as they thought best and send for others from the allies—and not less than five thousand hoplites in all, Athenian and allied, more if possible. The rest of the armament should be in proportion to that; archers from home and from Crete, slingers, and whatever else might seem desirable, should be made ready to be taken along.

[6.26] After they heard that, the Athenians voted at once that the generals should be in charge of the size of the army and of the expedition generally, and that they should do as they judged best for the interests of Athens. Then the preparations began. Messages were sent to the allies, and enlistment rolls were drawn up at home. The city had just recovered from the plague and the first part of the war, many young men had come of age, and capital had accumulated because of the truce, so everything was provided more easily.

[6.27] While all this was happening, most of the stone herms* in the city of Athens (according to native custom, these were square figures, common in the doorways of private houses and temples) in a single night had their faces mutilated.† No one knew who had done it, but large public rewards were offered to find the culprits. But it was voted also that

---

* Herms were pillars made of stone or (less expensively) of wood, sometimes topped with a portrait bust of a famous person or god, and usually adorned with an erect phallus, a symbolic means of warding off danger.

† Some of the phalluses were knocked off as well, to judge from a joke made by Aristophanes in his comedy *Lysistrata* (l.1094). The column of the herm showed an erect phallus in bas-relief, a token of fertility and hence good fortune.

anyone who knew of any other act of impiety* should give information without fear of consequences, whether he was a citizen, alien, or slave. The matter was taken up the more seriously as it was thought to be a bad omen for the expedition and part of a conspiracy to bring about a revolution and overturn the democracy.

[6.28] Information was thus given by some resident aliens and domestic servants, not about the herms, but about previous mutilations of other images perpetrated by young men in a drunken romp, and about mock celebrations of the Eleusinian Mysteries,† said to have taken place in private homes. Alcibiades was implicated in these celebrations. The issue was taken up by people who disliked Alcibiades because he stood in the way of their own undisturbed control of the people and who thought they would become more prominent if he were sent into exile. These men magnified the matter and proclaimed loudly that the affair of the Mysteries and the mutilation of the herms were a scheme to overthrow the democracy, and that none of this had been done without Alcibiades participating. The proof, they claimed, was the general undemocratic lawlessness of his life and habits.

[6.29] Alcibiades immediately defended himself against the charges in question. Before setting sail, he offered to stand trial, so that it might be determined whether he was guilty of the acts attributed to him. (The preparations for the expedition were now complete.) He wished to be punished if found guilty, but if acquitted, to take up his command. He objected to people entertaining slanders against him in his absence and asked them rather to execute him at once if he was guilty. He pointed out the imprudence of sending him out at the head of so large an army with so serious a charge still pending. But his enemies feared he would have the army on his side if he were tried immediately and that the common people were protecting him because it was on *his* account that the Argives and some Mantineans had joined in the expedition.‡ So his detractors brought in other speakers who said Alcibiades ought to sail *now* and not delay the army's departure, but should be tried within a fixed number of

---

* The herms were private property, but they also had religious significance because of their association with the god Hermes.

† The Eleusinian Mysteries were initiation rituals sacred to the goddesses Demeter and Persephone. The rituals included a procession from Athens to Eleusis, as well as a secret ritual that seems to have offered a positive picture of life after death for the initiates, both men and women.

‡ See 6.16 above and note.

days of his return. They wanted during his absence to have him recalled and brought home for trial on a more serious charge; this they could more easily arrange if he was away. So it was voted that Alcibiades should sail.

[6.30] After this, since it was now around midsummer, came the departure for Sicily. Most of the allies, with the grain transports and smaller craft and the rest of the expedition, had already received orders to muster at Corcyra* and to cross the Ionian Sea from there in a body to the Iapygian promontory.† But the Athenians themselves and the allies who happened to be with them went down to Piraeus at daybreak on the appointed day and began to man the ships for putting to sea. The whole population of the city, one could say, went down with them. There were both citizens and foreigners and people from the countryside escorting members of their families. Some brought friends, others relatives, and others sons, making their way both with hope and lamentation, as they thought of the conquests they hoped to make or of those men they might never see again; they knew what a long voyage it was that they were sending them on.

[6.31] Indeed, at this moment, when they were now on the point of parting from one another, the danger came home to them more than when they voted for the expedition. But the strength of the armament, and the extent of the provisioning before them, was a sight that could not help but comfort them. As for the foreigners and the rest of the crowd, they simply went to see a spectacle worth seeing, a thing beyond belief.

The armament that first sailed out was by far the most costly and splendid Greek force sent out by a single city up to that time.... The expedition was intended for a long term of service both by land and sea, and was furnished with ships and troops so as to be prepared for either, as required. The fleet had been elaborately equipped at great cost to the captains‡ and the state; the treasury was giving a drachma a day to each seaman and provided empty ships, sixty warships and forty transports, manning these with the best crews obtainable; the captains gave, in addition to the pay from the treasury, a bounty to the *thranitai*§ and the crews generally, besides spending lavishly on figureheads and all made equip-

---

* Corcyra was a convenient stopping point on the way to the heel of Italy.

† The tip of the heel of Italy.

‡ The captains (trierarchs) were rich men responsible for the maintenance of the triremes, recruitment of their crews, and command while at sea.

§ Experienced rowers, who sat on the topmost of the three tiers in a trireme.

ment. One and all made the utmost effort to enable their own ships to excel in beauty and fast sailing.

Meanwhile the land forces had been picked from the best enlistment rolls and vied with one another in paying great attention to their armor and personal gear. There was a competition in each unit, and it seemed to the other Greeks to be more like a show of power and resources than an armament against an enemy. For if someone had counted up the public expenditure of the state, and the private outlay of individuals—that is to say, the sums the state had already spent on the expedition and what was already in the hands of the generals, and what individuals had spent on their own gear, or what captains of triremes had spent and were still going to spend on their vessels—and if that person added to these expenses the money for the journey that each was likely to have in store for a voyage of such length (aside from the pay from the treasury), and what the soldiers or merchants took with them to use for trade, it would have been found that many talents of money had been taken out of the city. Indeed, the expedition became more famous for its wonderful boldness and for the splendor of its appearance than for its overwhelming strength (as compared to the peoples it would confront). This was the longest passage from home yet attempted, and the most ambitious in its goals in relation to the resources of those taking it on.

[6.32] The ships were now manned and everything they meant to bring with them was put on board. A trumpet blast signaled silence. The usual prayers before putting to sea were offered, not in each ship by itself, but by all together, in unison with a herald. Bowls of wine were mixed through all the fleet, and libations* were made in gold and silver goblets by the soldiers on board and their officers. They were joined in their prayers by the crowds on shore, the citizens and all who wished them well. After they sang the paean† and poured the libations, they put out to sea. At first, they sailed out in a column and then raced one another as far as Aegina.‡ Then they rushed on to get to Corcyra, where the rest of the allied forces were also assembling.

---

* It was customary to pour some wine on the ground as an offering to the gods before taking a drink oneself.

† A paean, a kind of hymn in honor of the gods, was sung at the beginning of undertakings like sea voyages and battles.

‡ A large island in the Saronic Gulf, south of Athens.

The Syracusans got word of the plans of the Athenian invasion. They debated what action to take; some disbelieved the reports and thought there was little to worry about, while others urged strenuous action. Both sides felt confident that Sicilian and Italian Greeks would unite against an Athenian invasion, which turned out to be the case. When the Athenians reached Rhegium, in southern Italy, the formerly friendly city refused to admit them or assist their war effort.

[6.45] Reliable reports came in from all quarters to the Syracusans, as well as from their own officers sent to reconnoiter, confirming that the Athenian fleet was at Rhegium. At that point, the Syracusans laid aside their incredulity and threw themselves intently into preparation. In some cases, guards were sent round to the Sicels, in other cases envoys. Garrisons were put into the posts of the Peripoli* in the country; horses and arms were reviewed in the city to ensure nothing was missing, and all other steps taken to prepare for a war that might start at any moment.

The Athenians sent three ships to Egesta, their firmest ally on Sicily, to see what money was available there. The Egestaeans had made huge promises of funds to induce the Athenians to sail.

[6.46] The three Athenian ships sent on ahead to Egesta came back to the Athenians at Rhegium. They reported that, far from the sums that had been promised, all that there appeared to be was thirty talents. The generals were disheartened at being thus disappointed at the start of their expedition and because the Rhegians had refused to join them. Those had been the people the Athenians had first tried to persuade and had had most reason to count on,† because of their relationship to the Leontines and constant friendship for Athens.

Nicias was prepared for the news from Egesta, but his two colleagues‡ were taken completely by surprise. The Egestaeans had made use of the following stratagem when the first envoys from Athens had come to inspect their resources. They took those envoys to the temple of Aphrodite

---

* Outposts in the countryside that in peacetime were staffed by young men.

† In 433–432 BC the Athenians had renewed an existing alliance with Rhegium.

‡ Lamachus and Alcibiades, the other two generals in charge.

at Eryx* and showed them the treasures deposited there:[†] bowls, wine-ladles, censers,[‡] and many other pieces. Because these items were made of silver, they gave an impression of wealth quite out of proportion to their small value. The envoys also entertained the ships' crews privately and collected all the gold and silver cups they could find in Egesta itself or could borrow in neighboring Phoenician and Greek towns, and each crew member brought them to the banquets as their own. Because they all used the same pieces, and everywhere a great amount of silver was shown, the effect was most dazzling on the Athenians from the triremes and made them speak loudly of the riches they had seen when they got back to Athens. Those who had been deceived, and had in their turn persuaded the rest, were much blamed by the soldiers when the news got around that the money that was supposed to be at Egesta did not exist. Meanwhile the generals met to decide what should be done.

[6.47] The advice of Nicias was to sail with all the armament to Selinus, the main object of the expedition, and if the Egestaeans could provide money for the whole force, to plan accordingly; but if they could not do so, to require them to supply provisions for the sixty ships they had asked for and stay and settle matters between Egesta and Selinus, either by force or agreement.[§] Then they should sail past the other cities, and after displaying the power of Athens and proving their zeal to their friends and allies, sail home again—unless they should have some sudden and unexpected opportunity to help Leontini or make alliances with some of the other cities—and not endanger Athens by wasting its resources.

[6.48] Alcibiades said that a great expedition like the present one must not disgrace itself by going away without accomplishing anything. Heralds needed to be sent to all the cities except Selinus and Syracuse. Efforts needed to be made to make some of the Sicels revolt from the Syracusans and to make allies of others so the Athenians could have their grain and troops. But first of all, they needed to persuade the Messanans to join them, because their city was situated directly on the strait and the

---

* Eryx, a city near the northwest corner of Sicily, was founded by Elymians, like Egesta, with which it was closely allied.

† Money and other treasures were commonly stored in temples.

‡ Dispensers of incense.

§ Support of Egesta against Selinus had been the pretext for the expedition and its most limited goal.

entrance to Sicily and would provide a harbor and a most advantageous starting point and base for the army.* Once they had made allies of the cities and knew who would be on their side in the war, they could attack Syracuse and Selinus, unless the Selinuntes came to terms with Egesta and the Syracusans allowed Athens to colonize Leontini.†

[6.49] Lamachus, on the other hand, said they ought to sail straight to Syracuse and fight their battle at once under the walls of the town while the people were still unprepared and their panic was at its height. Every armament, he said, was most terrible at the outset. If invaders allowed time to go by without showing themselves, the people would regain their courage and regard them with indifference. By attacking suddenly, while Syracuse was afraid to receive them, the Athenians would have the best chance of gaining a victory for themselves and of striking complete panic into the enemy, seeing how many they were (a number that would never again appear as large as it was now) and anticipating what they would suffer given the immediate danger of battle. He thought the Athenians might also count on surprising many still lingering in the fields outside the city (not believing the invaders were coming), and that when they brought their army, it would not need supplies when encamped in force before the city.‡ The rest of the Sicilians would thus be immediately less disposed to ally themselves with the Syracusans and would join the Athenians without waiting to see which side was strongest. They must, he said, make Megara§ their naval station as a place to retreat to and a base from which to attack, because it was an uninhabited place at no great distance from Syracuse either by land or by sea.

[6.50] After speaking to this effect, Lamachus nevertheless gave his support to the opinion of Alcibiades.¶ Alcibiades sailed across to Messana in his own ship with proposals for an alliance but had no success.

---

* Tragically for Athens, Alcibiades chose to rely on the diplomatic skills that had served him well in previous years, when he'd arranged the alliance between Athens and Argos. Sicilian cities were not as open to his persuasion.

† Leontini had been allied with Athens against the Syracusans in an earlier war (427–424 BC). Athens now wished to settle citizens there so as to firm up its presence on Sicily.

‡ That is, the fields and crops of the Syracusans would be theirs for the taking, and the rural population made hostages. If the Athenian generals had followed through on Lamachus' advice, they might well have succeeded in taking Syracuse.

§ Not the Megara in Greece, but Megara Hyblaea, north of Syracuse.

¶ After appointing three generals, Athens seems not to have given any one of them top rank or made allowances for differences of opinion. Nicias was senior commander, but Alcibiades had the most forceful personality.

The Messanans replied that they could not receive him within their walls, although they would provide him with a market outside. So he sailed back to Rhegium.

Immediately upon his return the generals manned and provisioned sixty ships out of the whole fleet and coasted along to Naxos, leaving the rest of the fleet behind them at Rhegium with one general. After they were welcomed by the Naxians, they sailed along the coast to Catana. But when the people of Catana did not receive them (there were men there who were on the side of the Syracusans), they were escorted to the river Terias.* Here they camped, and the next day sailed in single file to Syracuse with most of their ships (except for ten ships they sent on ahead to sail into the Great Harbor to see if any ships had been launched) and to proclaim by herald from shipboard that the Athenians were come to restore the Leontines to their country,† being their allies and kinsmen. Any Leontines, therefore, who were in Syracuse should leave it without fear and join their friends and benefactors, the Athenians. After making this proclamation and reconnoitering the city and the harbors, and the features of the country they would have to make their base of operations in the war, they sailed back to Catana.

———

Now that the Athenians were able to use Catana as a base, they tried again, but again failed, to make an alliance with Rhegium. Then a new development changed the fate of the expedition.

———

[6.53] Back at Catana, the Athenians found that the *Salaminia*‡ had come from Athens for Alcibiades with orders for him to sail home to answer the charges the city had brought against him, along with certain other soldiers who had likewise been accused of sacrilege in the matter of the Mysteries and the herms.§

Those in Athens, after the departure of the expedition, had continued to investigate as actively as ever the facts of the Mysteries and of the herms. [6.60] The Athenian Assembly was angry and suspicious of the persons charged in the affair of the Mysteries, and they thought that what had taken place was part of an oligarchical and monarchical conspiracy.

---

* A river south of Catana, near Leontini, now Fiumi di San Leandro.

† See 6.6 above and note.

‡ A very fast ship used for special errands.

§ See 6.28 above.

Because they were angry about this matter, many respectable men had been already put in prison. Far from showing any signs of abating, public feeling grew more savage every day, and more arrests were made. Finally, one of those in custody,* who was considered to be the guiltiest of all, was persuaded by a fellow prisoner to make a confession—whether true or not is a matter on which there are two opinions, since no one has been able, either then or since, to say for certain who did the deed. In spite of that, the first prisoner found arguments to persuade him, that even if he had not done the deed himself, he ought to save himself by receiving a promise of immunity, and free the city from its present suspicions, because he would be more certain of safety if he confessed after being promised immunity than if he denied his guilt and was then brought to trial. So he made a confession, involving himself and others in the affair of the herms.

The Athenian people were pleased to at last, as they supposed, get at the truth. Previously they had thought it intolerable that they had not been able to learn who had conspired against the people. They let the informer go, along with all the others he had not denounced. They brought the accused to trial and executed as many as were caught. They condemned to death those who had fled and offered a reward to anyone who killed them. In this it was, after all, not clear whether those accused had been punished unjustly, but for the moment the rest of the city was apparently better off.

[6.61] As for Alcibiades, because the same enemies were after him who had attacked him before he sailed out, the Athenians took a harsh view of him. Because they thought they knew the truth about the herms, they believed more firmly than ever that the affair of the Mysteries also, in which he had been implicated, was his work, and that he had done it for the same reason and with the same intent: to conspire against the democracy.

While this agitation was going on, it happened that a small force of Spartans had advanced as far as the Isthmus because they had something to do with the Boeotians. It was now believed that this force had come by previous arrangement at Alcibiades' instigation, not for the benefit of the Boeotians, and that, if the citizens had not acted on the information received and forestalled them by making arrests, the city would have been betrayed. They went so far as to spend one night armed in the temple of

---

* We know from his own surviving speeches that this informer was the orator Andocides.

Theseus within the walls.* The friends also of Alcibiades at Argos were just at this time suspected of a plot against the Argive democracy, and for that reason the Argive hostages who had been deposited in the islands by the Athenians† were surrendered to the Argive people to be executed. In short, everywhere something was found to create suspicion against Alcibiades. It was therefore decided to bring him to trial and execute him.

The *Salaminia* was sent to Sicily for him and the others named in the accusation. The envoys were instructed to order him to come and answer the charges against him, but not to arrest him, because the Athenians wished to avoid causing any agitation in the army or among the enemy in Sicily. Above all they wished to keep the Mantineans and Argives there, because they thought it was because of Alcibiades that these had been persuaded to join the expedition.‡

Alcibiades, with his own ship and his fellow accused, sailed off with the *Salaminia* from Sicily, as though to return to Athens. These men went with the ship as far as Thurii,§ and there they left the ship and disappeared because they were afraid to go home for trial with such prejudice against them. The crew of the *Salaminia* stayed some time looking for Alcibiades and his companions, and at length, since these were nowhere to be found, they left and sailed away. Alcibiades, now an outlaw, crossed in a boat not long afterward from Thurii to the Peloponnese. The Athenians passed sentence of death by default on him and his companions.

———

In the first major confrontation of the war, the Athenians managed to seize a favorable position near Syracuse after tricking the Syracusans into leaving it undefended. The Syracusans hurried into position and a battle took place, hard fought by both sides until the Athenians prevailed. Their gains were small, though, due to their inferiority in cavalry. They sent for more horsemen from Athens, while the Syracusans, for their part, asked the Corinthians and Spartans to assist them.

———

[6.88.7] When the Syracusans arrived at Corinth they made a speech calling on the Corinthians to assist them on the grounds of their common

---

* Not the temple of Hephaestus in the Athenian Agora now popularly known as the Theseion, but a temple north of the Acropolis. It was often used as a mustering point for those defending the city.

† These prisoners were oligarchs who in the summer of 416 had been defeated by democrats and turned over to the Athenians.

‡ See 6.16 above and note; Alcibiades had special connections to these two cities.

§ An Athenian colony on the southern end of the instep of the Italian boot.

origin.* The Corinthians immediately voted with great eagerness to defend Syracuse and sent envoys along with the Syracusans to Sparta in order to persuade the Spartans also to fight the Athenians more openly at home and to send aid to Sicily.

When the envoys from Corinth reached Sparta, they found Alcibiades there with his fellow refugees. They had come straight from Thurii in a cargo ship, first to Cyllene in Elis, and afterward from there to Sparta, because the Spartans had sent for him. He had been guaranteed safe conduct by them (he'd been afraid of them because of the battle at Mantinea).†
The result was that the Corinthians, the Syracusans, and Alcibiades all made the same request in the assembly of the Spartans and succeeded in persuading them. But the ephors and the authorities, though they decided to send envoys to the Syracusans to prevent their surrendering to the Athenians, were not inclined to send any military assistance. So Alcibiades now came forward and sharpened the Spartans' resolve, and he stirred the Spartans by speaking as follows:

[6.89] "I am forced first to speak to you about the prejudice with which I am regarded. I do not want suspicion to make you disinclined to listen to me about matters of concern to us both. The connection with you as your *proxenoi*,‡ which the ancestors of our family for some reason renounced, I personally have tried to renew by my good intentions toward you, especially on the occasion of the disaster at Pylos.§ But although I have maintained this friendly attitude, you nonetheless chose to negotiate the Peace with the Athenians through my enemies,¶ and thus to strengthen them and bring dishonor on me. Therefore you had no right to complain if I turned to the Mantineans and Argives and thwarted and injured you on other occasions.

"The time has now come when those among you, who in the bitterness of the moment may have been unfairly angry with me, should look at the

---

* See 6.6 above and note.

† See 6.6 above and note.

‡ Alcibiades, like his guardian (see 2.34.7), Pericles, was a member of the aristocratic Alcmeonid family, which had been under a curse since their ancestors had murdered some suppliants. A *proxenos* had certain privileges in a foreign city-state that considered him an ally.

§ Pylos was the site of a major Athenian victory in 425 BC, where the Spartan ships had not been able to come to the aid of their army on land (see 6.16 above and note).

¶ The Peace of Nicias. Nicias, who might have been thought a political rival (and was until recently a co-commander), is here described as an enemy.

matter in its true light and take a different view. Anyone who thinks the worse of me because I have leaned rather to the side of the common people should not suppose that he has reason to be angry with me. We Athenians have always been hostile to tyrants, and the people are called democrats because they oppose authoritarians. So for us democracy means the leadership of the common people. And because democracy was the city's government, one had to conform to established practice. But we* tried to behave more moderately in public affairs than the licentious attitude prevailing at the time. There were others, now and in the past, who tried to encourage the common people to do what was wrong. They were the ones who banished me.

"We worked on behalf of the whole people because we thought it right to maintain the kind of government under which the city had been its greatest and most free, and as we had inherited it. As for democracy, those who have sense understood what it was, and I as much as anyone the more because I have been injured by it. There is, however, nothing new to be said of this acknowledged folly. Meanwhile I did not think it safe to withdraw from it while you were my enemies.

[6.90] "So much then about the attacks against me. Now I call your attention to the questions you must consider and about which (since I know more about it) I need to speak.

"We sailed to Sicily first to conquer, if possible, the Sicilians, and after them the Greeks in Italy, and finally to assail the empire and citizens of Carthage.† If all or most of these plans succeeded, we were then going to attack the Peloponnese, bringing with us the entire force of Greeks we had acquired and hiring many foreigners as well, such as Iberians‡ and other foreign peoples who are considered particularly warlike. We would also have built many triremes in addition to those we have already, because timber is plentiful in Italy. With this fleet blockading the Peloponnese from the sea, and assailing it with foot-soldiers by land, taking some cities by storm and building siege walls around others, we hoped to con-

---

* In this and the following sentences Alcibiades uses "we" to refer to himself and his family.

† In chapter 6.15.2, Thucydides describes the conquest of Carthage as having been Alcibiades' ultimate goal, which was not necessarily shared by other members of the Athenian Assembly. The conquest of the rest of Greece (described in what follows) was not discussed on that occasion either, at least according to Thucydides.

‡ Iberians (a Celtic people) had immigrated to the western part of Sicily from Spain.

quer it easily, and after that to rule over the whole of the Greek world. Money and grain meanwhile would be more easily obtained from these cities and allow us to better carry out these plans without using our own revenue.

[6.91] "You have thus heard the history of the present expedition from the man who knows most accurately what our objectives were. The generals who remain in charge, if they can, will carry out these objectives. So you must understand that the Syracusans will not survive unless you come to help them, for the Sicilians are inexperienced, but if their forces were united they might even now be saved. The Syracusans alone, who have already been beaten in one battle with all their people and blockaded from the sea, will be unable to withstand the Athenian force that is now there. And if that city is conquered, all Sicily falls as well, and Italy immediately afterward. And the danger I have spoken of will, before long, arrive from there and fall upon you.

"So you need to think not only about Sicily but about the Peloponnese as well, if you do not immediately do as I've told you and send troops to Syracuse, troops that can row their ships themselves and fight as hoplites the moment that they land*—and what I consider to be even more important than troops, a Spartiate as commanding officer to discipline the forces already there and compel the unwilling to serve. That way the friends that you have already will become more confident, and those who have doubts will be encouraged to join you.

"Meanwhile you must carry on the war here more openly,† so that the Syracusans will see you have not forgotten them and will defend themselves, and also so that the Athenians will be less able to send reinforcements to their troops. You must fortify Decelea‡ in Attica. That is what the Athenians are always most afraid of and the only thing they think they have not experienced in the present war. The surest method of harming an enemy is to find out what they most fear, and once you know

---

* Ordinarily, oarsmen and hoplites belonged to different branches of the military. If oarsmen could also fight in armor, then each ship could bring over a greater number of infantrymen.

† Sparta had not "carried on war" with Athens, officially, since the Peace of Nicias in 421, but had made covert or nonmilitary moves that were obviously hostile.

‡ Decelea was a town thirteen or fourteen miles north of Attica and roughly the same distance east of Boeotia, hence of strategic value for the Spartans (see 7.19.2 and 7.27–28 below).

it to choose that means of attack. Presumably, every state knows better than anyone else what their own weak points are and fears for these. Your benefits from holding Decelea will cause problems for your enemies. Many of these problems I shall not discuss, but will only mention the most important. Most of the property in the countryside will automatically become yours, either captured or left behind. Also the Athenians will right away be deprived of their revenues from the silver mines at Laurium,* of their current profits from their land and from the law courts, and above all of the payments from their allies, which will be scanted by those who incline toward you because they'll see you devoting your strength to the war.

[6.92] "The zeal and speed with which all this shall be done depends, Spartans, on you. I am quite confident that you can do it, and I doubt I am mistaken.

"Meanwhile I hope that none of you will think any worse of me if, after having before this seemed a lover of my country, I now join its worst enemies in attacking it. I hope that no one will suspect that what I say is the usual zeal of an exile. I am an outlaw from the injustice of those who drove me away, but not, if you choose to believe me, a stranger to your service. *You* are not my worst enemies—you only harmed your foes—but rather those who have made enemies of their friends. Love of country is not something I feel when I'm wronged but what I felt when my citizen rights were protected.

"Indeed, I don't believe I'm attacking a country that's still mine. Rather, I'm trying to recover one that is mine no longer. The true lover of his country is not the man who consents to lose it unjustly and does not attack it, but the one who longs for it so much as to go to any length to recover it.

"Thus, Spartans, I ask you without hesitation to use me for danger and trouble of every kind. I ask you to remember an argument that everyone can make, that if I did you great harm as an enemy, I could likewise do you good service as a friend, because I know the plans of the Athenians while I only guessed about yours.

"As to yourselves, I ask you to think that you are deliberating about matters of the greatest importance to you. I urge you to send without

---

* The silver mines at Laurium (worked by slave labor) allowed Athens to produce their own coins and were an important source of revenue for the city.

delay expeditions both to Sicily and Attica. You'll protect important cities, and you'll destroy the power of Athens both as it now is and as it might become. After this you will dwell in security and be leaders of all Greece, not through force but consent and goodwill."

[6.93] Such were the words of Alcibiades.

The Spartans, who had themselves before intended to march against Athens but were still waiting and considering what to do, at once became much more serious after Alcibiades gave them this information. They considered that they had heard it from the man who best knew the truth of the matter. They now turned their attention to fortifying Decelea and sending immediate aid to the Sicilians. They put Gylippus, son of Cleandridas, in command of the Syracusans and told him to consult with them and with the envoys from Corinth and arrange for assistance to be sent to Sicily in the best and quickest way possible under the circumstances. Gylippus asked the Corinthians immediately to send him two ships to sail for Asine,* and to get ready the other ships they meant to send and have them prepared to sail at the proper time. After agreeing to this, the Corinthian envoys left Sparta.

Meanwhile the Athenian trireme that had been sent by the generals[†] to ask for money and cavalry arrived at Athens from Sicily. After hearing what was wanted, the Athenians voted to send the cavalry and the supplies for the army. And the winter ended, and with it ended the seventeenth year of the war of which Thucydides is the historian.

———

In the following summer (414 BC) the struggle for Syracuse moved to Epipolae, the high ground north of the city. Both sides realized that control of these heights by Athens would allow a walling-off of Syracuse, which, together with a naval blockade, would starve the city into surrender. The Athenians succeeded in seizing Epipolae and building a fort there from which to extend walls to the sea. Several Syracusan attempts to block this walling operation were defeated, but in one of these actions Lamachus, co-commander with Nicias, was killed.

With the walling-off of Syracuse well advanced, it seemed to all parties, even to the Spartan Gylippus, who was on his way to organize defense, that the fate of Syracuse was sealed. But in the seventh and most gripping of his work's eight books, Thucydides illustrates, in minute detail, how the tables turned.

---

* The Asine on the southwest coast of Messana.

† Nicias and Lamachus.

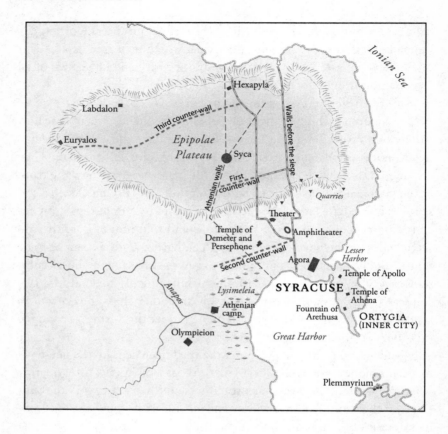

In the summer of 414, the Corinthians, allies of the Spartans, arrived in Syracuse just in time to prevent the Syracusans from surrendering. Right behind them came Gylippus, a highly trained Spartan commander, to organize the Syracusan resistance.

—

[7.2] The Corinthian fleet from Leucas* came to help [the Syracusans] with all speed. One of their commanders, Gongylus, who started last with a single ship, was first to reach Syracuse, a little before Gylippus. Gongylus found the Syracusans on the point of holding an assembly to consider whether to surrender to the Athenians. He prevented them and reassured them by telling them that more ships were on the way and that Gylippus, son of Cleandridas, had been dispatched by the Spartans to

---

* An island on the western coast of Greece.

take command. The Syracusans took courage and immediately marched out with all their forces to meet Gylippus, because they could see that he was now close at hand....

As it happened, he had arrived at a critical moment. The Athenians had already finished a double wall almost a mile long to the Great Harbor, except for a small portion next to the sea. They were still busied with that and the remainder of the circle toward Trogilus on the other sea.* Stones had been laid ready for building the greater part of the distance, and some points had been left half-finished, while others were entirely completed. So close had Syracuse come to being surrounded.

[7.3] At first the Athenians had been thrown into confusion by the sudden approach of Gylippus and the Syracusans, but they formed in order of battle. Gylippus halted at a short distance away and sent ahead a herald to tell them that, if they would evacuate Sicily with all their equipment within five days, he would make a truce. The Athenians treated this proposition with contempt and sent back the herald without an answer. After this both sides began to prepare for action.

When Gylippus saw that the Syracusans were in disorder and did not fall easily into line, he led his troops into open ground. Meanwhile, Nicias did not lead the Athenians forward but remained inactive near his own wall. When Gylippus saw that the Athenians did not come forward, he led his army away to the citadel known as Temnites[†] and spent the night there. On the following day he led out most of his army and drew them up in order of battle before the Athenians' walls to prevent them from going to the relief of any other of their troops. He also dispatched a strong force against Fort Labdalum.[‡] He took it and killed all those he found there. The place was not within sight of the Athenians. On the same day, an Athenian trireme that lay moored off the harbor was captured by the Syracusans.

[7.4] After this the Syracusans and their allies began to build a single wall, starting from the city, in a slanting direction up through Epipolae, so that the Athenians (unless they could hinder the work) might no

---

* Probably on the east coast of Epipolae, north of Syracuse. This wall was a counter-wall, intended to keep Syracuse from receiving supplies and reinforcements.

† Temnites, the site of a sanctuary of Apollo, was inside the wall the Syracusans had been building, Plemmyrium, northwest of the peninsula on which Syracuse was located.

‡ The Athenians had built this fort at the edge of the cliffs facing Megara (see 6.97.5).

longer be able to blockade them.* Meanwhile the Athenians had gone up to the heights because they had now finished their wall down to the sea. Because part of their wall was weak, Gylippus led out his army by night and attacked it. But the Athenians (for they happened to be camping outside the wall) went out to meet him. When Gylippus realized this, he quickly withdrew his men. The Athenians now built their wall higher, and in future guarded it at this point themselves and positioned their allies along the rest of the fortification at points where each could keep guard.

Nicias decided also to fortify a place called Plemmyrium, a promontory above and opposite Syracuse, which juts out and narrows the entrance of the Great Harbor. He thought that the fortification of this place would make it easier to bring in supplies. Also, the Athenians would be able to carry on their blockade from a shorter distance to the Syracusans' harbor, rather than be obliged, as they were at present, to set out from the bottom of the Great Harbor if they were disturbed in any way by the Syracusan navy. Besides that, he now began to pay more attention to the war by sea, because he saw that there was no hope for success by land now that Gylippus had arrived. So he brought over his ships and some troops and built three forts. He placed most of his equipment in these and moored there for the future the larger craft and men-of-war.

Then there first took place not the least of the misfortunes the crews experienced. The water they used was scarce and not available nearby, and whenever the sailors went out for firewood they were killed by the Syracusan cavalry, who were in control of the countryside. A third of the enemy's cavalry had been stationed at the little town of Olympieum in order to prevent plundering incursions on the part of the Athenians at Plemmyrium. Meanwhile, Nicias learned that the rest of the Corinthian fleet was approaching. He sent twenty ships to watch for them near Locris and Rhegium and the approach to Sicily.

[7.5] Meanwhile, Gylippus went on building the wall across Epipolae, using the stones the Athenians had laid down for their own wall. At the same time he constantly led out the Syracusans and their allies and formed them in order of battle in front of the wall. The Athenians formed

* This counter-wall was meant to cut across the line of the Athenian wall so that it could not be completed. If the cross-wall succeeded (as Nicias points out in 7.6 below), all the Athenian wall building would be rendered useless. Epipolae is the name of the high ground north and east of Syracuse, the roughest terrain and a place where the Athenian wall had not been completed.

in battle line against him. When he thought the time was right, he began to attack. A hand-to-hand fight ensued between the walls where the Syracusan cavalry could be of no use. The Syracusans and their allies were defeated. They took up their dead under a truce, while the Athenians erected a trophy.*

After this, Gylippus called the soldiers together and said that the fault was not theirs but his. He had kept their battle lines too much within the walls and had thus deprived them of the services of their cavalry and javelin men. So he would now lead them out a second time. He told them to remember that in physical force they would be fully a match for their opponents, and that they should keep in mind that it would be intolerable if Peloponnesians and Dorians did not feel confident that they could overcome Ionians and islanders and a mixed assortment of people and drive these out of the country.

[7.6] After that, when the time was right, he led his men out again. Now Nicias and the Athenians believed that even if the Syracusans did not want to start a fight, it was necessary for them to keep the Syracusans from building their cross-wall (it already almost overlapped the end of their own wall, and if the cross-wall went any further, it would from that moment make no difference whether they always kept winning skirmishes or whether they never fought at all). So they came out to meet the Syracusans. Gylippus led out his hoplites further from the fortifications than he had before, and so joined battle. He posted his cavalry and javelin men outside the flank of the Athenians in the open space, where the construction of the two walls terminated. His cavalry attacked the left wing of the Athenians that opposed it and routed them. The rest of the Athenian army was as a result defeated by the Syracusans and driven headlong inside their walls. The following night, the Syracusans brought their wall up to the Athenian construction and passed through it. As a result, the Athenians could no longer restrict them, and even if they won a battle, the Syracusans had deprived them of all chance of blockading the city in the future.

[7.7] After this, the remaining twelve vessels of the Corinthians, Ambraciots, and Leucadians sailed into the harbor under the command of Erasinides, a Corinthian. They eluded the Athenian ships on guard and helped the Syracusans complete the remainder of the cross-wall. Meanwhile Gylippus went into the rest of Sicily to raise land and naval forces

---

* A suit of enemy armor set on a wooden stake to mark a victory in battle.

and also to bring over any of the cities that either were lukewarm in the cause or had previously kept out of the war altogether. Syracusan and Corinthian envoys were dispatched to Sparta and Corinth to get another force sent over, in any way possible, either in cargo vessels or transports, or in any other manner likely to be useful, because the Athenians were also sending for reinforcements. The Syracusans proceeded to man a fleet and to practice, intending to try their fortune in this way also, and in other respects became very confident.

[7.8] When Nicias realized this and saw that the strength of the enemy and his own difficulties were increasing every day, he sent a message to Athens. He had before sent frequent reports of events as they occurred and felt it especially necessary for him to do so now, because he thought that they were in a desperate position, and that, unless they sent reinforcements now, they could not survive. He was afraid, however, that the messengers, either through inability to speak, or through failure of memory, or from a wish to please the common people, might not report the truth. So he thought it best to write a letter, to ensure that the Athenians would know his own opinion without its being lost in transmission and would be able to decide based on the real facts. His emissaries left with the letter and his verbal instructions. He then attended to the affairs of his army, and now he was more careful to uphold his defense and to avoid any unnecessary danger.

[7.10] As winter came on, the emissaries sent by Nicias came to Athens and gave the verbal messages entrusted to them, answered any questions that were asked of them, and delivered Nicias' letter. The clerk of the city now came forward and read out to the Athenians the letter, which was as follows:

[7.11] "What we have done up to now, Athenians, has been made known to you by many other letters. Now it's time for you to become equally familiar with our present condition and to plan accordingly. We had defeated the Syracusans against whom we were sent in most of our engagements, and we had built the fortifications we are now occupying. Then Gylippus arrived from Sparta with an army from the Peloponnese and from some of the cities in Sicily. In our first battle with him we were victorious. In the battle on the following day, we were overpowered by a multitude of cavalry and javelin men and compelled to retire within our lines. We have now, therefore, been forced by the numbers of the opposition to stop building a wall around Syracuse and to remain inactive. We are unable to make use of all the forces we have because a large portion of our hoplites is occupied in the defense of our lines. Meanwhile the enemy have carried a single wall past our lines, thus making it impossible for us to blockade them in future, unless someone can attack and take over their cross-wall. As it happens, the besieger in name has become in fact, from the land side at least, the besieged, because we are prevented by their cavalry from going any distance into the countryside.

[7.12] "In addition they have sent an embassy to the Peloponnese to procure reinforcements, and Gylippus has gone to the cities in Sicily to persuade those now neutral to join him in the war and also to get from his allies additional contingents for the land forces and material for the navy. They are planning, as I hear, a combined attack on our walls with their land forces and with their fleet by sea. No one should be surprised that I say 'also by sea.' For as our navy has discovered, though our ships were dry and in good shape and their equipment was intact, during this length of time the ships have become waterlogged; they've been exposed to the sea and their gear has deteriorated. It's impossible for us to beach our ships and dry them thoroughly, because the enemy has as many ships as we, or even more, and we are constantly anticipating an attack. They are clearly preparing to attack, and they will be able to attack when they please, because they do not need to maintain a blockade and can dry out their ships.

[7.13] "But we could hardly dry out our ships even if we had plenty of ships to spare and were relieved of our present need to spend all of our strength on the blockade. Even if we were to relax our vigilance for a short time we would not have the supplies we need, because it is already difficult to bring them in past Syracuse. Our crews have been killed and are still being killed by Syracusan cavalry when we go on expeditions for fuel and forage and because of the long distances required to fetch water. Our slaves are deserting because we have lost our previous advantage. Our foreign seamen, who were forced to serve us, take the first opportunity of departing to their respective cities. The foreign seamen originally seduced by the temptation of high pay, who expected little fighting and large profits, were surprised by the unexpected appearance of a navy against us and the strength of the enemy's resistance. So they are leaving us, either by deserting to the enemy or by availing themselves of one or another of the opportunities for escape that the size of Sicily offers. Some even engage in slave trading themselves and prevail on the captains to take on board slaves from Hyccara* in their place, and thus have ruined the efficiency of our navy.

[7.14] "I do not need to remind you that the time during which a crew is in its prime is short, and that the number of sailors who can start a ship on her way and keep the rowing together is small. But by far my greatest trouble as your general is to control them, since by nature you Athenians are difficult to command. Meanwhile we have no source from which to recruit our crews, and the enemy can harm them from many quarters. Instead, we are forced to depend on the men we brought with us both for supplying crews in service and for making good our losses. Our present allies, Naxos and Catana, are incapable of supplying us. There is only one thing more our opponents still lack: the defection to their side of the places in Italy that supply us, when these see the state we are in, since you are not helping us. The war would be over because we would be besieged and surrender without a fight.

"I might have written to you something more agreeable than this, but certainly not more useful, if you would like to know the real state of things here before making your plans. Besides, I know you like to be told the best part of things, and then blame the messenger if the expectations raised in your minds do not come out as you expect. I thought it safest, then, to tell you the complete truth.

[7.15] "Now do not think that either your generals or your soldiers are to blame. But since now a Sicilian coalition is being formed against us, and an additional army is expected from the Peloponnese, you must now consider—since we do not have enough forces here against our enemies— whether to recall us or to send out another army as large as the present one, with infantry, ships and a large sum of money, and someone to succeed me, since I cannot continue on account of kidney disease.† I think I deserve your indulgence, because I have often served as general while I had my health. But whatever you are going to do, do it at the beginning of spring and without delay, because the enemy will obtain their Sicilian reinforcements shortly, and, after that, those from the Peloponnese. If

---

* On their way to Egesta, the Athenians had sacked the city of Hyccara and enslaved its inhabitants.

† The connection between the kidneys and urination was probably understood by this time. Four different kidney diseases were described by physicians: kidney stones, infection, blood in the urine, and venereal disease. Since we cannot know from which kind Nicias was suffering, it is impossible to say whether the disease affected his judgment.

you do not keep your minds on this, they will elude you, and, as they did before, get here before you."

[7.16] Those were the subjects covered by Nicias in his letter. After the Athenians heard what he said, they refused to accept his resignation but chose two colleagues to assist him. They selected Menander and Euthydemus, two of the officers present with him in Sicily, to fill those places until the new colleagues could get there, so that Nicias might not be left to carry on alone in his sickness. They also voted to send out another army and navy, drawn partly from the Athenians on their register, partly from the allies. As colleagues for Nicias they chose Demosthenes,* son of Alcisthenes, and Eurymedon, son of Thucles. Eurymedon was sent off at once, around the time of the winter solstice, with ten ships, a hundred and twenty talents of silver, and instructions to tell the army that reinforcements would arrive and that care would be taken of them.

[7.17] Demosthenes stayed behind to organize the expedition, intending to start as soon as it was spring. He sent to Athens's allies for troops and meanwhile collected money, ships, and hoplites at home.

[7.18] Meanwhile, the Spartans made preparations for their invasion of Attica. They had resolved to do so and with the encouragement of the Syracusans and Corinthians. They had heard that Athens was about to send reinforcements to Sicily and wished to prevent the invasion from happening. Alcibiades had also emphasized to them that they should fortify Decelea and not stop the war. The Spartans had grown more confident because they believed that Athens, with two wars on her hands, one against themselves and the other against the Sicilians, would be easier to subdue, and because they thought that Athens had been the first to break the truce.... They spent that winter requesting iron from their allies and getting ready the other implements for building their fort at Decelea. Meanwhile they began recruiting at home. They also demanded requisitions from the rest of Peloponnese for an army to be sent out in cargo ships to their allies in Sicily. Winter ended, and with it the eighteenth year of this war of which Thucydides is the historian.

—

Amid the worsening situation for Athens, both at home and on Sicily, Thucydides gives his attention to a secondary episode involving a squad of Thracian merce-

---

* Not the famous fourth-century orator, but the Athenian general who was responsible for the Athenian victory at Pylos in 422 (see p. 171 above).

naries. The random, unprovoked savagery of the event seems, in context, to em-
blematize the terrible toll the war was taking on Greeks and non-Greeks alike.

[7.27] This same summer, thirteen hundred swordsmen arrived at Athens. They were Thracians of the tribe of the Dii, who were supposed to have sailed to Sicily with Demosthenes. Because they had come too late, the Athenians decided to send them back to Thrace where they had come from. Retaining them for the war around Decelea seemed too expensive, because the pay of each man was a drachma a day. Indeed, since Decelea had been first fortified by the whole Peloponnesian army during this summer,* and after that the Peloponnesians had been busy harassing the countryside, with garrisons from various cities relieving one another at stated intervals, Decelea had been doing great harm to the Athenians. In fact, the occupation of Decelea was one of the principal causes of the Athenians' defeat, owing to the destruction of property and loss of men that resulted from it. Previously the Spartan invasions had been short and had not kept the Athenians from enjoying their land the rest of the time. Now the enemy was permanently installed in Attica. Sometimes it was with a large number of troops, at other times it was the regular garrison overrunning the country and stealing property. When the Spartan king Agis was in the field and diligently directing the war, his army did great harm to the Athenians. So the Athenians had been deprived of their entire countryside. More than twenty thousand slaves had deserted, a great part of them craftsmen. All of their sheep and beasts of burden had been lost, and their horses as well; because the Spartan cavalry rode out daily on excursions to Decelea and to guard the country, the Athenians' horses were either lamed by being constantly worked on rocky ground or else wounded by the enemy.

[7.28] Moreover, the transport of provisions from Euboea, which had been done before so much more quickly overland toward Decelea from Oropus, was now accomplished at great expense by sea around Sunium. Everything the city of Athens required had to be imported from abroad, and instead of a city it became a fortress. Summer and winter the Athenians were worn out by having to keep guard on their fortifications, during the day by turns, at night all of them, except for the cavalry, at different military posts or on the city wall. But what most oppressed them was that they had two wars going on at once and had thus reached a pitch

---

* As advised by Alcibiades (see 6.91.1).

of determination that no one would have believed possible if they had heard of it before it happened. For could anyone have imagined that even when besieged by the Peloponnesians entrenched in Attica, instead of withdrawing, the Athenians would still be in Sicily continuing their siege of Syracuse, a city in itself no less significant than Athens? Would anyone have believed that they would show to the Greeks so thoroughly unexpected an impression of strength and audacity such as, at the start of the war, some thought might last one year, some two, none more than three, if the Peloponnesians invaded their country? Now seventeen years after the first invasion, after they had already suffered all the evils of war, they went to Sicily and undertook a new war in no way inferior to the one they had already with the Peloponnesians.

These causes—the great losses from Decelea and the other heavy expenses that fell upon them—caused their financial ruin. It was at this time that they imposed on their subjects, instead of the tribute, the tax of a twentieth upon all imports and exports by sea, which they thought would bring them more money. Their expenditures were now not the same as they were at first, but had grown with the war, while their revenues had been cut off.

[7.29] Thus, not wishing to incur expense in their present want of money, they had immediately sent back the Thracians who had come too late to join Demosthenes. These left under the supervision of Diitrephes. He had been instructed to make use of them if possible during their voyage to injure the enemy, because they were going to pass through the Euripus.* Diitrephes first landed them at Tanagra and hastily snatched some plunder. Then he sailed across the Euripus in the evening from Chalcis in Euboea. He disembarked in Boeotia and led them against Mycalessus.

He passed the night unobserved near the temple of Hermes, not quite two miles from Mycalessus. At daybreak he assaulted and captured the town, not a large one. Its inhabitants were off their guard and did not expect anyone to ever come up so far from the sea to attack them. Their wall was weak, and in some places it had tumbled down while in others it had not been built to any height. Also the gates had been left open because the people felt secure.

The Thracians burst into Mycalessus, sacked the houses and temples,

---

* The Euripus is a narrow strait between the mainland and the island of Euboea, from which it would be easy to disembark.

and butchered the inhabitants, sparing neither youth nor age, but killing everyone they encountered, one after the other, children and women, and even beasts of burden, and whatever other living creatures they saw. (The Thracians are very much like the Persians: most bloodthirsty when they are confident.)* Everywhere confusion reigned and death in all its manifestations, especially when they attacked a boys' school, the largest in the town, into which the boys had just gone, and massacred them all. In short, the disaster that fell on the whole town was unsurpassed in magnitude, and especially because it was so unexpected and terrible.

A type of Thracian warrior known as a peltast *because he often carried a light, crescent-shaped shield called a* peltē. WIKIMEDIA COMMONS

[7.30] Meanwhile the Thebans heard about it and came to the rescue. They overtook the Thracians before they had gone far, recovered the plunder, and drove them in panic to the Euripus and the sea, where the boats that brought them were docked. The greatest slaughter took place when the Thracians were embarking, since they did not know how to

---

* Athenians considered the Thracians (inhabitants of a territory west of the Black Sea and north of the Aegean) to be particularly cruel and uncivilized.

swim.* The men in the boats, when they saw what was going on ashore, had moored them out of bowshot. In the rest of the retreat the Thracians made a very respectable defense against the Theban cavalry, the first forces to attack them. They dashed out and defended themselves using the tactics of their country and lost only a few men in that action. A good number who were after plunder were caught in the town and killed. Altogether the Thracians had two hundred and fifty killed out of thirteen hundred. The Thebans and the rest who came to the aid of Mycalessus lost about twenty, troopers and hoplites, along with Scirphondas, one of the Boeotarchs.† The Mycalessians lost a large part of their population.

———

Having given us a brief glimpse of the Mycalessus horror, Thucydides returns to the Sicilian campaign. Reinforcements had by now begun to arrive for both the Athenians and the Syracusans, and the field of combat was becoming very crowded.

———

[7.42] While the Syracusans were preparing for a second attack by both land and sea, Demosthenes‡ and Eurymedon arrived with the reinforcements from Athens. These consisted of about seventy-three ships, including some from their allies: nearly five thousand hoplites, Athenian and allied; and many javelin men, Greek and foreign; and slingers and archers and every other warrior on a corresponding scale.

The Syracusans and their allies were for the moment not a little dismayed at the idea that there was to be no limit or ending to their dangers. They saw that despite the Spartan fortification at Decelea,§ a new army had arrived nearly equal to the former, and that the power of Athens had in every aspect proven so great. Some confidence, however, arose from the difficulties the first Athenian forces had encountered.

Demosthenes saw how matters stood and felt that he could not delay and fare as Nicias had done. Nicias had been formidable when he arrived, but he did not attack Syracuse immediately. He had spent the winter in Catana instead of at once attacking Syracuse, and now he was looked down upon. Gylippus had got ahead of him by arriving with a force from the Peloponnese, which the Syracusans would never have sent

---

* Hellenes found it remarkable that many foreigners did not know how to swim.

† That is, a chief magistrate in Boeotia, the region in which Thebes was the most important city.

‡ See 7.16 above and note.

§ The Spartan fort in Attica (see 6.91 above and note).

for if Nicias had attacked immediately. The Syracusans had imagined that they were a match for him by themselves and would not have discovered their inferiority until they were already blockaded, and, even if they then sent for reinforcements, they would no longer have been as able to profit from their arrival. Demosthenes thought about it and realized that it was now, on the first day after his arrival, that (as Nicias had been) he was most formidable to the enemy. So he decided to lose no time in getting the greatest advantage from the consternation inspired by his army.

Demosthenes saw that the Syracusans' counter-wall,* which prevented the Athenians from blockading them, was a single wall, and that whomever could control the way up to Epipolae† and the camp there would have no difficulty in seizing the wall because no one would be expecting an attack. So he acted in all haste to make the attempt, thinking that this strategy would be the quickest way to end the war. He would either succeed and take Syracuse or lead the army back instead of wasting the lives of the Athenians serving in the expedition and the resources of his city. So first the Athenians went out and laid to waste the lands of the Syracusans around the Anapus River.‡ They were as victorious as they had been at first by land and by sea, because the Syracusans did not oppose them in either, except with their cavalry and javelin men from the Olympieion.§

[7.43] Next, Demosthenes resolved to try to destroy the counter-wall¶ first by means of siege machines.** But the siege machines that he brought up were burned down by the enemy fighting from the wall, and the rest of his forces were driven back after he attacked at many different points. So he determined to delay no longer, and, having obtained the consent of Nicias and his fellow commanders, he proceeded to execute his plan of attacking Epipolae.

By day it seemed impossible to approach and climb up without being observed, so Demosthenes ordered provisions for five days and took all

* A counter-wall had been built by the Syracusans as a defense against the Athenian fortifications.

† A hilly area northwest of Syracuse where the Athenians had built a fort and had begun to build some fortification walls.

‡ A river southwest of Syracuse.

§ A sanctuary southwest of Syracuse.

¶ See note p. 210.

** Possibly battering rams, since they did not have large siege engines (see appendix).

the masons and carpenters, and other things, such as arrows and every-thing else they might need for the work of fortification if they were suc-cessful. Then at the beginning of night,* he set out for Epipolae with Eurymedon and Menander and the whole army, leaving Nicias behind inside the walls.

Demosthenes came up by the hill of Euryelus.... His men were not observed by the enemy's guards, so they went up to the fort the Syra-cusans had there and took it and killed part of the garrison. Most of the Syracusans, however, escaped and warned the other Syracusan camps. There were three of these camps on Epipolae, all defended by outer walls. One was manned by Syracusans, one by other Sicilians, and one by other allies. They also alerted the six hundred Syracusans who formed the original garrison for this part of Epipolae. These at once advanced against the assailants. But Demosthenes and the Athenians engaged them and, after a sharp resistance, immediately pushed on, eager to achieve the object of their attack without delay. Meanwhile others, from the start of the operation, were seizing the counter-wall of the Syracusans, which had been abandoned by its garrison, and tearing down its fortifications.

The Syracusans and their allies, and Gylippus with the troops under his command, advanced to the rescue from the outer walls. They were astonished (a night attack was an audacity which they had never ex-pected) and at first were compelled to retreat. But the Athenians, because they had been victorious, now advanced in some disorder. They wanted to make their way as quickly as possible through all the enemy forces that had not yet joined in the fight, without relaxing their attack or giving the enemy time to rally. The Boeotians† were the first to confront them, at-tack them, and rout them, and force them to retreat.

[7.44] The Athenians now fell into great disorder and confusion. It was not easy to get from either side a detailed account of what happened. In daytime, certainly, combatants have a clearer idea of what is happening (though even then by no means did they know everything), since no one knows much of anything happening beyond his immediate area. But in a night battle (and this was the only one that occurred between large armies during the war), how could anyone know anything for certain? Although there was a bright moon, they saw one another only as men do by moonlight. They could distinguish the form of a body, but could not

---

* Night attacks in Greek warfare were very rare.

† Allies of the Syracusans.

tell for certain whether it was that of a friend. Both sides had great numbers of hoplites moving around in a small space. Some of the Athenians were already defeated, while others were arriving, still unconquered, for their first attack. A large part also of the rest of their forces either had only just arrived or were still coming up, so they did not know which way to march. Because of the rout that had taken place everything in front of them was now in confusion, and it was difficult to recognize anything because of the shouting. The victorious Syracusans and allies were cheering one another on with loud cries, by night the only possible means of communication, and meanwhile engaging all who came against them. The Athenians were looking around for one another, thinking everyone in front of them were enemies even though these might have been friends who were now fleeing. They were constantly asking for the password, which was their only means of recognizing one another. That not only caused great confusion among themselves because they were asking all at once, but also made the password known to the enemy. But they could not learn their enemies' password because the Syracusans were winning and not scattered, and thus less easily mistaken. So if a more powerful group of Athenians encountered some enemies, these enemies were able to escape because they knew the Athenians' password, but when they themselves were unable to give the enemy's password, they were killed.

But what hurt them as much, or indeed more than anything else, was the singing of the paean.* That caused confusion because it was nearly the same on both sides. The Athenians were frightened whenever the Argives and Corcyraeans and any other Dorian peoples in their own army raised their paean, no less than did the enemy. In the end, once most of the army had been thrown into confusion, they ended up colliding with one another in many parts of the field, friends with friends and fellow citizens with fellow citizens. They terrified one another and even came to blows and could be parted only with difficulty. In the pursuit many perished by throwing themselves down from the cliffs, because the road down from Epipolae was narrow. Some got down safely into the plain, and many, especially those who belonged to the first group of attackers, escaped because they were more familiar with the locale. But some of the more recent arrivals lost their way and wandered around the

---

* Soldiers from certain Greek cities sang a paean (a prayer to Apollo to avert danger in battle) before battle, although the Athenians did not.

countryside. In the morning, the Syracusan cavalry rounded up these men and killed them.

[7.45] The next day the Syracusans set up two trophies, one on the hill of Epipolae where the ascent had been made, and the other on the spot where the first Athenian assault had been stopped by the Boeotians. The Athenians recovered their dead under a truce. A great many of the Athenians and allies had been killed, although still more weapons were captured than could be accounted for by the number of the dead, because some of those who were compelled to leap down from the cliffs died, but others survived.

[7.46] After this the Syracusans recovered their old confidence as a result of such an unexpected stroke of good fortune. They sent Sicanus with fifteen ships to Acragas,* where there was a revolution, to see if they could get that city to join them. Gylippus again went by land around the rest of Sicily to procure reinforcements. He now hoped that he could take the Athenian walls by storm because of what had happened at Epipolae.

[7.47] In the meantime, the Athenian generals were discussing the disaster that had occurred and their army's complete loss of morale. They saw they had been unsuccessful in their endeavors and that the soldiers' declining health had been worn out by their stay. These had become exhausted by sickness for two reasons: first because it was the season of the year in which men were weakest, and then because the area where they had camped was marshy and rough.† The whole situation seemed hopeless. Demosthenes thought they ought not to stay there any longer. In keeping with his original idea of risking the attempt upon Epipolae (since that had failed), he voted to leave without delay while it was still possible to cross the sea and the reinforcements just arrived on ships might give them an advantage. He also said it would be more profitable for Athens to carry on the war against those building fortifications in Attica‡ than it was to continue fighting against the Syracusans. It was no longer easy to defeat them; besides, it did not make sense to spend large sums of money to no purpose by continuing the siege.

* Modern Agrigento.

† In addition to malnutrition, dampness, and heat, their weakness appears to have been caused by malaria, which they did not know was carried by mosquitoes.

‡ Referring to the Spartan occupation of the fortress at Decelea.

[7.48] That is what Demosthenes had come to understand. Nicias did not deny that the state of their affairs was bad, but he did not wish to reveal that they were weak. Nor did he wish to have it reported to the enemy that the Athenians were voting for retreat openly, in the presence of many witnesses, because in that case they would be much less likely to retreat when they wanted to without being discovered. Moreover, the fact that the affairs of the enemy would soon be in a worse state than their own—he had learned more about these than the others had—gave him reason to hope, if the Athenians persevered in the siege. They would wear down the Syracusans by depriving them of money, especially with the more extensive command of the sea now given them by their current navy. Besides this, there was a party in Syracuse that wished to betray the city to the Athenians;* these people were sending him messages and telling him not to abandon the siege. He understood this, though in reality he was still wavering and debating which of the two courses to take and hoping to see his way more clearly. But in his public speech at the time he said that he would not let the army retreat.

Nicias was sure the Athenians would never approve of the army's returning unless they had authorized it to do so. They were the ones who would vote about the army and its actions, and they would not acknowledge the facts after listening to other people's assessment of them, but would go along with whomever denounced them persuasively. He said that many, indeed most, of the soldiers at Syracuse who now so loudly claimed to be in danger, once they were in Athens would claim the opposite just as loudly and would say that their generals had betrayed them because they had been bribed to retreat. Therefore, because he understood the natures of the Athenians, he would rather not be put to death under a dishonorable charge and an unjust sentence at Athenian hands. Instead he preferred to take his chances and die, if necessary, by the hand of the enemy, as an individual. Besides, the Syracusans were in a worse state than his own forces. What with paying mercenaries, expenditures for fortified posts, and now for a full year maintaining a large navy, they were already at a loss and would soon be at an impasse. They had already spent two thousand talents and incurred heavy debts besides. They could not lose even a small fraction of their present force because they could not pay for it without ruining their chance for success; they depended more on mercenaries rather than on soldiers required to serve (as his

---

* As had happened at Melos (see 5.116).

own were). He therefore said that they ought to stay and carry on the siege and not leave after being defeated merely because of money,* since they had more of that than the Syracusans did.

[7.55] The Syracusans had now gained a decisive naval victory (previously they had been afraid of the reinforcements brought by Demosthenes). The Athenians were in deep despair, and their disappointment was also great, and even greater was their regret that they had come on the expedition to Sicily.... They had failed in most of their attempts and were already unsure what to do. Now that they had been defeated at sea, which they had not thought possible, they were thus more at a loss than ever.

[7.56.] The Syracusans immediately began to sail freely along the harbor and decided to block its mouth so that the Athenians might not be able to get away from them in the future even if they wished. Indeed, the Syracusans were no longer considering only how to save themselves but also how they might keep the Athenians from escaping. They were thinking—and thinking correctly, because of what had recently happened—that they were now much stronger than the Athenians, and that if they could conquer the Athenians and their allies by land and sea, they would win great glory in Greece. Some Greeks would immediately be set free, and others released from fear, because the remaining forces of Athens would from now on be unable to sustain any war they had brought against them. Meanwhile they, the Syracusans, would be regarded as the authors of this deliverance, and they would be admired not just by all men now living but also by posterity. The struggle was worth it not only because they had overcome the Athenians as well as their numerous allies, but also because they had not done so alone, but with the men who had fought alongside them. They had become leaders side by side with the Corinthians and Spartans....

———

Thucydides now catalogs the allies on both sides of the conflict, who had come to Sicily from all over the Greek world, and then continues:

———

[7.59] The Syracusans and their allies thought it would win them great glory if they could follow up their recent victory in the naval battle by capturing the whole Athenian encampment, without allowing them es-

---

* In response to Demosthenes, who had argued that they should not continue to spend money on a lost cause (see 7.47.4).

cape either by sea or by land. They began at once to close the Great Harbor by means of boats, cargo ships, and triremes moored broadside across its mouth (nearly a mile wide), and they made all other arrangements in case the Athenians again ventured to fight at sea. There was, in fact, nothing at all small in their intentions.

[7.60] When the Athenians saw them close off the harbor and had other information about what they were planning, they called a council of war. The generals and commanding officers assembled and discussed the difficulties of the situation. Among other considerations, they no longer had provisions for immediate use (they had sent messengers ahead to Catana to tell them not to send any, because they thought they were going away). They would not have any provisions in future unless they could command the sea. They therefore determined to evacuate their upper walls and to enclose with a cross-wall and garrison a small space close to the ships, only just sufficient to hold their stores and their sick. They would man all their ships, seaworthy or not, with every man that could be spared from the rest of their land forces, to fight it out at sea, and, if victorious, to go to Catana. If they did not win, they would burn their ships, form in close order, and retreat by land for the nearest friendly place they could reach, Greek or barbarian. This plan was no sooner settled than carried out.

They came down gradually from the upper walls and manned all their vessels, compelling all to go on board who were of age to be in any way of use. They thus succeeded in manning about one hundred and ten ships in all. They put on board these ships archers and javelin men from the Acarnanians and other allies. They made all other provisions that their plans and necessity compelled them to do.

All was now nearly ready. Nicias saw that the soldiers were disheartened by their unprecedented and decided defeat at sea and were eager to fight it out as soon as possible because of the scarcity of provisions. He first called them all together and said the following:

[7.61] "Athenian soldiers and allies: The coming struggle is of common concern to us all, because life and country are at stake for us quite as much as for the enemy. If our fleet wins the day, each of us can see his native city again. You must not lose heart or be like men without any experience. If such men fail in a first attempt, ever after they are afraid that the future will be disastrous. But let the Athenians among you who have already had experience of many wars, and the allies who have joined us in so many expeditions, remember the surprises of war. They must hope that fortune will not be always against us and prepare to fight again in a manner worthy of the number you see yourselves to be.

[7.62] "Now we have provided for whatever we thought would be of use against the crowd of vessels in such a narrow harbor, and against the force on the decks of the enemy, from which we suffered in the past. All this has been considered together with the helmsmen, as far as our means have allowed. Many archers and javelin men will go on board. This is a large number that we would not employ in an action in the open sea, where we know we would be crippled by the weight of the ships. But in the present land battle we are forced to make on board ships, all these fighters will be useful. We have also made changes in the construction of our ships that we needed to make to confront theirs; and against the thickness of their ships' cheeks,* which have caused us the greatest harm, we have provided grappling irons.† These will keep an attacking ship from backing water after charging at us, if the soldiers on deck here do their duty. For in this case we are absolutely compelled to fight a land battle from the decks of the fleet, and it seems to be in our interest not to back water ourselves and not to let the enemy do so, especially since the land, except for what may be held by our infantry, is hostile territory.

[7.63] "You must remember this and fight on as long as you can and do not let yourselves be driven ashore. When your ship falls in with theirs you must make up your minds not to break ranks until you have swept the hoplites from the enemy's deck. I say this as much to the hoplites as to the seamen, because it is a job for the men on deck. It is possible for us even now to win mostly with our infantry. The sailors I both advise and require not to be overcome by our misfortunes, now that we have our decks better armed and a greater number of ships. Keep in mind that it is a pleasure worth preserving that you are regarded as Athenians even though you are not, because of your knowledge of our dialect‡ and imitation of our manners, and as such have been honored throughout Greece. You have had your full share of the advantages of our empire, not least because of the fear you inspired in our subjects and in the much greater share you have had in protecting them from being wronged. You are the only ones who have freely shared our empire with us; do not betray it

---

* The sides of the prows of the ships (see 7.36.2).

† Iron-clawed instruments attached to ropes to be thrown at the enemy's ships.

‡ Dialects varied all over Greece, because the distinctive mountainous geography of the area kept the various settlements apart from one another.

now, but look down on the Corinthians as inferior, since you have often beaten them, as well as the Sicilians, none of whom dared to stand against us when our navy was in its prime. We ask you to defend yourselves against them, and to show that even in sickness and disaster your skill is better than other men's good fortune and strength.

[7.64] "As for the Athenians among you, again I remind you: You left behind you in Athens no more such ships in your docks than these, no more hoplites in the prime of their strength. If you do anything but conquer, our enemies here will immediately sail *there*, and those that are left at Athens will be unable to repel their attackers and the reinforcements that will follow them. Here, you will fall immediately into the hands of the Syracusans—you remember the intentions with which you attacked them—and at home, your countrymen will fall into the hands of the Spartans. Since the fate of both thus depends on this single battle, now, if ever, stand fast. Remember, every one of you, that you who are now going on board are the army and navy of the Athenians and all that is left of the state and the great name of Athens. In her defense, if any man has an advantage in skill or courage, there is no better time for him to show it, and thus save himself and save us all."

[7.65] After this address, Nicias at once gave orders to man the ships. Meanwhile, Gylippus and the Syracusans could perceive by the preparations they saw going on that the Athenians meant to fight at sea. They had also found out about the grappling irons, against which they had provided by stretching hides over the prows and much of the upper part of their ships, so that the irons when thrown would slip off without taking hold. When all was ready, the generals and Gylippus addressed them in the following terms:

[7.66] "Syracusans and allies, most of you seem to know that this contest will be about the glorious character of our past achievements and the no less glorious results in the coming battle. Otherwise, you would never have thrown yourselves with such determination into it. And if anyone is not as fully aware of the facts as he should be, we will declare them to him. The Athenians came to this country first to enslave Sicily, and after that, if they accomplished that, to enslave the Peloponnese and the rest of Greece. They already possessed the greatest empire yet known among the Greeks, both in present times and in the past. You were the first men to stand up against their navy, which had made them masters everywhere. You have already defeated them in the previous naval battles and you will in all likelihood defeat them again now. When men have had an unexpected fall from what they are proud of, they give way despite their actual strength. That is likely to be what the Athenians are experiencing.

[7.67] "As for ourselves, in the past we had strength, with which we dared to oppose them in the days when we lacked skill. We are now more certain of that strength, and the conviction has now been added to it that we must be the best seamen of the time because we have conquered the best. So the hope of every one of us is doubled. Where there is the greatest hope, there is usually also the greatest enthusiasm for action. We know the methods of combating us they have tried to find by copying our armament, and we will not be unprepared for any of them. But they— although they will have a large number of hoplites on their decks, contrary to their custom, and while many javelin men (born landlubbers, surely, Acarnanians and others) will be on board—how will these not be a problem for the ships? They will be confused because they do not know how to throw their weapons while remaining seated, unable to run as they usually do.*

"The Athenians will not be helped by the number of their ships (just in case some of you are alarmed at the odds being against you). A quantity of ships in a confined space will be slower in executing the maneuvers required, and thus easily harmed by our preparations. In fact, you must realize (as we are credibly informed) that the truth is that they are overwhelmed by their sufferings and forced into desperate action because of the hopelessness of their present situation. They are running this risk not because they have confidence in their preparation. Rather, it is because they want to try their chances as best they can. Either they will force their way and sail out, or after that retreat by land, because they cannot be worse off than they are.

[7.68] "Against such disorder, and the fortune which has now betrayed into our hands our bitter enemies, we must fight in anger. We must believe it is entirely lawful for men to take vengeance against an aggressor. At the same time, it is natural for us and (as the proverb has it) sweetest to take vengeance on our enemies. You all know that they are enemies and mortal enemies, since they came here to enslave our country, and if successful they would have inflicted the most miserable suffering on our men and the most indignities on our children and women, and for the whole city, the most shameful ignominy. For that reason no one should pity them or think it will be better for them to go away without doing us

---

* Javelin throwers need to step back and run before throwing their weapons.

further harm. That they will do in any case, even if they win. But if we succeed in punishing them, as we most likely will do, and in returning to all Sicily her ancient freedom strengthened and confirmed, that will be a triumph. The rarest dangers are those in which failure brings the least loss and success the greatest advantage."

[7.69] The Syracusan generals and Gylippus, after speaking to their soldiers, immediately proceeded to man their ships when they saw the Athenians manning theirs. Meanwhile, Nicias was overcome by the present reality confronting him. He saw how great the danger was and that it was already near because they were not yet ready to set out from shore. He thought, as men are apt to think in great crises, that when all has been done, they have still something left to do, and when all has been said, they have not yet said enough. Again he called on the captains one by one, addressing each by his father's name, by his own, and by that of his tribe.* He told each man not to betray his reputation or whatever claim he had to glory, or the innate virtues for which their ancestors were famous. He reminded them of their country, the freest of all, and of the unfettered discretion it allowed to all to live as they pleased. He also said what men would say in such a crisis, things made to serve on all occasions alike with little change, by speakers who do not care if what they say is considered commonplace: appeals to wives, children, and ancestral gods—everything that men call out because they will be useful in the moment of crisis.

Even though he did not believe he had said enough, or what he needed to say, Nicias withdrew and led the troops to the sea. He arranged them in as long a line as he could, in order as far as possible to help sustain the courage of those on board. Demosthenes, Menander, and Euthydemus— the Athenian generals who had taken the command of the ships—set out from their own camp and sailed straight to the barrier across the mouth of the harbor and to the passage that had been left open, with the intention of forcing their way out.

[7.70] The Syracusans and their allies had already put out with about the same number of ships as before. Some of these kept guard at the outlet; the rest guarded all around the remainder of the harbor, in order to attack the Athenians on all sides at once, while the land forces held themselves in readiness at points where the vessels might put into shore. The

---

* An Athenian man was formally known by his own name, his father's name, and the name of his tribe. There were ten tribes, each named for an Athenian hero.

Syracusan fleet was commanded by Sicanus and Agatharchus. Each of them had a wing of the whole force, with Pythen and the Corinthians in the center.

The Athenians, having come up to the barrier, overpowered the ships stationed there with the first shock of their charge, then tried to cut them loose them from their moorings. After that, because the Syracusans and allies were bearing down upon them from all quarters, the action spread from the barrier over the whole harbor and was more violent than any of the preceding battles. On both sides the rowers showed great determination to move their vessels when they were commanded to, and the helmsmen showed great skill in maneuvering, and there was great competition against one another. Once the ships were alongside each other, the soldiers on board took care not to let their service on deck be outdone by the others. In short, every man was determined to prove himself first in his own assigned task.

Since many ships were engaging in a small area (these were the largest fleets fighting in the narrowest space ever known, just short of two hundred in total), there were few regular attacks with rams; there was no opportunity to back water or break the line. But the collisions caused by one ship chancing to run afoul of another, either while fleeing from or attacking a third, were more frequent. During the time that a vessel was coming up to attack an enemy ship, the men on the decks rained javelins, arrows, and stones upon her. But once the ships were side by side, the hoplites tried to board each other's vessels, fighting hand to hand. Because of the narrow space, it often happened that a vessel was attacking an enemy on one side and being attacked itself on another, and two or sometimes more ships thus became entangled around one another, forcing the helmsmen to attend to defense here, offense there, not to one thing at once but many on all sides.

Meanwhile the huge din caused by the number of ships crashing together not only spread terror but made the orders of the boatswains inaudible. The boatswains on either side were shouting in the discharge of their duty and in the heat of the conflict, incessantly calling out orders and appeals to their men. Some urged the Athenians to force the passage out, and now if ever to show their mettle and ensure a safe return to their country. Others called out to the Syracusans and their allies that it would be glorious to prevent the escape of the enemy and exalt their own countries by victory. Meanwhile the generals on either side called out to the captains by name, whenever they saw, in any part of the battle, ships backing ashore without being forced. The Athenians asked whether these were retreating because they thought the hostile shore more welcoming than the sea that had cost them so much labor to conquer. The Syracusans asked the captains if they were fleeing from the fleeing Athenians, who they well knew would be eager to escape in any way they could.

[7.71] Meanwhile, the two armies on shore, while the naval battle hung in the balance, suffered the most agonizing and conflicting emotions. The natives were eager to win more glory than they had already won, while the invaders were afraid they would do even worse than they already had. Because the fate of all the Athenians depended on their fleet, their fear of the future was like nothing they had ever felt before, and because of the uneven terrain they had different views of the sea-battle.* They were close to the scene of action and were not all looking at the same point at once; some saw their friends victorious and took courage, and fell to calling on the gods not to deprive them of salvation. Others had their eyes fixed on the losers, mourned and cried aloud, and, though they were spectators, were more overcome than the actual combatants. Still others were gazing at some spot where the battle was evenly contested. Whenever the strife was protracted and indecisive, their swaying bodies reflected the turmoil of their minds, and they suffered worst of all, ever just within reach of safety or just on the point of destruction. In short, in that same Athenian army, so long as the naval battle remained in doubt, every sound could be heard at once, shrieks, cheers, "We're winning," "We're losing," and all the other different exclamations that a great host would necessarily utter in great peril.

With the men in the fleet it was nearly the same; until at last the Syracusans and their allies, after the battle had lasted a long while, routed the Athenians, and with much shouting and cheering chased them in open rout to the shore. The naval force, one in one direction, another in another, all who had not been captured on the sea now ran ashore and rushed from their ships to their camp. Meanwhile the army, no longer divided, but carried away by one impulse, all with shrieks and groans were unable to endure what had happened. They ran down, some to help the ships, others to guard what was left of their wall, while most of the rest had already begun to consider how they should save themselves. Indeed, the panic of the present moment had never been surpassed. They now suffered very nearly what they had inflicted on the Spartans at Py-

---

* This is a possible translation of the transmitted text.

los.* The Spartans, along with the loss of their fleet, had also lost the men who had crossed over to the island. So now it was the Athenians who had no hope of escaping by land, unless something unexpected happened.

[7.72] The naval battle had been violent, and many ships and lives had been lost on both sides. The victorious Syracusans and their allies now picked up their wrecks and dead and sailed off to the city and set up a trophy.† But the Athenians were overwhelmed by their misfortune and never even thought of asking permission to take up their dead or wrecks. They wished to retreat that very night. Demosthenes, however, went to Nicias and proposed that they should man the ships they had left and make another effort to force their passage out next morning. He said that they still had more ships left that were fit for service than the enemy did—the Athenians had about sixty ships remaining as opposed to fewer than fifty of their enemies. Nicias agreed with him. But though they both wanted to man the vessels, the sailors refused to go on board, so utterly overwhelmed by their defeat that they no longer believed that they were capable of winning.

[7.73] And so they all now decided to retreat by land. But the Syracusan Hermocrates suspected what they would do and thought it would be dangerous to allow a force of that size to retreat by land, establish itself in some other part of Sicily, and renew the war from there. He went and stated his opinion to the authorities. He pointed out that they ought not to let the enemy get away by night, but that all the Syracusans and their allies should immediately march out and block up the roads and seize and guard the passes. The authorities were in complete agreement with him and thought this should be done. But they did not believe that the people would be willing to listen to them. They were taking their ease after a great battle at sea and it was a holiday (there happened to be a sacrifice to Heracles on that date). Most were so happy about the victory that they had begun drinking at the festival, and the authorities could expect them to do anything rather than take up their arms and march out at that moment. For these reasons the magistrates thought it seemed hopeless to pursue the Athenians.

Although Hermocrates had failed to persuade them, on his own he devised the following stratagem: He was afraid the Athenians would pass through the most difficult places during the night and quietly get the

* On Pylos, see 6.89 above and note.

† See 7.5.1.

advantage. So as soon as it was dusk, he sent some friends to the Athenians' camp with some horsemen. They rode up within earshot and called out to some of the men, as though they were friends of the Athenians, and told them to tell Nicias (who in fact had some correspondents who informed him of what went on inside the town) not to lead off the army by night because the Syracusans were guarding the roads, but to make his preparations at his leisure and to retreat during day. After saying this they departed; and those who heard them informed the Athenian generals. [7.74] They stayed where they were for that night on the strength of this message, because they did not think the advice was a trap.

Since after all the Athenians had not set out immediately, they now decided to stay the following day as well to give the soldiers time to pack up as best they could the most useful equipment and leave everything else behind. They would start out only with what was strictly necessary for subsistence. Meanwhile, the Syracusans and Gylippus marched out and blocked up the roads throughout the country by which the Athenians were likely to pass. The Syracusans kept guard at the fords of the streams and rivers and posted themselves where they could receive the Athenians and thought they would be best positioned to block them. Meanwhile, their fleet sailed up to the beach and towed off the Athenians' ships. (A few had been burned intentionally by the Athenians themselves.) The Syracusans lashed the remaining ships to their own at their leisure, where each had landed, without anyone's trying to stop them, and took them to the city.

[7.75] When Nicias and Demosthenes thought that enough had been done to prepare, the retreat of the army took place, on the second day after the naval battle.

It was a dreadful scene, for many reasons. They were retreating after losing all their ships, and instead of having realized their great hopes, both they and their city were in peril. Also, in their departure from camp there were things most painful for every eye and heart. The dead lay there unburied, and each man shuddered with grief and horror as he recognized a friend among them. The survivors they were leaving behind—the wounded or sick—were to the living far more pitiful than the dead. These men begged them and wept until their friends did not know what to do. They called out to each individual comrade or relative whom they saw and asked to be taken along. They hung on the necks of their tent-fellows as they departed and followed them as far as they could. When their strength and bodies failed, they called again and again to the gods and cried aloud as they were left behind. So the whole army was in tears and distracted, not knowing what to do. They found it was not easy to depart, even from enemy land, where they had already suffered evils too great for tears and were afraid of what more they might suffer in the unknown future.

There was great dejection and self-condemnation among them. Indeed, they could be compared to a city under siege, and not a small one, in their secret flight. The whole multitude that was marching were not fewer than forty thousand men.* All of them carried anything they could that might be of use. The hoplites and troopers, contrary to usual custom, carried their own food while wearing their armor, in some cases because there were no slaves, in others because they did not trust them (for a long time the slaves had been deserting and now did so in greater numbers than ever). Even so, they did not take enough with them; there was no longer any food in the camp.

Also there was their failure and the universality of their sufferings. These were somewhat less burdensome since they were shared by all, but at the time did not seem easier to bear, especially seeing that the expedition had begun with splendor and glory but had come to such a miserable end. For this was by far the greatest reverse ever experienced by a Greek army. They had come to enslave others but were departing in fear of being enslaved themselves. Instead of the prayers and paeans with which they had sailed out, they were starting back with the opposite, words of ill omen. They were traveling by land instead of by sea and depending on their hoplites instead of their fleet. All the same, because of the enormity of the danger still hanging over them, all this seemed tolerable.

[7.76] Nicias saw that the army was disheartened and greatly changed. He went along the ranks and encouraged and comforted them as far as was possible under the circumstances, and called out still more loudly as he went from one to another in his enthusiasm, and hoping that by shouting he could somehow help them:

[7.77] "Athenians and allies, even in our present position we must still hope. Before now men have been saved from worse situations than these. You must not blame yourselves too harshly either because of our misfortunes or because of your present undeserved misery. I myself am not better off than any of you in strength—indeed you see what a state I am in because of my illness. I believe I am the equal of anyone in respect to

---

* Thucydides must have exaggerated this number for dramatic effect.

good fortune,* whether in private life or otherwise, and now I am hanging suspended in the same danger as the least fortunate among you. This even though I have spent my life making the customary offerings to the gods, and acting justly and generously toward men.

"That is why I still have strong hopes for the future, and our misfortunes do not frighten me as much as they might. Indeed, they may soon be lightened. Our enemies have had good fortune enough, and if any of the gods was offended by our expedition, we have been already amply punished. Others before us have attacked other people and have done what men do without suffering more than they could bear, and it is likely we shall find that the gods will be more kind, because we deserve their pity more than their envy.

"Look at yourselves, what fine hoplites you are and how many are marching in your ranks, and do not give way too much to despair. Instead reckon that you yourselves are a city as soon as you set yourselves anywhere, and that there is no other city in Sicily that could easily resist your attack or dislodge you when established. The safety and order of our journey is for you yourselves to look to. Each one of you must have no other thought than this: that any spot on which he is forced to fight, he must take control of it and hold it as if it were his own country and stronghold.

"Meanwhile we will speed on our way night and day alike because our provisions are limited. If we can reach some friendly place inhabited by Sicels (they are still loyal to us because they fear the Syracusans), you may from then on consider yourselves safe. A message has been sent on to them with instructions to meet us with supplies of food.

"To sum up, soldiers, you must understand the need to be brave, because if you run away there is no place nearby to take refuge in. If you can now escape from the enemy, you others may see again what your hearts long to see, while those of you who are Athenians will restore the great power of your city, even though it is now fallen. Men make the city and not walls or ships without men in them."

[7.78] As he made this speech, Nicias went along the ranks and brought back into place any troops he saw dropping out of line. Meanwhile, Demosthenes did the same for his part of the army, addressing them in similar words. The army marched in a hollow square, the division under

---

* Nicias was widely considered lucky in his previous military career (see 6.17 above and note).

Nicias leading and that of Demosthenes following. The hoplites were on the outside, surrounding the baggage-carriers and the bulk of the army in the middle.

When they arrived at the ford of the river Anapus, they found the Syracusans and allies stationed there. They routed them, crossed the river, and went ahead. The Syracusan cavalry attacked them, and their light troops threw their javelins. On that day the Athenians advanced about four and a half miles, stopping for the night on a hill.

The next morning they started early and went on about two miles farther. They descended into a place in the plain and camped there. They wanted to take some food from the houses, because the place was inhabited, and bring water from there with them, because for a long distance ahead, water was scarce in the direction they were heading. The Syracusans meanwhile went on and fortified the pass in front, where there was a steep hill with a rocky ravine on each side, known as the Acraean cliff. The next day the Athenians advanced but were impeded by the cavalry of the Syracusans and their allies and many javelin men, who struck and charged from both sides. The Athenians fought for a long while, then retreated to the same camp, where they no longer had provisions as before; it was impossible to leave the place because of the cavalry.

[7.79] Early the next morning they started out again and forced their way to the hill, which had been fortified. There they found the enemy's infantry drawn up many shields deep to defend the fortification, where the pass was narrow. The Athenians assaulted the walls but were assailed by many arrows and spears from the hill (these came down more easily from the heights). The Athenians could not force their way through; they retreated again and rested. Meanwhile there was some thunder and rain, which often happens toward autumn. Because of that the Athenians became even more discouraged; they thought all these things were signs of their approaching destruction.

While they were resting, Gylippus and the Syracusans sent part of their army to put up fortification walls behind the Athenians, on the road by which they had come. But the Athenians immediately sent some of their own men and prevented this. After that the Athenians retreated toward the plain and halted for the night.

When they advanced the next day, the Syracusans surrounded them and attacked them on every side and wounded many. If the Athenians advanced, the Syracusans fell back. But if the Athenians retreated, the Syracusans attacked. In particular they assaulted their rear, in hope of routing these men quickly and causing the whole army to panic. For a long while the Athenians persevered in this fashion, but after advancing about three miles they halted to rest in the plain. The Syracusans also withdrew to their own camp.

[7.80] That night Nicias and Demosthenes saw that the troops were in bad shape and lacked every kind of necessity, and that many had been injured in the frequent attacks. So they decided to light as many fires as possible and lead off the army, no longer by the same route as planned, but in the opposite direction to that guarded by the Syracusans, toward the sea. (This route was leading the army not to Catana but to the other side of Sicily, toward Camarina, Gela, and the other Greek and barbarian towns in that area.) So they lit many fires and set out by night.

All armies, and the largest most of all, are subject to fears and alarms, especially when they are marching by night through an enemy's country with the enemy nearby. Nicias' division, which was in the lead, kept together and got a good way in front. But Demosthenes' division, rather more than half the army, got separated and marched on in some disorder. By morning, however, they reached the sea, and getting onto the Helorine road, pushed on to reach the river Cacyparis. They followed the river up through the interior, where they hoped to be met by the Sicels whom they had sent for.

When they arrived at the river, they found, there too, a Syracusan party engaged in barring the ford with a wall and pointed stakes. They forced their way across this blockade, crossed the river, and went on to another river called the Erineus, following the instructions of their guides.

[7.81] Meanwhile, when daylight came and the Syracusans and allies found the Athenians gone, most of them accused Gylippus of having let them escape on purpose. They rushed to pursue them and had no difficulty finding the road they had taken. They caught up with them about breakfast-time. They first engaged with the troops under Demosthenes, who were behind and marching somewhat slowly and in disorder, because they had fallen into a panic during the night. They immediately attacked and engaged these. The Syracusan cavalry surrounded them more easily now that they were separated from the rest and herded them into one place.

The troops under Nicias were about six miles in front of these. Nicias had led them on more rapidly because he thought that under the circumstances their safety lay not in staying and fighting, unless they were compelled to, but in retreating as fast as possible and fighting only when forced. But Demosthenes was more subject to trouble because his position in the rear left him first exposed to attack. Then, when he realized that the Syracusans were pursuing him, he did not advance but instead positioned his men for battle. He lingered until he was surrounded by his pursuers.

Demosthenes and the Athenians with him were in great confusion. They were huddled in an enclosure with a wall all around it, a road on either side, and olive-trees in great number. Missiles were being thrown all around them. The Syracusans sensibly had adopted this mode of attack instead of fighting at close quarters (risking a struggle with desperate men was now more to the advantage of the Athenians than to themselves). Besides, their success had now become so certain that they began to spare themselves a little in order not to be cut off in the moment of victory. They also thought that they would be able in this way to subdue and capture the Athenians.

[7.82] After pelting the Athenians and their allies all day long from every side with spears and arrows, they saw that their foe was now worn down by their wounds and other sufferings. So Gylippus and the Syracusans and their allies made an announcement, offering liberty to any of those from the islands* who chose to defect to them. A few of those cities went over. Afterward an agreement was made with Demosthenes on behalf of the others. They were to lay down their arms on condition that no one would be put to death either by violence or imprisonment or be deprived of the means of life. Six thousand surrendered, and set down all the money that they had, and put it into the hollows of their shields, and filled four of them. These men were immediately taken to Syracuse.

[7.83] Meanwhile, Nicias with his men arrived on that same day at the river Erineus. Nicias led them across and posted his army on high ground on the other side. The next day the Syracusans overtook him. They told him that the troops under Demosthenes had surrendered and invited him to follow their example. Nicias did not believe them and asked for a truce so he could send a horseman to inspect the situation. After the messenger returned and verified that they had surrendered, Nicias sent a herald to Gylippus and the Syracusans to say he was ready to agree with them on behalf of the Athenians to repay whatever money the Syra-

* Citizens of the subject states in the Athenian Empire. The troops were organized in units by their home city.

cusans had spent on the war, if they would release his army. He offered to give Athenians as hostages, one man for every talent, until the money was paid. The Syracusans and Gylippus rejected this proposal and attacked Nicias' men as they had the others, standing around them and hurling spears, slingshot, and arrows at them until evening.

The Athenians were badly in need of food and necessities, as Demosthenes' men had been. Nevertheless, they watched for the quiet of the night to resume their march. But while they were taking up their arms the Syracusans noticed them and raised their paean.* When the Athenians learned that they had not escaped the Syracusans' notice, they again laid down their arms, except for about three hundred men who forced their way through the guards and left during the night in any way they could.

[7.84] As soon as it was day, Nicias led his army out. The Syracusans and their allies pelted them with javelins and other weapons from all sides. The Athenians pushed on for the Assinarus River, assailed by attacks from every side by a numerous cavalry and the rest of the troops. They supposed it would be easier for them once they got across the river, and they were driven on also by their exhaustion and craving for water.

Once at the Assinarus, they rushed into the river in disorder. Everyone wanted to be the first to cross it, but the enemy attacks made it difficult to cross at all. Because they were forced to huddle together, they fell against and trampled one another. Some perished immediately among the javelins and baggage, others became entangled in it and were swept away by the river. Meanwhile the Syracusans were standing on the opposite bank, which was steep. They hurled weapons down on the Athenians, who were drinking eagerly while crowded together in disorder in the deep bed of the river.

The Peloponnesians came down and butchered the men in the river. The water was immediately spoiled, but they were drinking it all the same, mud and all, bloody as it was, and most of them were fighting to have it.

[7.85] At last, when many dead lay piled on one another in the stream, and part of the army had been destroyed at the river while those that escaped from there were killed by the cavalry, Nicias surrendered himself to Gylippus, whom he trusted more than he did the Syracusans. He told him and the Spartans they could do what they liked with *him* but to

* See 6.32 above and note.

stop the slaughter of the soldiers. Right away Gylippus gave orders to take prisoners. The survivors were gathered together (except for those— a large number—kept secretly by the Syracusan troops). Some riders were sent in pursuit of the three hundred Athenians who had got through the guard during the night, and these were now captured along with the rest.

The number of prisoners collected as public property was not great, but the number taken privately was very large. All Sicily was filled with them, because no arrangements for them had been made, as there had been for those who were captured along with Demosthenes. A large portion also had been killed. The carnage was very great, not exceeded by any in this war. Many had also fallen in the numerous other encounters. Nonetheless, many escaped. Some got away; others served as slaves and ran away subsequently. These found refuge at Catana.

[7.86] The Syracusans and their allies now came together and took up the spoils and as many prisoners as they could and went back to the city. The rest of their Athenian and allied captives had been sent down into the quarries because this seemed to be the safest way to keep guard over them. They cut the throats of Nicias and Demosthenes—even though Gylippus did not want them to, because he thought it would be the crown of his triumph if he could take the enemy's generals to Sparta. One of them, Demosthenes, happened to be one of Sparta's greatest enemies because of his role in the battle on the island and in Pylos.* The other, Nicias, was for the same reasons one of her greatest friends; he had persuaded the Athenians to make peace with the Spartans and release their prisoners. For these reasons the Spartans felt kindly toward him, and it was mainly for that reason that Nicias entrusted himself to Gylippus. But some of the Syracusans who had been in communication with him were afraid, it was said, of his being tortured and ruining their success by his revelations. Others, especially the Corinthians, were afraid that Nicias could escape by bribery (he was rich),† and that new harm might come from him in the future, so they persuaded their allies and had him put to death.

For this reason or something like it, Nicias was executed, though of all the Greeks in my time, he least deserved such a degree of misfortune,

* Demosthenes had been the general responsible for the Spartans' defeat at Pylos in 427 BC; see 6.89 above and note.

† Nicias' wealth came from the silver mines at Laurium; he owned a thousand slaves.

242 · The Greek Histories

because of the virtue he had made his practice during the whole course of his life.

[7.87] The prisoners in the quarries were at first treated cruelly by the Syracusans. Many were crowded in a hollow area, without any roof to cover them. The heat of the sun and the stifling closeness of the air tormented them during the day, and then the nights, which came on autumnal and chilly, made them ill by the violence of the change. Also they had to do everything in the same spot because space was limited.* The bodies of those who died of their wounds or from the variation in the temperature, or from similar causes, were left heaped together on top of one another. The stench was intolerable, and they were always afflicted by hunger and thirst, because for eight months each man had only a cup of water and two cups of grain given him daily. It seems that no single suffering experienced by men thrust into such a place was spared them.

For some seventy days they lived all together like that. After that, all, except for the Athenians and any Sicilians or Italian Greeks who had joined in the expedition, were sold as slaves. The total number of prisoners taken would be difficult to state exactly, but it could not have been less than seven thousand.

This was the greatest action of any in this war, or, in my opinion, of any that has been heard of among Greeks. It was at once most glorious to the victors and most calamitous to the defeated.[†] They were conquered in every respect and altogether; all that they suffered was great; they were destroyed, as the saying is, with a total destruction,[‡] both their fleet and their army. There was nothing that was not lost, and few out of many returned home. That is what happened in Sicily.

———

It would seem as though Athens was surely headed for defeat in the larger war against Sparta, but the city continued to fight on for another eight years—a source of astonishment to Thucydides (see pp. 216–217). There were even several important victories, some thanks to Alcibiades, who was taken back into Athens's good graces and given a command (but was soon booted out a second time). Fighting moved largely to the Aegean where a Spartan fleet, built with money supplied by the Per-

---

* A delicate reference to their excretory needs.

† In Greek the phrase "and most calamitous to the defeated" is a line of iambic trimeter verse, which Thucydides may have quoted from a tragedy that is now lost.

‡ The term "total destruction" (*panōlethria*) was Herodotus' term for the destruction of Troy (see 2.120.2).

⊂⟩10/25/24

sians, contested with Athenian ships for control of the sea. A Spartan admiral, Lysander, finally won that control after capturing most Athenian ships at Aegospotami,
on the Hellespont. That victory enabled Sparta to choke off food imports headed to
Athens and starve the city into submission, in 404 BC.

    Sparta's allies would have liked to see Athens annihilated, but Sparta held back
from such a cruel settlement. It demanded instead that Athens pull down a portion
of its walls, pay restitution, and change its government to a pro-Spartan oligarchy.
Lysander installed this government—the Thirty, as they were called—and under
this harsh regime Athens briefly became a police state with arrests and executions of
pro-democracy activists. Xenophon, the next author we feature in this volume, lived
through that era and recorded its terrors. Thucydides most likely witnessed it as
well, though his chronicle of the Peloponnesian War ends abruptly in 410 BC, unfin-
ished but nonetheless an enduring masterwork of historical prose.

Xenophon

XENOPHON

(c. 430–c. 355 BC)

Xenophon was a younger contemporary of Thucydides, and also like Thucydides was himself a military leader as well as an author. But there the similarities end. Where Thucydides put his all into a single work of historical prose, using it to explore the deepest questions of politics and morality, Xenophon wrote widely in many different genres and never approached in any the profundity of his predecessor. But he did write with vividness and verve, and also recorded important events in the Greek world for which we have no other surviving source.

Xenophon grew up in Athens during the Peloponnesian War, a member of the wealthy, horse-owning class. His later writings show an abiding interest in the pursuits of the aristocracy: hunting, horsemanship, military leadership. His politics were also very much those of his class: With a profound belief in the wisdom and skill of those he called the beltistoi *("best men"), the land-owning rich, he had little affection for the Athenian democracy and leaned strongly toward Sparta. His writings include* Agesilaus, *a biography that exalts to the skies the virtues of an authoritarian fourth-century Spartan king. Another strongly pro-Spartan text,* Constitution of the Lacedaemonians, *may also be his work, though there is some dispute about its authorship.*

While in his teens and twenties Xenophon spent much time with Socrates, as did other aristocratic youth, including Plato. Xenophon greatly admired Socrates and featured him as principal or sole speaker in many of his later writings. His Memorabilia *present a set of Socratic conversations very different in spirit from Plato's dialogues, and his* Apology *and* Symposium *seem to have been written in response to Plato's works of the same name. Ancient biographers class Xenophon as a philosopher rather than a historian, but it must be said that the ideas advanced in these Socratic works are largely conventional and not nearly as probing or challenging as those of Plato, his close contemporary.*

Pro-Spartan and pro-Socratic views made Xenophon an outlier in democratic

Athens, and he spent much of his life in exile from his native city. He became an expatriate in 401, shortly after Athens, defeated by Sparta in 404, threw off its Spartan-backed oligarchy, the regime called the Thirty, and restored its radical democracy. An offer came to Xenophon that year to join a mercenary army led by his friend Proxenus, a Boeotian, and serve under Cyrus the Younger, a brother of the Persian Great King. Socrates cautioned Xenophon, then aged twenty-nine, that Cyrus was no friend of Athens and fighting in his employ might incur political disfavor, but Xenophon went nonetheless. That decision led to the remarkable episode related below in the selections from Xenophon's most famous work, the Anabasis.

While serving in the army collected by Cyrus, and possibly because of that service, Xenophon was banished from Athens by official decree. He spent most of his adult life in the Peloponnese, either at Sparta, Corinth, or a small town called Scillus near Olympia. The Spartans awarded Xenophon an estate there in recognition of his service under Agesilaus, an aggressive Spartan king who employed Xenophon as a mercenary captain during his brief campaign against the Persians in western Asia. Xenophon's two sons were reportedly educated at Sparta in the famous Spartan training program, the agōgē, *though both later fought for their father's native Athens.*

At some point Xenophon returned to Athens and ended his life there, though nothing is known of his death. His latest surviving work, Revenues, *suggested ways Athens could revive its flagging fortunes by better harvesting the silver mines at Laurium. Spartan power had greatly declined by that time and Xenophon deeply disliked the Thebans, by that time a third rival for leadership of Greece. The inability of any leading city to establish hegemony in Greece deeply troubled Xenophon; his writings, especially* Hellenica, *illustrate the turmoil and decline that had set in among the Greeks owing to their lack of unity. At the time of his death, Philip of Macedon, the father of Alexander the Great, was just beginning to fill that leadership vacuum; Xenophon was barely aware of what was taking place on Greece's northern fringe or of the profound transformation it would bring to the city-states of the south.*

Because Xenophon wrote in so many genres and styles, it's difficult to represent him fully in this volume. We present below excerpts from his two surviving works that best qualify as historical writings, the Anabasis *and the* Hellenica. *But readers of history should also be aware of* The Education of Cyrus, *a romantic biography based on the life of Cyrus the Great, founder of the Persian Empire. This colorful text is more fiction than history but incorporates many fascinating details that Xenophon took from his own extensive experience of travel and warfare.*

THE *ANABASIS*

TRANSLATED BY CARLETON BROWNSON,
WITH REVISIONS BY JAMES ROMM

Xenophon's best-known work today goes under various English titles, since its Greek title, Anabasis, *is difficult to translate. The word literally means "the going-up," but to go "up" in Greek also meant to go inland from a coast (since land is always higher than sea). The military march Xenophon recounts in this work took him inland indeed—farther from the Aegean than any Greek army had ever gone, into what's now Iraq, and then back to the sea again (the Black Sea), a journey of more than two thousand miles.*

Xenophon never meant to go so far, but at around age thirty, while living in his native Athens, he received a letter from a friend, Proxenus. Proxenus had signed on as a mercenary captain in the employ of Cyrus the Younger, the brother of the reigning Persian king, Artaxerxes. Cyrus wanted Greek troops to help him (as he claimed) fight his foes in western Turkey, and he was offering handsome rewards. Xenophon joined the mercenary force and followed Cyrus eastward. Soon it became clear that the target was not local but very distant—the Great King himself, whom Cyrus hoped to overthrow. By the time the truth came out, it was too late to turn back, so Xenophon and the other Greek recruits—the Ten Thousand, as they became known—slogged onward into Asia.

Xenophon's narrative of the campaign and its aftermath has a uniquely personal voice that distinguishes it from his other writings. He was a participant in all that took place, indeed the central figure for most of the story. The details he gives of life on the march, and of the life of Greek mercenaries serving in foreign lands, are startlingly vivid. Xenophon's self-presentation is fascinating as well, especially since he speaks about himself in the third person (as does Julius Caesar in the similarly autobiographical Gallic War*).*

Among the work's most gripping passages is the account of the Battle of Cunaxa, in which the forces under Cyrus, having arrived in Mesopotamia after a long march, fought the army of the Great King, Artaxerxes.

[1.7.10] At this time, when the troops were marshaled under arms, the number of the Greeks was found to be 10,400 hoplites and 2,500 light-armed infantry men, while the number of the barbarians under Cyrus was 100,000 and there were about 20 scythe-bearing chariots.* The enemy,

---

* This uniquely Persian weapon is further described by Xenophon just below.

Black Sea

Sinope

THRACE

PAPHLAGONIA

Heraclea

BYZANTIUM   Chrysopolis

Propontis

BITHYNIA

MYSIA   PHRYGIA   *Haly*

THYMBRION

SARDIS   LYDIA   Iconium   Dana   C

IONIA   Celaenae

Maeander   Colossae   Tarsus

CARIA   PISIDIA

LYCIA

Rhodes

Cyprus

Mediterranean Sea

—— Route of Xenophon
      and the Ten Thousand

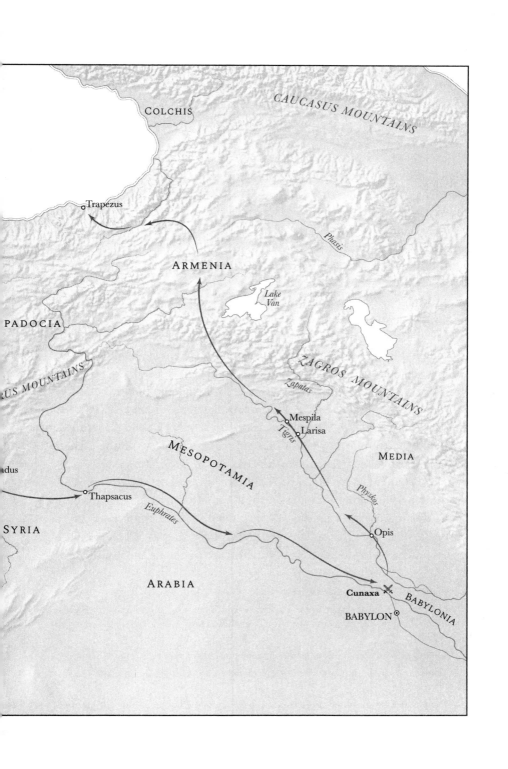

COLCHIS

CAUCASUS MOUNTAINS

Trapezus

ARMENIA

Phasis

PADOCIA

Lake
Van

US MOUNTAINS

ZAGROS MOUNTAINS

Zapatas

Mespila
Larisa

Tigris

MESOPOTAMIA

MEDIA

adus

Thapsacus

Euphrates

Physkos

SYRIA

Opis

ARABIA

Cunaxa

BABYLONIA

BABYLON

it was reported, numbered 1,200,000* and had 200 scythe-bearing chariots; besides, there was a troop of 6,000 horsemen under the command of Artagerses, stationed in front of the King himself.[†] ... Such were the reports brought to Cyrus by those who deserted from the Great King before the battle, and after the battle identical reports were made by the prisoners taken thereafter.

From there Cyrus marched one stage, three parasangs,[‡] with his whole army, Greek and barbarian alike, drawn up in line of battle, for he supposed that on that day the King would come to an engagement. About midway in this day's march there was a deep trench, thirty feet wide and eighteen feet deep. This trench extended up through the plain for a distance of twelve parasangs, reaching to the wall of Media,[§] and alongside the Euphrates there was a narrow passage, not more than about twenty feet in width, between the river and the trench.... Cyrus and his army went through by the passage just mentioned, and so found themselves on the inner side of the trench.[¶]

Now on that day the King did not offer battle, but tracks of both horses and men in retreat were to be seen in great numbers.... Since the King did not appear at the trench and try to prevent the passage of Cyrus' army, both Cyrus and the rest concluded that he had given up the idea of fighting. Hence on the following day Cyrus proceeded more carelessly. On the third day he was making the march seated in his chariot and with only a small body of troops drawn up in line in front of him, while the greater part of the army was proceeding in disorder and many of the soldiers' arms and accoutrements were being carried in wagons and on pack-animals.

[1.8] It was now about full market time** and the stopping-place where Cyrus was intending to halt had almost been reached when Pategyas, a trusty Persian of Cyrus' staff, came into sight, riding at full speed, with his horse in a sweat. He at once shouted to everyone he met, in the bar-

---

* Undoubtedly this is a vast exaggeration.

† The Persian King at this juncture was Artaxerxes II, half brother of Cyrus. By Persian convention the Great King went to war with his army and took his position in the center of the battle line.

‡ A parasang is a Persian unit of measurement equivalent to about three and a half miles.

§ A defensive wall built by the Babylonians to defend against the Medes, at this time already in ruins.

¶ The Great King must not have had time to complete the trench or block off this passage.

** That is, midmorning, the peak hour to be out shopping in most Greek cities.

barian tongue and in Greek, that the King was approaching with a large army, ready for battle. Then ensued great confusion; the thought of the Greeks, and of all the rest in fact, was that the King would fall on them immediately, while they were in disorder. Cyrus leapt down from his chariot, put on his breastplate, and then, mounting his horse, took his spears in his hands and passed the word to all the others to arm themselves and get into place, every man of them.

They proceeded in great haste to take their places. Clearchus occupied the right end of the Greek wing* close to the Euphrates, Proxenus next to him, and the others beyond Proxenus, while Meno and his army took the left end of the Greek wing.† As for the barbarians, Paphlagonian horsemen to the number of a thousand took station beside Clearchus on the right wing, as did the Greek peltasts; on the left was Ariaeus, Cyrus' lieutenant, with the rest of the barbarian army; and in the center [were] Cyrus and his horsemen, about six hundred in number. These troopers were armed with breastplates and thigh-pieces and, all of them except Cyrus, helmets— Cyrus, however, went into the battle with his head unprotected. . . .

It was now midday, and the enemy were not yet in sight. But when afternoon was coming on, a rising dust was seen; it appeared at first like a white cloud, but some time later like a kind of blackness on the plain, extending over a great distance. As the enemy came nearer, there were soon flashes of bronze here and there, and spears and the hostile ranks began to come into sight.

There were horsemen in white cuirasses on the left wing of the enemy, under the command, it was reported, of Tissaphernes.‡ Next to them were troops with wicker shields and, farther on, hoplites with wooden shields§ that reached to their feet, these latter being Egyptians, people

---

* As usual in land warfare, the strongest troops occupied the right wing; in Cyrus' army these were the Greek hoplites and, among these, those under Clearchus.

† Xenophon names the three principal generals of the Greek forces, each of whom commanded his own contingent (there were two others besides with smaller units). Clearchus, a Spartan leading other Spartans, was the best trained and oldest of the three; Proxenus was a Boeotian, and Meno a Thessalian. (Meno is encountered elsewhere as the principal speaker in Plato's dialogue *Meno,* where he is shown in conversation with Socrates during a visit to Athens.)

‡ Former satrap of Lydia, once a key player in the final phase of the Peloponnesian War (see p. 262). He was a close ally of Artaxerxes and a bitter foe of Cyrus.

§ Xenophon uses the term "hoplite" here even when describing non-Greek soldiers. The defining feature of the hoplite was the weight and sturdiness of the shield he carried (in this case, a large wooden one).

said; and then more horsemen and more bowmen. All these troops were marching in national divisions, each nation in a solid square. In front of them were the so-called scythe-bearing chariots, at some distance from one another, and the scythes they carried reached out sideways from the axles and were also set under the chariot bodies, pointing toward the ground, so as to cut to pieces whatever they met; the intention, then, was that they should drive into the ranks of the Greeks and cut the troops to pieces.

As for the statement Cyrus made when he called the Greeks together and urged them to hold out against the shouting of the barbarians, he proved to be mistaken in this point. They came on, not with shouting, but in the utmost silence and quietness, slowly, with equal step.

At this moment Cyrus rode along the line, attended only by Pigres, his interpreter, and three or four others, and shouted to Clearchus to lead his army against the enemy's center because the King was stationed there. "And if," he said, "we are victorious there, our whole task is accomplished." Clearchus, however, saw the compact body at the enemy's center and heard from Cyrus that the King was beyond Cyrus' left wing (for the King was so superior in numbers that, even at the center of his own line, he was beyond Cyrus' left wing), and he was unwilling to draw the right wing away from the river for fear that he might be turned on both flanks.* He told Cyrus, in reply, that he was taking care to make everything go well.

At this critical time the King's army was advancing evenly, while the Greek force, still remaining in the same place, was forming its line from those who were still coming up. Cyrus, riding along at some distance from his army, was taking a survey, looking in either direction, at both his enemies and his friends. Then Xenophon, an Athenian,[†] seeing him from the Greek army, approached so as to meet him and asked if he had any orders to give. Cyrus pulled up his horse and told Xenophon to tell everyone that the sacrificial victims and omens were all favorable. While saying this he heard a noise running through the ranks and asked what the noise was. Xenophon replied that the watchword was now passing

---

* The greatest danger to forces on the extreme ends of the battle line was being outflanked. Clearchus insisted on staying put so as to keep close to the river, his protection against this danger.

† Xenophon speaks of himself in the third person in the *Anabasis,* even after he becomes its central figure. This is his first appearance in the narrative.

along for the second time.* And Cyrus wondered who had given it out, and asked what the watchword was. Xenophon replied "Zeus Savior and Victory." And upon hearing this, Cyrus said, "Well, I accept it, and so let it be."[†] After he had said these words he rode back to his own position.

Artaxerxes II and his army, depicted on the façade of his rock-cut tomb in Iran.
WIKIMEDIA COMMONS

At last the opposing lines were not less than half a mile apart. The Greeks struck up the paean and began to advance against the enemy. And when, as they proceeded, a part of the phalanx billowed out,[‡] those who were left behind began to run, and they all set up the sort of war-cry they raise to Ares, and all alike began running. It is also reported that some of them clashed their shields against their spears, thereby frightening the enemy's horses. And before an arrow reached them, the barbarians broke and fled.[§]

---

* The watchword passed from the front line to the rear and then back again, to ensure everyone had it right.

† The content of the watchword is taken as a good omen by Cyrus. For similar superstitions regarding watchwords see Plutarch's *Demetrius*, p. 386 below.

‡ In the advance, some troops moved faster than others, causing a dangerous "billow."

§ A striking example of the known superiority of Greek to non-Greek infantrymen. The barbarian forces facing the Greeks were not willing to stand and face them.

The Greeks pursued with all their might, but they shouted meanwhile to one another not to run at a headlong pace but to keep their formation during the pursuit. As for the enemy's chariots, some of them plunged through the lines of their own troops; others drove through the Greek lines, but without charioteers. And whenever the Greeks saw them coming, they would open a gap for their passage; one fellow, to be sure, was caught, like a befuddled man on a racecourse,* yet it was said that even he was not hurt in the least, nor, for that matter, did any other single man among the Greeks get any wound in this battle—except that someone on the left wing was reported hit by an arrow.

Cyrus saw that the Greeks were victorious over the division opposite them and were in pursuit. Though he was pleased and was already being saluted with homage as King by his attendants, he nevertheless was not induced to join the pursuit. Keeping the six hundred horsemen of his troop in close formation, he was watching to see what the King would do. For he knew that the King held the center of the Persian army. (In fact, all the generals of the barbarians hold their own center when in command, for they think that this is the safest position, namely, with forces on either side, and also that if they want to pass along an order, the army will get it in half the time.) In this instance the King held the center of his army, but still he found himself beyond the left wing of Cyrus. Since, then, there was no one in his front to give battle to him or to the troops drawn up before him, the King proceeded to wheel round his line with the intention of encircling the enemy.

At this point Cyrus, seized with fear lest the King might get in the rear of the Greek troops and cut them to pieces, charged to meet him; and attacking with his six hundred, he was victorious over the forces stationed in front of the King and put to flight the six thousand, slaying with his own hand, it is said, their commander Artagerses. But when these turned to flee, Cyrus' six hundred, setting out in pursuit, became scattered also, and only a very few were left around him, chiefly his so-called table companions. While attended by these only, Cyrus caught sight of the King and the compact body surrounding him. On the instant he lost control of himself and with the cry "I see the man!" rushed upon him and struck him in the breast and wounded him through his

---

* As we might say, "like a deer in the headlights."

breastplate—as Ctesias the physician* says, adding also that he himself healed the wound.

While Cyrus was delivering his stroke, however, someone hit him a hard blow under the eye with a javelin; and then followed a struggle between the King and Cyrus and the attendants who supported each of them. The number that fell on the King's side is stated by Ctesias, who was with him; on the other side, Cyrus himself was killed and eight of the noblest of his attendants lay dead upon him.

It is said of Artapates, one of Cyrus' chamberlains who was his most faithful follower, that when he saw Cyrus fallen, he leapt down from his horse and threw his arms around him. One report says that the King ordered someone to slay him on the body of Cyrus, while others say that he drew his dagger and slew himself with his own hand; for he had a dagger of gold, and he also wore a necklace and bracelets and all the other ornaments that the noblest Persians wear (he had been honored by Cyrus because of his affection and fidelity).

[1.9] In this way, then, Cyrus came to his end, a man who was the most kingly and the most worthy to rule of all the Persians who have been born since Cyrus the Elder, as all agree who are reputed to have known Cyrus intimately....

What happened to Cyrus at the end of his life is a strong indication that he was a true man himself and that he knew how to judge those who were faithful, devoted, and constant. When he died, all his body-guard of friends and table companions died fighting in his defense, with the exception of Ariaeus. He, it chanced, was stationed on the left wing at the head of the cavalry, and when he learned that Cyrus had fallen, he took to flight with the whole army that he commanded.

[1.10] Then Cyrus' head and right hand were cut off. The King, pursuing Ariaeus, burst into the camp of Cyrus; and Ariaeus and his men no longer stood their ground, but fled through their own camp to the stopping-place from which they had set out that morning, a distance, it was said, of four parasangs. So the King and his troops proceeded to secure plunder of various sorts in great quantities. In particular he captured the Phocaean woman, Cyrus' concubine, who, by all accounts, was

* Ctesias was a Greek doctor serving at the Persian royal court and an eyewitness to this battle. He later published an account of Persian history (now lost) that included his own version of the events at Cunaxa.

clever and beautiful.* The Milesian woman, however, the younger one, after being seized by the King's men made her escape, lightly clad, to some Greeks who chanced to be standing guard amid the baggage train and, forming themselves in line against the enemy, had killed many of the plunderers, although some of their own number had been killed also. Yet they did not take to flight but saved this woman and whatever else came within their lines, whether persons or property.

At this time the King and the Greeks were distant from one another about seven miles, with the Greeks pursuing the troops ahead of them in the belief they were victorious over all the enemy, the King and his followers plundering in the belief that *they* were victorious. When the Greeks learned that the King and his forces were in their baggage train, and the King heard from Tissaphernes that the Greeks were victorious over the unit facing them and had gone on ahead in pursuit, the King proceeded to gather his troops and form them in line of battle. Clearchus called Proxenus (for he was nearest him in the line) and took counsel with him as to whether they should send a detachment or go in full force to the camp[†] for the purpose of lending aid. Meanwhile the Greeks saw the King advancing again, as it seemed, from their rear, and they therefore countermarched and made ready to meet his attack in case he should advance in that direction. The King, however, did not do so, but returned by the same route he'd followed before when he passed outside of Cyrus' left wing, and in his return picked up not only those who had deserted to the Greeks during the battle but also Tissaphernes and his troops. For Tissaphernes had not taken to flight in the first encounter, but had charged along the river through the Greek peltasts; he did not kill anyone in his passage, but the Greeks, after opening a gap for his men, proceeded to deal blows and throw javelins at them as they went through. The commander of the Greek peltasts was Episthenes of Amphipolis, and it was said he proved himself an intelligent man. At any rate, after Tissaphernes had thus come off the worst, he did not wheel around again but went on to the camp of the Greeks and there fell in with the King. So after forming their lines once more, these two were proceeding together.

When they were facing the Greek left wing, the Greeks became afraid

* We learn from other sources that her name was Aspasia, a Greek woman who had been brought to Cyrus as a concubine but attained a more elevated status as a result of her proud spirit. Later she also held high rank at the court of Artaxerxes.

† The "camp" is the baggage train. It's not clear how the Greek commanders had received news of what was taking place several miles away.

that the Persians might advance against that wing and, by outflanking them on both sides, cut them to pieces. They thought it best, therefore, to draw the wing back and get the river behind them. But while they were taking counsel about this matter, the King changed his line of battle to the same form as theirs and brought it into position opposite them, just as when he had met them for battle the first time.* When the Greeks saw that the enemy were near them and in battle-order, they again struck up the paean and advanced to the attack much more eagerly than before. The barbarians once again failed to await the attack but took to flight at a greater distance from the Greeks than the first time. The Greeks pursued as far as a certain village and then halted, for above the village was a hill on which the King and his followers rallied; they were no longer fighting on foot, but the hill was covered with horsemen, so the Greeks could not perceive what was going on. They did see, they said, the royal standard, a kind of golden eagle on a shield, raised aloft on a pole....

The Greeks halted, grounded arms, and proceeded to take their rest. At the same time they were surprised that Cyrus was nowhere to be seen and that no one else had come to them from him. They did not know that he was dead, but conjectured that he had either gone off in pursuit or pushed on to occupy some point. So they took counsel as to whether they should remain where they were and bring the baggage train there, or return to their camp. The decision was to return, and they reached their tents about supper-time.

Such was the conclusion of this day. The Greeks found most of their property pillaged, in particular whatever there was to eat or drink. As for the wagons loaded with flour and wine that Cyrus had provided in order that if ever serious need should overtake the army, he might have supplies to distribute among the Greeks (there were four hundred of these wagons, it was said), these also the King and his men had now pillaged. The result was that most of the Greeks had no dinner (they had had no breakfast either, for the King had appeared before the time when the army was to halt for breakfast). Thus it was that they got through this night.

———

With no way to get food and no guide to show them the roads, the Greeks were in a helpless position, but they had also shown in the recent battle that they were more than a match for the Persians. A tense standoff ensued between the Great King,

---

   * The two sides have by now re-formed and re-engaged, facing opposite to their original positions. The elite forces surrounding the King confront Cyrus' Greeks for the first time.

Artaxerxes and the collective Greek army under the lead of Clearchus. The King insisted that the Greeks disarm, but Clearchus refused, despite the warnings of the King's Greek herald that disarming was their only hope of survival. Eventually a truce was agreed on, under which the Greeks retained their weapons.

Clearchus and the other Greek leaders struck a bargain with Ariaeus, a Persian leader who had marched with them under Cyrus but had then deserted to the King in the heat of battle. Ariaeus was now leading his men back to the West and offered to take the Greeks with him, though not by the route they had followed before, for this was stripped bare of food. The Greeks and Ariaeus swore a pact of mutual trust, but Ariaeus was already in cahoots with Tissaphernes and the King in a plot to destroy the Greek army.

Their truce with the King required them to stay in their camp or they would be attacked; nevertheless they broke camp and started westward with Ariaeus and no attack came. The King was showing weakness, but the Greeks were weak as well, nearly faint from hunger. With neither side sure which one held the advantage, the King sent heralds to reopen negotiations. That gave Clearchus the confidence he displays in the exchange below.

———

[2.3] Though the day before the King had ordered the Greeks to give up their arms, he now, at sunrise, sent heralds to negotiate a truce. When these heralds reached the Greek sentinels, they asked for the commanders. And when the sentinels reported, Clearchus, who happened at the time to be inspecting the ranks, told the sentinels to direct the heralds to wait until he was free. Then, having arranged the army so it presented a fine appearance from every side as a compact phalanx, with no one visible outside the lines of the hoplites,* he summoned the messengers, and he himself came forward with the best-armed and best-looking of his own troops and told the other generals to do likewise.

Face-to-face with the messengers, he inquired what they wanted. They replied that they had come to negotiate for a truce and were empowered to report the King's proposals to the Greeks and the Greeks' proposals to the King. And Clearchus answered: "Report to him, then, that we must have a battle first; for we have had no breakfast, and there is no man alive who will dare talk to Greeks about a truce unless he provides them with a breakfast."

---

* Apparently Clearchus placed the sick and wounded, and noncombatants, inside the formation and had the battle-ready soldiers stand close together so that the others could not be seen.

Upon hearing these words the messengers rode away, but they quickly came back again; this made it clear that the King, or someone else charged with carrying on these negotiations, was somewhere near. They stated that what the Greeks said seemed to the King reasonable, and that they had now brought guides who would lead the Greeks, in case a truce should be concluded, to where they could get provisions. Then Clearchus asked whether he was making a truce merely with these go-betweens* or whether the truce would bind the others also. "Every one of them," they replied, "until your message is carried to the King." When they had said this, Clearchus had them withdraw and took counsel about the matter.

It was thought best to conclude the truce quickly so that they could go and get the provisions without being harassed. And Clearchus said: "I agree with this view, but I shall not say so at once; I'll delay until the messengers become afraid of our deciding against the truce. To be sure, I suppose our own soldiers will also feel the same fear." When it seemed that the proper time had come, he reported that he accepted the truce and directed the messengers to lead the way immediately to the provisions.

They proceeded, then, to lead the way, but Clearchus, though he had made the truce, kept his army in battle formation on the march and himself commanded the rear guard. And they kept coming upon trenches and canals full of water that could not be crossed without bridges. They made bridges of a kind, however, out of the palm trees that had fallen and others they cut down themselves. And here one could well observe how Clearchus commanded; he had his spear in his left hand and in his right a stick, and whenever he thought that any of the men assigned to this task was shirking, he would pick out the man and deal him a blow; at the same time he would get into the mud and lend a hand himself. The result was that everyone was ashamed not to match him in energy. The men detailed to the work were all those up to thirty years of age, but the older men also took hold when they saw Clearchus in such energetic haste.

Now Clearchus was in a far greater hurry because he suspected that the trenches were not always full of water in this way, since it was not a proper time to be irrigating the plain. His suspicion was that the King had let the water into the plain in order that the Greeks might see at the very start many things to make them fearful about their journey.

The march finally brought them to villages where the guides directed

---

* Literally, "with those coming and going." Clearchus is alert to Persian deceit at this stage, though he lets his guard down later.

them to get provisions. In these villages was grain in abundance and palm wine and a sour drink made by boiling that wine. As for the palm-dates, the sort that one can see in Greece were set apart for the attendants, while the choice ones, remarkable for their beauty and size and with a color like amber, were set aside for their masters; still others they dried and stored as sweets. These made a pleasant morsel along with wine-drinking, but were apt to cause headache. Here also the soldiers ate for the first time the heart of the palm,* and most of them were surprised not only at its appearance but at its peculiar flavor. This too was very apt to cause headache. And when the heart was removed from a palm, the whole tree would wither.

In these villages they remained three days.

———

Tissaphernes now arrived on the scene acting as the King's emissary, a man who had decades of experience dealing with Greeks. He convinced the Greek leaders that he was their advocate to the King and had secured safe passage for them out of the region. Oaths were sworn and conditions were agreed to, but then Tissaphernes disappeared for three weeks and Ariaeus began acting more standoffish; the Greeks became fearful that they were being misled. Then Tissaphernes reappeared with his army and, like Ariaeus before him, offered to lead the Greeks with him on his own journey back to the West.

The two armies marched side by side through Mesopotamia amid growing tensions. Clearchus requested a meeting with Tissaphernes to shore up trust. At that parley, Tissaphernes pulled the wool over Clearchus' eyes, convincing him not only that he meant no harm but even suggesting he, like Cyrus before him, wanted to overthrow the King with the help of the Greeks. Clearchus, spying the chance to recover all that had been lost when Cyrus was killed, agreed to return the next day and to bring the other Greek leaders. The Persian trap had been set.

———

[2.5.27] On the following day, when Clearchus returned to the Greek camp, he not only made it clear that he thought he was on very friendly terms with Tissaphernes and reported the words he had used, but he said that those whom Tissaphernes had invited must go, and that whoever among the Greeks was convicted of making false charges† ought to be punished as traitors and foes to the Greeks. Clearchus suspected that the

---

* Reflecting the fact that this delicacy comes from the top of the tree, Xenophon calls it "brain" of palm.

† That is, against Tissaphernes.

author of these slanders was Meno, for he was aware that Meno had not only had meetings with Tissaphernes, in company with Ariaeus, but was also organizing opposition to his own leadership and plotting against him with the intention of winning over the entire army and thereby securing the friendship of Tissaphernes. But Clearchus wanted to have the entire army devoted to *him* and to get the complainers out of the way.* As for the soldiers, some of them made objections to Clearchus' proposal, urging that the captains and generals should not trust Tissaphernes and should not all go to his dinner. But Clearchus vehemently insisted until he secured an agreement that five generals should go and twenty captains. About two hundred of the soldiers also followed along, with the intention of going to market.

When they reached Tissaphernes' doors, the generals were invited in—Proxenus the Boeotian, Meno the Thessalian, Agias the Arcadian, Clearchus the Spartan, and Socrates the Achaean—while the captains waited at the doors. Not long afterward, at a coordinated signal, those inside were seized and those outside were cut down.

After this, some of the barbarian horsemen rode about over the plain and killed every Greek they met, whether slave or freeman. The Greeks wondered at this riding about, as they saw it from their camp and were puzzled as to what the horsemen were doing. Then Nicarchus the Arcadian reached the camp in flight, wounded in his belly and holding his bowels in his hands, and told all that had happened. Then the Greeks, one and all, ran to their weapons, panic-stricken and believing that the enemy would immediately come against the camp.

They did not come en masse, however; Ariaeus, Artaozus, and Mithradates, who had been most faithful friends of Cyrus, arrived,† and the interpreter of the Greeks said that with them he also saw and recognized Tissaphernes' brother. These were followed by other Persians, armed with breastplates, to the number of three hundred. As soon as this party had come near, they directed whatever Greek general or captain there might be to come forward, in order that they might deliver a message from the King. Two generals went forth from the Greek lines under guard—Cleanor the Orchomenian and Sophaenetus the Stymphalian—

---

* The three Greek commanders had often been at odds with one another before this, and their contingents had sometimes come to blows.

† The envoys are the Persian officers who had formerly been fighting under Cyrus alongside the Greeks but who had since switched sides.

and with them Xenophon the Athenian, who wished to learn the fate of Proxenus.* Cheirisophus, however, happened to be away in a village in company with others who were getting provisions.

When the Greeks got within hearing distance, Ariaeus said: "Men of Greece: Clearchus, who was shown to be perjuring himself and violating the truce, has got what he deserved and is dead. Proxenus and Meno, because they gave information about Clearchus' plots, are held in high honor.† As for yourselves: The King demands your weapons, for he says that they belong to him, since they belonged to Cyrus, his slave." To this the Greeks replied as follows (Cleanor the Orchomenian acting as spokesman): "Ariaeus, you worst of men, and all you others who were friends of Cyrus: Are you not ashamed, before gods or men, that, after giving us your oath to have the same friends and foes as we did, you betrayed us—joining hands with Tissaphernes, that most godless and villainous man—and that you have destroyed the very men you gave your oath to, betrayed the rest of us, and come against us in company with our foes?" Ariaeus replied: "It was shown that long ago Clearchus was plotting against Tissaphernes and Orontas and all of us who are with them." Upon this Xenophon spoke as follows: "If Clearchus was really breaking the truce in violation of his oaths, he got what he deserved; it's right that perjurers should perish. But as for Proxenus and Meno: Since they are your benefactors and our generals, send them here. Surely since they are friends of both parties, they'll try to give both you and ourselves the best advice." To this the barbarians made no answer, but after talking for a long time with one another, they departed.

[2.6] The generals, then, after being thus seized, were taken to the King and put to death by being beheaded.‡

[3.1.2] After the generals had been seized and the captains and soldiers accompanying them had been killed, the Greeks were naturally in great perplexity. They considered that they were at the King's gates, that round

* Proxenus had been a friend of Xenophon and had recruited him for the army of Cyrus. Note that Xenophon, as yet an ordinary soldier, here boldly steps forward together with two "generals."

† All three accounts of the top commanders are lies. Clearchus had not yet been executed; Proxenus and Meno were under arrest.

‡ As Xenophon reveals farther on, only Clearchus and Proxenus were killed immediately; Meno the Thessalian was kept prisoner and cruelly tortured for a year before his execution. Another source reports that Meno was thought willing to betray the Greeks by helping the Persians destroy them.

about them on every side were many hostile tribes and cities, that no one would provide them a market any longer,* that they were distant from Greece not less than ten thousand stades,† that they had no guide to show them the way, that they were cut off by impassable rivers flowing across the homeward route, that the barbarians who had made the march inland with Cyrus had also betrayed them, and that they were left alone, without even a single horseman to support them, so that it was quite clear that if they should be victorious, they could not kill anyone, while if they should be defeated, not one of them would be left alive.‡ Full of these reflections and despondent as they were, only a few of them tasted food that evening, few kindled a fire, and many did not come that night to their quarters but lay down wherever they each happened to be, unable to sleep for grief and longing for their native cities and parents, their wives and children, whom they thought they should never see again. Such was the state of mind in which they all lay down to rest.

There was a man in the army named Xenophon, an Athenian, who was neither general nor captain nor private, but had accompanied the expedition because Proxenus, an old friend of his, had sent him at his home an invitation to go with him.... When the time of perplexity came, Xenophon was distressed as well as everybody else and was unable to sleep. But getting at length a little sleep, he had a dream. It seemed to him that there was a clap of thunder and a lightning bolt fell on his father's house, setting the whole house ablaze. He awoke at once in great fear, and judged the dream in one way an auspicious one, because in the midst of hardships and perils he had seemed to behold a great light from Zeus. But looking at it in another way he was fearful, since the dream came, as he thought, from Zeus the King and the fire appeared to blaze all about; he feared that he might not be able to escape out of the King's country,§ but might be shut in on all sides by difficulties. Now what it really means

* Soldiers on the march were normally expected to buy their own meals from local markets set up to serve them.

† Perhaps about 1,300 miles, though the measure of the Greek stade varied widely. In fact the distance spoken of here was a good deal longer than 10,000 stades, depending on the route taken and the final destination.

‡ The lack of cavalry meant that the Greeks could not effectively pursue a fleeing enemy, while the Persians, rich in cavalry troops, could easily pursue *them.* Most battlefield casualties occurred during these pursuits.

§ This interpretation relies on seeing Zeus, the "king" of the gods, as a stand-in for King Artaxerxes.

to have such a dream one may learn from the events that followed the dream—and they were these:

First, on the moment of awakening, the thought occurred to Xenophon: "Why do I lie here? The night is wearing on, and at daybreak it's likely the enemy will be upon us. If we fall into the King's hands, what will prevent our seeing all the most grievous sights and knowing all the most dreadful sufferings while we live, and then being put to a violent, disgraceful death? No one is making preparations or taking thought for defending ourselves, but we lie here as if it were possible to enjoy our ease. What about myself, then? From what city do I expect a general will arrive to perform these duties? What age must I wait to attain? For surely I'll never be any older, if today I give myself up to the enemy."

Then he arose and, as a first step, called together the captains who'd served under Proxenus. When these had gathered, he said: "Gentlemen, I am unable either to sleep, as I presume you are also, or to lie still any longer, when I see in what straits we now are. Clearly the enemy did not begin open war upon us until they believed their preparations had been adequately made. But on our side no one is planning any countermeasures at all to ensure that we put up the best possible fight. And yet if we submit and fall into the King's hands, what do we imagine our fate will be? This man cut off the head and hand of even his own brother, when he was already dead, and impaled them; what fate may we expect to suffer, then—we who have no one to intercede for us, who took the field against him to make him a slave rather than a king and to kill him if we could? Will he not do his utmost to inflict on us the most outrageous tortures and thus make all humankind afraid to undertake an expedition against him? We must make every effort not to fall into his power.

"For my part, so long as the truce lasted I never ceased feeling pity for us and congratulating the King and his followers. I saw plainly what a great amount of fine land they possessed, what abundant provisions, what quantities of servants, cattle, gold, and apparel. But whenever I thought about our own soldiers, I saw that we had no share in these good things, unless we bought them; I knew there were few of us who still had money for buying, and I knew that our oaths restrained us from getting provisions in any other way than by purchase.* With these considerations in mind, I used to fear the truce more than I now fear war. But seeing that

* That is, the Greeks were forbidden to live off the land by plundering and despoiling it.

their own act has put an end to the truce, the end has likewise come, in my opinion, both of their arrogance and of our envy. For now all these good things are offered as prizes for whichever of the two parties prove the braver men. The judges of the contest are the gods, who, in all likelihood, will be on our side. For our enemies have sworn falsely by these gods, while we, with abundant possessions before our eyes, have steadfastly kept our hands off because of our oaths by the gods. Therefore we, I think, can go into the contest with far greater confidence than can our enemies.

"Besides, we have bodies more capable than theirs of bearing cold and heat and toil, and we likewise, by the blessing of the gods, have better souls.* These men are more liable than we to be wounded and killed, if the gods again, as on that former day, grant us victory. And now, since it may be that others also have these thoughts in mind, let us not, in the name of the gods, wait for others to come to us and summon us to the noblest deeds. Let us take the lead ourselves and rouse the rest to valor. Show yourselves the best of the captains, more worthy to be generals than the generals themselves. As for me, if you choose to set out on this course, I am ready to follow you; but if you assign me the leadership, I do not plead my youth as an excuse. Rather, I think I am in the very prime of my power to ward off dangers from my own head."

Such were Xenophon's words. After hearing what he said, the officers told him to take the lead—all except a man named Apollonides, who spoke in the Boeotian dialect. This man said that anyone who claimed he could gain safety in any other way than by winning the King's consent through persuasion was talking nonsense. At the same time he began to recite the difficulties of their situation. Xenophon, however, interrupted him in the midst of his talk and said: "You amazing fellow, you have eyes but still do not see; you have heard but still do not remember. You were present, surely, with the rest of these officers when the King, after the death of Cyrus and in his elation over that event, ordered us by messenger to give up our weapons. But instead of giving them up, we equipped ourselves with them and went and encamped beside him. Then what means did he leave untried—sending ambassadors, begging for a truce, offering us provisions—until in the end he obtained a truce? When our

* Xenophon, like most Greeks of his time, believed that Greeks were innately more virtuous than non-Greeks, and especially more so than the decadent Persians whom they had several times routed in battle.

generals and captains, following precisely the plan that you are now urging, went unarmed to a conference, relying upon the truce, what happened in that case? Are they not at this moment being beaten, tortured, insulted, unable even to die (unfortunates that they are) even though they earnestly long, I imagine, for death? And do you, knowing all these things, say that those who urge self-defense are talking nonsense, and do you propose we should again go and try persuasion? In my opinion, gentlemen, we should not simply refuse to admit this fellow to our company but should deprive him of his captaincy, lay packs on his back, and treat him as that sort of a creature. For the fellow is a disgrace both to his native state and to the whole of Greece, since being a Greek he is still a man of this kind."

Then Agasias, a Stymphalian, broke in and said: "For that matter, this fellow has nothing to do either with Boeotia or with any part of Greece at all, for I have noticed that he has both his ears pierced, like a Lydian's."* In fact, it was so. He was therefore driven away, but the others proceeded to visit the various units of the army. Wherever a general was left alive, they would invite him to join them; where the general was gone, they invited the lieutenant-general; or, again, where only a captain was left, the captain. When all had come together, they seated themselves at the front of the encampment, and the generals and captains thus assembled amounted in number to about a hundred. By this time it was nearly midnight.

Then Hieronymus the Elean, who was the eldest of Proxenus' captains, began to speak as follows: "Generals and captains, we have deemed it best, in view of the present situation, both to come together ourselves and to invite you to join us, in order that we may devise whatever good counsel we can. Repeat now, Xenophon," he added, "just what you said to us."

Then Xenophon spoke as follows: "We all understand thus much, that the King and Tissaphernes have seized as many as they could of our number, and that they are manifestly plotting against the rest of us, to destroy us if they can. It is for us, then, in my opinion, to make every effort that we may never fall into the power of the barbarians, but that *they* may rather fall into *our* power. Be assured therefore that you, who have

---

* The wearing of earrings by a male was considered decadent and effeminate by mainland Greeks and was associated with "soft" barbarian races like the Lydians.

now come together in such numbers, have the grandest of opportunities. All our soldiers here are looking to you. If they see that you are faint-hearted, all of them will be cowards; but if you not only show that you are making preparations against the enemy and calling on the rest to do like-wise, be assured they will follow you and try to imitate you.

"But perhaps it is really proper that you should somewhat surpass them. For you are generals, you are lieutenant-generals and captains. While peace lasted, you had the advantage of them in pay and in stand-ing; now, therefore, when a state of war exists, it is right to expect you to be superior to common soldiers and to plan for them and toil for them whenever there is need.

"And now, firstly, I think you would do the army a great service if you see to it that generals and captains are appointed as soon as possible to take the places of those who are lost. Without leaders nothing fine or use-ful can be accomplished in any field, to put it broadly, and certainly not in warfare. For discipline, it seems, keeps men in safety, while the lack of it has brought many to destruction. Secondly, when you have appointed all the leaders that are necessary, I think you would act opportunely if you gather together the rest of the soldiers and try to encourage them. For, as matters stand now, you may have observed in what dejection they came to their quarters and in what dejection they proceeded to their picket duty. So long as they're in this state of mind, I know not what use one could make of them, if there should be need of them either by night or by day.

"If, however, we can turn the current of their minds, so that they think not merely of what they will suffer but of what they're going to do, they'll be far more cheerful. You understand, I'm sure, that it's neither numbers nor strength that wins victories; rather, adversaries generally refuse to stand against whichever of the two sides, by the gods' blessing, advances to the attack with stouter hearts. In my experience, gentlemen, I have observed this also: Those anxious in war to save their lives in any way they can are the very ones who usually meet a base and shameful death; while those who've recognized that death is the common, inevitable lot of all mankind, and who strive to meet death nobly, are precisely those more likely to reach old age and enjoy a happier existence while they do live. Taking to heart this lesson—so suited to the crisis that now con-fronts us—we must be brave ourselves and call forth bravery in our fel-lows." With these words Xenophon ceased speaking.

After him Cheirisophus* said: "Up to now, Xenophon, all I have known about you, by hearsay, is that you were an Athenian. Now I commend you for both your words and your deeds, and I'd be glad if we had very many of your sort. It would be a blessing to the entire army. And now, gentlemen," he went on, "let us not delay; go and choose your commanders at once, you who need them, and after making your choices come to the middle of the camp and bring with you the men you have selected. Then we'll call a meeting there of all the troops. And let's make sure that Tolmides, the herald, is present." With these words he got up at once, that there might be no delay in carrying out what was needed.

At that point the commanders were chosen: Timasion the Dardanian in place of Clearchus, Xanthicles the Achaean in place of Socrates, Cleanor the Arcadian in place of Agias, Philesius the Achaean in place of Meno, and Xenophon the Athenian in place of Proxenus.

———

With new leadership, and with Xenophon devising strategy, the Greeks burned their carts and excess gear and set off on a long and perilous road home. The Persians did them some harm with superior cavalry strength and long-range bows but were not willing to risk an infantry clash. Tissaphernes harassed the Greek army several times but finally gave up his pursuit and disappeared.

The Greek army moved north into the rugged mountains of Armenia, choosing their route to avoid regions stripped bare of food. Here they met a new foe, Tiribazus, the regional Persian governor and a close friend of the King. He too, like Ariaeus and Tissaphernes before him, concluded a truce with the Greeks but then treacherously plotted to destroy them. Meanwhile winter had arrived and a peril with which the Greeks were unfamiliar—snow and extreme cold. Under grave duress, the Greeks found refuge in one of their strangest, most remote bivouacs, amid a rural people who surely had no concept of who they were.

———

[4.5] The next day it seemed the Greeks must continue their march with all speed, before the enemy's army could be gathered again and take possession of the narrow passes. They therefore packed up and set out at once, marching through deep snow with a large number of guides. Before the day ended they crossed over the summit at which Tiribazus was intending to attack them and went into camp. From there they marched

* A Spartan commander who (unlike the freebooter Clearchus) had marched with Cyrus' army on the orders of the Spartan state. Xenophon, who in his writings constantly extols the virtues and strength of Spartan society, clearly takes great pride in being praised here by a Spartan.

three stages through desert country, fifteen parasangs, to the Euphrates, and crossed it, wetting themselves up to the navel. The report was that the sources of the river were not far off.

From there they marched over a plain and through deep snow three stages, thirteen parasangs. The third stage proved a hard one, with the north wind, which blew full in their faces, absolutely blasting everything and freezing the men. Then it was that one of the soothsayers bade them offer sacrifice to the wind, and sacrifice was offered; it seemed quite clear to everybody that the violence of the wind abated.* But the depth of the snow was six feet, so that many of the baggage animals and slaves perished, and about thirty of the soldiers. They got through that night by keeping up fires, for there was plenty of wood at their next stop. Those who came up late, however, had none, and consequently the men who had arrived early and were keeping a fire would not allow the latecomers to get near it unless they gave them a share of their wheat or anything else they had that was edible. So then they shared with one another what they each possessed. Where the fire was kindled the snow melted, and the result was great holes clear down to the ground; and there, of course, one could measure the depth of the snow.

From there they marched all the following day through snow, and many of the men were faint with hunger. Xenophon, who was marching with the rear guard, did not know what the trouble was as he came upon men falling by the way. But a person who was acquainted with the condition told him they had hunger-faintness, and if they were given something to eat would be able to get up; so he went around among the pack-animals and wherever he saw anything that was edible, he distributed it among the sick men, or sent those who had the strength to run along the lines and give it to them. And when they had eaten something, they would get up and continue the march.

As the army went on, Cheirisophus reached a village about dusk and found at the spring outside the wall women and girls who had come from the village to fetch water. They asked the Greeks who they were, and the interpreter replied in Persian that they were on their way from the King to the satrap.† The women answered that he was not there, but about a parasang away. Then, since it was late, the Greeks accompanied the

* An important point for Xenophon, who revered religious traditions.

† A lie, but the real story would have been unintelligible. A satrap is a Persian provincial governor.

water-carriers within the wall to visit the village chief. So it was that Cheirisophus and all the troops who could muster strength enough to reach the village went into quarters there, but others who were unable to complete the journey spent the night in the open without food or fire, and in this way some soldiers perished.

Meanwhile they were being followed by the enemy,* some of whom had banded together and were seizing the pack-animals that lacked the strength to go on, fighting over these with one another. Some of the Greeks likewise were falling behind—those whose eyes had been blinded by snow, or whose toes had rotted off by reason of the cold.† It was a protection to the eyes against the snow if a man marched with something black in front of them, and a protection to the feet if one kept moving and never quiet and if he took off his shoes for the night. But in all cases where men slept with their shoes on, the straps sunk into their flesh and the shoes froze on their feet; for what they were wearing, since their old shoes had given out, were moccasins made of freshly flayed ox-hides.

Under compulsion of such difficulties, some soldiers were falling behind; and seeing a spot that was dark because the snow just there had disappeared, they surmised that it had melted (in fact it had melted on account of a spring nearby, steaming in a dell). Here they turned aside and sat down, refusing to go any farther. But when Xenophon with some of the rear guard observed them, he begged them by all manner of means not to be left behind, telling them that a large enemy force had gathered and were pursuing. Finally he became angry. They told him to kill them, for they could not go on.

In this situation it seemed to be best to frighten the pursuing enemy, if they could, to prevent their falling on the sick men. It was dark by this time, and the enemy were coming on with a great uproar, quarreling over the booty they had. Then the men of the rear guard, who were sound and well, started up and charged the enemy, while the invalids raised as big a shout as they could and clashed their spears on their shields. The enemy, seized with fear, threw themselves down over the snow into the dell, and not a sound was heard from them afterward.

Then Xenophon and his men continued their march, after telling the

---

* The forces led by Tiribazus.

† Snow blindness and frostbite were little known to the Greeks, and Xenophon has no words for them.

invalids that the next day people would come back for them. But before
they had gone half a mile they came on their comrades lying down in the
road on the snow, wrapped up in their cloaks, and without so much as a
single guard posted. They tried to get them up, but the men said that the
troops in front would not make way for them. Xenophon passed along
and, sending forward the strongest of the peltasts, directed them to see
what the hindrance was. They reported back that the whole army was
resting in this way. So Xenophon and his party camped where they were,
without a fire and without dinner, after stationing such guards as they
could.

When it came toward morning, Xenophon sent the youngest of his
troops to the sick men with orders to make them get up and force them
to proceed. Meanwhile Cheirisophus sent some of the troops quartered
in the village to find out how the people at the rear were faring. Xenophon's party were glad enough to see them, and they turned over the
invalids to them to carry on to the camp while they themselves continued
their journey, and before completing two and a half miles they reached
the village where Cheirisophus was quartered.

When all had come together, the generals decided it was safe for the
different divisions of the army to take up quarters in the several villages.
Cheirisophus stayed where he was while the other generals distributed
by lot the villages within sight, and all set off with their respective commands. Then Polycrates, an Athenian captain, asked to be detached from
his division; with an active group of men he ran to the village which had
fallen to Xenophon's lot and there took possession of all the villagers, the
village chief included, seventeen colts being reared for tribute to the
King, and the village chief's daughter, who had been married eight days
before (her husband, however, was off hunting hares and was not taken in
the village).

The houses here were underground, with a mouth like that of a well,
but spacious below; and while entrances were tunneled down for beasts
of burden, the human inhabitants descended by a ladder. In the houses
were goats, sheep, cattle, fowls, and their young; and all the animals were
reared and took their fodder there in the houses. Here were also wheat,
barley, and beans, and barley-wine in large bowls. Floating on the top of
this drink were the barley-grains and in it were straws, some larger and
others smaller, without joints; and when one was thirsty, he had to take
these straws into his mouth and suck. It was an extremely strong drink

unless one diluted it with water, and extremely good when one was used to it.

Xenophon made the chief man of this village his guest at dinner and bade him be of good cheer, telling him that he should not be deprived of his children, and that before they went away they would fill his house with provisions by way of reward if he proved to have given the army good guidance until they reached another tribe. He promised to do this, and in a spirit of kindliness told them where there was wine buried. For that night, then, all Xenophon's soldiers, in this village where they were thus separately quartered, went to bed amid an abundance of everything, keeping the village chief under guard and his children all together within sight.*

The next day Xenophon took the village chief and set out to visit Cheirisophus; whenever he passed a village, he would turn aside to visit the troops quartered there, and everywhere he found them faring sumptuously and in fine spirits. There was no place from which the men would let them go until they had served them a meal, and no place where they did not serve on the same table lamb, kid, pork, veal, and poultry, together with many loaves of bread, some of wheat and some of barley. Whenever a man wanted to drink another's health out of good fellowship, he would draw him to the bowl, and then one had to stoop over and drink from it, sucking like an ox. To the village chief they offered the privilege of taking whatever he wanted. He declined for the most part to accept anything, but whenever he caught sight of one of his kinsmen, he would always take the man to his side.

When they reached Cheirisophus, they found his troops also feasting in their quarters, crowned with wreaths of hay and served by Armenian boys in their strange, foreign dress; and they were showing the boys what to do by signs, as if they were deaf and dumb. As soon as Cheirisophus and Xenophon had exchanged warm greetings, they together asked the village chief, through their Persian-speaking interpreter, what this land was. He replied that it was Armenia. They asked him again for whom the horses were being reared. He answered, as tribute for the King; and he

---

* This last clause reveals the darker undertones of the seemingly congenial scene. Not trusting the villagers, Xenophon and his men effectively treat the chief and his children as hostages. Later, when leaving these villages, the Greeks took the chief and his son along as guides, and trust broke down when the way to the next village proved long. The chief ran off in the night leaving behind his son, who was brought along with the army and ended up in Greece.

said that the neighboring country was that of the Chalybians, and told them where the road was.

Then Xenophon took the village chief back for the time to his own household, and gave him a horse that he had got when it was rather old, to fatten up and sacrifice, for he understood that it was sacred to the sun god. He did this out of fear that the horse might die, for it had been injured by the journey; and he took for himself one of the colts and gave his captains also a colt apiece. The horses of this region were smaller than the Persian horses but much more spirited. The village chief instructed them about wrapping small bags around the feet of their horses and beasts of burden when they were going through the snow; for without these bags the animals would sink in up to their bellies.

———

Not all interactions between the Greek army and remote mountain tribes went as well as in Armenia. Xenophon was clearly pained by his tragic encounter with the Taochians, related below.

———

[4.7.1] The army marched into the country of the Taochians five stages, thirty parasangs. Their provisions were running low, for the Taochians dwelt in strongholds, and in these strongholds they kept all their provisions stored away. Now when the Greeks arrived at one of them which contained no town nor houses, but was only a place where men and women and a great number of cattle were gathered, Cheirisophus proceeded to attack this stronghold as soon as he reached it; and when his first battalion grew weary, another advanced to the attack, and yet another; for it was not possible for them to surround the place in continuous line, because its sides were precipitous.

The moment Xenophon came up with the rear guard, consisting of both peltasts and hoplites, Cheirisophus said to him: "You have come in the nick of time. The place must be captured; the army has no provisions unless we capture this place." They took counsel together, and when Xenophon asked what was stopping them from gaining an entrance, Cheirisophus replied: "There is this one approach, the one you see; but when one tries to go along by this way, they roll down stones from this overhanging rock. Whoever is caught gets *this* result"—and he pointed out men with their legs and ribs crushed.

"But suppose they use up their stones?" said Xenophon. "There's nothing else, is there, to prevent entry? Surely we don't see anything on the other side except those few men there, and only two or three of them are armed. And as you can see for yourself, the distance we must cross under attack is about a plethrum and a half.* Now as much as a plethrum of that distance is covered with tall, scattered pine trees. If men should stand behind them, what harm could they suffer either from the flying stones or the rolling ones? The remaining space, then, amounts to about half a plethrum, and that we must cross on the run at a moment when the stones stop coming." "But," said Cheirisophus, "the very moment we begin to push out toward the trees, the stones fly in quantities." "Just the thing we want," said Xenophon. "They'll use up their stones more quickly. Let's make our way to a spot where we'll have only a short run to cross the space, if we can do that, or an easy retreat if we choose to come back."

At that Cheirisophus and Xenophon set forth, and with them Callima-chus of Parrhasia, a captain, the officer of the day in command of the captains of the rear guard. The other captains remained in a place of safety. Following this lead, about seventy men got under shelter of the trees, not all together but one by one, each protecting himself as best he could. But Agasias and Aristonymus, who were also captains of the rear guard, and others took places outside the cover of the trees (no more than one company could stand among them with safety). Callimachus hit on a plan: He would run forward two or three steps from the tree he was under and, when the stones began to fly, would draw back without any trouble. At every one of his dashes more than ten cart-loads of stones were used up.

When Agasias saw what Callimachus was doing, with the whole army for spectators, he became fearful that Aristonymus would be first to make the run across to the stronghold. So without asking Aristonymus to join him, or Eurylochus of Lusi (though the former was close by and both were his friends), or anyone else, he dashed forward and proceeded to pass everybody. Callimachus, however, when he saw him going by, seized the rim of his shield. At that moment Aristonymus ran past both of them, and on his heels Eurylochus. These four were rivals in valor and always striving with one another. In this competition they captured the strong-hold, for once they had rushed in not a stone came down from above.

Then came a dreadful spectacle: The women threw their little chil-dren down from the rocks and then threw themselves down after them, and the men did likewise. In the midst of this scene, Aeneas of Stympha-lus, a captain, catching sight of a man wearing a fine robe who was run-

* A plethrum is about a hundred feet.

ning to cast himself down, seized hold of him in order to stop him. But the man dragged Aeneas along after him, and both went flying down the cliffs and were killed.

In this stronghold only a very few human beings were captured, but the army secured cattle and donkeys in large numbers, and sheep.

———

After the mass suicide of the Taochians, the Greeks faced still more harsh terrain and hostile encounters, but their goal soon came into view: the Black Sea, a waterway that offered a passage home to their native cities. In the most celebrated passage of the Anabasis, *the exhausted, haggard troops first glimpse an end to their sufferings.*

———

[4.7.15] The army marched through the land of the Chalybians seven stages, fifty parasangs. These were the most valiant of all the peoples they passed through, willing to fight hand to hand. They had corselets of linen reaching down to the groin with a thick fringe of plaited cords instead of flaps. They had greaves on their shins also and helmets, and at the waist a knife about as long as a Laconian dagger with which they would slaughter whomever they could vanquish; then they would cut off their heads and carry them along on their march. They would sing and dance whenever they were likely to be seen by their enemy. They each carried also a spear about five cubits long, with a point at only one end. These people stayed within their towns, and when the Greeks had passed by, they followed them, always ready to fight. Their dwellings were in strongholds and they had stored all their provisions in these, so the Greeks could get nothing in this country, but subsisted on the cattle they had taken from the Taochians.

Leaving this land, the Greeks arrived at the Harpasus River, which was four plethra in width. From there they marched through the territory of the Scythinians four stages, twenty parasangs, over a level plain. They arrived at some villages and there remained for three days and collected provisions.

From there they journeyed four stages, twenty parasangs, to a large and prosperous inhabited city called Gymnias. From this city the ruler of the land sent the Greeks a guide to lead them through territory that was hostile to his own. When the guide came, he said that he would lead them within five days to a place from which they could see the sea; if he failed to do so, he was ready to accept death. Thus taking the lead, as soon as he had brought them into the hostile territory, he kept urging them to spread fire and ruin, making it clear he had come for this purpose and not out of goodwill toward the Greeks.

On the fifth day they did in fact reach the mountain; its name was Theches. As soon as the vanguard got to the top of the mountain, a great shout went up. When Xenophon and the rear guard heard it, they imagined that other enemies were attacking in front (for enemies were following behind from the district that was in flames, and the rear guard had killed some and captured others by setting an ambush and had also taken about twenty wicker shields covered with raw, shaggy ox-hides). But the shout kept getting louder and nearer, and the ranks that came up all began to run at full speed toward the ranks ahead that were one after another joining in the shout. The shout kept growing louder as the number of men grew greater, and it became clear to Xenophon that here was something of unusual importance. So he mounted a horse, took with him Lycius and the cavalry, and pushed ahead to lend aid; and in a moment they heard the soldiers shouting, "The sea! The sea!" and passing the word along.

Then all the troops of the rear guard likewise broke into a run, and the pack-animals began racing ahead and the horses. And when all had reached the summit, then indeed they fell to embracing one another, and generals and captains as well, with tears in their eyes. And suddenly, at the bidding of someone or other, the soldiers began to bring stones and to build a great cairn.* Thereon they placed as offerings a quantity of raw ox-hides and walking-sticks and the captured wicker shields; and the guide not only cut these shields to pieces himself, but urged the others to do so.† After this the Greeks dismissed the guide with gifts from the common stock—a horse, a silver cup, a Persian dress, and ten darics; but what he particularly asked the men for was their rings, and he got a considerable number of them. Then he showed them a village to encamp in and the road they were to follow to the country of the Macronians, and, as soon as evening came, took his departure.

———

Between a quarter and a third of the Greek soldiers had been lost during the arduous march and an even greater percentage of servants and noncombatants. But the

* This heap of stones served as a makeshift altar.

† Unmoved by the pious devotion of the Greeks, the guide seems concerned only to destroy the armaments of his tribe's enemies.

majority of the party had gotten through despite long odds. Xenophon's generalship had been key to their survival. The Anabasis *is in part a great adventure story but also a study of leadership in action, as its author evolves, in the course of its first four books, from a common soldier to a commander revered by his troops.*

That reverence, however, was largely born of privation and peril. Once the army was in more settled circumstances, it fractured into contentious factions and argued over how it should be led. Xenophon was even put on trial at one point for having struck exhausted men who could not otherwise be made to march, and had to strenuously defend his own actions. The story of these later books of Anabasis *(not excerpted here) centers not around survival and innovation, but around the problem of preserving unity among proud, headstrong Greeks belonging to different city-state cultures—in essence, the problem of all Greek history in the classical age.*

2. THE *HELLENICA*

Xenophon framed his only work of general history, Hellenica, *in such a way that it seemed to be a continuation of Thucydides'. The work begins precisely where that of Thucydides leaves off, in 410 BC, and it employs many of the same techniques, for example, the use of diplomatic speeches to dramatize foreign policy decisions. But Xenophon is not as successful as Thucydides in forcing the reader to confront the problems these decisions raise.*

The Hellenica *is also shorter and less detailed than the works of either Herodotus or Thucydides. Events that loom large in the record are sometimes omitted by Xenophon entirely, some out of carelessness, others intentionally. In particular the rise of Thebes in the 370s and 360s BC is given short shrift here, because Xenophon (like many Greeks) looked down on the Thebans (sometimes also called Boeotians) and resented their growing power. Xenophon's own political leanings made him strongly pro-Spartan, so he passes quickly over episodes that had embarrassed Sparta, or even leaves them out of his chronicle entirely.*

The five selections that follow are chosen to give insight into the three major cities of fourth-century Greece (Athens, Sparta, and Thebes), and also to illustrate the rise of warlords in places that had not before held much power or posed a threat to their neighbors. Jason of Pherae, who acquired rule over Thessaly in the 370s, was among the first of this new breed of leaders, but he would soon be followed by others even more aggressive and expansionist, Philip of Macedon and his son Alexander.

Xenophon ended the Hellenica *with the Battle of Mantinea in 362 BC, though he lived well beyond that time. He seems to have felt that with the indecisive results of that battle (described in the final selection below), the confusion and lack of leadership in Greece had become a hopeless condition.*

A. THE FALL OF THERAMENES (ATHENS, 403 BC)

TRANSLATED BY PAMELA MENSCH

The Thirty were a board of oligarchic rulers put in place by Sparta to keep Athens in line following Sparta's victory in the Peloponnesian War. Theramenes, a leading Athenian of moderate political views, at first went along with the regime of the Thirty, but he tried to extricate himself when their actions against their enemies became too repressive and cruel.

———

[2.3.11] The Thirty were chosen as soon as the Long Walls and those that surrounded Piraeus had been razed.* But though they had been chosen to frame a constitution according to which they would govern, they constantly delayed writing and publishing it, though they set up a Council and other offices as they thought suitable.† Then, to begin with, they arrested and charged with capital crimes those who they knew had earned a living under the democracy by acting as informers and who had vexed the aristocracy. The Council was glad to find them guilty, and the rest of the citizens—those, at any rate, who knew they were not men of that sort—were not at all unhappy about it.

But when the Thirty started to think about how they might acquire the power to manage the city however they pleased, they began by sending Aeschines and Aristoteles‡ to Sparta to persuade Lysander to provide them with a Spartan garrison, which would remain until, as they put it, they could rid themselves of the rascals and establish their regime. The Thirty also undertook to pay the costs of maintaining the garrison. Ly-

---

* The Long Walls, connecting Athens to its harbors in Piraeus, were deemed essential to its naval power, so the Spartans had insisted on their destruction as part of the settlement at the end of the Peloponnesian War.

† The Council (*Boulē*) consisted at first of four hundred, later of five hundred citizens, responsible for setting the agenda of the Assembly and overseeing other government functions. The Thirty had to stock it with their own partisans in order to effect their agenda.

‡ Both Aeschines and Aristoteles are different people than their more famous namesakes (the orator Aeschines and the philosopher Aristotle).

sander gave his consent and arranged for the garrison and for Callibius to be sent to them as its harmost.* But when they had received the garrison, the Thirty paid court to Callibius in every way so that he would approve of everything they did; and when he sent a detachment of guardsmen to accompany them, they arrested not only the men they were targeting—the worthless and those of little worth—but also those they thought least likely to tolerate being thrust aside,† and who, if they attempted to oppose the Thirty, could obtain the greatest number of partisans.

At first, Critias‡ and Theramenes were like-minded and friendly to each other. But when it emerged that Critias was bent on killing many, given that he had once been banished by the democracy, Theramenes interfered, saying it was not seemly to put a man to death for being honored by the people as long as he was doing the aristocracy no harm—"since even you and I," he said, "have done and said many things to gratify the city." To this, Critias replied (for he still treated Theramenes as a friend) that those who wanted to gain more power could hardly avoid eliminating those most able to thwart them. "And if," he continued, "you suppose that because we are thirty and not one, we need concern ourselves less with safeguarding our authority than we would as a tyranny, you are being naïve." But when several men were put to death unjustly, and it became clear that many citizens were banding together wondering where the regime was headed, Theramenes spoke up again and said that unless the oligarchy involved a sufficient number of citizens in managing the city's affairs, it could not survive.

Thereafter Critias and the rest of the Thirty, already fearing, principally, that the citizens might join together and lend their support to Theramenes, enlisted three thousand citizens who, they said, would take part in managing public business. Theramenes, however, argued against this as well, saying, firstly, that it would be strange if those who wished to make partners of the best citizens should fix their number at three thousand, as if that number must somehow include worthy men and there could be no men of integrity outside this cohort and no mediocrities within it. "Furthermore," he said, "I observe that we are doing two con-

---

* A harmost was a garrison commander empowered to use force against a subject population. Sparta began using harmosts extensively after the Peloponnesian War, much to the displeasure of other Greeks.

† That is, those who would resent being pushed out of office or out of public life.

‡ The leading member of the Thirty.

trary things: We're founding our regime on violence and rendering it weaker than its subjects."

So said Theramenes. The Thirty then held a review of the Three Thousand in the marketplace, while those excluded from the list were convened at various other locations. These latter were ordered to lay down arms, and when they had left, the Thirty sent along the guardsmen and their own partisans, confiscated all the weapons except those of the Three Thousand and had them conveyed to the acropolis and deposited in the temple. Once this was done, the Thirty, who assumed they now had the power to do whatever they wanted, killed many men out of personal hostility and many for the sake of acquiring their property. It was also decided that in order to raise funds to pay the garrison, each of them should seize one of the metics,* put him to death, and confiscate his property. But when they urged Theramenes to seize anyone he chose, he answered, "I don't think it honorable for those who claim to be the best citizens to be more unjust than paid informers. They, at any rate, allowed those from whom they took money to live, whereas we are proposing to kill men who have done no harm, in order to get their property. How will this not be, in every sense, more unjust than what the informers did?" The Thirty, then, concluding that Theramenes would interfere with what they wanted to do, plotted against him and privately slandered him to the Council, approaching the members individually and claiming that he was undermining their regime. They also summoned the boldest of the young men, ordering them to come with little daggers concealed under their arms. Then they convened the Council. When Theramenes arrived, Critias rose up and spoke as follows:

"Members of the Council, if any one of you feels that more people are being put to death than is proper, let him reflect that these things always happen whenever and wherever governments are being transformed. The men who are changing the form of our government to an oligarchy are bound to have a great many enemies, both because our city has the largest population of all the Greek cities, and because our citizenry has for the longest time been reared in liberty. Aware as we are that for men such as yourselves† and us, democracy is a harsh form of government,

---

* The metics, or resident aliens, were non-Athenians living in Athens or Piraeus but not enjoying citizen rights.

† The newly constituted Council was composed of wealthy citizens who favored oligarchic government.

and knowing that the masses would never be friendly to the Spartans (who keep us safe), but the aristocracy would always be loyal to them, we have, with the Spartans' blessing, established our present regime. And if we sense that someone is opposed to the oligarchy, we rid ourselves of him insofar as we are empowered to do so. And it strikes us as particularly fair that if any one of us is harming this regime, he pay the penalty.

"We now discern that Theramenes here, as far as is in his power, is seeking to destroy both us and you. And that this is true you will realize, if you think about it, given that no one faults our present proceedings more than Theramenes here, or is more resistant whenever we want to get rid of one of the popular leaders. Now if he had taken this position from the outset, he'd surely have been our enemy, though it wouldn't have been fair to regard him as a villain. But as matters stand, it was he who initiated our loyal friendship with the Spartans and the dissolution of the democracy,* and who most of all incited you to inflict penalties on those whose crimes you were called on to judge. But now that you and we have clearly incurred the democrats' hate, he's no longer happy with the present situation, and he's aiming to guarantee his own safety while we suffer punishment for all that's been done. Consequently, he should be punished not only as an enemy, but also as a traitor to you and to us. For treason is more terrible than war to the extent that it's harder to guard against the invisible than the visible; and it's much more hateful, given that whereas men make peace with their enemies and learn to trust them again, no one can ever make peace with a man, or trust him again, once he's been exposed as a traitor.

"And just so you know that there's nothing new in what this man is doing, and that he's a traitor by nature, I'll recall some of his previous actions. From the beginning, though honored by the people like his father, Hagnon, he was exceptionally eager to transform the democracy into the oligarchical regime of the Four Hundred,† and he served as a leader in their government. But when he became aware that an opposition to the oligarchy was coalescing, he emerged as the first leader of

---

* In the previous year, Theramenes had been chief among those who advised the Athenians to accept Sparta's terms for surrender, which included the dissolution of the democracy.

† The Four Hundred was an earlier, more moderate oligarchic regime, installed in 413 BC in the crisis of the defeat in Sicily. Theramenes was at first one of its leading members, but he then worked against the regime when it seemed to be going too far in a pro-Spartan direction.

common people against the oligarchs. And this is why he's nicknamed Cothurnus.* For the *cothurnus* appears to fit both feet, and he looks toward both camps.

"A man who deserves to live, Theramenes, should not be adept at leading his associates into trouble, and then, on meeting with a reverse, to instantly turn about. Instead, like a ship's pilot, he should persevere until he and his passengers encounter a favoring wind. Otherwise how would sailors ever reach their appointed destination, if whenever they encounter some obstacle they immediately change course and sail in the opposite direction? All changes of government invariably entail loss of life. But you, Theramenes, because you're so fickle, are responsible both for the enormous losses of oligarchs at the hands of the common people and the enormous losses of democrats at the hands of the aristocracy. It was this man who, though posted by the generals to retrieve the Athenians whose ships were sunk in the sea-battle off Lesbos, neglected to do so, though he nevertheless took it upon himself to accuse the generals and had them condemned to death so that he himself would survive.[†]

"Now if a man is invariably always seeking his own advantage and paying no heed to honor or to his friends, how should one ever spare him? Shouldn't we take precautions against him, aware as we are of his fickleness, lest he treat us likewise? We are therefore indicting him for plotting against and betraying both you and ourselves. And as proof that we are acting reasonably, consider this as well: The finest form of government is naturally thought to be that of the Spartans. And if any of the ephors[‡] should venture to criticize that government, and instead of obeying the majority should oppose the government's actions, wouldn't he be regarded, both by the ephors themselves and by all the rest of the city, as deserving the severest punishment? So if you are sensible, you will not spare this man, but will instead protect yourselves, since he, if allowed to

---

* A kind of boot worn by actors in tragedies. Unlike other shoes, it did not have a right and left version.

† Xenophon himself gives an account of this battle (at Arginousae) and subsequent trial earlier in *Hellenica.* Theramenes was not a commander but a ship's captain in the battle. The Athenians won but then were unable to retrieve their dead and wounded afterward. The generals were indicted and tried for this impiety; Theramenes joined in accusing them, though the generals suggested at the trial that Theramenes himself, whom they'd told to go back for the bodies, was largely to blame. In the end the generals were condemned to death while Theramenes went unpunished.

‡ Civic magistrates at Sparta.

live, would encourage many who oppose you to have grand ambitions, whereas his death would undercut the hopes of all your opponents, both within the city and outside it." So saying, Critias sat down.

Theramenes, rising to his feet, replied, "Well, first of all, gentlemen, I will remind you of the last thing Critias said about me: He says that I, by accusing the generals, caused their death. But it was not I, certainly, who issued the first accusations; it was they who declared that I had failed to perform my duty to rescue the unfortunate men in the sea-battle off Lesbos. And when I defended myself by claiming that on account of the storm it was not possible even to sail, much less to retrieve the men, I was thought by the city to have made a reasonable argument, whereas the generals were shown to be accusing themselves. For though they said that the men could have been rescued, they themselves departed and sailed away, leaving them to perish. But I'm not surprised that Critias has a mistaken notion of what happened. For when these events were unfolding, he was not here but in Thessaly, with Prometheus, setting up a democracy and arming the servants against their masters.* May nothing of what he was up to there come about here!

"Yet I agree with him in this: That if anyone is aiming to depose you from office and is strengthening those who are plotting against you, it would be right for him to meet with the severest punishment. But I think you'll be the best judges of who's doing this if you consider what each of us has done and is doing now. Up to the time you became Council members, and magistrates were appointed, and the false informers were brought to trial, we all held the same views. But once these Thirty began to arrest worthy men, I began to hold views opposed to theirs. I knew, for example, that when Leon of Salamis† perished—who was, and was thought to be, a man of integrity who had done no wrong—that those like him would be alarmed and in their fear would oppose this regime. I realized that when Niceratus, son of Nicias,‡ was arrested—a wealthy man who, like his father, had never courted the common people—that those like him would become ill-disposed to us. And when Antiphon§

---

* Nothing else is known of this episode in Critias' career.

† A staunch defender of the democracy. According to Plato, Socrates was enlisted by the Thirty to arrest Leon but declined to do so.

‡ Nicias had led the Athenian expedition to Sicily in the previous decade (see Books 6 and 7 of Thucydides above).

§ Not the more famous orator whose speeches partly survive, but another Antiphon

286 · *The Greek Histories*

perished at our hands—a man who during the war contributed two swift-sailing triremes—I knew that everyone who eagerly supported the city's cause would be suspicious of us. I also protested when the Thirty said we should each seize one of the metics; for it was clear that once these had perished, all the metics would be hostile to our regime. I likewise protested when they confiscated the people's weapons, since I thought we ought not to make the city weak.

"I saw that the Spartans preserved us not because they wished us to be few and incapable of helping them; had that been what they wanted they would have been able, by briefly prolonging the famine, to leave no one alive.[*] Nor was I happy with the hiring of the garrison, since it was in our power to hire the same number of our own citizens until such time as we, the rulers, could easily control our subjects. When I saw, at any rate, that many in the city were hostile to this regime and many were becoming exiles, it did not seem right to me to banish Thrasybulus or Anytus or Alcibiades.[†] For I knew that this would strengthen the opposition, if the common people acquired able leaders, and if those who wished to lead them attracted many partisans.

"Now would the man who openly offers this advice be justly considered well-meaning, or would he be thought a traitor? Those who prevent us from making enemies, Critias, or who teach us how to acquire a lot of allies, are not the ones who strengthen our enemies, but rather those who confiscate others' property unjustly and put to death men who have done no wrong. These are the persons who swell the numbers of their opponents[‡] and betray not only their friends but themselves through their shameful lust for gain. And if it is not otherwise obvious that I speak the truth, consider the question in this light: Do you think Thrasybulus and Anytus and the other exiles would prefer that we adopt here the policy I advocate or the one these Thirty are putting into effect? I imagine the exiles now think all places full of allies. But if the most powerful citizens

---

[*] Theramenes refers to the events earlier in the current year. Sparta had cut off food supplies to Athens and caused a famine in order to force a surrender. But after that surrender, Sparta refrained from destroying Athens (or in Theramenes' terms, "preserved us"), though some of its allies recommended destruction.

[†] Three prominent Athenian democrats who had, at one point or another, fallen afoul of the state and got kicked out. All three were now in exile, and Theramenes worries that they could rally the other exiled opponents of the Thirty. Thrasybulus indeed would lead the counterrevolution that overthrew the Thirty soon after this speech was delivered.

[‡] Theramenes speculates that by going too far, the Thirty are playing into the hands of the democrats.

were friendly to us, the exiles would consider it unsafe to set foot anywhere in our land.

"As for Critias' charge that I am the sort who always changes sides, give thought to this as well: The popular party itself, as we know, voted for the constitution of the Four Hundred, being informed that the Spartans would trust any form of government rather than a democracy.* But the Spartans did not slacken their war effort, and Aristoteles, Melanthius, and Aristarchus and their fellow-generals were found to be constructing fortifications on the promontory† where they wanted to admit our enemies and make the city subject to themselves and their allies. If I became aware of this and prevented it, was that a betrayal of my friends?

"Critias calls me Cothurnus, claiming I try to accommodate both sides. But what about the man who pleases neither side—what, in the name of the gods, are we to call him? You, Critias, when the democracy was in place, were regarded as the greatest hater of the common people; under the aristocracy you became the greatest hater of the upper class. But I, Critias, am always at odds with those who think a democracy cannot be excellent unless slaves are included and those who, through poverty, would sell out the city for a drachma. I am likewise opposed to those who think an oligarchy can't be excellent until the city has been subjected by the few to a tyranny. But to manage the government with the help of those who can serve, whether with horses or shields—that is what in the past I considered best, and I do not change my views now.

"If you are able, Critias, to cite a single occasion when I tried, with the help either of democrats or would-be tyrants, to deprive respectable men of their right to participate in government, speak out. For if I am convicted either of doing so now or of having ever done so in the past, I agree I deserve to suffer the severest of all penalties—death."

On speaking these words, he stopped, and the councilmen, who were clearly well disposed, applauded. Critias, realizing that if he permitted the Council to pass judgment about Theramenes, the man would be acquitted, and regarding this as insufferable, conferred briefly with the Thirty. Then he stepped outside and ordered those with daggers to stand at the railing where they could be seen by the Council.

---

* The oligarchy of the Four Hundred was voted in by the Assembly in 413, following a devastating loss of Athenian power in Sicily. Those advocating for it claimed it would win Athens clemency from Sparta.

† A wall that was begun in Piraeus under the Four Hundred seemed to some to be a means for Sparta to occupy the port.

Coming back in, Critias said, "Councilmen, I consider it the task of a leader worthy of the name, if he sees his friends being deceived, not to allow it. I shall act accordingly. The men standing out there say they will not permit us to release a man who is clearly harming the oligarchy. Now according to our new laws, none of the Three Thousand may be put to death without your vote, though the Thirty are entitled to put to death those not on the list of Three Thousand. I therefore," he said, "with unanimous consent of the Thirty, erase Theramenes' name from the list. This man," he said, "we condemn to death."

On hearing this, Theramenes leapt to the hearth* and said, "I beg you, gentlemen, for what is most just of all things: Let it not be in Critias' power to erase my name, or that of any of you he chooses. Let this be done only in accord with the law concerning those on the list, the law these very men have enacted. By the gods, I know full well that this altar will be of no use to me, yet I also want to make clear that these Thirty are not only utterly unjust toward men but also utterly irreverent toward the gods. And I am surprised that you, worthy gentlemen, don't come to your own defense, knowing as you must that my name is no easier to erase than any of yours."

At that point the herald of the Thirty ordered the Eleven† to seize Theramenes. These men came in with their henchmen, led by Satyrus, the boldest and most shameless of them all. Then Critias said, "We are putting Theramenes here in your custody, condemned according to the law. May you, the Eleven, take him to the proper place and do what must follow."

When Critias had spoken thus, Satyrus, with the others' help, dragged Theramenes from the altar.

Then Theramenes, as one might expect, called on gods and men to witness what was happening. The councilmen kept still, seeing men at the railing of the same stamp as Satyrus and noticing that the area in front of the Council was filled with guardsmen, these too, as the councilmen were aware, in possession of daggers.

As they led the man away through the marketplace, he continued to proclaim in a loud voice the wrongs he was suffering. It's been reported

---

* As in any building, the hearth of the Council chamber was sacred and could serve as a place of refuge for those in peril.

† An enforcement squad serving the will of the Thirty.

that when Satyrus told him that if he did not keep silent he would regret it, Theramenes replied, "And if I do keep silent, I won't regret it?"

When, compelled to die, he drank the hemlock, they said that he flung out the last drops and declared, as if he were playing *kottabos,** "Here's to my beloved Critias." Now I realize full well these anecdotes may not be worth recording, yet I find it admirable that with death looming, the man lost neither his wit nor his playfulness.

———

As predicted by Theramenes, the gross abuses committed by the Thirty deeply alienated many Athenians and energized exiled democrats. Thrasybulus, who had gone into exile at Thebes, crossed into Attica in 403 BC with a small band and seized an outlying fort. The populace quickly rallied to his side. It was not long before the Thirty were ousted and democracy was restored. Sparta, riven by divisions between its leaders, did not put down the uprising when it might have done so.

The course of the next two decades, in mainland Greece, was the one Theramenes had predicted for Athens: Overreach by Sparta led other states to block and counterweight. Sparta was sole superpower of Greece after its victory over Athens; its power extended farther than ever, even into Asia, where Spartan-led armies invaded the lands of the Persian Great King in the 390s. But Sparta's exertion of control alienated other cities, especially Thebes, a formidable force in land warfare. As the fourth century dawned, Thebes moved from alignment with Sparta to opposition and reached an entente with Athens. Even Corinth, traditionally a firm Spartan ally, briefly joined Sparta's foes in a grinding seven-year conflict called the Corinthian War (395–388).

The Persians helped foment that war, once again using their wealth to keep the Greeks fighting one another (as they had done in the Peloponnesian War). But Persian interests gradually converged with those of Sparta. In 388, the two great monarchs of the age, Agesilaus of Sparta and Artaxerxes of Persia, collaborated on a novel treaty arrangement—a Common Peace, as the Greeks termed it: a security framework for all the states of mainland Greece, guaranteeing mutual noninterference, overseen by the Persian Great King (hence termed the King's Peace). Sparta was anointed the enforcer of the treaty; in return, it ceded to Persia control over the coast of Asia Minor, putting an end to the freedom of the Ionian Greeks.

Enforcing the King's Peace (sometimes also called the Peace of Antalcidas) gave

———

* *Kottabos* was a drinking game in which the dregs at the bottom of the wine cup were flung out at a target. The player might dedicate his throw to a lover or favorite, a custom mocked by Theramenes here.

Sparta the right to make war on those it could cast as treaty violators. Before long Agesilaus was using the Peace as a club to beat up on his rivals, including, principally, Thebes. For nearly a century, Thebes had headed a union of all the cities in its region, an ethnically based super-state called the Boeotian League. Sparta challenged the League on the grounds that it violated the autonomy guarantee of the King's Peace, setting Sparta and Thebes even further at odds. Then in 382 a Spartan army, while apparently marching northward past Thebes, suddenly entered the city and, with the help of the pro-Spartan faction there, seized the Theban acropolis, a strongly fortified hill.

For three years the Spartans controlled Thebes by way of puppet rulers and garrison troops. Those opposed to Spartan rule took up exile in Athens and plotted a counterstroke. The Athenian experience of twenty years before provided them with a model: Just as Thrasybulus had overthrown Critias and the Thirty by invading from Thebes, so the Theban exiles, led by Pelopidas and Melōn, might overthrow their own city's oppressors, named Leontiades, Philip, and Archias, by invading from Athens.

The coup was carefully planned to be executed on a winter solstice holiday called the Aphrodisia, a night when the puppet rulers would have their guard down as they feasted, drank, and cavorted with Theban women. In Xenophon's retelling below, Melōn led the revolutionary plot, aided by a mole inside the regime, Phillidas. But we know from other sources that Pelopidas—whom Xenophon hated for his later victories over Sparta—was even more instrumental than these two men.

B. THE RETAKING OF THEBES (379 BC)

TRANSLATED BY PAMELA MENSCH

[5.3.27] The Spartans' success had been such as to render the Thebans and other Boeotians utterly subservient, the Corinthians perfectly dependable, the Argives abject (given that their "sacred months" excuse could no longer help them),* the Athenians bereft of allies, and their own allies punished if they'd shown ill will toward Sparta. Spartan supremacy† seemed to have been made perfectly sound and secure.

[5.4] One might mention many other occasions, among both Greeks and barbarians, showing that the gods do not ignore the impious and those who commit impious acts; at the moment, however, I will limit myself to the events before us. The Spartans had sworn to leave the cities autonomous, but they had seized the acropolis at Thebes. They soon found themselves punished by the very men who had been injured (and only by them), though they had never, until then, been overpowered by anyone. As for the Theban citizens who had brought the Spartans into the acropolis—preferring that the city be subject to Sparta so that they themselves might hold absolute power—it needed only seven of the exiles to overthrow them. I'll now relate how these events unfolded.

There was a man, called Phillidas, who served as secretary to Archias and the other polemarchs‡ and attended to their other affairs with excep-

---

* Some years before this, the Argives had changed the usual timing of a sacred truce to forestall a Spartan attack, but the Spartans had obtained oracles that allowed them to disregard the truce.

† The Greek word here translated "supremacy" can also mean "empire." In truth Sparta had become an imperial power in the past two decades, using many of the tactics for which they had reviled the Athenians.

‡ Archias was one of three polemarchs governing Thebes on behalf of its Spartan masters; his colleagues were Leontiades and Hypates. Philip, mentioned just below, seems also to have had a lead role in this pro-Spartan government.

tional ability—or so it appeared. Some business matter having taken him to Athens, Phillidas ran into Melōn, one of the Theban exiles who had fled to Athens and whom he had also known previously. When Melōn learned about the machinations of the polemarch Archias and of Philip's tyranny, and discerned that Phillidas detested how matters stood at home even more than he did, the two men exchanged pledges and agreed as to how each aspect of the situation should be handled.

Then Melōn, taking with him the six fittest exiles armed only with daggers, entered Theban territory by night.* Passing the day in some out-of-the-way spot, they arrived at the gates of Thebes as if coming from the fields, at the very time when the last laborers returned home. They entered the city and spent that night and the next day at the house of a man called Charon.

Phillidas, meanwhile, was catering to the polemarchs' other needs, since they were then engaged in celebrating the Aphrodisia, which took place at the close of their terms.† He had promised long before to bring them the most revered and beautiful of the Theban women, and he said he would do so at that time. And the polemarchs, who were men of that type, were anticipating a highly pleasurable evening. When they had dined and (with Phillidas' eager assistance) quickly become drunk, and had been asking for a while that the courtesans be brought in, the secretary finally went out and brought in Melōn and his companions, having clothed three of them as women of rank and the rest as their maids. He led these men into the polemarchs' anteroom and then went himself to Archias and his colleagues and told them that the women had refused to come in if any of the polemarchs' servants were there.

The polemarchs at once told all their servants to depart, and Phillidas, after providing one of the servants with wine, sent them on their way. He then brought in the [supposed] courtesans and seated each of them next to one of the polemarchs. The members of Melōn's party had agreed that on taking their seats they would immediately remove their veils and strike. This, according to some, is how the polemarchs died; others report that they were killed when Melōn and his comrades entered as if they were a party of revelers.

---

* The distance between the border of Attica and the gates of Thebes could easily be covered on foot in one night, especially as this was late December, affording the longest nights of the year.

† The Theban term of office expired at the winter solstice. That was also the occasion of the Aphrodisia, a religious festival marked by drinking, revelry, and sex.

Then Phillidas, with three of his associates, went to the house of Leontiades.* Knocking on the door, he said he wished to convey a message from the polemarchs. It turned out that Leontiades was still reclining on his couch after dining alone, and his wife was seated beside him, weaving wool. Thinking Phillidas trustworthy, Leontiades told him to come in. Phillidas entered with his men and they killed Leontiades and terrorized his wife into silence. On departing, they told her to keep the door locked, threatening that if they found it unlocked they would kill everyone in the house.

This mysterious scene, on a fourth-century gold vessel found in Bulgaria, may represent a mythicized version of the retaking of Thebes by Melōn, Phillidas, and other Theban patriots. NIKOLAY GENOV

This done, Phillidas took two of his men, proceeded to the prison, and told the jailer he was delivering a man from the polemarchs who had to be incarcerated. When the jailer opened the door, they killed him at once and freed the prisoners.† Taking weapons from the stoa,‡ they quickly armed the prisoners, led them to the Amphieium,§ and ordered them to

* The senior member of the pro-Spartan regime. He had stayed home that night instead of attending the revels of the Aphrodisia.

† According to other accounts there were more than a hundred Thebans in the jail, some of them political prisoners due to be executed. The pro-Spartan regime had instituted roundups of its enemies, just as the Thirty had done at Athens.

‡ In the stoa, or colonnade surrounding the market square, the Thebans had hung weapons captured in battle as a memorial.

§ A shrine to the hero Amphion.

remain there under arms. Then they immediately issued a proclamation, urging all Thebans to come forward, both horsemen and hoplites, since the tyrants were dead.

Now the citizens, during the night, kept still, not believing the news. But when day dawned and what had happened became clear, the horsemen and hoplites immediately hastened with their weapons to lend aid. Meanwhile, the exiles* sent horsemen to the Athenian troops massed at the borders under two Athenian generals. These troops, understanding why the horsemen had been sent to them, rushed to the rescue.[†]

When the Spartan commander on the acropolis became aware of the nighttime proclamation, he instantly sent for help from Plataea and Thespiae.[‡] But when the Theban horsemen realized that the Plataeans were approaching, they went out to confront them and killed more than twenty of them. And when they had returned from this encounter and the Athenians had arrived from the borders, they jointly attacked the acropolis. Those on the acropolis, seeing that their own numbers were scanty and having noted the zeal of all their attackers (handsome rewards had been promised to the first men to climb the hill), grew frightened and said they would depart if they were given a safe conduct, provided they could take their weapons with them.[§]

The Thebans, delighted, granted the request, and after pouring libations and solemnizing oaths sent the men off, having agreed to these terms. But as the Spartans were departing, the Thebans, recognizing men who had been their enemies, grabbed and killed them.[¶] Some who were departing were stolen away and saved by the Athenians who had come from the borders to aid the Thebans. Yet the Thebans even arrested the children of those who were killed—those, at any rate, who had children—and slaughtered them.

---

* Meaning Melōn and his confederates, newly arrived from Athens. Pelopidas, who in other accounts was the leader of the exile band, goes unmentioned by Xenophon.

† Much is unclear about Athenian participation in the Theban coup. Athens later repudiated the move and put these generals to death, evidently fearful of angering Sparta.

‡ Two Boeotian towns quite close to Thebes, both controlled at this time by Spartan puppet regimes.

§ A startling surrender, given the Spartan reputation for defiance to the death. Other sources make clear that the garrison chief had by chance been away from Thebes at the time of the coup.

¶ These "enemies" included not only Spartan garrison troops but the Theban citizens who had helped them, now going with them out of Thebes.

When the Spartans learned of these developments they executed the commander who'd abandoned the acropolis—since he'd not waited for help that was on the way*—and declared war on the Thebans. Agesilaus then declared he had become eligible for military service more than forty years before and pointed out that just as his age-mates were no longer obliged to serve in the military, the same law applied to the kings. So saying, he declined to serve in the campaign. But this was not the reason he stayed home; he was well aware that if he served as general his fellow citizens would say he was making trouble for his city in order to help tyrants.† He therefore left them free to decide this question for themselves.

When the ephors learned of the slaughter at Thebes from the men who'd escaped it, they sent out Cleombrotus,‡ though it was his first command and winter was upon them.... On reaching Thespiae, Cleombrotus proceeded to Cynoscephalae, in Theban territory, and encamped. After remaining there about sixteen days he withdrew to Thespiae. He left Sphodrias there as governor, along with a third of each of the allies' contingents. He also turned over to Sphodrias all the money he'd brought with him from home and urged him to hire a force of mercenaries,§ which Sphodrias proceeded to do.

Cleombrotus then conducted his army home along the road that leads through Creusis. His soldiers were quite at a loss to know whether they were at war with Thebes or at peace, since he'd led them through Theban territory and departed after inflicting the least possible damage.

---

* A Spartan relief force was a day or two away when the garrison surrendered. We learn from other sources that two subcommanders were executed, but the garrison chief, who had been off the scene on official business, was fined and banished.

† An interesting insight into the complexities of Spartan politics. Agesilaus had strongly supported (and, some suspect, instigated) the Spartan takeover at Thebes, but another faction at Sparta clearly felt it was improper and that the puppet rulers it had empowered were no better than "tyrants." A similar split in Spartan opinion had accelerated the downfall of the Thirty at Athens, some twenty-five years before this.

‡ The younger of the two Spartan kings, several decades junior to Agesilaus. Cleombrotus had come to the throne shortly before this and, as the account below demonstrates, was unsteady in his command.

§ In the fourth century BC, Greece was increasingly beset by stateless or landless men whose best way of earning a living was through paid military service. All the major powers, including Sparta, came to rely on mercenary forces to augment citizen armies. In this instance, Sparta sought to strengthen its principal base in Boeotia by means of money rather than commitments of manpower. Perhaps also they were preparing for a commando raid on the Athenian dockyards, for Sphodrias launched such a raid a month or two after this time.

On his return journey a violent wind arose, which some regarded as a portent. For in addition to all the other considerable damage it did, when he'd departed Creusis and was crossing the mountain ridge that slopes down to the sea, the wind blew many pack-animals down from the cliffs along with their baggage. Many of the soldiers' weapons were snatched away and fell into the sea.* In the end, many who were unable to advance with their weapons left them here and there on the heights, turning their shields facedown and filling them with stones. They then took a meal, insofar as this was possible, at Aegosthena, in Megarian territory. On the following day they went back to retrieve their weapons. Then they returned to their various homes, since Cleombrotus dismissed them.

———

The revival of independent Thebes after 379 BC, and its hardened opposition to Sparta, profoundly altered the power balance in Greece. Thebes became a force to be reckoned with, a threat to the Spartans and, increasingly, the Athenians (though they for the moment considered Thebes an ally). Athens was also reviving from its defeat in the Peloponnesian War and re-forming its Aegean naval alliance, though on more modest, and voluntary, terms. Greece had become a "three-headed monster," according to a lampoon of the day.

Sparta's fortunes were on the wane for one overriding reason: Its population had been declining for a century and had by now reached alarmingly low levels. Its wars were fought by small contingents of Spartiates—full citizens—and a much greater number of perioikoi, *residents of towns and villages surrounding Sparta, and recruits from allied cities, many of whom served unwillingly. Some spots in the ranks were even filled by helots, state-owned slaves who were promised freedom in exchange for military service.*

The problem of Spartan depopulation comes through clearly in the episode related below: An attempt by a Thessalian leader, Polydamas, to enlist Sparta's help in resisting a local tyrant, Jason of Pherae. Jason had come to power in Pherae, a city in Thessaly, by hiring a huge army of mercenary soldiers. In modern terms he was a warlord, a man whose power rested purely on the loyalty of armed toughs. He aspired to become tagus, legitimate ruler of all Thessaly, despite the opposition of most of the region.

Sparta traditionally disliked tyrants like Jason and often put them down with military force. So Polydamas, a leader of Thessalian opposition to Jason, had every

---

* The meaning of the "portent," left implicit by Xenophon, derives from the fact that the Spartans had been stripped of their weapons. In fact the Thebans' recapture of their acropolis, and the failure of Cleombrotus to do much about it, marked the start of a precipitous decline of Spartan power.

right to expect help when he went to Sparta in 375, especially after making clear the danger Jason posed to Thessaly, and after that all of Greece. But the outcome of his visit was not what he had hoped.

 Xenophon uses an unusual speech-within-a-speech structure here, allowing Polydamas to quote, to the Spartans, a long harangue he had heard from Jason. Neither speech should be taken as a historical record; together they represent Xenophon's depiction of how a dangerous warlord dreaming of world domination might interact with a lawful, respected leader who stands in his way.

C. A THESSALIAN'S PLEA FOR HELP (SPARTA, 375 BC)

TRANSLATED BY CARLETON BROWNSON, WITH REVISIONS BY JAMES ROMM

[6.1.2] At about this time, Polydamas of Pharsalus arrived from Thessaly and presented himself before the general assembly of the Spartans. This man was not only held in very high repute throughout all Thessaly, but in his own city was regarded as so honorable a man that when the Pharsalians fell into factional strife, they put their acropolis in his hands.... Besides, he was hospitable and he was generous to guests and grand in style, in the Thessalian manner. Now when this man arrived at Sparta, he spoke as follows:

"Men of Sparta, I am your diplomatic agent and benefactor,* as all my ancestors have been of whom we have any knowledge. I therefore deem it proper, if I am in any difficulty, to come to you, and if any trouble is gathering for you in Thessaly, to make it known to you.

"I am sure you often hear the name of Jason, for the man has great power and fame. This man, after concluding a truce with my city, had a meeting with me and spoke as follows: 'Polydamas, you may conclude from the following facts that I could gain power over your city— Pharsalus—even against its will. You know,' he said, 'that I have as allies the greater number and the largest of Thessalian cities, and I subdued them when you were fighting by their side against me. Furthermore, you're aware that I have men of other states as mercenaries, as many as six thousand, with whom, I think, no city could easily contend.

---

* "Benefactor" translates the Greek term *euergetēs*, an official title for a foreigner who had benefited the state.

"'As for numbers,' Jason told me, 'of course, some other city might field as large a force. But armies made up of citizens have men advanced in years and others not yet come to their prime. What's more, in every city very few men do bodily exercise, but among my mercenaries no one serves unless able to endure toils as severe as mine.' Jason himself— I must tell you the truth—is exceedingly strong of body and a lover of toil besides. Every day he tests the men under him; he leads them in full armor, both on the drill-ground and whenever he's on a campaign. And those among his mercenaries he finds weak, he casts out, but those he sees to be fond of toil and fond of war's dangers he rewards—some with double pay, others with triple pay, others even with quadruple pay, and with gifts besides, as well as care in sickness and splendor in burial. Thus all his mercenaries know that martial prowess assures them a life of greatest honor and abundance.

"Jason pointed out to me (though I knew it before) that he already has as subjects the Maracians, the Dolopians, and Alcetas, ruler of Epirus. 'Therefore,' Jason said to me, 'why should I fear that I won't subdue *you* easily? One who did not know me might perhaps retort, "Why do you delay? Why not launch your campaign against the Pharsalians at once?" Because, by Zeus, it seems to me better to bring you over to my side willingly rather than unwillingly. If you were constrained by force, you would be planning to harm me however you could, while I would want to keep you as weak as possible. But if I persuade you to join me, it's clear we would advance one another's interests to the best of our ability.

"'Now, I know, Polydamas,' Jason said to me, 'that your city looks up to you. If you make her friendly to me, I promise to make you the greatest, next to myself, of all men in Greece. Hear now what manner of fortune it is in which I offer you second place (and believe nothing I say unless it holds up to your examination). This much is plain to us: That if Pharsalus and the cities dependent on you are added to my power, I could easily become *tagus** of all the Thessalians; and whenever Thessaly is under a *tagus,* her horsemen amount to six thousand, and more than ten thousand men become hoplites. When I see both the bodies and high spirits of Thessalians, I think they would not agree to submit to any other people, if someone organizes them well. And while Thessaly is an exceedingly flat land, all the peoples round about are subject to her as soon

---

* The Thessalian *tagus* was a commander in chief elected by the leading cities of Thessaly, empowered to levy a national army. The office was not always filled.

as a *tagus* is established here, and since these neighbors are mostly javelin-men, it's likely that our combined force would be far superior in peltasts also.*

"'Furthermore,' Jason went on, 'the Boeotians and all the others at war with the Spartans are my allies, and ready to be my followers too, if I free them from the Spartans. The Athenians also, I know very well, would do anything to become allies of ours, but I do not think it best to establish ties with them, for I believe I could obtain empire by sea even more easily than by land. To see if my reasoning is sound,' he said, 'consider these points also. With Macedonia in our possession—the place where the Athenians get timber—we'll be able to build more ships than they. And who are likely better able to supply these ships with men, the Athenians or ourselves—we who have so many excellent serfs?† And who are likely better able to maintain the sailors—we, who with our abundance, ship surplus grain to other lands, or the Athenians, who have not even enough for themselves unless they buy it?

"'As for money,' said Jason, 'we'd likely enjoy a greater supply of it, for we would not rely on little islands for revenue‡ but draw on the resources of mainlanders. (Naturally, all our neighbors pay tribute as soon as Thessaly is under a *tagus*.) And you know well that it is by drawing on the resources of the mainland, not of islands, that the King of the Persians is the richest of mortals. Still, I think it easier to subdue him than to subdue Greece. For I know that everyone over there, except one person, has accustomed himself to slavery rather than courage, and I know what kind of force it was—both the one that marched with Cyrus and the one with Agesilaus§—that made the King risk his all.'

"In answer to Jason's statements, I replied that while the other matters he mentioned were worth considering, nevertheless for friends of the Spartans to secede and go over to their enemies, without any complaint

* That is, the peltasts of the neighboring regions would supplement Thessaly's traditional strength in cavalry (the result of its flat topography, conducive to charges on horseback).

† The Thessalian *penestai* were a class of hereditary slaves, not unlike Spartan helots. In Greek navies it was poor men (or slaves) who rowed the triremes, and huge numbers were needed to man large fleets.

‡ Jason here belittles the Athenian Empire, which included a multitude of small islands.

§ Referring to the army of the Ten Thousand (see glossary and selections from Xenophon's *Anabasis*) and the Spartan campaign in Anatolia under Agesilaus in 395. In both instances Persian armies had fared very poorly against Greek hoplites.

to bring against them—this, I said, seemed to me to be impossible. Then Jason (after commending me and saying he must keep me even closer because I was that sort of a man), allowed me to come to you and tell the truth: That he intends to campaign against the Pharsalians if we do not yield to him. He told me to ask you for help. 'And if,' said Jason, 'the gods grant that you persuade them to send a supporting force large enough to make war with me, so be it. Let us abide by the result of the war. But if it seems to you they don't give you adequate help, wouldn't you be blameless if you then follow the best course for the city that honors you?'

"It's about this, Spartans, that I've come. I tell you the whole situation as I myself see it and as I heard it from Jason's lips. And I believe this, men of Sparta: That if you send us a force that seems, not to me only but to the rest of the Thessalians, large enough to make war on Jason, the cities will revolt from him. All of them are afraid of the lengths to which the man's power will go. But if you imagine that freed helots, with a private citizen as commander, will suffice,* I advise you not to get involved. Be assured, the war will be against strong forces and against a man who is so clever a general that he achieves whatever he undertakes, whether by secrecy, or by getting ahead of his enemy, or by sheer force. He can make as good use of night as of day, and when he's in haste, to take breakfast and dinner together and go on with his task. He thinks it proper to rest only after reaching his goal and accomplishing what's needed. He has accustomed his followers also to the same habits.

"Yet he also knows how to gratify his soldiers when by added toil they achieve some success. All those with him have learned this lesson: That from toils come the easy life. He has greater self-control than any man I know as regards physical pleasures, so that he's not prevented by such things from doing what needs to be done. Consider, therefore, and tell me, as is fitting for you, what you will be able to do and intend to do." Thus Polydamas spoke.

At the time the Spartans deferred their answer; but after counting up, the next day and the day after, their units abroad to see how many they were, and the units near Sparta detailed to meet Athenian naval sorties and wars with their neighbors, they replied that at the moment they could not send Polydamas adequate support. They told him to go home and arrange his affairs and those of his city as best he could.

---

* Beset by declining numbers of citizens, Sparta had filled its ranks with sub-citizen soldiers.

Polydamas had little choice but to submit his city to Jason of Pherae. Jason became tagus of Thessaly and seemed to be on his way to achieving his grandiose plans when assassins abruptly ended his life in 370 BC. One threat to mainland Greece was thereby eliminated, but others loomed on the horizon. Philip of Macedon was barely a teenager at the time of Jason's death, but the lesson of Jason's career—that the populous, resource-rich regions of northern Greece, if united under one leader, might be more than a match for the war-ravaged city-states of the south— undoubtedly was not lost on the future monarch.

Jason had counted on exploiting the split in Greece between pro-Spartan and anti-Spartan states, a split that became far wider in the 370s. A new leader at Thebes, Epaminondas, pressed the Thebans toward a showdown with Agesilaus, king of Sparta, still determined to weaken Thebes by dissolving the Boeotian League. Epaminondas understood that Sparta had weakened considerably since its victory over Athens, and that Sparta's "allies" were in fact often forced to fight in its wars. In a skirmish in 375, Thebes had shown that its new infantry unit, the Sacred Band—supposedly made up of pairs of male lovers fighting side by side— could defeat a more numerous Spartan force. The time was ripe for a direct Theban challenge to Agesilaus.

In 371, Sparta hosted a new Panhellenic treaty conference in hopes of renewing a common commitment to autonomy for all (the King's Peace of 387 had long since fallen apart). In Sparta's interpretation, "autonomy" meant the breakup of the Boeotian League, the foundation of Theban power. Epaminondas, representing Thebes at that conference, demanded that Sparta give up its own control of its Peloponnesian "allies" if it indeed endorsed the autonomy principle. The diplomatic dispute, as Xenophon described below, soon led to an all-out Spartan invasion of Boeotia and the most consequential battle in thirty years.

D. THEBES CONFRONTS SPARTA
(LEUCTRA, NEAR THEBES, 371 BC)

Translated by Pamela Mensch

[6.3.18] The Spartans voted to accept the Peace on condition that the garrison commanders be removed from the cities, that the armed forces, both naval and infantry, be disbanded, and that the cities be left autonomous. If anyone violated these terms, any city that so desired could aid the injured city, while those that did not so desire were not obliged by oath to give aid. On these conditions the Spartans swore the oath on behalf of themselves and their allies, while the Athenians and their allies each swore on their own behalf. Thebes was among the cities that had sworn the oath, but the Theban ambassadors came forward the next day and demanded that the wording be altered to read that "the Boeotians" rather than "the Thebans" swore.*

Agesilaus replied that he would change nothing they had sworn to and committed to writing. If the Thebans preferred not to be part of the truce, he said, he would remove their names at their behest. Thus all the others concluded the Peace, and Thebes was the only dissenter. In the Athenians' opinion, one could now hope that the Thebans would, so to speak, be "tithed."† The Thebans themselves, utterly despondent,‡ departed.

After this, the Athenians removed their garrisons from the cities.... The Spartans, however, though they removed the commanders and garrisons from all other cities, made one exception: Cleombrotus was in charge of the army in Phocis,§ and he asked the authorities at home what he should do. Prothoös¶ said he thought they should disband the army in accord with the oath** and send word to the other cities to amass contributions for the temple of Apollo (each city contributing as much as it wished). Then, if any among them refused to leave the cities autonomous, the Spartans should again summon everyone who wished to establish and support autonomy and lead them against those who opposed. By

---

* At issue in this change was the legitimacy of the Boeotian League, a point Sparta and Thebes had contested for decades. If the League was a legitimate body, then Thebes was entitled to swear on behalf of all Boeotia. But Sparta maintained that the League violated earlier treaties that included an autonomy clause.

† Under standing conventions, one-tenth of the booty captured in war was dedicated to Apollo at Delphi. So for Thebes to be "tithed" meant to be destroyed, with a tenth of the booty and sale price of slaves going to Delphi.

‡ This judgment about Theban state of mind seems to arise out of Xenophon's extreme pro-Spartan, anti-Theban bias. In fact Thebes had sought the coming fight and had grounds for thinking it would win.

§ The Spartans had sent a large army into Phocis, north of Boeotia, prior to convening the treaty conference, no doubt to put pressure on Thebes. King Cleombrotus was field commander; Agesilaus, who was directing Spartan policy, had phlebitis of the leg and could not fight.

¶ An otherwise unknown Spartan leader.

** "The oath" refers to the Peace just adopted. It required joint rather than unilateral action against violators, so, in the view of Prothoös, Sparta had to disband the army in Phocis (dispatched by Sparta alone) and form a new one, if warranted, from a coalition of cities.

adopting this course, he said, the gods would be most well disposed to them and the cities least burdened. The assembly, however, when it heard his proposal, thought Prothoös was talking nonsense. Already, as it appeared, the divine was leading them forward.*

The Spartans therefore sent word to Cleombrotus ordering him not to disband the army but to lead it at once against the Thebans unless they left the cities autonomous. And when Cleombrotus learned that the Thebans were not freeing the cities, and that not only were they not disbanding their army but were arraying it against him, he at once led his forces into Boeotia.

He did not, however, invade from Phocis at the point where the Thebans expected and where they were keeping watch at a narrow pass.

---

* An unusual instance in which Xenophon sees *to theion,* the collective will of the gods, behind historical events. Earlier he had pointed out the pattern of divine retribution seen in the Thebans' recapture of their acropolis (see p. 291 above), after Sparta had violated an earlier treaty by seizing it.

Instead, having advanced through Thisbe over a mountainous and un-expected route, he arrived in Creusis, where he seized the wall and cap-tured twelve Theban triremes. After doing so and marching up from the coast, he camped at Leuctra, in the district of Thespiae. The Thebans camped not far off, on the hill opposite, having no allies but the other Boeotians.*

Cleombrotus' friends came to him and said, "Cleombrotus, if you let the Thebans go without a battle, you are likely to suffer the ultimate punishment at your city's hands. For your fellow citizens will remember both that when you reached Cynoscephalae you failed to lay waste the Thebans' territory, and that on a subsequent occasion when leading the army you were repulsed from making an inroad, though Agesilaus always used to invade by way of Cithaeron.† So if you care about your own well-being and want to return to your native land, you should lead us against these men." So spoke his friends. His enemies, on the other hand, said, "Now the man will reveal whether he indeed favors the Thebans, as some claim."

Cleombrotus was goaded by these words to engage the enemy. The leaders of the Thebans, in turn, reasoned that if they did not fight, the neighboring cities would revolt from them and they themselves would be besieged, and that if the people of Thebes had no provisions, the city was likely to turn against them. And since many of them had been in exile previously,‡ they reasoned it would be better to die fighting than to be exiled again. They were also heartened by the oracle that had declared that the Spartans were fated to be overthrown near the grave monument of the virgins. (The virgins were said to have killed themselves after being raped by certain Spartans.)§ The Thebans adorned that monument

---

* Athens was still nominally allied with Thebes but increasingly mistrustful, and the terms of the new Peace spelled out that no state was required to help any other if it didn't want to. In coming years Athens would abandon its Theban alliance and side with Sparta.

† The Spartan advisers here recall the two previous occasions when Cleombrotus led troops into Boeotia. The first campaign, in 378, suffered from lack of resolve (see the de-scription above, pp. 295–96); the second, in 376, did not even reach Boeotia but turned back after meeting resistance in the passes of Mount Cithaeron. The unflattering comparison the Spartans draw here, between the two kings, reflects their very different temperaments; Cleombrotus was perceived as weak-willed compared to the imperious, ambitious Agesi-laus.

‡ After the Spartan seizure of the Theban acropolis (see pp. 290–91).

§ Legend had it that the girls, known as the Leuctridae, or "women of Leuctra," had been the daughters of a simple Boeotian farmer and had been raped and killed (or, in Xenophon's

before the battle. Also, word reached them from the city that all the temples were spontaneously opening their doors and that the priestesses maintained that the gods were signaling a victory. It was also reported that the weapons had disappeared from the temple of Heracles—a sign that the god had gone forth to battle.

There were some, of course, who said that all these portents had been concocted by their leaders.* Yet everything that occurred in the battle either thwarted the Spartans or favored their adversaries, including chance events. For example, it happened that Cleombrotus' final council about the battle took place after the first meal of the day; and since at noon they took some refreshment, it's said that the wine they drank was spurring them on.† And when both sides were donning their armor (as it was by then clear that there would be a battle), the people who had furnished the market,‡ together with some baggage-carriers and others who did not wish to fight, got up and left the Boeotian army; the Spartan mercenaries under Hieron, along with the Phocian peltasts and the Heracleot and Phliasian horsemen, attacked them as they were leaving, forced them to turn back, and even pursued them to the Boeotian camp. The result was that they swelled the Boeotian numbers and made their force more massive.§

Then, since the land between the two sides was a plain, the Spartans stationed their horsemen in front of the phalanx, and the Thebans facing them did likewise. The Thebans' cavalry was then in top form as a result of their battles with both the Orchomenians and the Thespians,¶ whereas at that period the Spartan cavalry was in the worst possible condition. For the wealthiest Spartans kept the horses, and it was only when a call to

---

version, killed themselves) while their father was away. The father, named Scedasus, went to Sparta to demand justice but was mocked and ignored. He called on the Furies, underworld deities charged with avenging murder, then hanged himself. Since that time the Spartans had been warned, "Beware the wrath of Leuctra."

* Other sources charge that Epaminondas, now leading the Theban army, falsified these apparitions.

† Xenophon's implication that Cleombrotus and his officers were somewhat intoxicated is no doubt meant to shift blame for Leuctra away from Agesilaus, whom Xenophon deeply admired.

‡ Noncombatants who set up food stalls for the soldiers to purchase meals.

§ It's not clear why the Spartans would want their foes' numbers increased, or whether Xenophon regards this Spartan move as a mistake.

¶ In the past eight years the Thebans had gradually reclaimed the Boeotian League by driving out Spartan forces, and Spartan sympathizers, from Boeotia.

arms had been sounded that the assigned rider appeared. Getting whatever horse and weapons were provided to him, he would go into battle at that instant. What's more, the Spartan horsemen were the worst in physical condition and the least warlike.

Such were the cavalries on each side. As for their infantries, it has been reported that each Spartan half-company was led three files abreast; the result was that their phalanx was no more than twelve rows deep. The Thebans, on the other hand, were arrayed no less than fifty shields deep, their leaders reckoning that if they prevailed over the company that surrounded the king, the rest of the enemy forces would easily be subdued.*

When Cleombrotus started to lead his forces against the enemy, and before the men under his command had even noticed he was advancing, the two cavalries engaged, and that of the Spartans was swiftly overpowered. As they fled, they fell back on their own hoplites, and then too the Theban squadrons were coming at them. The fact that the troops surrounding Cleombrotus had the upper hand when the battle began can be inferred from this: They would not have been able to take Cleombrotus up and carry him away alive unless the men posted in front of him had at that point been getting the better of their opponents. But once Deinon the polemarch had perished along with Sphodrias, who shared the king's tent, and Sphodrias' son Cleonymus, then the horsemen and the polemarch's aides (as they were called), along with others who had been pushed back by the Theban throng, retreated; and when those on the Spartan left wing saw the right wing thrust back, they gave ground.†

* This strategy, called "cut off the snake's head," was supposedly demonstrated by Epaminondas to his troops before the battle (using an actual snake). The goal was to knock out the leadership of the Spartan wing, and therefore the Spartans themselves (who made up only a small percentage of the mixed forces in this army). The Spartan allies who made up the rest of the line, it was thought, would turn and run if they saw the Spartans defeated. To that end, the Thebans put their strongest troops on the left, facing the Spartans and Cleombrotus, rather than on the right as tradition dictated. The added depth of this left wing—fifty rows instead of the usual eight or sixteen—added impetus and also made it harder for the Spartans to outflank them.

† Xenophon's account of the battle is impressionistic and vague, but the following stages can be discerned: (1) As the phalanxes advanced, both cavalries came forward into the ground between them and clashed; the Spartan horsemen were defeated and thrust back on their own lines, disrupting cohesion. (2) Theban infantry squads charged the disrupted Spartan lines and caused huge losses, including the wounding of Cleombrotus and the deaths of several high-ranking officers. (From other accounts, we know this charge was led by the Theban Sacred Band, an elite squad made up of 150 male couples; but Xenophon never mentions this squad and barely takes note of its leader, Pelopidas.) (3) The Spartans fled the field; their allies on the opposite wing also took flight before even making contact with the enemy.

Many Spartan troops had fallen and been overpowered; yet when they crossed the ditch, which happened to lie in front of their camp, they grounded their weapons at the place from which they had originally marched forth. (Their camp did not lie on level terrain, but on the slope of a hill.)* Some of the Spartans, finding their misfortune unbearable, declared they ought to prevent the enemy from erecting a trophy and ought to retrieve their dead not under a truce but by fighting.† Their polemarchs, however, seeing that nearly a thousand of all the Spartans had perished and that roughly four hundred Spartiates of the seven hundred present had died,‡ and noticing that all their allies were reluctant to fight and that some were not sorry about what had happened,§ assembled their most capable men and deliberated about what to do. Everyone thought it best to retrieve the dead under truce, and they sent a herald to request one. After this, the Thebans erected a trophy and gave back the dead under truce.

After the battle, the man sent to report the disaster reached Sparta on the last day of the Gymnopaedia,¶ during the men's chorus at the theater. When the ephors** heard of the disaster, they must, I assume, have been grieved. Yet they did not dismiss the chorus but allowed it to complete its performance. Meanwhile they gave out the names of each of the dead to that man's relatives and warned the women not to raise a wail but to bear their calamity in silence.

On the following day one could see the kinfolk of those who had died going about in public looking bright and cheerful. You would have seen

* The point of this comment is that the Spartan forces were safe from further attack once they attained their camp.

† The conventions of war required the loser to admit defeat by asking the winner for permission to recover the dead; the winner had the right to erect a trophy, made up of captured enemy weapons, to advertise the victory. The Spartans seeking to prevent these two outcomes are unwilling as yet to accept defeat.

‡ Spartiates, or full Spartan citizens, were far more valuable (because of their years of intensive training) than the "Lacedaemonians" who fought beside them (inhabitants of villages and towns surrounding Sparta). The loss of four hundred Spartiates, perhaps a third of all that Sparta had, was devastating.

§ A shocking admission by Spartophile Xenophon: Not all of Sparta's "allies" fought for her voluntarily or wanted her to succeed.

¶ A Spartan religious festival held in summer. It was one of few occasions when large numbers of Greeks from other cities visited Sparta, which partly explains the desire of the ephors to keep the news of Leuctra under wraps.

** The five elected officials in charge of domestic policy.

few of the survivors' kinfolk, and these were going about looking down-hearted and despondent.*

———

The Theban victory at Leuctra made Thebes the leading power in Greece, and Epaminondas, its visionary leader, moved quickly to press his advantage. He invaded the Peloponnese and dislodged many of Sparta's so-called allies, cities that were in fact longing to be free of Spartan oppression. The Arcadians, in the center of the Peloponnese, formed a league not unlike that of Thebes and dedicated themselves to containing Spartan power. Meanwhile Epaminondas, after threatening Sparta itself—a place that had never yet, according to legend, seen the smoke of an enemy's campfires—led his army west and founded Messene, a fortress city designed to protect helots who had escaped their servitude to Sparta.

The Peloponnese, reorganized by Thebes in multiple invasions in the 360s, soon became a prison for the isolated Spartans rather than their power base. But the containment system set up by Thebes began to collapse as that decade neared its close. The Arcadian League split apart into pro-Theban and pro-Spartan factions, and Thebes felt compelled to invade once more to support its side of the schism, the faction based at Tegea. Sparta and Athens, now allies, took the field in support of the other Arcadians, based at Mantinea, and a major confrontation began to take shape.

Xenophon observed the clash at close quarters (he was living in Corinth at the time) and also had a first-rate informant: his own son, who fought with the Athenian cavalry. Another son, Gryllus, was killed in action in the same unit.

E. THE LAST CAMPAIGN OF EPAMINONDAS OF THEBES (MANTINEA, IN THE PELOPONNESE, 362 BC)

Translated by Pamela Mensch

[7.5.9] Epaminondas learned that his enemies had acquired a strong position near Mantinea and were sending for Agesilaus and all the Spartans, and that the latter had set forth and had now reached Pellene. He ordered his troops to have supper, then led them straight to Sparta.† And if, by some divine luck, a Cretan had not approached Agesilaus and re-

———

* Xenophon's portrait captures the power at Sparta of deeply ingrained statist ideology. Those whose sons had died at Leuctra were considered more fortunate—or behaved as though they were—than the parents of the living.

† Epaminondas was starting from Tegea, about thirty miles north of Sparta, so he planned to cover that ground in an all-night march with a select, fast-moving force.

ported that the Theban army was on its way, Epaminondas would have captured the city like a nest deserted by its protectors. But Agesilaus, having had a timely warning, was able to get back to Sparta ahead of the enemy. The Spartiates posted themselves at several points and stood guard, though few in number; all their horsemen were away in Arcadia, along with their mercenary force and three of their twelve battalions.

Epaminondas arrived at Sparta. He did not enter at a point where his men would be forced to fight on level ground and could be pelted from the rooftops, nor where, though fighting against few, their superior numbers would give them no advantage. Instead he seized a place he saw as advantageous, from which he would be marching downhill, not up, to the city.

As for what ensued: One might say either that some god was responsible or that no one can resist men who are desperate. When Archidamus led out his men (fewer than a hundred) and crossed a stretch that one might think would pose difficulties, he advanced uphill against the enemy. At that, his adversaries, the "fire-breathers,"* who had defeated the Spartans and who not only had strength of numbers but occupied higher ground, did not stand the charge of Archidamus and his troops but drew back. The men in Epaminondas' front ranks perished. But when the Spartans, thrilled at their victory, pursued the enemy farther than was prudent, they too were dying; it appeared that the measure of victory granted to them had been circumscribed by the god. Archidamus proceeded to erect a trophy at the place where he had triumphed and gave back, under a truce, the enemy's dead.

Epaminondas, guessing that the Arcadians would be coming to Sparta's aid,† did not want to engage all the Spartans' assembled forces, given that these had had success while his own men had been defeated. He therefore marched back as speedily as possible to Tegea, where he gave his hoplites a rest but sent his horsemen on to Mantinea. He begged them to persevere and informed them that all the Mantineans' cattle and all its people were probably outside the city,‡ especially since it was the harvest season. They then set forth.

---

* Xenophon, clearly peeved at earlier Theban victories over his admired Spartans, uses this term sarcastically.

† Archidamus had summoned the Mantineans when he learned of the Theban attack on Sparta (see above).

‡ A surprise attack, if it caught the rural population outside the walls (as Epaminondas here hoped), could easily force its target to surrender, since the captured farmers and flocks effectively became hostages.

The Athenian horsemen,* meanwhile, having ridden out from Eleusis, had taken their supper at the Isthmus. They had passed through Cleonae, and a number of them happened to be nearing Mantinea or finding lodgings in the houses within its wall. Then the Thebans were seen advancing on the city. The Mantineans pleaded with the Athenian horsemen to aid them in any way they could, since all their cattle and workmen were outside the wall, as were many freeborn children and elderly men. Hearing this, the Athenians hastened to the rescue, though they and their horses had not yet taken food. Who, then, would not marvel at the bravery of these men? For though they saw they were far outnumbered, and though their horsemen had suffered a reverse at Corinth, they gave this no thought and didn't reflect that they were about to do battle with Theban and Thessalian horsemen, who were reputed to be the strongest. Instead they considered it shameful, being on the spot, not to help their allies. The moment they caught sight of the enemy, they charged, eager to uphold their ancestral renown.

Because they joined battle they brought about the rescue of everything outside the city belonging to the Mantineans. A number of their brave men were slain, and they slew men who were clearly of comparable courage. For none on either side wielded weapons too short to reach their foe. The Athenians did not abandon the corpses of their own troops and gave back the enemy's corpses under truce.†

Meanwhile, Epaminondas, bearing in mind that within a few days he'd have to depart (since the campaign's term had expired),‡ and that if he were to leave defenseless the people he'd come to as an ally, they'd be besieged by their enemies, and his own reputation would be utterly ruined (since with a large number of hoplites he'd been defeated at Sparta by a small force, and had then suffered another defeat in the cavalry clash at Mantinea; and by invading the Peloponnese had occasioned the union of the Spartans, Arcadians, Achaeans, Eleans, and Athenians). With all these considerations in mind, he thought it impossible to leave without

---

* Xenophon shifts scene to follow the progress of the Athenian cavalry, dispatched to the Peloponnese to aid the Spartans. His two sons were part of this unit.

† The request for permission to retrieve one's dead was a formal admission of defeat.

‡ Xenophon earlier reported that the Theban government had given Epaminondas a time limit for this campaign, and he here assumes that this limit dictated the general's strategy. But we do not hear of this factor in our other source for these events, Diodorus Siculus, and in any case it seems unlikely that Epaminondas would have felt bound by such constrictions.

again engaging the enemy. He calculated that if he prevailed he would redeem all his errors, whereas if he perished his death would be honorable, the consequence of his attempt to bequeath to his country control of the Peloponnese.

Such calculations on his part I find not at all surprising, since men who pursue glory are apt to entertain such thoughts. But I do consider this remarkable: He had trained his army in such a way that his men shirked no effort, day or night, and held aloof from no danger; and though their equipment was meager they were nevertheless poised to obey him. When he issued his final order, telling them to prepare themselves as there would soon be a battle, his horsemen eagerly whitened their helmets in obedience to his command; the Arcadian hoplites painted clubs on their shields, as if they were Thebans; and everyone sharpened their lances and swords and polished their shields.

When his men, prepared in this manner, were led out, Epaminondas' actions should be noted. To begin with, as was reasonable, he drew them up in battle-array. By doing so he made clear he assumed he was preparing to engage. But when his men had been drawn up as he wished, he led them not by the shortest route against the enemy, but toward the mountains that face Tegea from the west. He thereby made his enemy think he would not, on that day, engage in battle. As soon as he reached the mountain, and his phalanx had been stationed, he had his men plant their weapons at the foot of the heights, giving the impression that he would encamp there. By doing so, he prompted most of the enemy to slacken their readiness both to engage in battle and to maintain formation.

It was only when he had led his companies to his wing and bolstered the wedge-shaped array around him* that he ordered his men to take up arms and led them forward. They followed his lead. And as soon as the enemy saw their opponents unexpectedly approaching, none of them could keep still. Some ran to their posts, others arrayed themselves for battle, others bridled their horses, still others donned their breastplates. All resembled men who were about to suffer harm rather than inflict it.

* The strategy used here by Epaminondas, like that of Leuctra (see p. 306 above), was an attempt to "cut off the snake's head"—that is, knock out the best troops first. The left wing of the Theban line, which would face the Spartan contingent, was strengthened and made "wedge-shaped"; the right wing was told to hang back and avoid making contact with the opposing left, made up of Sparta's allies (including, now, the Athenians). In the description below, Xenophon memorably compares this strong Theban left wing to the ram of a warship.

Epaminondas now advanced his army like a ship with the prow forward, assuming that wherever he attacked and broke through the enemy's line he would destroy their entire army. For he was preparing to deploy the strongest part of his force, and he had posted the weakest part in the rear, knowing that if he were overpowered it would discourage his own troops and hearten his opponents. Furthermore, whereas the enemy had arrayed their horsemen like a hoplite phalanx (six ranks deep and excluding foot-soldiers), Epaminondas had formed a strong wedge of his horsemen and posted foot-soldiers among them, thinking that once he broke through the enemy's cavalry he would defeat the entire force. For it's not easy to find men willing to stand their ground when they see some of their comrades fleeing. And to deter the Athenians on the left wing from coming to help the troops stationed beside them, he posted horsemen and hoplites on some hills across from them, hoping to make them afraid to lend aid lest the men on the hills attack them from the rear.

So he launched his assault, and his hopes were not disappointed. After gaining control at the point where he attacked, he put the entire enemy force to flight. Yet when he himself had fallen,* his other troops were unable to take full advantage of the victory. Instead, though the phalanx opposite them had fled, his own hoplites failed to kill a single man or advance past the point where the clash had occurred. And though the enemy cavalry had also fled, his own troops did not pursue or kill either horsemen or hoplites, but retreated fearfully through the ranks of their fleeing enemy. The foot-soldiers and peltasts who had taken part in the cavalry's victory† arrived like victors at the enemy's left wing, most of them perished there at the hands of the Athenians.

In the aftermath of these events, the opposite of what everyone expected came to pass. Given that almost all the Greeks had assembled, arraying themselves on opposite sides, no one imagined that if a battle were fought the victors would not rule, the defeated not be their subjects. But the god arranged matters so that both sides erected trophies on the assumption that they had won (since no one attempted to prevent this), and both sides, assuming themselves victors, gave back corpses under a

* As in his other battle descriptions, Xenophon leaves the turning point vague and understated. As we know from other sources, Epaminondas was felled by a spear thrust to the chest as he led the pursuit of the fleeing Spartans. The wound was not immediately fatal, but he died soon after when he pulled the spearhead from his own chest. His troops had halted when they saw him fall, so the routed Spartans got away with light losses.

† That is, the Theban infantry who had been mixed in with the cavalry.

truce, and, assuming themselves defeated, took back the corpses of their own men under a truce. Neither side was shown to be better off, either in territory or city or authority, than it had been before the battle. On the contrary, Greece was in greater perplexity and turmoil after the battle than before it.

Let this conclude my narrative. Someone else will perhaps take up the sequel.*

———

Those who "took up the sequel" from Xenophon, to write the story of the next forty years and the last phase of classical Greek history, are mostly mere names to us today. That was the era that saw the rise of Macedon as the superpower of the Greek world, the defeat in battle of Athens and Thebes at the hands of Philip of Macedon, and the Asian campaign led by Alexander the Great, resulting in the conquest, by Greek and Macedonian forces, of the vast Persian Empire. Contemporary historians wrote about these events, but their works did not survive into modern times, except for a few quotations by later authors or fragments of recovered papyri.

In lieu of true primary sources—records left by eyewitnesses to history, or by those who could speak to eyewitnesses—today's Hellenists use a variety of later, secondhand writers to "fill in the gap." One is Diodorus Siculus, a very uneven and inelegant writer of the first century BC, *whose* Library of History *includes accounts of Philip and Alexander in its sixteenth and seventeenth books. Another is Arrian, a Greek military man who served under Roman emperors in the late first and second centuries* AD *and whose* Anabasis Alexandrou, *"The Inland March of Alexander the Great"—the title is a deliberate echo of Xenophon's* Anabasis— *supplies our most reliable record of Alexander's campaign of 334–323* BC.

Looking farther down the time line of the Hellenistic age—the era begun by the conquests of Alexander—we come to Polybius, an important Greek historian who lived through much of the second century BC. *He described and analyzed the principal developments of his own lifetime, the Roman subjugation of Greece and Carthage, often from the perspective of a participant (he was a close friend of the leading Roman commander of the day and accompanied him on his final campaign against Carthage). In his depth of insight and his proximity to the events he describes, Polybius ranks among the greatest of Greek historians, but his focus is more on Rome than on his native Hellas.*

---

* Xenophon ended *Hellenica* at this point, though he lived perhaps seven or eight years longer. Nothing during those years changed his assessment that Greece had become confused and leaderless.

A more comprehensive volume than this one would include all the above-mentioned writers, but we have opted instead to include substantial selections from Plutarch's Lives. *Though usually classed as a biographer and moralist, not a historian, Plutarch relied on primary sources now lost to us and preserves a wealth of data not found elsewhere. He is also an insightful and compelling writer, whose shrewdly selected anecdotes bring his subjects vividly to life, and whose penetrating metaphors and analogies allow us to probe the larger dimensions of historical events.*

The inclusion of Plutarch also allows us to document the eight decades between the Battle of Mantinea, where Xenophon ended his Hellenica, *and the last of the wars between the Successors of Alexander the Great, the point at which the Hellenistic world attained a degree of stability, until the arrival of the Romans in the next century.*

PLUTARCH

PLUTARCH

(C. AD 45–C. AD 120)

Unlike the three authors presented thus far, Plutarch was neither an eyewitness to the events he describes nor an investigator of the recent past. The Greeks he profiled in his masterwork, Parallel Lives, *lived several centuries before his time; he learned about them through books (or more accurately, papyrus scrolls) he found in libraries. He stands at the same distance from Alexander the Great and Demosthenes, to take two examples, as we do from Shakespeare, or from the very first English settlers to arrive in North America. And just as in the case of those modern figures, much lore and legend had accreted over time around Plutarch's subjects, complicating his task as he set out to probe the essence of who these men were.*

Plutarch is also unique in this volume in that he did not claim to be writing history, but rather historical biography with a strong moral flavor. He draws the distinction between his own approach and that of others—say, Herodotus or Thucydides—by an analogy with portraiture: Whereas the historian needs to portray the whole figure from head to toe, Plutarch limits himself to carving busts, where "the marks of the soul" can be read in the subject's face. He does not feel obliged to cover every event in which his subjects took part, or to give more weight to events of greater importance, for, as he says, a single quip or remark can be more revealing than a battle that results in thousands dead. The search for character, not for a record of fact, drove Plutarch's investigations, which makes his Parallel Lives *an uneven and sometimes unreliable resource for modern historians.*

But while scholars may be frustrated by the Parallel Lives, *moralists, dramatists, and students of human nature have found it endlessly fascinating. Shakespeare used it heavily in his Roman plays,* Julius Caesar, Antony and Cleopatra, *and* Coriolanus, *and essayists such as Michel de Montaigne and Ralph Waldo Emerson took inspiration from it as well. Plutarch's insights into character, into the ways in which people's virtues and flaws interact with the nations they govern, convey a kind of truth that transcends mere historical fact. For this reason, we have chosen him as the fourth of our Greek historians, giving preference to literary merit and cultural influence over comprehensiveness.*

Plutarch was a native of Chaeronea, in central Greece. In his lifetime, all of Greece had become a province of the Roman Empire, then at its height of power and wealth. Roman officials were frequent visitors to Greece, and Greek intellectuals were in high demand as teachers of upper-class Romans. Plutarch visited Rome as a young man and made quite an impression there for his learning and eloquence; he attained Roman citizenship thanks to the help of a sponsor, Lucius Mestrius Florus, and he took that man's middle name (perhaps his first as well) as part of his own. Though he might have prospered and gained fame in Rome, Plutarch went back to Chaeronea, an undistinguished place, and spent most of his adult life there, serving both as magistrate of the town and as head priest of the nearby shrine at Delphi.

Like Xenophon, Plutarch wrote widely and prolifically, and a huge number of his works survive. The surviving Parallel Lives *comprises twenty-three pairs, each one matching a Greek with a "parallel" Roman (a few others have been lost), and there are four independent (unpaired) biographies extant as well. Less often read today, but of huge importance in the Renaissance, are the seventy-eight essays, speeches, and dialogues that collectively go under the title* Moralia. *Many of these are ethical inquiries, such as "How to Control Anger" or "How to Tell a Flatterer from a Friend"; others are collections of clever apothegms or amusing stories and facts; still others are didactic and parental, like "Advice to a Bride and Groom." A few of these works are startlingly original, like "Gryllus," a dialogue in which Odysseus converses with a talking pig, or "On the Face of the Moon," which features an account of a fictional transatlantic voyage. Many, however, are talky and moralistic, not much in line with modern tastes. Plutarch wrote more works than survive, and a list of his titles stretches to over two hundred.*

Plutarch's moral and religious preoccupations can be clearly felt in his Lives *as well as in the moral essays. He gives more space even than Herodotus to dreams, oracles, portents, and other manifestations of the divine (though he takes little interest in the Olympian gods; he was an adherent of Platonism, a belief system that in his day regarded divinity as nonanthropomorphic). In his character portraits he clearly seeks to highlight virtues as qualities to be emulated and vices as things to avoid. In the prologue to* Demetrius, *the third of the* Lives *presented here, he indicates that vices and flaws are part of his subject matter because we can learn from them what their opposites look like, so as to cultivate the latter while rejecting the former. Yet even "bad boy" Demetrius has his good qualities, for none of Plutarch's figures are complete sinners or saints. All are a mixture, which is to say, all are human.*

In one of his comments on the project of the Lives, *Plutarch says that he wel-*

comed his subjects in as though they were dinner guests. His portraits, even that of Demetrius, are suffused by a warm glow, made up partly of an instinctive admiration of "great" men but partly also of an affection for the quirks and foibles of human nature. Plutarch pays far greater attention than other historical writers to the private lives of his subjects: their familial or sexual relationships, their behind-the-scenes moments or unscripted remarks. Such material, of course, came to Plutarch from highly dubious sources, so historical scholarship largely passes it by; but readers are often delighted to find that ancient leaders were not marble statues but flesh-and-blood human beings.

There are still more caveats for those reading Plutarch as a historical source. He has little interest in chronology, sometimes presenting events out of sequence or giving no sense at all of their relative time frames. He indulges in personal bias, as can be seen when he recounts a single event in two different lives: The two versions can differ widely, as Plutarch strove to put the subject of each in the best possible light. And, since he was writing parallel biographies—contrasting a Greek and a Roman figure—he often "bends" the arc of one man's career to align it more closely with that of the other. His tales of Demetrius' exploits with the courtesan Lamia, for example, were probably exaggerated to better parallel the all-consuming love of Antony, Demetrius' Roman counterpart, for Cleopatra.

Despite all these shortcomings, Plutarch's Lives remains an enduring masterwork and an important piece of the ancient historical record.

A. Demosthenes stands up to Philip (Athens, 350s–336 bc)

Demosthenes (384–322 bc) is among the only figures in Plutarch's Lives who had no military achievements. Indeed, Plutarch repeats a story, possibly apocryphal, that Demosthenes threw away his shield and ran from the enemy on the only occasion when he fought at arms, at the Battle of Chaeronea. Plutarch nevertheless admires Demosthenes for eloquence, tireless pursuit of political goals, and what he regarded as ideologic constancy (opinions have differed on this point, as Plutarch acknowledges in chapter 13). He gives Demosthenes a noble, and highly moving, exit from the historical stage.

The events of Demosthenes give us our only Plutarchan narrative of the rise of Philip, king of Macedon starting in 358 bc. By any measure, Philip was an extraordinary leader who brought Macedonia from humble status to domination of the entire Balkan Peninsula in a single generation. He reorganized the Macedonian army and outfitted it with new weapons, a lighter shield and a longer spear, that made it more than a match for the hoplite phalanxes of the Greek states to his south. With this military machine, Philip began to make inroads into central Greece, where Thebes was dominant, and into Thrace and the Chalcidice peninsula, where Athens had major strategic interests.

Opinions were divided in Athens over how to respond to Philip. Some "philippizers" preferred to collaborate with the rising monarch or at least look the other way as his power grew. Others, like Phocion (see the selection below), recognized the threat Philip posed but thought Athens too weak to resist. Demosthenes pressed for confrontation and, if necessary, war. His showdown with Philip came to define his political career and ultimately cost him his life.

—

[4] When Demosthenes, at age seven, was left well provided for by his father (the value of his entire estate fell little short of fifteen talents), he was ill-used by his guardians, who embezzled part of his fortune and neglected the rest, and consequently even his teachers were robbed of their wages. That was one reason he appears not to have been instructed in the subjects suitable and proper for a freeborn lad; another was his physical weakness and delicacy, since his mother would not permit him to engage in physical exercise, nor did his instructors insist that he do so. For Demosthenes was scrawny and sickly from the start, and it is said that the boys who made fun of him for his physique gave him the derogatory nickname Stutterer.

[6] When he came of age, Demosthenes began by taking his guardians to court and writing speeches denouncing them, in response to which they devised many evasions and additional trials. Having gained practice by these exercises, in which, to use the phrasing of Thucydides, he took on challenges both boldly and energetically, he achieved considerable success. Though he was unable to recover even a small portion of his patrimony, he acquired confidence and sufficient practice in public speaking; and once he had tasted the prestige and the feeling of power associated with contests, he ventured to come forth and take part in public affairs....

Yet when he first appeared in the Assembly he met with uproars and was laughed at for his inexperience, since his discourse seemed to have been muddied up by his long sentences and too harshly and immoderately strained by his rhetorical syllogisms. It also appears that the weakness of his voice, a tendency to slur his words, and shortness of breath further confused the sense of his remarks by throwing his complicated sentences into disarray.

[11] To overcome his physical disadvantages, Demosthenes adopted the practices described by Demetrius of Phalerum,* who claims he heard about them from Demosthenes himself when the latter was an old man. Demosthenes corrected his lisp and the indistinctness of his speech by reciting with pebbles in his mouth; he exercised his voice at the racecourses, by declaiming as he scaled a flight of steps, and by reciting speeches or verses while holding his breath; and he had a large mirror at home, before which he would stand as he practiced his speeches.

[12] Demosthenes embarked on his public career when the Phocian War† was in progress, as he himself says, and as one may gather from his orations against Philip.‡ . . . Once he had adopted the noble civic purpose of pleading against Philip on behalf of the Greeks, and had made a worthy success of that cause, he soon gained renown and was admired everywhere for his eloquence and outspokenness. He was revered in Greece, was courted by the Great King,§ and won more respect from Philip than did all the other public speakers. Even those who disliked him considered him a worthy opponent; Aeschines and Hyperides¶ certainly expressed their regard even when they were attacking him.

[13] With this in mind, I cannot understand how it occurred to Theopompus to say that Demosthenes was of an unstable character and could not remain faithful for any length of time to the same policies or men. For it is clear that Demosthenes maintained to the very end the line and

---

* Chief executive in Athens starting in 318 BC, after the city had become a protectorate of the Macedonians.

† A war that began around 355 BC when the Phocians, in a bid for regional supremacy, took over the shrine of Apollo at Delphi and began using its wealth to hire mercenaries.

‡ The so-called *Philippics,* which have given a new word to the English language, were a series of speeches calling on the Athenians to oppose Philip II of Macedon (father of Alexander the Great). The first was delivered in 351 BC.

§ The king of Persia, at that time Artaxerxes III, had just as much reason as Demosthenes to oppose Philip, seeing that the rise of Macedon threatened Persia's interests as well as those of Athens.

¶ Aeschines, another leading Athenian orator during this era, was often on the opposite side from Demosthenes in matters regarding the Macedonians, and there was a deep personal hatred between the two men; Aeschines brought charges in 330 BC that Demosthenes rebutted, successfully, in his famous speech "On the Crown" (see chapter 15). Hyperides, by contrast, was usually a political ally and friend of Demosthenes, but attacked him bitterly in a prosecutorial speech at Demosthenes' bribery trial in 323.

position to which he committed himself at the start of his public career. And not only did he *not* alter his position during his lifetime,* but he gave up his life in the cause of not altering it, unlike Demades,† who, when defending his change of policy, said that he often spoke at variance with himself but never at variance with the city's best interest.... As for Demosthenes, we cannot speak of him as we would of a man given to altering course and adapting to circumstance, either in word or deed. For just as he adhered to one unalterable conception of public policy, he held to one course in public affairs. Panaetius the philosopher states that most of Demosthenes' speeches share the premise that only the honorable is to be chosen for its own sake. Panaetius cites the speeches "On the Crown," "Against Aristocrates," "In Defense of Indemnities," and the speeches against Philip, in all of which Demosthenes guides the citizens not toward the pleasantest course or the easiest or the most profitable, but at many points deems that their security and safety ought to hold second place to honor and decency. And that is why, had martial courage and an unshakable incorruptibility been added to the distinction of his principles and the nobility of his speeches, Demosthenes would have deserved to be ranked not with such orators as Moerecles, Polyeuctus, and Hyperides, but on high with Cimon, Thucydides, and Pericles.‡

[14] Among his contemporaries, at any rate, Phocion,§ though he advocated a policy by no means praiseworthy and was reputed to favor Macedonia, was nevertheless, because of his courage and honesty, thought to be in no way inferior to Ephialtes, Aristides, or Cimon.¶ Demosthenes, on the other hand, was neither a reliable soldier (as Demetrius says) nor completely immune to bribery (though incorruptible by

---

* Plutarch goes unusually far out of his way to defend his biographical subject. In fact, Demosthenes' record is not nearly as uniform as Plutarch claims, since, though he started out as a bitter foe of Macedonian power, he made various accommodations with it in later life.

† Another orator contemporary with Demosthenes, notorious for corruption and opportunism.

‡ The same contrast between strength of arms and strength of judgment is found in the inscription that adorned Demosthenes' memorial statue at Athens. Unlike the leaders of a previous era, or his own contemporary Phocion, Demosthenes had eloquence and political skill but no military experience.

§ Phocion the Good, an aristocratic soldier-statesman educated by Plato, had a long and esteemed political career (see the selection below on Phocion's fall).

¶ The great leaders of Athens in the century preceding the time of Demosthenes.

gold from Philip and Macedonia, he proved susceptible and was over-whelmed by the stream that flowed in from Susa and Ecbatana);* and while supremely adept at praising our noble forebears, he was unequal to emulating them.

But except for Phocion, Demosthenes surpassed the orators of his own day even in his manner of living. He clearly excelled at reasoning frankly with the people, resisting the inclinations of the multitude and attacking their faults, as one may gather from his orations.... In the case of Antiphon,† his procedure was highly aristocratic. When the man was acquitted by the Assembly, Demosthenes had him arrested and brought before the council of the Areopagus,‡ whereupon, taking no account of the fact that he was displeasing the people, he convicted Antiphon of having promised Philip to set the dockyards on fire.§

[15] As for Demosthenes' public orations,¶ his speeches against Andro-tion, Timocrates, and Aristocrates were written for others to deliver, as Demosthenes had not yet embarked on his public career. (He evidently produced those speeches when he was twenty-seven or twenty-eight.) He appeared in person in the action against Aristogeiton and delivered the speech about the indemnities.... It is not clear whether his speech denouncing Aeschines' dishonest embassy** was ever delivered, though Idomeneus says that Aeschines won acquittal by a mere thirty votes. But it appears unlikely that this is true, if one must judge by the "On the

---

* That is, from the Persian king. Demosthenes was accused at Athens of taking Macedo-nian money as well, despite what Plutarch says here.

† Not the famous orator of the late fifth century BC but a less prominent citizen of the mid-fourth century. Demosthenes himself refers to the incident related here in his speech "On the Crown."

‡ That is, Demosthenes brought Antiphon to trial before a small, elite group of jurors (the Areopagus) after the broader citizen body (the Assembly) had acquitted him.

§ That is, to sabotage the Athenian navy, the principal bastion of Greek military strength.

¶ In the Athenian judicial system, many cases were brought to advance political agendas, for example, by indicting someone on procedural grounds for espousing a certain foreign policy. Defendants in such cases were called upon to justify their politics as much as their actions. Demosthenes wrote many speeches for such defendants, including the three re-ferred to here, as well as for contestants in purely private legal actions. It was customary in all Athenian trials to hire a professional speechwriter, much as a modern defendant hires a lawyer.

** In 346 BC, Demosthenes accused Aeschines of malfeasance in negotiating a peace treaty with Philip of Macedon. His oration "On the False Embassy" survives.

Crown" speeches written by both orators.* For neither of them refers to that conflict clearly and distinctly as one that ever came to trial. But that is a question for others to decide.

[16] Demosthenes' public policy was apparent even while the peace lasted,[†] as he allowed none of the Macedonians'[‡] actions to go uncriticized, but stirred the Athenians up at each affront and inflamed them against him. As a result, Philip held Demosthenes in the highest regard, and when the orator arrived in Macedonia as one of an embassy of ten, though Philip listened to everyone, he responded to Demosthenes' speech with particular care. Yet when it came to other honors and friendly overtures, Philip did not treat Demosthenes equally well, but made a greater effort to win over Aeschines and Philocrates. Consequently, when these men praised Philip for being an excellent speaker, extremely good-looking, and a champion drinker, Demosthenes felt compelled to disparage him and joked that this was proper praise for a sophist, a woman, and a sponge—not for a king.

[17] When matters were tending toward war because Philip could not remain quiet, and the Athenians were stirred up by Demosthenes, the orator began by urging the Athenians toward Euboea, which had been made subject to Philip by its tyrants.[§] When Demosthenes had written the decree, the Athenians sailed across the strait and expelled the Macedonians. Then, when Byzantium and Perinthus had been attacked by the Macedonians, Demosthenes lent aid to both cities,[¶] having persuaded

---

* Plutarch refers here to the great showdown between Aeschines and Demosthenes in 330 BC. Aeschines brought suit against Ctesiphon for proposing that an honorary crown be awarded to Demosthenes for public service; at issue was the propriety of Demosthenes' policies over the course of two decades. After a ringing rebuttal, Demosthenes won such a huge majority of the votes that Aeschines was forced into exile.

† The "peace" refers to an entente between Macedon and Athens known as the Peace of Philocrates, negotiated in part by Aeschines in 346 BC.

‡ Referring to Philip II, father of Alexander the Great.

§ Demosthenes in his third *Philippic* (341 BC) called attention to the threat posed by Philip's incursions into Euboea. The island, lying just off Attica's shores, was of crucial strategic concern to Athens.

¶ The Hellespont was even more vital to Athens than Euboea because the city's food supplies were shipped through that strait. Philip's attacks in 340 BC on two Hellespont cities, Perinthus and Byzantium, were aggressive moves against Athenian interests. Demosthenes rallied Athens to send troops and ships, and, together with other forces sent by the Persians, these succeeded in driving Philip out of the region.

the Athenians to relinquish their enmity, forget the wrongs each people had committed in the allies' war,* and send out the force that saved both cities. Then, serving as an ambassador, he engaged the Greek states in an exchange of views, sharpened their resentment, and succeeded in setting all but a few against Philip. As a result, the Greeks mustered a mercenary force of fifteen thousand foot-soldiers and two thousand horsemen (apart from the militias) and eagerly contributed money to pay their wages....

This Roman bust of Demosthenes, based on a lost Greek original, conveys the sorrow of a man who spent his career resisting Macedonian power but failed to achieve his goals. WIKIMEDIA COMMONS

When Greece had been stirred up about her future, and a league had been formed that included the tribes and cities of the Euboeans, Achaeans, Corinthians, Megarians, Leucadians, and Corcyraeans, Demosthenes was left with the most important challenge, namely, to induce the Thebans to join the military alliance, since they occupied a position that commanded a full view of Attica, possessed a force fully equal to the struggle, and were considered the finest warriors in Greece at the time. It was not easy to sway the Thebans, as they had been pacified by favors

---

* Byzantium had revolted from the Second Athenian League in 357 BC.

recently conferred by Philip during the Phocian War,* and particularly because, given the two cities' proximity, each skirmish reopened the wounds caused by their standing differences.

[18] But when Philip...launched a surprise attack on Elatea and occupied Phocis,† the Athenians were utterly taken aback. And when no one dared to ascend to the speaker's platform (as no one had any idea what should be said), and a puzzled hush fell on the Assembly, Demosthenes alone came forward and advised the Athenians to stand by the Thebans. Raising his fellow citizens' spirits in various ways, and encouraging their hopes, as he was accustomed to do, he was sent with others as an ambassador to Thebes. According to Marsyas, Philip sent two Macedonians, Amyntas and Clearchus, Daochus the Thessalian, and Thrasydaeus to counter the Athenians' arguments.

Now the Thebans, as they deliberated, were not unmindful of their own interests. Each man possessed a clear vision of the horrors of war, their recent defeats in the Phocian War still fresh in their minds. But Theopompus reports that the orator's power stirred their spirits, fired their ambition, and blinded them to all other considerations. Inspired by his speech to embrace a noble cause, they cast aside fear, calculation, and gratitude. Demosthenes had achieved an effect so powerful and brilliant that Philip immediately sent ambassadors to treat for peace, and Greece was aroused and up in arms to face what lay ahead. And it was not only the generals who served Demosthenes and carried out his orders; the boeotarchs‡ did so as well. Demosthenes took charge of all the Thebans' assemblies no less than those of the Athenians, was greeted with affection by both peoples, and exerted his power neither unfairly nor unworthily, but with great propriety.

[20] It is said that Demosthenes, who had complete confidence in the Greeks' armaments and was clearly elated by the strength and zeal of so many men defying their enemy, forbade them to pay heed to oracles or

---

* See note to chapter 12 above. Philip had carefully leveraged the antipathies in the Phocian War (also sometimes called the Third Sacred War) to his own advantage so that he came out of it as both the ally of Thebes and the champion of Delphi.

† In 339 BC, Philip swerved from his apparent route of march and seized Elatea, a town that commanded one of the routes through the mountains into southern Greece. By this gesture he proclaimed that he was willing to fight for hegemony of the Greek world rather than continue to nibble away at it by diplomacy and proxy wars. Athens and Thebes were both now directly in his line of advance.

‡ The boeotarchs formed an annually elected executive board governing the whole Boeotian confederacy.

listen to prophecies (he even suspected the Pythian priestess of siding with Philip), and he reminded the Thebans of Epaminondas and the Athenians of Pericles,* pointing out that those men had believed such things to be pretexts for cowardice and had grounded their calculations on reason. So in *that* sense Demosthenes was a brave man. But in the battle itself[†] he showed no valor and performed no deed in keeping with his words. Instead he deserted his post, bolted disgracefully, and flung away his weapons.[‡] Nor did he even feel shame with regard to the inscription on his shield—"with good fortune"—engraved, as Pytheas says, in letters of gold.

Immediately after the victory, Philip gave insolent expression to his joy, and in a drunken state he went about among the corpses with a party of revelers, chanting the opening line of Demosthenes' decree: "Demosthenes, son of Demosthenes, of Paeania, moves thus," having divided it into meter, and beating time to it.[§] But when he had slept off his drunkenness and realized the magnitude of the struggle in which he had involved himself, he shuddered at the cleverness and power of the orator who had forced him, in the small space of a single day, to risk his hegemony and his life.[¶] Demosthenes' renown penetrated even to the Persian King, who sent letters to his satraps on the coast, commanding them to give Demosthenes money and to pay more attention to him than to all the other Greeks, as he had been capable of distracting the Macedonian and embroiling him in the Greek troubles.

[21] In the aftermath of the Greeks' misfortune, some political rivals, seeking to attack Demosthenes, prepared audits** and trumped up charges against him. The people, however, not only acquitted but continued to honor Demosthenes, and they called on him again and again as a man sincerely concerned for the city's well-being. And when the bones of the

---

* The greatest leaders of each city.

† The Battle of Chaeronea, fought on the Boeotian plain near Thebes in 338 BC.

‡ Plutarch accepts without hesitation a story that might well have arisen as a slanderous attack by Demosthenes' enemies. It is credible, however, that Demosthenes, who had never before this battle seen military action, might have turned and run from danger, as did many Athenian hoplites.

§ That is, Philip made the legal language of an Assembly decree into a singsong poem.

¶ By arranging the alliance with Thebes, Demosthenes had put Philip in a much weaker position than he would have liked.

** Since bribery was rife in Athenian politics, financial inquiries were often used as political weapons.

The Lion of Chaeronea marks the grave of the Sacred Band, the elite Theban infantry corps that perished in battle there in 338 BC when attacked by Alexander the Great. TANYA MARCUSE

fallen were conveyed from Chaeronea and honored with funeral rites, the people allowed Demosthenes to deliver the eulogy for their men.[*] Nor did they bear their misfortune basely or ignobly, as Theopompus reports in his lofty style, but made it evident, by taking special pains to revere and honor their counselor, that they did not regret having been guided by his advice. So Demosthenes delivered the eulogy, though he now stopped affixing his own name to decrees, inscribing instead the names of his friends, one after another, and avoiding the use of his own as ill-omened until after Philip's death, when he regained confidence. For Philip did not long survive his success at Chaeronea.[†]

———

Victory at Chaeronea did not protect Philip from the blade of an aggrieved junior officer, Pausanias by name. This young man, apparently enraged at ill treatment by Philip (who had once been his lover), rushed at and stabbed the king to death during a festal procession in 336 BC. The Greeks who had opposed Philip were elated; Demosthenes wore the white garb of celebration in the streets of Athens even though his daughter had recently died, a display some of his countrymen found unseemly.

Rule over Macedon passed to Alexander, Philip's twenty-year-old son, and the

———

[*] At Athens, a funeral oration over the war dead was delivered by a leading orator chosen by the people. The funeral oration of Pericles survives in Thucydides' famous version, but the one given on this occasion by Demosthenes has perished.

[†] Philip was assassinated in 336 BC, two years after his great victory over Athens and Thebes.

Greeks tried to regain the freedoms they'd lost under Philip. But Alexander forced them back into line, with brute force in the case of Thebes: The city was entirely destroyed and its population killed or sold into slavery after an armed rebellion was put down. Demosthenes supported that revolt but failed to motivate Athens to take action in time.

Alexander embarked in 334 on his Asian campaign, as described in depth in the following Life. Demosthenes stayed quiet during this eleven-year span and did not go directly against Alexander's interests, though clearly he was not happy about Athens's future. When word arrived in 323 that Alexander was dead, Athens went into revolt from Macedon, and Demosthenes—then in exile after his conviction in an embezzlement trial, but soon reinstated—took active part. But the rebellion failed and Athens was forced back into line, this time under the watchful eye of a Macedonian garrison force.

Demosthenes left Athens before that force arrived and sought refuge in a shrine on the small island of Calauria. A Macedonian squad surrounded the shrine and promised him clemency, but Demosthenes knew his fate was already sealed. Before the squad could apprehend him, he swallowed poison and died. He knew, as he took his own life, that his policy choices had failed to keep Athens free of control by the new superpower.

B. ALEXANDER

Plutarch's Alexander *is among the longest of his* Lives, *both because of Alexander's constant, unceasing activity and because of the complexity of his character. Plutarch seems to have admired Alexander immensely at the time he wrote his two speeches, "On the Fortune or Virtue of Alexander"—probably well before he wrote the* Lives—*referring to the Macedonian king as a "philosopher in arms" who tried to bring Greek enlightenment to the barbarian world. In the account below, Plutarch takes a more measured view of Alexander while still giving him the benefit of many doubts.*

Alexander (356–323 BC*) transformed Greece, and the ancient world as a whole, more thoroughly than any other leader. The league established by his father, Philip, consisting of all the European Greek states except Sparta, would surely have come apart had Alexander not thrown himself into action upon taking the throne. Then the conquest of the Persian Empire that followed—a project undertaken, at least ostensibly, as a Greek crusade—made Asia subordinate to European power for the first time ever. Hellenism became the dominant culture in urban centers from the*

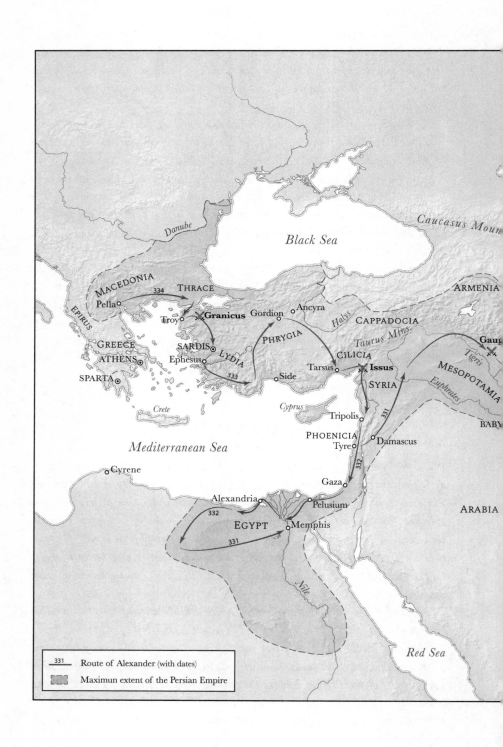

Danube

Black Sea

Caucasus Moun

MACEDONIA

THRACE

ARMENIA

Pella

334

Troy

Granicus

Gordion

Ancyra

CAPPADOCIA

Halys

EPIRUS

GREECE

SARDIS

LYDIA

PHRYGIA

Taurus Mtns.

CILICIA

Gaug

Tigris

ATHENS

Ephesus

CILICIA

Tarsus

Issus

MESOPOTAMIA

SPARTA

333

Side

SYRIA

331

Euphrates

BABY

Crete

Cyprus

Tripolis

Mediterranean Sea

PHOENICIA

Tyre

Damascus

332

Cyrene

Gaza

ARABIA

Alexandria

Pelusium

332

EGYPT

Memphis

331

Nile

Red Sea

---

331   Route of Alexander (with dates)

     Maximun extent of the Persian Empire

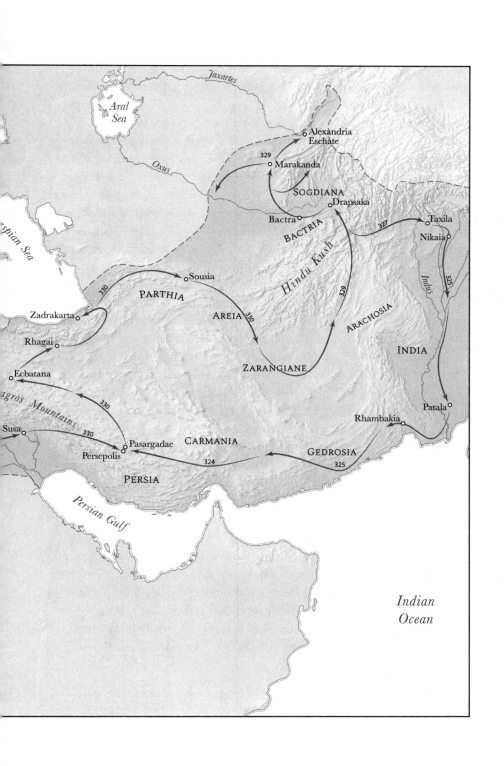

Aral
Sea

Jaxartes

Oxus

Alexandria
Eschàte

329
Marakanda

SOGDIANA

Drapsaka

Bactra

BACTRIA

Taxila

Nikaia

327

Caspian Sea

330

Sousia

PARTHIA

Hindu Kush

329

325

Indus

Zadrakarta

AREIA

330

ARACHOSIA

Rhagai

INDIA

Ecbatana

ZARANGIANE

Zagros Mountains

330

Susa

330

Pasargadae

CARMANIA

Persepolis

324

Patala

Rhambakia

GEDROSIA

325

PERSIA

Persian Gulf

Indian
Ocean

Aegean to modern Afghanistan and Pakistan and would continue to hold sway over much of the world for centuries thereafter—the so-called Hellenistic Age. Had Alexander lived longer, he might have brought Greek culture westward to the Atlantic, but a fatal illness cut short his life in 323.

The selection below begins shortly after Alexander, in his late teens, ascended the throne of his father, Philip, assassinated in 336 BC. After stunning the Greek cities into submission and stabilizing the empire, Alexander took up the invasion of Asia that his father had been preparing at the time of his death. In the first episode below, Alexander wins from the Greeks gathered in Corinth—all except the Spartans, who held aloof—an appointment as supreme commander of the army of invasion, a largely Macedonian force to which most Greek cities, especially Athens, also contributed. While overseeing this vote, Alexander had a famous encounter with an ascetic sage, Diogenes the Cynic.

———

[14] The Greeks had assembled at the Isthmus* and voted to march against Persia with Alexander, and Alexander was proclaimed commander. Since many statesmen and philosophers had met and congratulated them, Alexander was hoping that Diogenes of Sinope,† who was living near Corinth, would do the same. But as Diogenes had very little regard for the king, and remained quietly in Craneion, Alexander went to *him,* and came upon him lying in the sun. Diogenes sat up a little, at the approach of so many men, and squinted at Alexander, who greeted him and asked if there was anything he needed, to which Diogenes replied, "Only for you to move a little out of the sun." It is said that Alexander was so affected by this, and so admired the haughtiness and grandeur of the man who despised him, that when they were departing, and his attendants were laughing and making fun of the philosopher, Alexander said, "Well, had I not been Alexander, I'd have been Diogenes."

[15] As for the size of the expedition, those who give the smallest figures write that it included thirty thousand foot-soldiers and four thousand horsemen; those who give the largest, forty-three thousand foot-soldiers and five thousand horsemen. For provisioning these men, Aristobulus says that Alexander had no more than seventy talents, Duris maintains that he was in possession of only thirty days' sustenance, and Onesicri-

———

* The Isthmus of Corinth was the designated meeting place for the League, a confederation of Greek states (Sparta excluded) established by Philip under Macedonian leadership.

† A famous Cynic philosopher who rejected the values espoused by Greek society, especially the pursuit of power and wealth.

tus that he was two hundred talents in debt.* But though he started out with such small and meager means, he did not board his ship until he had looked into the circumstances of his Companions† and distributed to one a farm, to another a village, and to still another the revenue of some hamlet or harbor. And when almost all the royal property had been spent or allocated, Perdiccas‡ said, "But what, sire, do you leave for yourself?" When Alexander replied, "My hopes," Perdiccas said, "Then surely we too, who serve with you in the expedition, will share also in these." And when Perdiccas had declined the property that had been allotted to him, some of his other friends did the same. But Alexander eagerly gratified those who accepted or requested allotments, and most of what he possessed in Macedonia was spent in this way. With such ardor and his mind so disposed he crossed the Hellespont.§

Ascending to Troy, he sacrificed to Athena and poured a libation to the heroes. And when he had anointed Achilles' gravestone with oil, he and his Companions ran a race around it, naked, as is the custom, and crowned it with a garland.¶

[16] Meanwhile, since Darius' generals had mustered and arrayed a mighty force at the crossing of the Granicus,** it was necessary to fight at the gates of Asia, as it were, for an entrance and dominion there.

Most of the Macedonian officers feared the depth of the river and the unevenness and ruggedness of the farther banks, which they would have to scale during battle.... And when Parmenio†† tried to prevent Alexander from running risks, as it was late in the season, Alexander said that

---

* Plutarch here names three of the historians who had written about Alexander during his own time. There were many such primary sources that Plutarch was able to consult, but all have since perished, leaving modern historians with only the secondary sources that drew on them. A talent consists of six thousand drachmas, each drachma being about a day's wage for a common soldier.

† The inner circle of nobles and chiefs attending the Macedonian king were formally known as Companions.

‡ One of Alexander's oldest Companions and highest officers.

§ In the spring of 334 BC, almost two years after taking the throne.

¶ One of many symbolic rites Alexander performed to evoke the ancestral link between himself and Achilles, and to portray his invasion of Asia as a new Trojan War.

** A river in northern Turkey, the spot at which the regional Persian forces had elected to oppose Alexander's progress. The Persians had not defended the Hellespont crossing because Macedonian advance forces had well before established a beachhead there.

†† The senior general and right-hand man of Alexander's father and now of Alexander as well.

the Hellespont would be ashamed if, now that he had crossed *it*, he feared the Granicus. He then plunged into the stream with thirteen companies of cavalry.* Charging toward enemy missiles and steep positions fortified with infantry and cavalry, and across a stream that was surging around his men and sweeping them away, his actions seemed those of a mad and desperate commander, rather than one whose judgment was sound. But he persevered in the crossing, and when he had with difficulty scaled the opposite banks, though these were wet and slippery with mud, he was instantly forced to fight in disorderly, headlong haste, and to engage his attackers man by man, before his men who were crossing could form up in any order. For the enemy assaulted with a roar; and matching horse against horse, they made good use of their spears, and of their swords once the spears were shattered. Many thrust themselves at Alexander, who was easily distinguished by his light shield and the crest of his helmet, on either side of which was fixed a plume of marvelous size and whiteness. Though hit by a javelin at the joint of his breastplate, he was not wounded; and when the generals Rhoesaces and Spithridates rushed at him together, he avoided Spithridates and struck Rhoesaces, who was wearing a breastplate. After his own spear broke, Alexander used his sword. When the two men were engaged at close quarters, Spithridates rode up on one side, raised himself up on his horse, and brought his battle-ax down with main force on Alexander's helmet. His crest was broken off, along with one feather, and his helmet could barely and with difficulty resist the blow: The edge of the ax grazed Alexander's topmost hairs. And when Spithridates was rising up for another blow, Cleitus—the one known as Black Cleitus—anticipated him and ran him through with his spear. At that very moment Rhoesaces fell, struck by Alexander's sword.

While this dangerous cavalry combat was under way, the Macedonian phalanx completed its crossing of the river, and the two infantry forces came to blows. But the enemy infantry did not hold its ground firmly for long; it was routed and put to flight, except for the Greek mercenaries.[†] These men, making a stand on a certain ridge, asked Alexander for quar-

---

* The heroic account given here of the Battle of Granicus is one of two extant versions. Diodorus (*Library of History* 17.18.4–21) records a very different battle, in which Alexander approached the river cautiously, avoiding Persian strongpoints, and crossed more stealthily.

[†] The Persians employed many thousands of Greek infantrymen, who were better trained and equipped than the native peoples from whom they could levy troops. Alexander had, before starting his invasion, gotten a decree passed by the Greek cities forbidding Greek soldiers to fight for the Persians.

ter. But he, more in anger than by calculation, charged at them ahead of his men and lost his horse, which was struck through the ribs with a sword (this was not Bucephalus, but another). And it was there, as it turned out, that most of the Macedonians who died and were wounded fought and fell, engaging at close quarters with warlike and desperate men.*

It is said that twenty thousand barbarian foot-soldiers fell, and twenty-five hundred horsemen. On Alexander's side, Aristobulus says there were thirty-four dead in all, nine of whom were foot-soldiers.† Alexander ordered that bronze statues of these men be set up. (The statues were sculpted by Lysippus.)‡ Wishing to share the victory with the Greeks, he sent the Athenians in particular three hundred shields taken from his captives; and on all the remaining spoils, grouped together, he ordered that this highly ambitious inscription be engraved: "Alexander, son of Philip, and the Greeks, except for the Spartans, from the barbarians who inhabit Asia."§ But the drinking cups, purple robes, and any articles of that kind that he took from the Persians were sent, with a few exceptions, to his mother.

———

Alexander made a sweep through Asia Minor after the Granicus battle, "liberating" Greek cities (which meant transferring them from the Persian Empire to his own) and chasing out Persian satraps. The following year (333 BC) he brought his army deeper into Asia, a move opposed by a much larger Persian army than he had faced at the Granicus, commanded this time by the Great King, Darius III, himself. Darius had assembled forces many times as numerous as Alexander's and had chosen a level, open battlefield where he could deploy his superior numbers. But after Alexander delayed longer than expected in Cilicia, Darius grew impatient and decided to march out and meet the Macedonians rather than awaiting them on his chosen ground.

---

* Plutarch does not record the grim result of this attack: Some ten thousand Greek mercenaries were slaughtered by Alexander's forces, partly as a warning to other Greeks serving the Persians.

† These lopsided casualty figures are no doubt exaggerated.

‡ Lysippus was the most talented Greek sculptor of the day and the only one Alexander permitted to carve his portrait.

§ This inscription was designed to highlight Alexander's self-proclaimed partnership with the Greek cities of the league, even if that alliance had been achieved only by his show of cruelty at Thebes. The omission of the Spartans, who were not league members, reinforces the point. By sending the spoils to Athens, Alexander hoped to curry favor with the most powerful and politically influential Greek city, which had thus far regarded him with deeply mixed feelings.

The Alexander Mosaic, found on the floor of a house in Pompeii, was probably based on a painting made in Alexander's own day, depicting his victory in battle over King Darius. WIKIMEDIA COMMONS

———

[20] In Darius' army there was a Macedonian, Amyntas, who had fled from Macedonia and was fairly well acquainted with Alexander's nature. This man, when he saw Darius eager to advance into the narrow passes against Alexander, begged him to stay where he was and contend, with his enormous numbers, against the inferior force of the enemy in plains that were broad and open. When Darius replied that he was afraid the enemy might escape by stealth and Alexander elude him, Amyntas replied, "Rest assured, sire, on that score; for this man will march against you, and indeed will soon be at hand." Despite what he had said, Amyntas failed to persuade the king. Setting forth, Darius marched into Cilicia, and at the same time Alexander advanced into Syria against him. Missing each other overnight, they turned back.* Alexander was de-

---

* Plutarch seems not to have understood these movements very well. The two armies marched past one another unawares, separated as they were by a tall mountain range. Darius' army thus got around to the north of Alexander, cutting him off from his supply lines and escape route. After realizing his unexpected good fortune, Darius turned southward again, hoping to trap and destroy Alexander's army, and Alexander moved northward to meet him.

lighted with this turn of events and eager to encounter Darius near the passes, while Darius was glad to extricate his forces from them and regain his previous encampment. For he now realized that it was not to his advantage to launch himself into a region flanked by the sea and mountains, bisected by a river (the Pinarus), and riddled with broken ground—a setting that favored the small numbers of his enemy. Alexander's good fortune provided the site,* though his victory was due more to generalship than to luck. For though in numbers he was inferior to the barbarians by so large a multitude, Alexander gave them no chance to surround him, whereas he himself outflanked their left wing with his right, and on getting opposite their flank put the enemy to flight. Through it all he contended in the front ranks, and as a result was wounded in the thigh with a sword while contending with Darius at close quarters, according to Chares, though Alexander himself, in the letters about the battle that he dispatched to Antipater, does not say who wounded him, reporting only that he had been stabbed in the thigh with a dagger but was not seriously inconvenienced by the wound.

Winning a splendid victory and destroying more than one hundred and ten thousand of his enemies, Alexander nonetheless did not capture Darius, who had got the start in the escape by half a mile or more;† but by the time Alexander had turned back, he had captured Darius' chariot and bow.

[21] Among the captives were Darius' mother, wife, and two daughters. . . . But Alexander, considering it more kingly to master himself than to conquer his enemies, laid no hand on these women nor consorted with any other before marriage‡ besides Barsine, who had become a widow after the death of Memnon and was captured near Damascus.§

[23] Where wine was concerned he was less susceptible than was gen-

---

* Close to Issus, the city that has given its name to the battle.

† In the heat of the battle, Darius, standing in his war chariot at the center of the Persian line, had perceived that Alexander's forces were penetrating. Realizing that he was in danger of being captured, Darius turned and fled at top speed, escaping with his life but precipitating the total collapse of his army.

‡ The romantic legends surrounding Alexander made much of his chivalrous treatment of Persian royal women. Alexander later married Stateira, the eldest daughter of Darius (see chapter 70).

§ Barsine was a half-Greek, half-Persian noblewoman with whom Alexander carried on an affair in the 330s BC. With her he had a son, Heracles, whom he never knew or acknowledged.

erally thought. He came by that reputation because of the time he spent, talking more than drinking, over each cup, always engaging in some long discussion when he had nothing else to attend to.*...

But though in other respects he was the pleasantest of all kings to consort with, and lacked none of the social graces, he had now become unpleasant in his arrogance and very much the rude soldier; not only was he carried away when it came to boasting, but he also allowed himself to be ridden by his flatterers, by whom the more refined among the company were irritated, since they wished neither to compete with these men nor to fall short of them in praising Alexander. For the former course seemed shameful, the latter dangerous. After the carousal, Alexander would bathe and then retire to sleep, often until midday; there were even times when he spent the entire day sleeping.

———

After defeating Darius and putting him to flight at Issus, Alexander swept down the coast of Phoenicia, taking over the port cities that the Persian navy might use as a base. The Persians were at this time using their naval superiority to good advantage in the Aegean, and Alexander recognized that he could not challenge them on the sea; indeed, he had already dismissed his Greek-led fleet. Instead he tried to neutralize Persian naval strength by taking over all the anchorages and harbors along the coast of Asia. This required him to fight a long, grueling siege at Tyre, a nearly impregnable island city, in 332 BC.

After capturing the entire Phoenician coast, Alexander turned westward, toward Egypt. This province of the Persian Empire was happy to welcome him, having long hated its Persian masters. Here Alexander's army spent a cheerful and restful sojourn in late 332 and early 331. During this time Alexander founded the most famous of the many cities that were to bear his name.

———

[26] They say that on conquering Egypt, Alexander wanted to found a large and populous city and to name it after himself, and on the advice of his architects he was just about to measure off a certain site and build a wall around it. Then, one night in his sleep, he saw an astonishing vision:

———

* One of the many points on which Plutarch has trusted the more pro-Alexander sources, in this case Aristobulus, who was at pains to defend Alexander from charges of excessive drinking. But when in the next paragraph Plutarch reports that Alexander sometimes slept the whole day through, one has to believe that overindulgence in wine was involved.

A man of majestic appearance, with a great thatch of gray hair, stood beside him and uttered these epic verses:*

An island lies in the high-surging sea
Before Egypt; Pharos is what men call it.

As soon as he had risen, he went to Pharos, which at the time was still an island (it lay a short distance off the Canopic mouth), though today it is connected by a pier to the mainland. When he saw a surpassingly fertile spot—a strip of land, nearly equivalent in breadth to an isthmus, that separates a large lagoon and an arm of the ocean that terminates at a large harbor—he declared that Homer was not only admirable in other respects, but also the cleverest of architects, and he gave orders for his builders to trace the city's outline to conform to that site.... He ordered his contractors to get the work under way, while he himself set out for Ammon.† This was a long journey, one that furnished considerable trouble and hardship.

[27] When Alexander had crossed the desert and reached the site of the oracle, the prophet hailed him with a greeting from the god as from a father, whereupon Alexander inquired whether any of the murderers of his father had escaped him. When the prophet urged him to guard his tongue, as his father was not mortal,‡ Alexander rephrased the question and inquired whether the murderers of Philip had all been punished; he then inquired about his own empire, asking whether the god had granted him supreme power over all mankind. When the god had answered that this too had been granted, and that Philip had been fully avenged, Alexander presented the god with splendid votive offerings, and the priests with gifts of money.

That is what most writers report about the oracles. But Alexander himself, in a letter to his mother, says that he has been given certain secret prophecies, which on his return he will reveal to her alone. Some say that the prophet, wishing to hail him with the affectionate Greek greet-

---

* Homer's *Odyssey* 4.354–55.

† Ammon was an Egyptian god, equated with Zeus by the Greeks. The oracle of Ammon, in a remote oasis west of Egypt, was considered one of the most reliable sources of prophecy.

‡ The oracle hereby implied that Alexander was the son of a god rather than of Philip.

ing *"O paidion,"* misspoke, owing to his barbarian accent, and pronounced the last word with an *s* instead of an *n*, saying *"O pai Dios,"* and that the slip delighted Alexander, whereupon the story spread abroad that the god had addressed him as "son of Zeus."*

[28] On the whole, Alexander treated the barbarians haughtily and behaved as if he actually believed in his divine begetting and birth, but to the Greeks he was moderate and restrained when it came to assuming his own divinity,[†] except when, writing to the Athenians about Samos,[‡] he said, "I cannot have given you that free and famous city, for you received it from the man who was then your master and was called my father," meaning Philip....

When Darius sent a letter to Alexander and his friends requesting him to accept ten thousand talents in return for his captives, to keep all the territory east of the Euphrates, to marry one of his daughters, and to be his friend and ally,[§] Alexander shared the letter's contents with his Companions. When Parmenio said, "Well, if *I* were Alexander, I would accept these terms," Alexander replied, "And so would *I,* by Zeus, if I were Parmenio." He therefore wrote in reply that if Darius came to him, he would be shown every courtesy; if not, Alexander would march against him at once.

———

In the spring of 331 BC, *Alexander left Egypt and headed east, having heard that Darius had gathered a new army to defend his empire. Plutarch says this force numbered one million, but that is doubtless an exaggeration. By any measure, though, it was huge and included Darius' most fearsome weapons: expert Bactrian cavalrymen, scythed chariots with blades protruding from their wheels, and even a handful of trained Indian war elephants. Determined to preserve the advantage of favorable ground, Darius brought this force to an open plain near Gaugamela, in*

---

* In Greek, *paidion* is a way of hailing a friend, "hey, young man," whereas *pai Dios,* heard as two words, means "son of Zeus."

[†] Alexander's Greek subjects were much more wary of human pretensions to divinity than were Egyptians and Asians. The Greeks eventually passed resolutions giving Alexander divine worship, but the measures were very controversial.

[‡] In 323 BC, near the end of his life, Alexander decreed that all those exiled by the Greek cities must be returned to their homes, a measure that would have resulted in Athens's losing Samos, a territory from which it had expelled all the native inhabitants. The Athenians appealed to Alexander to exclude them from the decree, but their request was denied.

[§] The different Alexander sources give varying accounts of what Darius offered Alexander and when, but all of them make clear that the price Darius was willing to pay to buy Alexander off was huge.

what is now Iran, and cleared the land of rocks and obstructions so that his cavalry would not be impeded. Alexander approached this battleground cautiously, in late September 331, and prepared for his most important showdown yet.

———

[33] And now, after Alexander had addressed the Thessalians and the other Greeks at great length, and they had urged him, with a roar, to lead them against the barbarians, he shifted his spear to his left hand and with his right called on the gods, as Callisthenes* says, beseeching them, if he was truly the offspring of Zeus, to defend and strengthen the Greeks. The seer Aristander, wearing a white shawl and a golden crown, rode by and pointed out an eagle soaring over Alexander's head and flying straight toward the enemy, at the sight of which the men grew bold and encouraged one another, the cavalry charged at full speed against the enemy, and the phalanx surged forward like a wave. But before the first ranks had come to blows, the barbarians gave ground and there was a relentless pursuit, Alexander driving the conquered force toward their center, where Darius was. For Alexander saw him from a distance—a tall, handsome man mounted on a high chariot, fenced about with many splendid horsemen, who stood in compact array around the chariot to resist the enemy's attack. But once Alexander, formidable when seen at close range, had charged after the fugitives toward the ranks who were standing their ground, he astounded and scattered almost all of them. The best and noblest, however, who were slain in front of their king and falling in heaps on one another, hindered the Macedonians' pursuit, struggling convulsively and flinging themselves around the men and horses.

But Darius, faced with all these horrors and seeing his defenders retreating toward him and making it impossible to turn his chariot around and drive through easily, since its wheels were obstructed and jammed by the large numbers of fallen bodies, while his horses, overcome and hidden by the masses of corpses, were rearing up and alarming his charioteer, abandoned his chariot and weapons, mounted a mare that, according to report, had just foaled,† and fled. But it is thought that he would not have escaped had other horsemen not come from Parmenio, summoning Alexander with the plea that a large enemy force was still in formation

---

* The expedition's official historian, a Greek intellectual and kinsman of Aristotle, Callisthenes was later killed on Alexander's orders after defying the king's policies, in an episode not included in this volume.

† Mares that had recently given birth were thought by the Greeks to have extra speed.

there and would not give ground. In fact Parmenio is generally criticized for having been sluggish and idle in that battle, either because old age was already impairing his courage, or because he was oppressed by the arrogance and pomp, as Callisthenes phrases it, of Alexander's sovereignty and regarded it with envy. At the time, though the king was vexed by the summons, he did not tell his men the truth, but signaled retreat, declaring that he would refrain from further slaughter since darkness was falling. And as he drove toward the division that was in danger, he heard on the way that the enemy had been roundly defeated and was fleeing.*

[34] The battle having had this outcome, the empire of the Persians appeared to have been utterly destroyed, and Alexander, proclaimed king of Asia,† performed splendid sacrifices to the gods and presented his friends with large sums of money, houses, and commands. In his eagerness to be honored by the Greeks, he wrote that all their tyrannies had been abolished and that they might govern themselves autonomously.‡

[36] On becoming master of Susa,§ Alexander came into possession, in the palace, of forty thousand talents of coined money and all the other trappings of untold wealth¶....

[38] After this, when he was about to march against Darius,** Alexander chanced to take part in a playful carousal with his Companions that was also attended by women who came to revel with their lovers. The most

---

* Plutarch had little interest in military history, and his account of the Battle of Gaugamela is only a rough outline. The outcome at least is clear: Darius once again turned his chariot and fled the field rather than risk being taken prisoner by Alexander. The center of his line followed him in flight, but his right wing had already made good inroads against Alexander's left, led by Parmenio, and continued to threaten it. Alexander had to turn back from pursuit of Darius in order to aid Parmenio, allowing the Persian king to get away unscathed with a few followers.

† Alexander assigned himself this unprecedented title.

‡ Upon gaining control of Asia Minor three years earlier, Alexander had removed the Persian-installed puppet governments in the Greek cities and installed democracies. In theory these cities were now free, but in practice, of course, they could not defy Alexander, and many had to pay "voluntary" tribute to him. The idea that Alexander's campaign was in fact a Greek war of liberation from Persia was thereby maintained.

§ Susa was the principal Persian capital, though Babylon, Persepolis, and Pasargadae were also royal seats.

¶ A fantastic sum of money, and yet this was only a small portion of the total that Alexander captured after all the Persian treasuries had been emptied. The Persians had been hoarding the tribute money collected from all of Asia for more than two centuries.

** After resting his troops and enjoying the pleasures of Babylon and Persepolis, Alexander set out for Bactria in the spring of 330 BC to find and capture Darius.

popular among them was Thaïs, an Athenian by birth, and the mistress of Ptolemy, who subsequently became king.* Partly wishing to praise Alexander properly, and partly in jest, she was moved during the carousal to make a speech in keeping with the character of her native land, though it was too high-flown for a person of her sort. She said that for all she had suffered wandering about Asia she was on that day receiving her reward, enjoying a luxurious party in the splendid palace of the Persians. But it would be pleasanter still to go on a revel and burn down the house of Xerxes, who had burned Athens,† she herself kindling the fire while Alexander looked on, so that a legend might be preserved for humankind that the women of Alexander's entourage imposed a greater punishment on the Persians on behalf of Greece than all her naval and infantry commanders. This speech was received with uproarious applause, and the king's Companions eagerly cheered him on. Captivated, the king leapt up with a garland and a torch and led the way. The other revelers, following with a merry shout, stood around the palace, and other Macedonians who learned of it ran there with torches and were filled with joy. For they were hoping that the burning and destruction of the palace were the acts of a man who had fixed his thoughts on home and would not settle among barbarians. Some say that these events came about in this way, while others say they were planned;‡ but it is agreed that Alexander quickly repented and gave orders for the fire to be extinguished.

Alexander now marched out in the belief that he would again do battle with Darius. But on hearing that the king had been captured by Bessus,§ Alexander sent the Thessalians home, giving the mercenaries a gift of two thousand talents over and above their pay. And in the course of the pursuit, which proved troublesome and prolonged (in eleven days he covered upward of four hundred miles on horseback), most of his men

---

* Ptolemy, son of Lagus, was one of Alexander's oldest friends and top commanders. After the death of Alexander in 323 BC, Ptolemy became satrap of Egypt, and some sixteen years later, after Alexander's royal family had been killed off by those competing for control of the empire, he and several other former generals crowned themselves kings.

† In 480 BC, when the Athenian population had been evacuated to Salamis.

‡ Plutarch gives a nod to the alternative, and in most historians' eyes more likely, version recorded in Arrian's *Anabasis:* Alexander soberly decided to burn the palace, as a signal to the Persians that the Achaemenid dynasty was over and also as a sign to the Greeks that the promised revenge on the Persians had been achieved.

§ Bessus, satrap of Bactria, had accompanied Darius in flight, but when it was clear that Alexander was overtaking the fugitives, Bessus and his followers staged a coup and put Darius in chains. Thereafter Bessus tried to claim the throne that Darius had lost.

344 · *The Greek Histories*

gave out, mainly from lack of water.... It is said that only sixty rushed together into the enemy's camp, where they actually rode over much silver and gold that had been discarded, passed many wagons of children and women being carried this way and that, bereft of drivers, and pursued the first fugitives, thinking that Darius was among them. They finally found Darius lying in a wagon, his body full of javelins, on the point of death. Yet he asked for something to drink, and on taking some cool water said to Polystratus, who had given it to him, "This, my good fellow, is the climax of all my bad luck—to be treated well without being able to make a return. But Alexander will thank you for the favor, and the gods will reward Alexander for his kindness to my mother, wife, and children. To him, through you, I give this right hand." So saying, and taking Polystratus' hand, he died. When Alexander arrived, he was visibly grieved by the man's death; loosening his own cloak, he threw it over the body and shrouded it. And later on, when he found Bessus, he had him dismembered. Bending two straight trees toward each other, he attached a part of the man's body to each; then, when the trees were let go, and swung back with a rush, the part attached to each went with it.*

[45] From there, after moving the army into Parthian territory, Alexander found himself at leisure, and for the first time donned barbarian attire, either because he wanted to adapt himself to the local customs (in the belief that community of race and custom is a great humanizer of men), or as an attempt to introduce the practice of ritual bowing† to the Macedonians by gradually accustoming them to tolerate changes in his way of life and habits.‡...And the sight pained the Macedonians. But since they admired all his other virtues, they supposed they should forgive some of the things he chose to do for the sake of his own pleasure and renown.

---

* This account of Bessus' death is probably fanciful, but it is clear from other sources that Alexander had Bessus tortured and mutilated before his execution. Arrian's *Anabasis* takes Alexander to task for this, but it seems to be in line with Persian (though not Macedonian or Greek) norms.

† In one of his most controversial moves, Alexander attempted to have his officers bow down to him in greeting as the Persians did before the Great King.

‡ Plutarch presents the two contrasting views of his sources, some of which excused Alexander's Asianizing dress as an attempt to gain authority among his new Asian subjects, while others blamed him for arrogance and pomp. This was the first of many steps in Alexander's "fusion" program, his attempt to meld European and Asian political cultures and even force their aristocratic families to intermarry.

[47] Alexander now adapted his way of life more and more to that of the local inhabitants, and encouraged the latter to adopt Macedonian customs, thinking that by means of assimilation and fellowship—by goodwill rather than by force—he would ground his authority more securely while he himself was far away. That was why, upon selecting thirty thousand boys, he gave orders that they were to study Greek literature and be trained in Macedonian warfare, having assigned them several instructors.* As for his union with Roxane,† while it is true that, charmed by her youth and beauty, he fell in love when he saw her dancing at a drinking party, the match was also thought to accord well with his immediate aims. For the barbarians were heartened by the fellowship his marriage created, and they admired Alexander beyond measure because he had proved so temperate in these matters that he would not even consent to touch, without legal right, the only woman by whom he had been vanquished.

———

Once Darius and Bessus were dead, Alexander was the unchallenged ruler of the former Persian Empire, but he elected not to stop his campaign. He spent two years in Bactria and Sogdiana (modern Afghanistan, Tajikistan, and Uzbekistan), the wild frontier of the Persian world, subduing tribes that had no inclination to respect his authority. Here several incidents occurred that revealed tensions, or even breakdown of unity, in Alexander's army. Two plots against Alexander's life were uncovered during these two years, and purges were conducted after each. Alexander personally punished a grumbling dissident, a high officer named Cleitus, by killing him with a spear in full view of the whole senior staff. But ultimately Alexander's authority stood the test, and his army, now reorganized to give the king added security, held together.

In 327 BC, Alexander left Bactria, headed not homeward but farther east. He had accepted an alliance with Taxiles, a ruler near the Indus River, and took his army across the Hindu Kush mountains and into the land he knew as India (modern northern Pakistan). This region had once belonged to the Persian Empire, so Alexander had a slight political pretext for entering it. But he also needed to give his army, now indisputably the world's most powerful, something to do, and he himself

---

* This corps of select Asian youths was trained to fight in Macedonian fashion, beginning probably in 327 BC.

† Alexander's first wife, Roxane, was the daughter of a Bactrian chieftain. Alexander married her in 327 BC, largely in an effort to make allies and willing subjects of the recalcitrant Bactrian tribes.

longed to make a journey that only the gods Heracles and Dionysus, according to
Greek legend, had made before him.

———

[57] When Alexander was about to cross the mountains into India, he saw that his army was overburdened, its mobility impaired by its vast spoils. At dawn, when the wagons had been packed up, he burned his own wagons first, along with those of his Companions, and then commanded that those of the Macedonians be set on fire. And the ambition that prompted this exploit seemed greater and more formidable than the deed itself. For though a few of his soldiers were vexed, most of them, raising an impassioned war cry, shared their necessities with those who needed them and burned and destroyed their own superfluous goods, thereby filling Alexander with zeal and eagerness. By then he had also become a fearsome and implacable punisher of any who misbehaved. For after appointing Menander, one of his Companions, as chief of a garrison, he had the man killed for declining to remain in office, and he personally dispatched Orsodates, one of the barbarians who revolted from him, with a bow shot.

[59] Taxiles is said to have been in possession of a portion of India no smaller in size than Egypt—a region especially rich in pastures and land that bore fine fruit—and to have been, in his own way, a clever man. Welcoming Alexander, he said, "What need have we, Alexander, to fight with one another if you have come intending to deprive us neither of water nor of necessary sustenance, the only things for which sensible men are compelled to fight? As for the other riches and possessions so called—if I prove the stronger man, I am ready to treat you well, but if the weaker, I do not hesitate to show my gratitude when treated well." Delighted, Alexander clasped Taxiles by the hand and said, "Do you somehow imagine that after such friendly words our meeting will not lead to a battle? But you will not get the better of me; for I shall contend against you and fight on behalf of the favors *I* bestow, that you may not surpass me in generosity." Receiving many gifts, and giving more, Alexander finally made Taxiles a present of one thousand talents of coined money. In doing so, though he greatly pained his friends, he made many of the barbarians regard him more kindly.

But the most warlike of the Indians, who were mercenaries, went about to the various cities, defending them stoutly and doing Alexander great harm. Eventually, after making a truce with them in a certain city, Alexander caught them on the road as they were departing and killed them all.* And this adheres like a stain to his military record; in all other instances he waged war lawfully and in a manner worthy of a king. No less than the mercenaries, the philosophers† made trouble for him by abusing any kings who allied themselves with him, and by encouraging free peoples to revolt—which was why he had many of these men hanged as well.

[60] Alexander himself, in his letters,‡ has described his campaign against Porus.§ He says that their two camps were separated by the river Hydaspes, and that Porus, stationing his elephants on the opposite bank, kept constant watch on the crossing. In response, day after day Alexander created plenty of noise and uproar in his camp, and thereby accustomed the barbarians not to be alarmed. And then, one stormy, moonless night, taking a detachment of his infantry and his best horsemen, he marched a distance from the enemy and crossed to a smallish island. Rain poured down furiously there, and many hurricanes and lightning bolts assailed his men. But though he saw some of them perishing and burned to death by the lightning, he nevertheless set forth from the island toward the opposite bank. But the Hydaspes, swollen and agitated by the storm, forced a large breach in its bank, and a large part of the stream surged through it; and the ground between the two channels was too slippery and jagged to provide any secure footing. At that point Alexander is said to have cried, "Athenians, can you believe the dangers I undergo to earn your praise?" ... Alexander himself says that after abandoning their rafts they crossed the breach with their armor on, the water coming up to their chests; and that after getting across he led his horsemen two and a half miles in advance of his infantry, calculating that if the enemy attacked with their cavalry, he would prove superior, whereas if they advanced their phalanx, his own infantry would arrive in time. And his expectation was justified. For after routing a thousand horsemen and the sixty chari-

---

* This occurred at the town called Massaga, near the end of 327 BC. According to Arrian's account (*Anabasis* 4.27), Alexander attacked the mercenaries after learning that they intended to break their oath and desert him.

† Like many Greeks, Plutarch was deeply impressed by the religious ascetics of India, known to the Greeks variously as Brahmans, gymnosophists, wise men, or (as here) philosophers. The various religious orders in the region—Hindus, Jains, and perhaps also early Buddhists—were deeply opposed to Alexander's occupation.

‡ Plutarch evidently had access to a collection of Alexander's letters, of uncertain authenticity. They have become almost entirely lost.

§ An important local leader, an enemy of Taxiles with whom Alexander had allied.

ots that had attacked him, he seized all the chariots and killed four hundred of the horsemen. As Porus now guessed that Alexander himself had crossed the river, he advanced against him with his entire force, except the party he left behind to prevent the Macedonians from crossing.* But Alexander, dreading the beasts and the enormous numbers of the enemy, attacked the left wing himself and ordered Coenus to assault the right. A rout occurring at each wing, and Porus' men, forced back, retreated in each case toward the beasts, and crowded in among them. From then on the battle was a scramble until, in the eighth hour, the enemy gave up. This is the account the victor himself gives in his letters.

Most of the historians agree that Porus' height exceeded four cubits by a span,[†] and that because of his stature and the dignity of his physique, his size in relation to his elephant was proportional to that of a horseman's to his horse. Yet his was the largest elephant; and it showed a wonderful understanding and concern for the king, angrily warding off his attackers and repulsing them while the king was still vigorous. But when it sensed that he was wearied by scores of missiles and wounds, and dreaded that he might slip off, it lowered itself gently to its knees; and gently grasping the spears with its proboscis, drew each of them from Porus' body. When Alexander asked the captive Porus how he should treat him, Porus replied, "Like a king"; and when Alexander then asked whether he had anything else to say, Porus answered, "Everything is comprehended in 'like a king.'" Alexander not only allowed Porus to rule the territories over which he had been reigning, appointing him as satrap, but added another territory, having subdued its autonomous tribes, in which there were said to be fifteen peoples, five thousand noteworthy cities, and a great many villages. And he appointed Philip,[‡] one of his Companions, as satrap over a territory three times as large.

[62] The battle with Porus sapped the Macedonians' vigor and discouraged them from advancing farther into India. After barely repelling Porus, who had arrayed twenty thousand infantry and two thousand cav-

* A detachment of Macedonians had been left in position on the riverbank opposite Porus while Alexander led the rest to the crossing point. Porus wanted to deter this squadron, which included cavalry horses, from crossing, so he left some of his elephants there, knowing that horses were not willing to approach elephants.

† Making him over six feet tall, large for his time.

‡ No relation to Alexander's father.

alry against them, they firmly opposed Alexander when he insisted on crossing the river Ganges;* for they had learned that it was four miles wide and one hundred fathoms deep, and that the opposite banks were concealed by enormous numbers of infantry, horses, and elephants. For it was said that the kings of the Gandarites and Praesii were awaiting him with eighty thousand horsemen, two hundred thousand foot-soldiers, eight thousand war chariots, and six thousand warrior elephants.† And this was no idle boast. For Androcottus,‡ who reigned shortly thereafter, made Seleucus a present of five hundred elephants, and with an army of six hundred thousand invaded and subdued all of India.

At first, in his despair and anger, Alexander shut himself up in his tent and lay there, claiming no satisfaction with what he had accomplished unless he crossed the Ganges and regarding retreat as an admission of defeat. But when his friends, who gave him suitable consolation, and his men, who stood weeping and wailing by his door, appealed to him, he relented and broke up camp, fashioning many false and deceptive devices to enhance his renown; for he ordered the manufacture of armor that was larger than usual, taller horse stalls, and heavier bridles,§ and left these items behind, scattered about, and built altars of the gods, which to this day are held sacred by the kings of the Praesii, who cross the river and perform sacrifices on them in the Greek manner.¶

[63] From there, eager to see the outer sea,** he built many rafts and ferry-boats furnished with oars and was transported down the rivers†† in a leisurely manner. But the voyage was not free of toil or even of battles:

---

* Plutarch's error for the Hyphasis River. Alexander's army refused his order to cross this river and proceed toward what he claimed was the eastern edge of the world.

† The Nanda kingdom in the Ganges valley, the people apparently known to the Greeks as the Praesii, was indeed quite powerful at this time, and reports of their resources may well have played a part in the unwillingness of the troops to proceed.

‡ Chandragupta, the founder of the Maurya Empire.

§ The outsized gear was intended to give the impression that the realm was ruled by giants, to deter potential invaders.

¶ A fascinating statement, though how Plutarch could have known this is unclear. The altars of Alexander, if they ever really existed, have disappeared entirely today.

** With his vague notions of geography, Alexander imagined that the Arabian Sea, the body of water by the Indus River mouth, was in fact part of the world-encircling Ocean or "outer sea" that stretched around both Africa and northern Asia to join the Atlantic.

†† That is, the tributaries of the Indus and the Indus itself.

On landing and disembarking at the cities, he subdued them all.* Against the so-called Malli, who they say were the most warlike of the Indians, he just missed being cut to pieces. For he dispersed the Indians from their walls with spears, and was the first to mount the wall by a ladder; and when the ladder was shattered, and he was sustaining blows from the barbarians who were resisting from below, he wheeled about, though he had few companions, and leapt down into the midst of his enemies, and luckily landed on his feet. When he brandished his weapons, the barbarians imagined that some flamelike specter hovered before his body, which was why they fled at first and scattered. But when they saw him with two of his shield-bearers, they rushed at him, some of them trying to wound him with their swords and spears as he defended himself; and one, standing a little way off, released from his bow an arrow so forceful and steady that on piercing Alexander's breastplate it lodged in the bones near his chest. He himself yielded to the blow, his body bending double, whereupon his assailant, having hit him, advanced with his scimitar drawn, while Peucestas and Limnaeus† stood over the king. When both of these men were struck, Limnaeus perished, but Peucestas held out, and Alexander slew the barbarian.

After sustaining many wounds, Alexander was finally hit on the neck with a cudgel, at which point he planted his body against the wall and merely gazed at his enemies. Thereupon the Macedonians crowded around him, and he was seized, already unconscious, and carried to his tent. And at once there was a rumor in the army that he had died. When with great difficulty and effort they had excised the arrow's shaft, which was made of wood, and succeeded in removing his breastplate, they had to excise the barb that had entered one of his bones. It is said that the barb was three finger-breadths wide and four long. That was why, as it was being extracted, he fainted repeatedly and nearly died; but he nonetheless recovered. And when he was out of danger, but still weak and receiving prolonged care and treatment, he became aware, from the disturbance outside, that the Macedonians were longing to see him. He then donned

* The army's voyage down the Indus and its tributaries saw some of the hardest fighting, and harshest treatment of enemies, in all of Alexander's campaigns. Either Alexander wanted to terrorize the region in hopes of keeping it tractable, or he wanted to punish his men for defying him at the Hyphasis, or both.

† The two men who had accompanied Alexander over the wall. Other writers say the second was not Limnaeus but Leonnatus, or they include a third man, Abreas.

a cloak and went out.* After sacrificing to the gods, he again set sail and voyaged along the coast, subjugating great cities and extensive territory.

[66] His voyage down the rivers to the sea took seven months.† When he surged into the ocean with his fleet, he sailed out to an island that he called Scillustis, though others call it Psiltucis.‡ Disembarking there, he sacrificed to the gods and observed the natural features of the sea and the points on the coast that were accessible. Then, on praying that no man after him might travel beyond the bounds of his own expedition, he turned back. Appointing Nearchus as admiral and Onesicritus as chief pilot, he gave orders for the fleet to sail along the coast, keeping India on its right.§ He himself, advancing on foot through the Oreitans' territory, was led into the direst hardship and lost an enormous number of men, so that not even a fourth of his fighting force was brought back, though his infantry had numbered a hundred and twenty thousand, and his cavalry fifteen thousand.¶ Virulent diseases, bad food, the burning heat, and famine destroyed most of them, as they were crossing the untilled country of men who lived poorly and owned only a few miserable sheep whose flesh was inferior and foul-smelling, since the animals had been fed on ocean fish. After crossing the region with great difficulty in sixty days, he reached Gedrosia, where he suddenly had all things in abundance, since the nearest satraps and kings had provided them.

[68] When Nearchus and his men reached him from the coast, Alexander so enjoyed hearing in detail about their voyage that he himself

---

* Plutarch's brief finale does little justice to the intensely emotional episode. According to Arrian, Alexander's troops were ready to riot, believing him dead, until he summoned enough strength to mount a horse and ride out among them. The response of the troops was ecstatic.

† Roughly, the first half of 325 BC.

‡ Arrian gives the name as Cilluta (*Anabasis* 6.19.3). Its location is unknown.

§ With these orders, Alexander gave his old friend Nearchus a formidable task. The coast of Carmania, modern eastern Iran, was nearly barren, harborless, and totally unexplored. Alexander's plan was for a portion of the army to march along the coast and keep in contact with the fleet, finding water and anchorages for the sailors, while the ships supplied the land army with food. But the fleet and army became separated early on, and both endured terrible hardships. Nearchus' account of his voyage has been largely preserved in Arrian's *Indica*.

¶ The numbers and the scale seem fantastic, but some historians have found Plutarch's figures—the only surviving estimate for Gedrosia losses—credible. Hard evidence is lacking, but there is no doubt that the trip (in 325 BC) was a harrowing ordeal.

decided to sail down the Euphrates with a large armament, and then, after circumnavigating Arabia and Africa, to pass through the Pillars of Heracles and into the inner sea.* He had vessels of all sorts built for him at Thapsacus, and sailors and helmsmen were assembled from all quarters. But his difficult return march, the wound he sustained among the Malli, and the reports of his army's heavy losses raised doubts about his survival, which in turn incited his subject peoples to revolt, and occasioned great iniquity, greed, and insolence among his generals and satraps. In short, unrest and revolutionary impulses spread everywhere....

For these reasons he sent Nearchus back to the coast (for he was determined to fill the entire seaboard with wars), while he himself proceeded to punish the rogues among his generals.[†] He himself killed one of Abulites'[‡] sons, Oxyartes,[§] by running him through with a spear; and when Abulites failed to furnish him with the necessary provisions, bringing him three thousand talents of coined money instead, Alexander ordered the money to be thrown to the horses. When they would not touch it, he said, "What use to us are these provisions of yours?" and cast Abulites into prison.

[70] Holding a wedding for his Companions at Susa, he himself married Darius' daughter Stateira and assigned the noblest women to the noblest men;[¶] and for the Macedonians who had already married** he provided a public wedding feast at which he is said to have given each of the nine thousand invited guests a golden drinking cup for the libations. Distinguishing himself admirably in every way, he even cleared the debts his men had incurred, which amounted to 9,870 talents.

---

* Other sources also credit Alexander with this plan, to reach home by circumnavigating Africa and entering the Mediterranean (the "inner sea") at the Strait of Gibraltar ("Pillars of Heracles"), but it is doubtful that he really entertained it.

† This purge of unreliable satraps in 324 BC resulted in the flight of Harpalus to Athens, among other upheavals.

‡ Abulites the Persian was satrap of Susiana, first under the Persians, then under Alexander.

§ His name was Oxathres; Plutarch has confused him with Oxyartes, Roxane's father.

¶ The mass marriage Plutarch refers to occurred in the spring of 324 BC. Alexander matched nearly a hundred of his high officers with Persian and Bactrian brides, selected from the royal and noble families of Asia. The goal was to create a closer collaboration between the elites of the Greek and Persian worlds. Alexander himself married not only Stateira, as Plutarch says here, but also Parysatis, daughter of the Persian king who had preceded Darius. Alexander remained wedded to Roxane.

** That is, those who had Asian mistresses.

[71] Since the thirty thousand boys he had left behind for training and exercises* had acquired manly physiques and handsome looks, and displayed a wonderful ease and lightness in their drills, Alexander was delighted, though the Macedonians grew despondent and feared that he would regard *them* as less valuable. That was why, when he sent the weak and disabled to the coast,[†] they said it was insulting and humiliating that after using men in every capacity he discarded them in disgrace and cast them back to their native cities and parents, no longer the men they had been when he recruited them. They therefore urged him to send them *all* away and to consider all the Macedonians useless, since he now had these young dancers of the war dance[‡] with whom he could go forth and conquer the world.

To this Alexander responded harshly, and in his anger showered them with abuse. On driving them away, he gave his guard posts to Persians, out of whom he chose his body-guards and heralds. When the Macedonians saw him escorted by Persians, while they themselves were excluded and dishonored, they were humbled; and in talking among themselves, they realized that they had been almost mad with envy and rage. Coming to their senses at last, they visited Alexander's tent, unarmed and wearing only their tunics.... For two days and nights they persisted in standing at his door, weeping and appealing to him as their master. On the third day, coming forth and seeing them humbled and sobbing pitiably, he wept for a long time;[§] then, after duly scolding them, he addressed them kindly and released the men who were unfit, giving them splendid gifts and writing to Antipater[¶] that at all public games and theaters they were to occupy the front seats, crowned with laurel. He also awarded pensions to the children, now orphans, of the men who had died.

[73] As he was advancing to Babylon, Nearchus, who had rejoined him

---

* For Alexander's decision some years earlier to train a corps of Asian youths to fight alongside the Macedonians, see chapter 47 above.

† Alexander decommissioned not only the "weak and disabled" but also many of the most egregious troublemakers from the Hyphasis mutiny. About ten thousand Macedonian veterans were to be sent "to the coast"—that is, the west coast of Asia—and then home to Macedonia by ship, under the leadership of Craterus. The events described here occurred at the town of Opis, on the Tigris River, in the spring of 324 BC.

‡ Evidently a sarcastic reference to the youth and vigor of the new recruits. The veterans taunting Alexander were in their fifties and sixties.

§ Arrian, in his account of the same episode (*Anabasis* 7.11), does not show Alexander behaving nearly so emotionally.

¶ Antipater was in command of the Macedonian home front in Alexander's absence.

after sailing through the ocean to the Euphrates,* said that some Chaldaeans† had met him and recommended that Alexander keep away from Babylon. But Alexander ignored this advice and proceeded onward.... He was also perturbed by many other signs. For example, a tame ass, attacking the largest and most beautiful lion in his menagerie, kicked it to death. And when Alexander had stripped to anoint himself and exercise and was playing ball, and the young men who were playing went to put on their clothes, they found a fellow sitting silently on the throne, wearing the diadem and cloaked in the royal robe. The man, when asked who he was, was silent for a long time. Then, collecting himself, he said that his name was Dionysius, a Messenian by birth, and that charged with some crime he had been brought there from the coast and kept in chains for a long time; but just now the god Sarapis,† standing before him, had removed his chains, led him to that spot, and told him to don the robe and diadem, sit on the throne, and remain silent.

[74] On hearing of this, Alexander obeyed the seers and did away with the man. He himself now lost heart and grew dubious about divine protection and suspicious of his friends. He particularly feared Antipater and his sons, one of whom, Iolaus, was his chief cup-bearer; the other, Cassander, had lately arrived.§ And when Cassander, on catching sight of some barbarians performing a ritual bow, could not help laughing, since he had been reared in the Greek manner and had never seen such a thing before, Alexander flew into a rage, grasped Cassander's hair firmly with both hands, and knocked his head against the wall.

[75] Once Alexander had permitted himself to believe in divine influences, his mind grew so troubled and apprehensive that he regarded any odd or unusual occurrence, no matter how trivial, as a sign or portent;

---

* That is, through the Persian Gulf.

† A caste of Mesopotamian priests, famous for their powers of divination.

‡ Sarapis was a god worshipped primarily in Egypt during the post-Alexander period, thought by some to have been invented by Ptolemy, the ruler there. But the mention of Sarapis here and of a temple called the Sarapeion in chapter 76 predate Ptolemy's sovereignty. The discrepancy has been variously dealt with by modern historians.

§ Antipater was presumably an enemy because Alexander had ordered him to step down from his post in Macedonia and report to Babylon. But it is unclear whether Alexander was displeased with Antipater or meant him harm. Antipater did not comply, indicating he felt at least some misgivings, but sent his son Cassander to Babylon in his place. Those who suspected Alexander was poisoned (see chapter 77) largely believed that Cassander had brought poison with him to Babylon, at his father's behest; but Plutarch rejects that theory.

and his palace was full of people sacrificing, performing ritual purifications, and prophesying....

After entertaining Nearchus and his men with a brilliant banquet, he bathed, as was his habit before going to bed; but then he joined Medius* in a carousal, at that man's invitation. Then, after drinking all the next day, he fell into a fever.

[76] The royal diaries† give the following account of his disease: On the eighteenth of the month of Daesius‡ he slept in the bathhouse because of his fever. On the next day, after bathing, he moved back to his bedroom and spent the day playing at dice with Medius. Then, after bathing late in the day, he performed his sacrifices to the gods, took a little food, and was feverish during the night. On the twentieth, after bathing again, he performed his customary sacrifice; reclining in the bathhouse, he devoted himself to Nearchus, listening to his account of his voyage and of the Great Sea.§

On the twenty-first, a day spent in the same way, his fever worsened; he passed a difficult night, and on the next day was in a raging fever. After being carried outside, he lay down beside the great bath, where he talked with his officers about the vacant posts of his realm and how they might be filled by able men. On the twenty-fourth, though in a high fever, he had himself carried out to perform his sacrifices. He gave orders for his most important officers to wait in the courtyard, and for the taxiarchs and pentacosiarchs¶ to pass the night outside. On the twenty-fifth, he was carried to the palace on the other side of the river, where he slept a little,

---

* This man, evidently a trusted friend of Alexander, is unknown apart from the large role he played in Alexander's final days.

† There is great dispute as to what this document was or how much it can be trusted. Apparently a set of diaries was kept throughout Alexander's campaign, recording events day by day. Whether the account of Alexander's illness that Plutarch drew on here actually came from that set is unclear. Arrian also claims to quote from royal diaries in his narrative of Alexander's fever (*Anabasis* 7.25–26), but the two versions differ in some details.

‡ The beginning of June 323 BC. Alexander died, as we know from a Babylonian record, on June 11.

§ Plutarch refers to the Arabian Sea as though it were a part of the world-encircling Ocean.

¶ The various commanders and subcommanders of the army brigades. It is unclear why Alexander wanted them all present. In Arrian's account of the fatal illness, which overlaps closely with that of Plutarch but is not identical, Alexander was about to launch an invasion of Arabia.

though his fever did not let up. When his officers came to him, he could not speak. His condition was unchanged on the twenty-sixth, which was why the Macedonians, thinking he had died, came shouting to his door, threatened his Companions, and forced their way in. And when the doors had been thrown open to them, they all filed past his couch, one by one, wearing only their tunics.... And on the twenty-eighth, toward evening, he died.

[77] Most of these details have been set down here exactly as recorded in the diaries. In the immediate aftermath, no one suspected poisoning; but five years later, they say, when information was given, Olympias had many persons put to death* and cast out the ashes of Iolaus,[†] alleging that he had administered the poison.... But most think that the story about the poisoning is a complete fabrication.[‡]

C. THE FALL OF PHOCION

As the civil war between rival Macedonian leaders Cassander and Polysperchon heated up, Phocion found himself caught in the middle. He was a natural ally of Cassander, who favored keeping Athens an oligarchy as his father, Antipater, had fashioned it; but Polysperchon, who was nominally in control of Macedonian policy, had passed a decree restoring Athens and other Greek cities to their former democratic constitutions. After this decree took effect and Athens's oligarchic government fell, Phocion was kicked out of the city, along with several followers. He went north to see Polysperchon and ask for support, but the Macedonian leader, desperately clinging to power himself, chose not to make an exemption to his new freedom decree.

—

[34] A guard now surrounded Phocion and his associates; and all of his friends who were not standing nearby, on seeing this, covered their faces

* Olympias, Alexander's mother, got power in Macedonia in 317 BC by a strange series of twists and turns. While in power Olympias had one of Cassander's brothers, and many of his supporters, executed. Rumors that had spread through the Greek world accused Cassander and his father, Antipater, of having masterminded the poisoning of Alexander.

† Iolaus was Cassander's brother; he had been serving as Alexander's wine pourer at the time his illness began.

‡ Of the surviving sources, several support the theory that Alexander was poisoned, while only Plutarch explicitly rejects it; Arrian implies that he believes Alexander died of illness. Modern historians remain divided on this question, or on whether it can even be answered.

and saved themselves by fleeing. Cleitus* brought the captives to Athens, ostensibly to stand trial but in fact already sentenced to die. And the manner of their conveyance was also distressing, since they were carried on wagons through the Cerameicus to the theater.† After bringing them there, Cleitus kept them confined until the magistrates had filled the Assembly—opening the speaker's platform and the theater to everyone, male and female, even slaves, foreigners, and criminals.‡ And when they had read the king's letter§ aloud, in which he said that though he had determined that these men had betrayed him, he was handing them over to be tried by their fellow citizens, who were free and autonomous, Cleitus brought the men in.

The noblest citizens, when they saw Phocion, covered their faces, hung their heads, and wept. One of them, rising to his feet, had the courage to say that since the king had entrusted so important a trial to the people, it was just as well that slaves and foreigners leave the Assembly. And when the multitude bridled at this, and shouted that the oligarchs and haters of democracy should be stoned, no one else ventured to speak on Phocion's behalf, whereupon Phocion himself, though he could hardly make himself heard, said, "Do you want to put me to death unjustly or justly?" When some answered "Justly," he said, "And how will you reach a decision unless you have listened?" But when they would hear no more, he drew near and said, "Then I admit that I have done wrong, and I accept the death penalty for the policies I enacted. But why, men of Athens, will you kill *these* men, who have done no wrong?" When the crowd replied, "Because they are your friends," Phocion stood apart and remained silent. And Hagnonides,¶ holding the decree he had written, read it aloud. It said that the people should vote as to whether they thought these men had done wrong; and if convicted, they should be put to death.

[35] When the decree had been read aloud, a number of people demanded an additional clause, that Phocion should be tortured before ex-

---

* A top Macedonian officer.

† The theater of Dionysus at Athens was normally the site of performances of tragedies and comedies, but it was occasionally used as space for political proceedings. It is not clear what disgrace was involved in bringing Phocion there by cart.

‡ Against constitutional law, the leaders of the new democracy had allowed noncitizens into the Assembly.

§ That is, the letter of King Philip III of Macedon, the mentally incompetent monarch now in the control of Polysperchon.

¶ Leader of the democratic counterrevolution.

ecution, and said that the rack should be brought in and the executioners summoned. But Hagnonides, who felt that such a proceeding was barbaric and abominable, and saw that even Cleitus was disgusted by it, said, "When we catch that rogue Callimedon,* gentlemen of Athens, let us torture *him*. But where Phocion is concerned I shall not write such an order." At this some decent fellow called out in answer, "You do right! For if we torture Phocion, what are we to do to *you*?" When the decree had been ratified and a vote by show of hands was taken, no one remained seated; all stood up, many having donned garlands,† and voted to condemn the prisoners to death.

[36] When the Assembly was dismissed, the condemned men were led to the prison. The rest of them, receiving the embraces of their friends and relatives, walked along weeping and wailing; but the onlookers who gazed at Phocion's face, which looked just as it had on those occasions when he was sent forth from the Assembly to serve as general, marveled at the man's impassivity and greatness of heart.

[37] It was the nineteenth day of the month of Munichion,‡ and the cavalry, conducting the procession in honor of Zeus, was passing by the prison. Some of the horsemen removed their garlands, while others, gazing at the prison door, shed tears. And it was clear to persons not altogether savage or debased by spite and envy that it was terribly impious for the city not to exercise restraint on that day and keep itself unpolluted by a public execution while holding a festival. Nevertheless, as if their triumph over him left something to be desired, Phocion's enemies passed a decree stipulating that Phocion's body was to be sent beyond the border and that no Athenian was to kindle a pyre in honor of his burial. Thus no friend dared to touch his body. But a certain Conopion, a man in the habit of rendering such services for a fee, conveyed the corpse beyond Eleusis, obtained fire in Megara, and burned it. Phocion's wife, who was present with her female slaves, heaped up an empty tomb there and poured a libation. Putting the bones in the fold of her dress and conveying them home by night, she buried them beside the hearth, saying, "Dear hearth, I entrust you with the remains of a good man. Restore them to his ancestral tombs once the Athenians have come to their senses."

---

* A fugitive member of the fallen oligarchic regime.

† As a gesture of celebration.

‡ The day of an Athenian festival in honor of Zeus. The date is 318 BC.

[38] And indeed, when a short time had elapsed, and their state affairs taught them what sort of steward and guardian of temperance and justice they had lost, the people erected a bronze statue of Phocion and buried his bones at public expense.

D. PLUTARCH, *DEMETRIUS*

This volume concludes with a complete Plutarchan Life, *one of Plutarch's richest and most unusual creations. In nearly all the* Parallel Lives, *Plutarch holds up models of moral virtue, often bending the record to cast historical figures in a positive light. In* Demetrius, *as he tells us in the prologue, Plutarch elects to depict a figure from the opposite end of the moral spectrum—someone whose example we should shun, not follow. Because of his party-boy ways—a love of drink, extravagance, sexual excess, and showy displays of status—Demetrius offended Plutarch's sense of political propriety. The typical statesman of the* Lives *is sober and self-restrained, while Demetrius is flamboyant and dissolute.*

However, the tone of this Life *is not as clear-cut as Plutarch might have intended. As the narrative progresses we sense an abiding affection for Demetrius and an admiration for the way he bounces back after nearly every reversal. It seems the allure of this "bad boy" celebrity was stronger than Plutarch was willing to admit. The final chapter, with its description of the rites of mourning over Demetrius' cremated remains, conveys a sense of reverence that Plutarch seems to share, or at least does nothing to undermine.*

The events of this Life *take us into the confused period following the death of Alexander the Great in 323 BC, an era sometimes characterized as the Wars of the Successors. Alexander's generals vied with one another for control of an empire that encompassed most of the known world, stretching from Greece to what is now Pakistan. These Successors, as they are termed (a rough translation of the term the Greeks applied to them, Diadochoi), were expert commanders and tacticians but less adept at long-term strategy, diplomacy, or statecraft. They battered at one another for decades without achieving lasting gains, creating instabilities across three continents, squandering much of the wealth and manpower Alexander had accrued, and wreaking havoc among the city-states of the Greek mainland, which were forced to choose sides and often then punished for their choices. When the dust settled, the empire of Alexander had fragmented into several independent states, each ruled by an aging warlord who had, by that time, proclaimed himself a king. The Hellenistic age, as it is now termed, was under way.*

The Successors used various means, not only warfare, to build power and establish legitimacy. They drew on the already mythic stature of Alexander, by imitating his personal style or displaying his effects (even, in the case of Ptolemy, his corpse). They married women with high dynastic standing, the widows or daughters of those who had served with Alexander or the offspring of marriages he had arranged. Demetrius employed both these strategies: His bravado, both in civic arenas and on the battlefield, was cut from the same cloth as Alexander's, and his marriage to Phila, widow of one of Alexander's high-ranking officers, was a huge boost to his fortunes. But he took other wives too, and his greatest affections tended toward Lamia, the sex symbol of her day, as Plutarch relates with a certain salacious pleasure.

Plutarch's Demetrius *reveals the scope and richness of historical biography at its finest. In the character of Demetrius, a man of grand ambitions but dangerous instabilities, Plutarch found the key themes of a grandiose, unstable age—the age of the Successors.*

———

[1] It seems to me that those who first likened the arts to the senses perceived, very clearly, the power of making distinctions that both possess—the power, as strong in the arts as in the senses, that enables us to perceive opposites. The arts and the senses share this power, but they differ in the use to which we put the distinctions we make. Sense-perception, on the one hand, can equally well distinguish white objects as black, or sweet things as well as bitter, or soft and yielding substances as well as hard and resistant ones (since its function is to receive impressions from all objects alike and then report that perception to the brain). The arts, on the other hand, use reason to select and adopt what belongs to their realm and to avoid and reject what is alien; they contemplate the former by preference and intent but the latter only incidentally, in order to ward them off. Thus, the art of healing examines disease only incidentally, just as the art of harmony examines the discordant—that is, in order to produce the opposite.

The most consummate arts of all—temperance, justice, and wisdom—distinguish not only what is good and just and beneficial, but also what is bad and unjust and disgraceful. These arts have no regard for an innocence that styles itself ignorant of evils.* They consider this foolishness,

---

* A difficult sentence, but the idea is that to be properly trained in the moral virtues requires familiarity with the vices too.

and ignorance of what those who seek to live rightly most need to know. It was thus that the ancient Spartans forced their helots to drink much unmixed wine at festivals and then brought them into the public dining halls, in order to show their young men what it was like to be drunk.*

I do not think that perverting some to correct others is humane or good civil policy. Still, when men have led reckless lives and become prominent for badness in wielding power or in great endeavors, perhaps it will not be amiss for me to introduce one or two pairs of them into my biographies. My purpose is not to divert and amuse my readers by varying my writing, but to do as Ismenias the Theban did: He used to exhibit both good and bad flutists to his music students and say "You must play like this one," or again, "You must not play like this one." And Antigenidas† used to think that young men would listen with more pleasure to good flute-players if they were given an experience of bad ones. So I think we too shall be more eager to observe and imitate better lives if we have narratives of the blameworthy and bad.

This book will therefore contain the Lives of Demetrius the Besieger and Antony the army chief,‡ men who bore most ample testimony to the truth of Plato's dictum: "Great natures exhibit great vices as well as great virtues."§ Both men were given to sex, drink, and battle; both were free in their giving and spending and had proud and insolent natures; and their fortunes were similar as a result. For all through their lives they not only won great successes but met with great reverses; they made innumerable conquests but suffered innumerable losses; they unexpectedly fell low but unexpectedly recovered themselves again. One reached his end imprisoned by his enemies, and the other on the verge of that calamity.

---

* Plutarch repeats this charge against Spartan mistreatment of helots in another *Life*, that of Lycurgus (28.4), adding there that the helots were forced to dance and sing in vulgar ways as forms of humiliation. The substance of these charges is hard to determine.

† Another Theban musician, like the aforementioned Ismenias. Thebans were especially good at playing the *aulos*, the double-reeded wind instrument favored by the Greeks (here rendered as "flute").

‡ As is usual in the *Lives*, Plutarch's introduction serves to preface a pair of biographies, one Greek and one Roman. The Roman life is not included here, nor is the Syncrisis or Comparison in which Plutarch drew a set of parallels and contrasts between Demetrius and Antony.

§ None of Plato's extant works have this dictum, but at *Republic* 491 d–e Plato has Socrates advance a similar idea.

[2] Antigonus* had two sons by Stratonicē, the daughter of Corrhagus, one of whom he named Demetrius, after his brother, and the other Philip, after his father. This is what the majority of writers say. But some have it that Demetrius was not the son but the nephew of Antigonus, claiming his own father died when the boy was quite young and his mother immediately married Antigonus, so that Demetrius was considered to be that man's son. Anyhow, Philip, who was a few years younger than Demetrius, died. Demetrius, the surviving son, was shorter than his father (though he was a tall man), but his features had a rare and astonishing beauty that no painter or sculptor could ever capture. His face showed grace and strength together with dignity and beauty; blended with its youthful eagerness was a certain heroic look and kingly majesty that were hard to imitate. His temperament was similarly framed to inspire both fear and affection in others. He was a very amiable companion, and most self-indulgent of monarchs in the leisure he gave to drink and high living, but he also had a very energetic and eager tenacity and purposefulness. Thus he used to take as his model Dionysus more than any other deity, since this god was most terrible in waging war and yet most skillful, when war was over, in making peace serve joy and pleasure.[†]

[3] Demetrius was extremely fond of his father, and from his devotion to his mother it was clear that he honored his father from genuine affection rather than out of deference to his power.[‡] On one occasion, when Antigonus was busy receiving ambassadors, Demetrius came home from a hunt, went up to his father and kissed him, then sat down by his side just as he was, hunting javelins in hand. Antigonus, as the ambassadors were going away with their answers, called out in a loud voice: "Fellows, make this report about us, that *this* is the way we feel toward each other"—implying that his harmonious and trusting relations with his son showed a certain vigor in the royal house and gave proof of its power. Thus it

---

* Antigonus Monophthalmus ("One-eye") was a Macedonian general who accompanied Alexander the Great into Asia in 334 BC, leaving his son Demetrius, then three years old, behind in Macedon with his mother. Antigonus was soon sidelined from the campaign and given a rearguard post as governor of conquered Phrygia, in what is now western Turkey, in 333; Demetrius and the rest of the family joined him there soon afterward.

† Alexander the Great had also modeled himself on Dionysus for similar reasons. Though known primarily as a kindly god who frees mortals from their cares (in part through the effects of wine), Dionysus could also destroy his enemies with ferocity, as seen in Euripides' *Bacchae*.

‡ That is, his love for his mother, who had no political power, proved that his filial affections were sincere.

seems that sovereignty is so opposed to social relations, so full of ill-will and distrust, that the oldest and greatest of the Successors of Alexander could make this a thing to glory in: He was not afraid of his own son, but allowed him near his person, lance in hand.*

The Antigonid house was virtually unique in keeping itself pure from this sort of crime for many generations. To be more specific, Philip V was the only one of the descendants of Antigonus who put a son to death.† But almost all the other Successor families afford many examples of men who killed sons and of sons who killed mothers and wives; and as for men killing brothers, just as geometricians assume their postulates, so fratricide came to be a common and recognized postulate wherever monarchy seeks security.

[4] From the start Demetrius was naturally humane and fond of his companions, as may be seen in the following example: Mithridates, son of Ariobarzanes,‡ was a companion of Demetrius and an intimate of the same age. He was one of the courtiers of Antigonus, and though he neither was nor was thought to be a villain, still, as the result of a dream, Antigonus became suspicious of him. (Antigonus dreamed he was traversing a large, beautiful field while sowing gold-dust. From this, at first, a golden crop sprang up, but when he came back a bit later he could see nothing but stubble. In vexation and distress, he heard in his dream sundry voices saying that Mithridates had reaped the golden crop for himself and gone off to the Black Sea.) Antigonus was much disturbed by this vision, and he told it to Demetrius after making him swear an oath of silence, adding that he had fully determined to destroy Mithridates and get him out of the way. On hearing this, Demetrius was greatly distressed. When Mithridates, as was his custom, came to spend some free time with him, Demetrius did not venture to open his lips on the matter or warn him by word of mouth, because of his oath. Rather, he gradually drew Mithridates away from the rest of his friends, and when they were by themselves,

* Plutarch's observations on the perils of power, here and throughout the *Lives,* establish the moral framework in which historical events are to be understood.

† Philip V, the great-great-grandson of Antigonus, was king of Macedonia in the late third and early second centuries BC. Near the end of his life he had his younger son, Demetrius II, killed to ensure that his older son, Perseus, would have no rival for power. This was about 150 years after the birth of Demetrius.

‡ A Persian nobleman who, in the late fourth century BC, founded the kingdom of Pontus in northeastern Turkey, carving off a chunk of what would have been Antigonid land. The foundation of Pontus is prefigured in the dream that Plutarch recounts in what follows.

with the sharp butt of his lance he wrote on the ground so that his friend could see: "Flee, Mithridates." Mithridates understood and ran away by night to Cappadocia. And soon fate caused the dream of Antigonus to be accomplished in real life. For Mithridates made himself master of a large and fine territory and founded the line of Pontic kings, which, in the eighth generation, was brought to an end by the Romans.* This, then, is an illustration of Demetrius' strong natural bent toward kindness and justice.

[5] But just as among elements of the universe (according to Empedocles), Strife produces mutual tension and warfare,[†] particularly among elements that touch or lie near one another, so the continuous wars waged by the Successors of Alexander were aggravated and inflamed when their interests or lands adjoined. Such was the case with Antigonus and Ptolemy. Antigonus was lingering in Phrygia when he heard that Ptolemy had crossed over from Cyprus and was ravaging Syria and reducing its cities or turning them from their allegiance.[‡] To counter Ptolemy he sent his son Demetrius, who was only twenty-two and was then for the first time sole commander of an expedition where great interests were at stake. But since he was young and inexperienced and had as adversary a man trained in the school of Alexander, a veteran of many great contests, Demetrius met with utter defeat near Gaza. Eight thousand of his troops were taken prisoner and five thousand were slain. Demetrius lost also his tent, his money, and, in a word, all his personal effects. But Ptolemy sent these back to him, together with Demetrius' friends and a considerate and humane message that the two sides must not wage war for all things alike but only for glory and dominion.[§] Demetrius accepted

---

* The rump state the Greeks called Pontus was at first an ally of Rome but came to be staunchly opposed to Roman intrusion into Asia Minor. Its last king, the famous Mithridates VI, led a series of wars against Roman forces in the region and was subdued only with great difficulty in the 60s BC.

† Empedocles, a Greek natural philosopher of the fifth century BC, believed that all matter was formed by combinations of four elements; the forces of Love and Strife govern these combinations and lend them different characteristics. Plutarch focuses only on Strife, for obvious reasons, though some manuscripts also include Love here.

‡ Ptolemy Soter, a Successor ruler based in Egypt, strove on several occasions to expand northward into Syria and Phoenicia. This brought him into conflict with his former ally Antigonus, who ostensibly controlled all that region.

§ The point of the remark is unclear here. In a version of this letter given by another source, Ptolemy says, more directly, that his objective in Syria was not mere conquest but restoration of honor, since Antigonus (he claims) had slighted him by not sharing the spoils of war when the two had been allies in a previous struggle.

the kindness and prayed to the gods that he might not long be in Ptolemy's debt but might soon return the favor.* He accepted his disaster not like a young boy thwarted at the start of an undertaking but like a sensible general acquainted with reverses of fortune; he busied himself with levying troops and preparing arms, while he kept the cities well in hand[†] and drilled his new recruits.

[6] When his father, Antigonus, learned of the battle, he said that Ptolemy had conquered beardless youths but must now fight with men.[‡] But not wishing to humble or curtail the spirit of his son, Antigonus did not oppose his son's request that *he* might fight Ptolemy again on his own, but allowed him to do it. Not long after, a general of Ptolemy, Cilles, arrived on the scene with a splendid army, intending to drive Demetrius out of Syria and looking down on him because of his previous defeat. But Demetrius fell on him suddenly and took him by surprise, put him to rout, and captured his camp, general and all; he also took seven thousand prisoners and made himself master of vast treasures. Demetrius rejoiced to have won the day, not because of what he would get but because of what he could restore; he was delighted not so much with the wealth and glory his victory brought as with the power it gave him to pay back Ptolemy's kindness and return his favor. But he did not do this on his own authority; he first wrote to his father about it. And when his father gave permission and told him to dispose of everything as he liked, he sent back to Ptolemy both Cilles himself and that man's friends, having loaded them with gifts. This reverse drove Ptolemy out of Syria and brought Antigonus down from Celaenae;[§] he rejoiced at the victory and yearned to get sight of his son.

[7] After this, Demetrius was sent to bring into subjection the Arabs known as Nabataean, and incurred great peril by getting into regions

---

* That is, he prayed that he might soon defeat Ptolemy and have occasion to practice similar magnanimity.

[†] By "cities" Plutarch means the Greek cities of the Asian coast (Miletus, Ephesus, Halicarnassus, and the rest). These valuable power bases, with their fortified walls and harbors, had no great allegiance to any of the Successors and were prone to switch sides unless closely guarded.

[‡] The Battle of Gaza fell in 312 BC. Demetrius was then about twenty-four, so hardly a "beardless youth," but the generation of leaders who followed Alexander kept themselves clean-shaven in adulthood as Alexander had done.

[§] Celaenae was the capital of Phrygia and Antigonus' home base. In the account of Diodorus (19.93.5) it is Antigonus' arrival on the scene, not the victory led by Demetrius, that drives Ptolemy out of the region.

that had no water. But he was neither terrified nor greatly disturbed, and his demeanor overawed the barbarians, so that he took much booty and seven hundred camels from them and returned.

Seleucus,* who had once been expelled from Babylonia by Antigonus but had succeeded in recovering the realm and was wielding the power there, marched inland with an army, intending to annex the tribes on the confines of India and the provinces about Mount Caucasus.† Demetrius, expecting that he would find Mesopotamia unprotected, suddenly crossed the Euphrates and invaded Babylonia before Seleucus could stop him. He expelled from one of its citadels (there were two of them) the garrison left there by Seleucus, got it into his power and stationed in it seven thousand of his own men. But after ordering his soldiers to take as booty everything they could carry or drive from the country, he returned to the sea-coast, leaving Seleucus more confirmed than before in his possession of the realm. For by ravaging the country, Demetrius seemed to admit that it no longer belonged to his father.‡

Meanwhile, Ptolemy was besieging Halicarnassus; Demetrius came swiftly to the aid of the city and rescued it.

[8] The glory won by this noble deed inspired Antigonus and Demetrius with a wonderful eagerness to give freedom to all Greece, which had been reduced to subjection by Cassander and Ptolemy.§ No nobler or juster war than this was waged by any one of the kings, for the vast wealth they together had amassed by subduing the barbarians was now lavishly spent on the Greeks, to win glory and honor.¶ As soon as father and son determined to sail against Athens, one of his friends said to An-

---

* A second enemy to the Antigonids, Seleucus, now emerges into Plutarch's narrative (in fact he had earlier aided Ptolemy at the Battle of Gaza, and the victory there had enabled him to establish himself in Babylon). Originally an officer in Alexander's army, Seleucus had only minor standing at the start of the Successor era but ended up one of its biggest winners.

† The Hindu Kush range.

‡ An interesting point, revealing the complexity of the politics of this era. Antigonus and Demetrius could not claim to control territory if they were also plundering it.

§ Cassander, based in Macedon, had established a power base in Europe in part by garrisoning the cities of mainland Greece and installing puppet governments loyal to him. It was he who had brought the line of Alexander to an end by killing Alexander IV, the conqueror's son. The Antigonids hoped to win the mantle of liberators by restoring (or at least appearing to restore) to the Greek cities, especially Athens, their ancient autonomy.

¶ As often, Plutarch is quick to put his faith in the declarations of his subjects. Most historians today view the call of Greek freedom, when sounded by Antigonus, more skeptically.

tigonus that they must keep that city, if they took it, in their own hands, since it was a scaling-ladder by which to vault into Greece.* But Antigonus would not hear of it; he said that the goodwill of a people was a noble and unshakable ladder, and that Athens, the beacon-tower of the whole world, would speedily flash the glory of their deeds to all mankind. So Demetrius sailed, with five thousand talents of money and a fleet of two hundred and fifty ships, against Athens, where Demetrius of Phalerum† was governing the city for Cassander and a garrison was set in Munychia.‡ By virtue of forethought combined with good fortune, he appeared off Piraeus on the twenty-sixth of Thargelion. No one knew beforehand of his approach, but as soon as his fleet was seen nearby, everyone thought that the ships belonged to Ptolemy and prepared to receive them.

At last the generals discovered their mistake and brought up support troops; there was confusion, as is natural when men are forced to defend themselves against enemies making an unexpected landing. For Demetrius had found the harbor entrances open and had sailed through them. He was soon inside, as all could see, and he signaled from his ship a demand for silence. When this was secured, he proclaimed by the herald at his side that he had been sent by his father on what he prayed might be a happy errand: to set Athens free, to expel its garrison troops, and to restore to the people their laws and their ancient form of government.

[9] On hearing this proclamation, most of the people at once threw their shields down in front of them and with clapping of hands and loud cries urged Demetrius to land his ship, hailing him as their savior and benefactor. The party of Demetrius of Phalerum also thought they must by all means receive the conqueror, even if he was not going to make good on his promises, but nevertheless sent ambassadors to supplicate his mercy. These Demetrius met in a friendly spirit, and sent back with them one of his father's friends, Aristodemus of Miletus.

---

* A metaphor from siege warfare, implying that all Greece would "fall" (i.e., come over to Antigonus and Demetrius) once Athens did.

† This puppet ruler, to our great dismay, bears the same name as our subject. To distinguish the two Demetriuses, this ally of Cassander is often called "the Phalerite," or, as here, Demetrius of Phalerum. The name Demetrius without qualifier stands for the subject of this *Life*.

‡ The hill of Munychia, in Piraeus (the harbor serving Athens), was so well fortified that a garrison housed there could control the harbor and therefore the food supply of Athens itself.

Now Demetrius of Phalerum, owing to the change of government, was more afraid of his fellow citizens than of the enemy. Demetrius, however, was not unmindful of him, but out of regard for the man's good reputation and excellence, sent him and his friends under safe conduct to Thebes, as he desired. As for himself, he declared that, although he wanted to see Athens, he would not do so before he had completed his liberation by ridding the city of its garrison. Meanwhile, after running a trench and a palisade around Munychia, he sailed against Megara, where a garrison had been stationed by Cassander.

But Demetrius learned that Cratesipolis (who had been the wife of Polyperchon's son Alexander) was lingering at Pagae* and would be very glad to pay him a visit, and she was a famous beauty, so he left his forces in the territory of Megara and set forth, taking a few light-armed attendants with him. Turning aside from these also, he pitched his tent in a separate place so Cratesipolis might visit him unobserved. Some of his enemies learned of this and launched a sudden attack. Terrified, he donned a shabby cloak, ran for his life, and got away, narrowly escaping a shameful capture that nearly resulted from his rash ardor. His tent, together with his belongings, was carried off by his enemies.

Megara meanwhile was captured, and Demetrius' soldiers would have plundered it if the Athenians had not strongly pleaded on behalf of its citizens. Demetrius expelled its garrison and gave the city its freedom. While he was engaged in this he thought of Stilpo the philosopher,† who was famous for choosing a life of tranquility. Demetrius summoned him and asked him whether anyone had robbed him of anything. "No one," said Stilpo, "for I saw no one carrying away knowledge." But nearly all the slaves in the city were stolen away. When Demetrius once more tried to deal kindly with the philosopher, and as he was leaving, said "Stilpo, I leave your city in freedom," Stilpo replied: "You speak true, for you have not left us a single one of our slaves."

[10] Coming back again to Munychia and encamping before it, he drove

---

* The manuscripts read "Patrae" here, but that place, as scholars have noted, is too far away for Demetrius to have gone there for a tryst; Pagae, however, is an easy day trip from Megara. So the story that follows becomes credible if we read "Pagae" for "Patrae," though there is no other confirmation of it. Alexander, son of Polyperchon, had governed the Peloponnese on behalf of Cassander until he was assassinated in 314 BC; his widow, Cratesipolis, took charge of his forces thereafter.

† Stilpo (whose works have perished) belonged to the Megarian school of philosophy. His views were closely aligned with those of the Cynics, who disdained all material wealth and comfort (as seen in the anecdote that follows).

out the garrison* and demolished the fortress, and with this feat accomplished, on the urgent invitation of the Athenians, at last made his entry into Athens, where he assembled the people and gave them back their ancient form of government.† He also promised that they would receive from his father a hundred and fifty thousand bushels of grain and enough ship timber to build a hundred triremes.‡ It had been fourteen years since the Athenians had lost their democracy; during the period after the Lamian War and the Battle of Crannon,§ their government had been nominally an oligarchy but really a monarchy, owing to the great influence of Demetrius of Phalerum. And now that the new Demetrius had shown himself great and splendid in his benefactions, the Athenians made him seem odious and obnoxious by voting him extravagant honors.¶ They were the first people in the world to give Demetrius and Antigonus the title of king, though both had up to that time shrunk from using the word since this was the only royal prerogative still left to the descendants of Philip and Alexander that others could not assume or share, as it was thought.**

The Athenians too were the only people to give Demetrius and Antigonus the appellation of Savior-gods, and they put a stop to the ancient custom of designating the year with the name of the annual archon, instead electing every year a priest of the Savior-gods whose name they prefixed to their public edicts and private contracts.†† They also decreed

---

* The troops installed there by Cassander in support of the puppet Demetrius of Phalerum.

† The Athenian democracy had been replaced by a narrow oligarchy under Cassander, so its restoration was considered a moral triumph. The year was 307 BC.

‡ Triremes, or oar-powered warships, were seen as central to Athenian power and also to democracy, since the poor were the primary source of the rowers they needed.

§ The war and the battle in which an Athenian rebellion against Macedon was defeated by Antipater, Cassander's father.

¶ There follows a long catalog of obsequious honors paid by Athens to Demetrius, extending to the end of chapter 13. Some of these belong to Demetrius' first entry into Athens in 307, but others, most likely, date from two later visits in the subsequent fifteen years.

** During the period following Alexander's death, the Macedonians bestowed the kingship on his two closest kin, his half brother and his son, both of whom were considered kings. But both were dead by 309 BC and the throne had become vacant. None of the Successors belonged to the royal family, so none had as yet claimed a royal title.

†† Lacking a system of numbered years, the Athenians used the name of the chief archon, an annually elected civic official, to indicate dates. As also with later Roman consuls, this archonship attained greater stature because the officeholder's name would be immortalized on documents and legislation. By awarding this honor instead to the priests of the Antigonid cult, the Athenians indirectly paid homage to Demetrius.

that the figures of Demetrius and Antigonus should be woven into the sacred robe,* along with those of the gods; and the spot where Demetrius first alighted from his chariot they consecrated and covered with an altar, which they styled the altar of Demetrius Alighter;† they also created two new tribes, Demetrias and Antigonis; and they increased the number of council members from five hundred to six hundred, since each tribe had to furnish fifty councilors.‡

[11] But the most monstrous thing that came into the head of Stratocles—the man who invented these elegant and clever bits of flattery—was his motion that envoys sent by public decree and at public expense to Antigonus and Demetrius should be called "sacred deputies"—like those who conducted to Delphi and Olympia the ancient sacrifices on behalf of the cities at the great Hellenic festivals—instead of "ambassadors."§ In all other ways, Stratocles was an audacious fellow; he lived a life of abandon and was thought to imitate the vileness and buffoonery of Cleon¶ before him in his familiarities with the people. He had taken up with a mistress named Phylacion, and one day when she had bought in the market-place some brains and neck-bones for his supper, "Aha!" he cried, "you've bought just such delicacies as we statesmen play ball with." Again, when the Athenians suffered their naval defeat near Amorgus,** before news of the disaster could reach the city he put a garland on his head and drove through the Cerameicus,†† and after announcing that the Athenians had won, sponsored a motion for a good-news sacrifice and made a generous distribution of meat to the people by tribes. Then, a little later, when the wrecks were brought home from the battle and people in their wrath called him out, he faced

* A ceremonial piece of clothing offered to the goddess Athena, on the Acropolis, in an annual rite.

† The use of an epithet like "Alighter" puts Demetrius on the plane of the Olympian gods, who were often called by such epithets ("Zeus the Thunderer," e.g.).

‡ The Athenian *Boulē* was an executive board overseeing the Assembly; it had had at first four hundred and later five hundred members, composed of fifty citizens from each of the city's ten tribes, a system that had been in place for two centuries by this time.

§ Once again the point of this change in nomenclature was to put the Antigonids on the plane of the gods.

¶ Cleon dominated the Athenian Assembly in the 420s BC, after the death of Pericles. He is described in our sources as a demagogue of low morals.

** The naval battle at Amorgus, in 322 BC, was a decisive defeat for Athens in its rebellion from Macedon and led to the further defeat at Crannon (see 10 above and note).

†† A neighborhood outside the walls of Athens.

the tumult unfazed and said: "What harm have I done you, I ask, if for two days you have been happy?" Such was the effrontery of Stratocles.

[12] But there are things hotter even than fire, as Aristophanes puts it. Someone else outdid Stratocles in servility by proposing that whenever Demetrius visited the city he should be received with the rites of welcome paid to Demeter and Dionysus,* and that a sum of money for a dedicatory offering should be granted from the public treasury to the citizen who surpassed all others in the splendor and costliness of the reception he staged. And finally, they changed the name of the month Munychion to Demetrion, and that of the last day of a month (called the "Old and New Day") to Demetrias, and to the festival called Dionysia they gave the name of Demetria.

But the gods marked most of these innovations with their displeasure. The sacred robe, for instance, in which the Athenians had decreed that the figures of Demetrius and Antigonus should be woven along with those of Zeus and Athena was torn through the middle when a hurricane struck it as it was being carried in procession through the midst of the Cerameicus; the soil all around the altars of the Savior-gods teemed with hemlock,[†] a plant that did not grow in many other parts of the country; and on the day for the celebration of the Dionysia, the sacred procession had to be canceled on account of severe cold weather that came out of season. A heavy frost followed, and the cold not only blasted all the vines and fig-trees but also destroyed most of the grain as it was sprouting. Therefore Philippides, who was an enemy of Stratocles,[‡] assailed him in a comedy with these verses:

Through him *the hoar-frost blasted all the vines,*
Through his *impiety the robe was torn in two—*
Because he gave gods' honors to a man.
It's this, not comedy, that ruins the state.

* These two gods were annually "brought in" to the city (symbolically) with festive processions and hymns. A hymn to Demetrius by an Athenian poet, done in the style usually reserved for Dionysus, survives.

† A plant of ill omen, since a deadly poison was distilled from it.

‡ Comic playwrights at Athens freely expressed their political views on the stage and often made fun of contemporary leaders. Sometimes their targets hauled them into court; this seems to have happened to Philippides, to judge by the last line of the quote below. Doubtless his opponent was Stratocles, whom he often poked fun at.

Philippides was a friend of Lysimachus,* and for his sake that king bestowed many favors on the Athenian people. Moreover, when Lysimachus was about to undertake anything or make an expedition, he thought it a good omen to meet or catch sight of Philippides. And in general Philippides was well regarded for his character, since he was no troublemaker and had none of the officious ways of a courtier. On one occasion Lysimachus wished to do him a kindness and said: "Philippides, what have I that I can share with you?" "Sire," said Philippides, "anything but one of your state secrets." This is the kind of man I purposely compare with Stratocles—the man of the stage with the man of the speaker's platform.

[13] But there was one honor proposed for Demetrius that was more strange and monstrous than any other. When the dedication of certain shields at Delphi was being debated, Dromocleides of Sphettus† moved that the Athenians should get an oracle from Demetrius. I will transcribe his very words from the decree; they run thus:‡ "May it be for the best. Decreed by the people that the people elect one man from the Athenians, who shall go to the Savior-god, and, after a sacrifice with good omens, shall inquire of the Savior-god in what most speedy, decorous, and reverent manner the people may accomplish the restoration to their places of the dedicatory offerings; and that whatever answer he shall give, the people shall act accordingly." With such mockery of adulation they finally corrupted Demetrius' mind, which even before was not wholly sound.

[14] While staying at Athens at this time, Demetrius married Eurydicē, a widow. She was a descendant of Miltiades from days of yore;§ she had married Ophelas, the ruler of Cyrene, and after his death had come back to Athens. The Athenians took her marriage to Demetrius as a graceful compliment to their city, but in general Demetrius made light of mar-

---

* Yet another Successor enters the narrative, soon to play a far larger role. Lysimachus fought beside Alexander during the Asia campaign and then was assigned to govern Thrace, where he established his power base.

† This politician, from the Athenian village of Sphettus, is barely known, but Plutarch mentions him again later in this *Life* (see p. 391 below). The proposal related here treats Demetrius as an incarnation of Apollo.

‡ The wording of this quote follows the formulae of known Athenian decrees by which messengers were sent to consult the Delphic oracle.

§ Miltiades, the hero of the Battle of Marathon in 490 BC, belonged to a prominent aristocratic family.

riages and had many wives at the same time.* Phila enjoyed the greatest esteem and honor among them, both because of her father, Antipater, and because she had been the wife of Craterus, the one of all the Successors of Alexander who left behind him the most goodwill among the Macedonians.† Antigonus, Demetrius' father, had persuaded Demetrius to marry this woman when he was quite young, although she was not of his age, but older;‡ and when his son was disinclined to the match, it is said that Antigonus whispered in his ear the verse of Euripides:

Where there's gain, one must wed, though nature be against it.

—substituting the more candid "one must wed" for the grammatically parallel "one must serve."§ However, so lightly did Demetrius respect Phila and his other wives that he consorted freely with many courtesans and with many women of free birth. In regard to this pursuit of pleasure he had the worst reputation of all the kings of his time.

[15] At this time Demetrius was called on by his father to wage war against Ptolemy for control of Cyprus. He had to obey the summons but was reluctant to abandon the war for the liberation of Greece—a nobler and more glorious war—and therefore sent to Cleonides, Ptolemy's general who headed the garrisons of Sicyon and Corinth, and offered him money to set those cities free. But Cleonides would not accept the bribe. Demetrius therefore put to sea in haste, and, taking additional forces, sailed against Cyprus. There he joined battle with Menelaus, a brother of Ptolemy, and promptly defeated him, but Ptolemy himself appeared on the scene with a large combined land and naval force. There were various exchanges of threats and boasts, with Ptolemy ordering Demetrius to sail away before his entire force assembled and crushed him, and Demetrius offering to spare Ptolemy if he agreed to withdraw his garrisons

* In Macedonian society, polygamy was the unique prerogative of the king, so Demetrius' adoption of this practice signifies his growing self-definition as royal in stature.

† Phila was highly esteemed in the Greek world for her noble nature. As eldest daughter of Antipater, a powerful and revered Macedonian general, she was a valuable prize in the contest among the Successors to gain legitimacy by marital means.

‡ Demetrius was about seventeen at the time he married Phila. Phila's exact age is not known, but she had already been married twice over the previous fifteen years and had a son who was perhaps four or five.

§ The line spoofed by Antigonus comes from Euripides' *Phoenician Women*, where Polynices, a son of Oedipus, describes how he reconciled himself to servitude. In the new version created by Antigonus, dynastic marriage is equated with servitude.

from Sicyon and Corinth. And not only Demetrius and Ptolemy but all the other dynasts too awaited expectantly the uncertain outcome of the impending struggle; they felt that not just Cyprus or Syria but absolute supremacy would at once be the prize of the victor.

[16] Ptolemy sailed to the attack with a hundred and fifty ships and ordered Menelaus to put out from Salamis with sixty ships and, when the struggle was fiercest, to attack the ships of Demetrius from the rear and throw them into confusion. To these sixty ships Demetrius opposed only ten ships (for that small number sufficed to block the narrow exit from the harbor), while he himself, after first drawing out his land forces and placing them around the headlands that extended into the sea, put out to battle with a hundred and eighty ships. He made his onset with great impetus and force and utterly routed Ptolemy. Ptolemy himself, after his defeat, fled swiftly with eight ships only (for only that number were left from his whole fleet); of the rest, some had been destroyed in the sea-fight and seventy had been captured, crews and all. Of the throng of attendants, friends, and women riding in cargo ships nearby, and of all Ptolemy's arms, money, and engines of war, nothing at all escaped Demetrius; he took everything and brought it safely to his camp. Among this booty was the famous Lamia, originally held in esteem for her artistic skill (she was thought to play the flute quite admirably), but later illustrious in the annals of love also.* At this time, at any rate, although she was past her prime and saw that Demetrius was much younger, she so mastered and swayed him by her charms that he was a lover for her alone, a beloved for all other women.†

After the sea-fight, Menelaus made no further resistance but handed over Salamis to Demetrius, together with his fleet and his land forces including twelve hundred horsemen and twelve thousand hoplites.

[17] This victory, so fine and brilliant, Demetrius adorned still more by his humanity and kindness of heart. He gave the enemy's dead a magnificent burial and set his captives free,‡ and he bestowed on the Athenians twelve hundred suits of armor from the spoils.

---

* Plutarch's term here refers specifically to sexual love. Lamia was a hetaera, a woman who was paid to supply sex, but also refined company and cultural diversion, to a male partner.

† The terms here translated "lover" and "beloved" are *erastēs* and *erōmenos,* more usually used in the context of male homosexual relationships to designate the older man, who typically took the role of pursuer, and the younger who was pursued.

‡ Under the conventions of warfare, Demetrius was entitled to ransom the dead bodies and sell the prisoners into slavery.

Demetrius sent Aristodemus of Miletus as his special messenger to tell his father of the victory—the arch-flatterer among all his courtiers, ready now, as it appeared, to crown his flatteries with the grossest one of all.* For when he had crossed over to Phrygia from Cyprus, he did not bring his vessel to land but ordered all his crew to drop anchor and stay quietly on board while he got into the ship's small boat, landed alone, and went on his way to Antigonus, who was anxiously awaiting news of the battle and was disposed as men are apt to be when contesting for so high a stake. When he heard Aristodemus was coming, he grew more disturbed than before. Keeping himself indoors only with difficulty, he sent servants and friends, one after the other, to learn from Aristodemus what had happened. Aristodemus, however, would make no answer to anybody, but step by step and with a solemn face drew near in perfect silence. Antigonus, thoroughly frightened and no longer able to restrain himself, came to the door to meet Aristodemus, who was now escorted by a large throng hurrying to the palace. When he had come near, he stretched out his hand and cried with a loud voice: "Hail, *King* Antigonus! We have conquered Ptolemy in a sea-fight and now hold Cyprus, with twelve thousand eight hundred soldiers as prisoners of war." To this Antigonus replied: "Hail to you also, by Zeus! But for torturing us in this way, you shall be punished; you'll get only later rewards for your good news."

[18] At this the crowd for the first time saluted Antigonus and Demetrius as kings. Antigonus was immediately crowned by his friends, and Demetrius received a diadem from his father, with a letter in which he was addressed as King. For their part, the followers of Ptolemy in Egypt, when these things were reported to them, gave him the title of King so that they might not appear to lose morale on account of their defeat. And thus their emulation extended to the other Successors of Alexander. For Lysimachus began to wear a diadem, and Seleucus also in his interviews with the Greeks (he had already before this posed as king when dealing with barbarians). But Cassander, though the others gave him the royal title in their letters and addresses, wrote his letters in his own untitled name as he usually did.

This crowning did not mean merely the addition of a name or a change of fashion. It stirred the spirits of the men, lifted their thoughts high, and

---

* That is, by saluting Antigonus as king, as related in the story that follows. None of the Successors had as yet claimed a royal title (see note 6, p. 369).

Demetrius was celebrated for his handsome features, and he used his image, idealized as in this portrait bust, to win support, especially in the Greek world where male beauty was highly prized. His coin portraits went even further, depicting him with bull's horns as though he were a divine being.

introduced pomp and gravity into their lives and dealings with others, just as tragic actors adapt their gait, voice, posture at table, and manner of addressing others to their grand costumes.* As a result, the rulers became harsher in their judicial decisions; they laid aside that ironic stance toward power that formerly had often made them more lenient and gentle with their subjects. Such great influence lay in a flatterer's single word,† and with so great a change did it fill the entire world.

[19] Antigonus, elated by the achievements of Demetrius at Cyprus, at once made an expedition against Ptolemy; he himself led his forces by land while Demetrius with a great fleet linked up with him by sea. What the outcome of the expedition was to be, Medius, a friend of Antigonus, was warned by a vision in his sleep. He dreamed that Antigonus with his whole army was competing in a race over the course and back; Antigonus ran vigorously and swiftly at first, then, little by little, his strength failed

---

* Plutarch's simile from the tragic theater calls attention to the artificial nature of these new royal titles. Like theatrical costumes and roles, they could be "put on" at will.

† That is, the use of the word "King" by Aristodemus.

him, and at last, after he had made the turn, he became weak, breathed heavily, and made the finish with difficulty. Bearing out this vision, Antigonus encountered many difficulties by land, and Demetrius also encountered a great storm and a heavy sea and was cast upon a rough coast that had no harbors, losing many of his ships. He returned without accomplishing anything.

[20] Antigonus was at this time almost eighty years old, and his great size and weight, even more than his old age, made it difficult for him to go along on campaigns. He therefore made use of his son instead, whose good fortune and experience now enabled him to conduct the greatest affairs successfully, and whose luxuries, extravagances, and drinking parties gave his father no concern. For in time of peace, Demetrius plunged deep into these excesses and devoted his leisure to pleasures without restraint and intemperately, but in time of war he was as sober as those who were abstemious by nature. And we are told that once, when Demetrius was known by all to be completely in thrall to Lamia, he came home from abroad and greeted his father with a kiss, and Antigonus said with a laugh, "One would think, my son, that you were kissing Lamia." On another occasion, when Demetrius had been drinking and reveling for several days, and excused his absence by saying that he was troubled with a flux, "So I learned," said Antigonus, "but was it Thasian or Chian wine that flowed?" Yet another time, learning that his son was sick, Antigonus went to see him and met a certain beauty at his door; he went in, however, sat down by his son, and felt his pulse. "The fever has left me now," said Demetrius. "No doubt, my boy," said Antigonus, "I met it just now at the door as it was going out." These failings of Demetrius were treated with such leniency by his father because of the young man's achievements. The Scythians, in the midst of drinking and carousing, twang their bow-strings as though summoning back their courage at the moment when it is dissolved in pleasure;* but Demetrius, giving himself up completely, now to pleasure and now to duty, keeping one completely separate from the other, was no less formidable in his preparations for war.

Demetrius was thought to be an even better general in building up military force than in using it. He wished everything to be ready in abundance for his needs and could never be satisfied with the size of his undertakings in building ships and engines of war; nor could he get enough

---

* Scythians, inhabitants of the Ukraine and parts of Central Asia, were known to the Greeks both as hard drinkers and, in warfare, expert horse archers.

of gazing at these things with delight. He was perceptive and naturally gifted and did not use his ingenuity on things that gave useless pleasure or diversion, like other kings who played on the flute or painted or did metalwork. Aeropus the Macedonian,* for instance, used to spend his leisure time making little tables or lamp-stands, and Attalus Philometor[†] used to grow poisonous plants, not only henbane and hellebore, but also hemlock, aconite, and dorycnium, sowing and planting them himself in the royal gardens, learning their juice and fruits and the proper seasons to harvest them. And the kings of the Parthians used to take pride in notching and sharpening with their own hands the points of their arrows and spears. But with Demetrius, even the work of his hands was kingly, and his method had grandeur about it, since what he produced displayed loftiness of purpose and spirit combined with elegance and ingenuity. People thought the result was equal not just to the design and resources of the king but also his own handicraft. Its magnitude terrified even his friends, and its beauty delighted even his enemies—a formula containing more truth than bombast. His enemies would stand on shore and admire his galleys of fifteen or sixteen banks of oars as they sailed past, and his "City-takers" were a spectacle to those whom he besieged, as the facts testify. For Lysimachus, though the bitterest enemy Demetrius had among the kings, when arrayed against him at the siege of Soli in Cilicia, sent and asked Demetrius to show him his engines of war and his ships on the sea; and when Demetrius had shown them, Lysimachus marveled at them and went away. The Rhodians also, after they had been for a long time besieged by Demetrius and had come to terms with him, asked him for some of his siege engines that they might keep them as a reminder of his power as well as of their own bravery.

[21] Demetrius made war upon the Rhodians because they were allies of Ptolemy.[‡] He brought up against their walls his greatest City-taker. Its base was square, and each of its sides measured at the bottom seventy-two feet. It rose to a height of a hundred feet and tapered from base to summit. Inside it was divided into many stories and chambers, and the

---

* King of Macedon in the early fourth century BC.

† King of Pergamon in the late second century BC.

‡ Rhodes, an independent state not part of any Successor's territory, had for many years preserved neutrality in the wars between Alexander's generals, but gradually tilted toward Ptolemy because of the rich profits to be made off of Egyptian trade. Antigonus provoked hostilities with the Rhodians by demanding that they come over to his side and abandon Ptolemy; they refused to do so.

side facing the enemy had windows in every story through which issued spears, arrows, and slingshot of every sort—for it was full of men who fought in every style. It did not totter or lean when moved but remained firm and erect on its base, advancing evenly with much noise and great impetus. This astounded the minds and at the same time greatly charmed the eyes of those who beheld it.

For his use in this war there were brought to Demetrius from Cyprus two iron coats of mail, each of which weighed thirty-five pounds. Wishing to show their strength and resistance, Zoilus, their maker, gave orders that a catapult's missile should be shot at one of them from twenty paces; in the place where it struck, the iron remained intact, although it did get a faint scratch such as an engraver might make. This coat of mail Demetrius wore; the other was worn by Alcimus of Epirus, the sturdiest and most warlike of all the men under him, and the only one whose suit of armor weighed a hundred pounds (the rest used suits of fifty pounds' weight);* he fell in battle at Rhodes near the theater.

[22] But the Rhodians on their part vigorously resisted, and Demetrius, although he was accomplishing nothing worthy of mention, nevertheless kept up the fight, in a rage because when Phila his wife sent him letters, bedding, and clothing, the Rhodians captured the ship and sent it, contents and all, to Ptolemy. (In this they did not imitate the kindness of the Athenians, who, having captured Philip's letter-carriers when he was making war upon them, read all the other letters but would not open one, from Olympias; they sent that one back to Philip with its seal unbroken.) Though Demetrius was exasperated by this, when the Rhodians soon after gave him a chance to retaliate, he would not do so. It happened that Protogenes the Caunian had been making a painting for the Rhodians that illustrated the story of Ialysus,† and this picture, nearly finished, was captured by Demetrius in one of the suburbs of the city. The Rhodians sent a herald and begged Demetrius to spare and not destroy the work. He replied that he would rather burn the likenesses of his father than so great a labor of art. For we are told that it took Protogenes seven years to complete the painting. And Apelles says Demetrius was so smitten with amazement on beholding the work that his voice actually failed him, and when at last he recovered it, he cried, "Great is

---

* These weights (in Greek terms, two talents' weight for Alcimus, one for the rest, even greater amounts than the round figures in the translation) seem inconceivable.

† A mythic figure associated with the Rhodian town that bore her name.

the toil and astonishing the work," remarking, however, that it lacked the grace that made the fame of his own paintings touch the heavens. This painting was stored in the same place as many others at Rome and was destroyed by fire.

As for the Rhodians, they continued their strenuous resistance until Demetrius, who wanted a pretext for abandoning the war, was induced to make terms by a deputation of Athenians, on condition that the Rhodians be allies of Antigonus and Demetrius except against Ptolemy.*

[23] Next the Athenians called upon Demetrius because Cassander was besieging their city.† So Demetrius sailed to their aid with three hundred and thirty ships and a great number of hoplites, and not only drove Cassander out of Attica but actually pursued him in his headlong flight as far as Thermopylae. Demetrius then took Heracleia, which joined him of its own accord, and six thousand Macedonians also came over to him. On his return he gave freedom to the Greeks south of Thermopylae, made the Boeotians his allies, and captured Cenchreae;‡ he also reduced Phyle and Panactum, Attic fortresses in which Cassander had garrisons, and gave them back to the Athenians. And they, though they had used up all the honors that could be bestowed on him, nevertheless devised a way to prove themselves innovators in flattery. They assigned Demetrius the rear chamber of the Parthenon for his quarters;§ and there he lived, and there it was said that Athena received and entertained him, although he was not a very orderly guest and did not occupy his rooms with the decorum due to a virgin.¶ And yet on one occasion when Antigonus understood that Demetrius' brother, Philip, was quartered in a house occupied by three young women, he said not a word to Philip, but in his presence

* Plutarch passes very quickly over one of the longest, most intense sieges in all antiquity. According to other sources, Demetrius brought massive force to bear against the walls of Rhodes, including his massive City-taker, for an entire year before deciding to negotiate a settlement. The abandoned City-taker was sold off for scrap by the Rhodians, and the proceeds funded the famous Colossus of Rhodes, a giant statue of the god Helios.

† Though driven out of Athens several years earlier, Cassander had not given up on the city and had reoccupied several forts while Demetrius was busy at Rhodes.

‡ One of the ports serving Corinth.

§ The Parthenon had two interior rooms, the larger of which housed a huge cult statue of Athena. Demetrius was installed in the smaller room, normally used for the weaving of Athena's sacred robe and other purposes.

¶ The reference is to the virgin goddess Athena, here playfully imagined by Plutarch as Demetrius' "roommate."

said to the quartermaster whom he had summoned, "You there, won't you get my son out of his tight spot?"*

[24] But Demetrius, who ought to have revered Athena, if for no other reason than because she was his elder sister (for this was what he liked to have her called), filled the acropolis with such wanton treatment of free-born youth and native Athenian women that the place was thought to be very pure, by comparison, when he shared his dissolute life there with Chrysis and Lamia and Demo and Anticyra,† well-known prostitutes.

To give all the particulars plainly would disgrace the fair fame of the city, but I will not pass over the modesty and virtue of a young boy named Democles. Demetrius did not fail to notice that Democles had a nickname based on his good looks (he was called Democles the Beautiful). But the boy yielded to none of the many who sought to win him by prayers or gifts or threats, and finally, shunning the *palaestras* and the gymnasium, he used to go for his bath to a private bathing-room.‡ Here Demetrius, who had watched for an opportunity, came upon Democles when he was alone. And the boy, when he saw that he was quite alone and in dire straits, took off the lid of the cauldron and jumped into the boiling water, thus destroying himself and suffering an unworthy fate but showing a spirit worthy of his country and his beauty. It was a different case with Cleaenetus, son of Cleomedon, who, in order to obtain a letter from Demetrius to the people and thereby get a pardon for a fine of fifty talents imposed on his father, not only disgraced himself§ but got the whole city into trouble. For the citizens released Cleomedon from his fine but passed an edict that no citizen should bring a letter from Demetrius before the Assembly. When Demetrius heard of it and was greatly enraged,

---

* The Greek word translated "tight spot" refers both to cramped quarters and to difficult circumstances. Antigonus' remark seems to contain a winking father-son jest about the sexual possibilities of sharing a house with three women (like the jests Antigonus directed toward Demetrius in chapter 20 above).

† Lamia has been discussed in the first note on p. 374 above; the other women mentioned here are far less well known. Plutarch implies his disapproval by using the severe word *pornai,* "prostitutes," rather than the more elevated *hetaerae.*

‡ The following story takes as its context the well-accepted pederastic traditions of Athens, in which beautiful boys or adolescents were courted as lovers by older men, often in the settings of *palaestras* (wrestling gyms) or public baths where males could be seen unclothed. Vase paintings often show bearded men courting these youths with gifts or attempting to fondle them, sometimes seemingly against their will.

§ Plutarch's language discreetly implies the offer of sexual favors.

the citizens took fright again and not only rescinded the decree but actually put to death some of those who had introduced and spoken for it, and drove others into exile; furthermore, they voted besides that it was the pleasure of the Athenian people that whatsoever King Demetrius should ordain in future, should be thought righteous toward the gods and just toward men. And when one of the better class of citizens declared that Stratocles was insane to introduce such a motion, Demochares of Leuconoë said: "He would indeed be insane not to be insane." For Stratocles reaped much advantage from his flatteries. Demochares, though, was indicted for this and sent into exile. So things went for the Athenians; they imagined, wrongly, that because they were rid of their garrison they had gained their freedom.

[25] And now Demetrius proceeded into the Peloponnese, where not one of his enemies opposed him but all abandoned their cities and fled. He received into allegiance Acte (as it is called)* and Arcadia except Mantinea, and freed Argos, Sicyon, and Corinth by bribing their garrisons† with a hundred talents. At Argos, where there was a celebration of the festival of Hera, he presided at the games and attended solemn assemblies with the Greeks, and married Deïdameia,‡ the daughter of the Molossian king Aeacides and sister of Pyrrhus. As for the Sicyonians, he told them their city was in the wrong place and persuaded them to change its site to that which it now has; he also changed the name of the city from Sicyon to Demetrias. At the Isthmus of Corinth, where a general assembly was held and throngs of people came together, he was proclaimed commander in chief of the Greeks like Philip and Alexander before him.§ To these men he considered himself not a little superior, lifted up as he was by the good fortune and power he then enjoyed. Indeed, Alexander never refused to bestow the royal title on others nor proclaim himself King of Kings, although many kings received their position and title from him; whereas Demetrius used to rail and mock at

---

* Acte ("the Coast") was a colloquial term for the northeastern spur of the Peloponnese.

† The posts installed by Cassander and his allies.

‡ Another dynastic prize in the marital sweepstakes, Deïdameia had earlier been betrothed to Alexander IV, the only legitimate son of Alexander the Great.

§ In 338 BC, following his defeat of the Greeks at Chaeronea, Philip of Macedon had organized the cities of mainland Greece into a league, meeting at Corinth, and established himself as commander of its forces. In 335, after Philip's death, the league (sometimes known today as the League of Corinth) had affirmed Alexander the Great as its head. Demetrius therefore was attempting to make himself third in line after these two great leaders.

those who gave the title of King to anyone except his father and himself, and was well pleased to hear his drinking-companions toast Demetrius as King but Seleucus as Master of Elephants, Ptolemy as Admiral, Lysimachus as Treasurer, and Agathocles of Sicily as Lord of the Isles.* When this was reported to these kings, they all laughed at Demetrius, except Lysimachus; he was incensed that Demetrius considered him a eunuch (it was the general practice to have eunuchs for treasurers).

Of all the kings, Lysimachus had most hatred for Demetrius. He once reviled the man's passion for Lamia, saying that this was the first time he had ever seen a whore come forward onto the tragic stage. Demetrius, however, declared that his own "whore" was more chaste than the Penelope of Lysimachus.†

[26] But to resume the story: When Demetrius was getting ready to return to Athens, he wrote letters to the people saying that he wished to be initiated into the Mysteries‡ as soon as he arrived and to pass through all the grades in the ceremony from the lowest to the *epoptica,* the highest. This was not lawful and had not been done before, since the lesser rites were performed in the month Anthesterion, the great rites in Boëdromion; and the supreme rites (the *epoptica*) were celebrated after an interval of at least a year from the great rites.§ And yet when the letter of Demetrius was read, no one ventured to oppose the proposition except Pythodorus the Torch-bearer, and he accomplished nothing. Instead, on motion of Stratocles, it was voted to name the current month Munychion as Anthesterion and to regard it as such, and the lesser rites at Agra were performed for Demetrius; afterward Munychion was again changed and became Boëdromion instead of Anthesterion, Demetrius received the remaining rites of initiation, and at the same time was also admitted to

* These mocking titles effectively made the other Successors into officers in Demetrius' regime. Seleucus had gathered a massive herd of war elephants after signing a treaty with a monarch of India.

† The point of both jests is unclear. Lamia was a master *aulos* ("flute") player, and the *aulos* accompanied tragic performances, so that perhaps explains Lysimachus' insult. Lysimachus was at this time married to a daughter of Ptolemy, Arsinoe, but why Demetrius would call her Penelope—after the famously faithful wife of Odysseus—is obscure.

‡ The cult rites of the goddess Demeter, celebrated at Eleusis (west of Athens), were known as the Mysteries and those initiated were said to enjoy a happy afterlife in Hades. The nature of the rites was kept a strict secret from outsiders, giving rise to our word "mystery."

§ The months named here correspond to our February/March and September/October, so the complete course of initiation normally took at least eighteen months.

the highest grade of *epoptos*. Hence Philippides, in his abuse of Stratocles,* wrote:

Who abridged the whole year into a single month,

and with reference to the quartering of Demetrius in the Parthenon:

Who took the acropolis for a hostelry,
And brought in courtesans to room with the virgin goddess.†

[27] But among the many lawless and shocking things done by Demetrius in the city at this time, the following is said to have most displeased the Athenians: After he had ordered them to quickly raise two hundred and fifty talents for his use, and after they had levied the money rigorously, granting no exemptions, when he saw the heap of coin that had been collected, he commanded it to be given to Lamia and her fellow courtesans to buy soap. The shame this produced in the citizens galled them more than the loss, and the report of the deed was worse than the deed itself. But some say it was the Thessalians, not the Athenians, who received this injury. What's more, Lamia, when she was preparing a supper for the king, exacted money from many citizens on her own authority. The costliness of this supper gave it so wide a renown that it was described in full by Lynceus the Samian, and a comic poet spoke of Lamia as "a veritable City-taker," not inaptly.‡ And Demochares of Soli called Demetrius "the Myth," because he too, like the annals of myth, had a Lamia.§

Not only among the wives of Demetrius, but also among his friends, the favor and affection he bestowed on Lamia aroused envy and spite. Some ambassadors from Demetrius once came to Lysimachus, and Lysimachus, in an hour of leisure, showed them on his thighs and shoulders

* On the comic playwright Philippides and his penchant for political satire, see third note on p. 371 above.

† The second line of the quote contains an untranslatable pun: Demetrius' women are here called *hetaerae*, a word that literally means "companions"—hence "companions for Athena"—but in common use denoted a high-status sex worker.

‡ The City-taker (Helepolis) is described on pp. 378–79 above. Lamia here is compared to it in her capacity to "sack" cities (i.e., shake down Athenians for money).

§ In Greek mythology the Lamia was a woman, a monster, or a woman turned into a monster, associated with cannibalism and/or sexual predation.

deep scars of wounds made by a lion's claws; he also told them about the battle he had fought against the beast, with which he had been caged by Alexander the Great.* Then they laughingly told him that their own king also carried, on his neck, the bites of a dreadful beast—a Lamia. And it was astonishing that while in the beginning he was displeased that Phila and he were unequal in age, he was vanquished by Lamia and loved her so long though she was already past her prime. In illustration, when Lamia was playing on the flute at a supper, Demetrius asked Demo, nick-named Mania,† what she thought of her. "O King," said Mania, "I think her an old woman." And at another time, when some sweetmeats were served up, and Demetrius said to Mania, "Do you see how many presents I get from Lamia?" "My mother," said Mania, "will send you more, if you will sleep with *her* as well."

There is on record also Lamia's comment on the famous judgment of Bocchoris. There was a certain Egyptian who was in love with Thonis the hetaera, and she was asked a great sum of money for her favors; then he dreamed that he lay with her, and after the dream he ceased from his desires. Thereupon Thonis brought an action against him for payment due. Bocchoris, on hearing the case, ordered the man to bring into court the sum demanded of him, in a small box, and to move it back and forth with his hand, and the hetaera was to grasp its shadow—since a thing imagined is a shadow of reality. This judgment Lamia thought to be unjust; for though the dream put an end to the young man's passion, the shadow of the money did not set the hetaera free from her desire of it. So much, then, for Lamia.

[28] But the fortunes and achievements of the man whose life I am narrating brings my narrative back, as it were, from the comic to the tragic stage.‡

All the other kings joined together against Antigonus and united their forces. So Demetrius set forth from Greece, and finding his father eager beyond his years for the war, was himself still more encouraged. And yet it would seem that if Antigonus had made some trifling concessions and

---

* According to other sources, Alexander became enraged with Lysimachus for furnishing one of his prisoners with poison to do away with himself; he put Lysimachus into a cage with a lion, but Lysimachus managed to overcome the beast.

† Demo was another of Demetrius' hetaerae. The name Mania translates to "madness."

‡ Plutarch associates with comic drama the ribald stories he has just been telling of Demetrius' escapades with hetaerae. War and battle, as all Greeks believed, belonged to the more elevated genre of tragedy. The tale of the Battle of Ipsus, in 301 BC, now follows.

had slackened his excessive passion for rule, he might have retained supremacy for himself and left it to his son. But he was naturally stern and haughty, harsh in words and deeds; he therefore exasperated and incited against himself many young and powerful men. He said he would scatter the groups and partnerships they formed with a single stone and a single shout, as if they were a flock of seed-eating birds.

Antigonus took the field with more than seventy thousand infantry, ten thousand horses, and seventy-five elephants, while his adversaries had sixty-four thousand infantry, five hundred more horses than he, four hundred elephants, and a hundred and twenty chariots.* After he had drawn near them, the cast of his expectations changed, though his purpose stayed as it was. He was normally lofty and boastful as he engaged in conflict, making pompous speeches in a loud voice, and many times also by a casual jest or joke; when the enemy was close at hand he would show the firmness of his spirit and his contempt. Now, though, he seemed mostly thoughtful and silent, and he presented his son to the army and pronounced him his successor.† But what more than anything else astonished everybody was his conversing alone in his tent with his son, though it was not his custom to have secret conferences even with *him*. Instead, he made his own plans, followed his own counsels, and *then* gave his orders openly. (We are told that Demetrius, when he was still a youth, asked his father when they were going to break camp, and that Antigonus replied in anger: "Are you afraid that you alone won't hear the trumpet sound?")‡

[29] Bad omens also dampened the spirits of father and son at this moment. Demetrius dreamed that Alexander, in brilliant array of armor, asked him what watchword§ they were going to give for the battle, and when Demetrius replied "Zeus and Victory," Alexander said: "Then I'll go and join your enemies; they'll surely welcome me." Moreover, Antigonus, when his phalanx was already forming and he was leaving his tent,

---

   * These enormous troop counts make the Battle of Ipsus the largest fought by Greek commanders to this point.

   † This last point is taken by Plutarch as a sign that Antigonus did not expect to survive the battle.

   ‡ Effectively Antigonus was telling his son to wait for the signal to march, along with the rest of the army.

   § Armies agreed on these watchwords just before battle, such that in the confusion of the clash soldiers could distinguish friend from foe. It's not clear what was objectionable, in the dream that follows, about this particular watchword.

stumbled and fell prone on his face, injuring himself severely; but he rose to his feet, stretched out his hands toward heaven, and prayed that the gods would grant him victory or else a painless death before defeat.

After the armies engaged, Demetrius, with the largest and best part of the cavalry, clashed with Antiochus, son of Seleucus;* he fought brilliantly and routed Antiochus, but threw away the victory by pursuing him too fiercely and eagerly. He was not able to turn back and rejoin his infantry, since the enemy's elephants were in his way.† Seleucus, observing that the opposing phalanx troops were unprotected by cavalry, did not charge but kept them in fear of a charge by continually riding around them, thus giving them an opportunity to come over to his side. And this was what happened; a large body of them, detached from the rest, came over to Seleucus of their own accord‡ and the rest were routed. Then, as throngs of enemies bore down on Antigonus, one of his followers said, "They're coming at you, sire," and Antigonus replied: "Who else would they aim at? But Demetrius will come to my aid." This was his hope to the last, and to the last he kept watching for his son. Then many javelins were let fly at him and he fell. The rest of his friends and attendants abandoned him, and one only remained by his dead body, Thorax of Larissa.

[30] The battle was decided in this manner, and the victorious kings carved up the entire domain of Antigonus and Demetrius like a great carcass; each took his portion, adding new provinces to those they already had. But Demetrius, with five thousand infantry and four thousand horses, drove straight on to Ephesus in his flight. Here everyone thought that, since he lacked money, he would not forbear to seize the temple;§ but Demetrius, fearing that his soldiers might indeed do this, departed speedily and sailed for Greece, putting his chief remaining hopes in Athens. For he had left ships there, and money, and his wife Deïdameia; he had supposed that no refuge in misfortune could be more secure than the

---

* In warfare between coalition armies, each side arranged its units to face other units over which it might prevail. In this battle Demetrius' cavalry, on his own right wing, was facing the cavalry of Antiochus; Antigonus led the infantry phalanx in the center of the field, facing Seleucus and Lysimachus.

† Horses were reluctant to approach elephants on the battlefield.

‡ Such desertions were not unusual in the Wars of the Successors, for all the participants were of the same nationality; veteran soldiers easily transferred allegiance to whoever was winning.

§ The shrine of Artemis at Ephesus was one of the ancient world's most splendid. Temple robbing was a sacrilege, but other generals had by this time already made a practice of it.

goodwill of Athens. That's why his wrath went beyond all proper bounds when, as he drew near the Cyclades islands, an embassy from Athens asked him to keep away from the city on the grounds that the Athenians had voted to admit none of the kings, and informing him that Deïdameia had been sent to Megara with fitting escort and honor. Demetrius had borne his other misfortunes easily, and in so great a reversal of fortunes had shown himself neither mean-spirited nor ignoble; but it was painful to him that the Athenians should disappoint his hopes and play him falsely, and that their apparent goodwill should prove on trial to be false and empty.

[31] It seems to me that the worst indicator of a people's goodwill toward a king or potentate is the extravagant bestowal of honors; for the beauty of such honors lies in the motives of those who bestow them, and fear robs them of their worth (since the same decrees may be passed out of fear and out of love). Therefore men of sense look first of all at their own acts and achievements and *then* gauge the value of statues, paintings, or deifications offered to them, trusting these as genuine, or not trusting them on grounds they are compulsory. It's certainly true that citizen bodies will often, even as they confer honors, most despise those who accept such honors immoderately, ostentatiously, and from the unwilling.

Be that as it may, in this case Demetrius thought himself grievously wronged. Since he was unable to avenge himself, he sent a message to the Athenians in which he mildly rebuked them and asked that his ships, including the "thirteener,"* be given back. These he obtained; then he coasted along to the Isthmus, where he found his affairs in a very sorry state. His garrisons were everywhere being expelled and there was a general defection to his enemies. He therefore left Pyrrhus[†] in charge of Greece while he himself put to sea and sailed to the Chersonese. Here he ravaged the territory of Lysimachus, thereby enriching and consolidating his own forces, which were beginning to recover their spirit and to show themselves formidable again. The other kings did not try to help Lysimachus. They thought he was no better than Demetrius, and because Demetrius had more power, he was even more to be feared.

Not long afterward, Seleucus asked by messenger to wed Stratonicē,

---

* In addition to building enormous siege engines, Demetrius also engineered hugely powerful warships, far bigger than any seen before. "Thirteeners" shipped many more oars than the standard Greek trireme.

† King of Epirus (roughly, modern Albania), now Demetrius' brother-in-law.

the daughter of Demetrius and Phila. He already had a son, Antiochus, by Apama the Persian, but he thought that his realm was large enough for more than one heir and that he needed this alliance with Demetrius, since he saw that Lysimachus was wedding one of Ptolemy's daughters and giving another in marriage to his son, Agathocles. Now, to Demetrius, a marriage alliance with Seleucus was an unexpected piece of good fortune. So he took his daughter and sailed with his whole fleet to Syria. He was obliged to touch at several places along the coast and made landings in Cilicia, a country held by Pleistarchus, having been allotted to him by the kings after their battle with Antigonus. Pleistarchus was a brother of Cassander. He thought his territories were violated by these landings of Demetrius and also wished to rebuke Seleucus for allying with a common enemy independently of the other kings. So he went up to see him.

[32] On learning of this, Demetrius set out from the coast for the city of Cyinda.* Finding twelve hundred talents of its treasure still left, he packed them up, got them safely on board ship, and put to sea with all speed. His wife Phila was already with him, and at Rhosus he was met by Seleucus. Together they at once made their parley royal in style, without trickery or suspicion. First Seleucus entertained Demetrius at his tent in the camp, then Demetrius in turn received Seleucus on board his "thirteener." There were also amusements, long conversations, and whole days spent together, all without guards or weapons, until at length Seleucus took Stratonicē and went up in great state to Antioch.† Demetrius took possession of Cilicia‡ and sent his wife Phila to Cassander, her brother, to dispel the denunciations of Pleistarchus. Meanwhile, Deïdameia came by sea from Greece to join Demetrius, but was with him only a short time before she died of some disease. Then, by the intervention of Seleucus, Demetrius made friends with Ptolemy and it was agreed he should marry Ptolemaïs, Ptolemy's daughter.§

---

* This obscure fort in eastern Anatolia had served as a treasury for much of the plunder Alexander took out of the Persian palaces.

† A city just recently founded by Seleucus and named after his son, Antiochus.

‡ A wealthy portion of what is today southeast Turkey.

§ In this whirlwind of comings and goings, we can discern the diplomatic complexities of the age of the Successors. Demetrius was simultaneously using one wife (Phila) to mend fences with Cassander (her brother) while marrying another (Ptolemaïs) to forge bonds with Ptolemy (her father). Meanwhile the death of another wife (Deïdameia) had broken his link to a valuable ally, Pyrrhus (her brother).

So far all was courtesy on the part of Seleucus. But soon he asked Demetrius to cede Cilicia to him for a sum of money, and Demetrius would not consent. Seleucus then angrily demanded Tyre and Sidon from him. It seemed violent and outrageous that one who had possessed himself of the whole domain from India to the Syrian sea should be so needy still and so beggarly as for the sake of two cities to harass a man, Demetrius, who was his relative by marriage and had suffered a reverse of fortune. In this Seleucus beautifully affirmed the wisdom of Plato, who urged the man who wants to be truly rich not to make his possessions greater but his insatiability less; he who puts no end to his greed is never free of poverty and want.

[33] Demetrius was not cowed but declared that not even if he should lose ten thousand battles like Ipsus would he consent to pay for the privilege of having Seleucus as a son-in-law.* Then he strengthened his cities with garrisons, while he himself, learning that Lachares had became tyrant over the Athenians in a factional struggle,† thought he would easily capture the city if he made an appearance there. So he crossed the sea in a great fleet without incurring losses, but as he was sailing along the coast of Attica he encountered a storm in which most of his ships were sunk and a great number of men perished. He himself escaped death and began a petty war against the Athenians, but since he could accomplish nothing, he sent men to collect another fleet for him, while he himself passed on into the Peloponnese and laid siege to Messene.‡ Here, in an attack upon the walls, he nearly lost his life when a projectile from a catapult struck him in the face and passed through his jaw into his mouth. But he recovered, and after bringing back into line certain cities that had revolted, he invaded Attica again, got Eleusis and Rhamnus into his power,§ and ravaged the country. He also seized a ship laden with grain for Athens and hanged its cargo master and its steersman. All other ships were thus frightened into turning back, and famine became acute in the city, where there was a shortage not only of food but of merchandise. A

---

* That is, he would not maintain an alliance with Seleucus if it meant being extorted.

† Lachares seized power in Athens around 300 BC, probably with assistance from Cassander.

‡ A well-fortified city in the western Peloponnese, at this time allied with Lysimachus.

§ These two strongholds in the Attic countryside allowed Demetrius to cut Athens off from its farmlands and therefore from a large part of its food supply. This and the subsequent seizure of the grain ship were intended to starve Athens into submission.

bushel of salt sold there for forty drachmas and a peck of wheat was worth three hundred.

The Athenians gained some relief from the appearance off Aegina of a hundred and fifty ships that Ptolemy sent to assist them. Then numerous ships came to Demetrius from the Peloponnese and Cyprus, so that his entire assemblage numbered three hundred. As a result the ships of Ptolemy fled off to sea and Lachares the tyrant abandoned the city and made his escape.

[34] The Athenians, although they had decreed death to anyone who should so much as mention peace and reconciliation with Demetrius, straightaway threw open the nearest gates and sent ambassadors to him. They did not expect any kindly treatment from him, but they were driven by destitution. Among many other grievous things, the following is said to have occurred: A father and a son were sitting in a room and had abandoned all hope. Then a dead mouse fell from the ceiling, and the two, when they saw it, sprang up and fought with each other for it. At this time also, we are told, the philosopher Epicurus sustained the lives of his followers by counting out and distributing beans.

Such, then, was the plight of the city when Demetrius made his entry and ordered all the people to assemble in the theater. He surrounded the stage-buildings with armed men and encircled the stage itself with his body-guards, while he himself, like tragic actors do, came down into view through one of the upper side-entrances. The Athenians were more frightened than ever, but with the first words that he uttered, Demetrius put an end to their fears. Avoiding all harshness and bitterness of speech, he merely chided them lightly and in a friendly way and then declared himself reconciled. He gave them besides a hundred thousand bushels of grain and put in place the magistrates who were most acceptable to the citizens. So Dromocleides the orator, seeing that the people in their joy were shouting all sorts of proposals and were eager to outdo the eulogies that public speakers deliver from the bema, put forth a motion that Piraeus and Munychia should be handed over to King Demetrius. This was passed. Demetrius also put a garrison on the Mouseium,* so that the people might not again shake off the yoke and give him further trouble.

---

* The Mouseium hill dominated the southwest quadrant of Athens, including the entrance to the city from the Long Walls (a corridor leading to Piraeus). With this position garrisoned, Demetrius could control Athens itself; previously he and Cassander had only occupied Piraeus.

[35] Now that he was in possession of Athens, he at once laid plans against Sparta. Near Mantinea, where King Archidamus* confronted him, he conquered and routed his foe, then invaded Laconia. After fighting a second pitched battle very near Sparta itself, where he captured five hundred men and killed two hundred, he all but got the city into his power, though up to this time it had never been taken. But Fortune seems not to have taken such great and sudden turns with any of the other kings as it did with Demetrius, and in no other careers did she so many times show herself now small, now great, nor move from brilliance to baseness or back again from smallness to strength. For this reason, we are told, in his worst reverses Demetrius would address Fortune in the words of Aeschylus:[†]

You fan my flame, yet seem to quench me too.

At this time, when events so generously favored his sovereignty and power, word was brought to him first that Lysimachus had deprived him of his cities in Asia, and next, that Ptolemy had taken all Cyprus except the city of Salamis, and among those under siege in Salamis were his children and his mother. But even Fortune—who like the woman in Archilochus, "in one deceitful hand bore water, and in the other fire"[‡]— drew him away from Sparta with such dreadful and terrifying reports, but then immediately inspired him with other hopes of new and great achievements.

[36] The reason was this: After Cassander died, his eldest son Philip reigned for a short time over the Macedonians and then died. The two remaining brothers quarreled with each other over the succession. One of them, Antipater, murdered his mother, Thessalonicē, and the other, Alexander, summoned Pyrrhus from Epirus to help him and also summoned Demetrius from the Peloponnese. Pyrrhus was first to answer the summons, and, after cutting off a large part of Macedonia as a reward, he'd become a threat on Alexander's borders. Demetrius, when he received Alexander's letters, set out with his forces to join him but frightened the young man even more because of his high position and

---

* Archidamus IV, one of Sparta's two reigning kings.

† The tragedy from which this line was taken has been lost.

‡ Archilochus was a lyric poet of the seventh century BC; the poem from which the line comes has been lost.

reputation. Alexander therefore met Demetrius at Dium* and gave him a friendly welcome, but he declared that the situation no longer demanded his presence. As a result, the men were suspicious of each other, and besides, as Demetrius was on his way to a dinner at Alexander's invitation, someone told him that there was a plot to kill him amid the drinking. Demetrius was not at all disturbed, but he delayed a little, ordering his officers to have his troops under arms and telling all his attendants and servants (far more numerous than the retinue of Alexander) to go with him into the banquet-hall and remain there until he rose from the table. This frightened Alexander, and he did not attempt anything. Demetrius also made the excuse that he was not in condition to take wine and left the party early. The next day he busied himself preparing for departure, telling Alexander that unexpected troubles had arisen that demanded his attention and asking pardon for leaving so quickly. He assured Alexander that he would pay a longer visit another time when his affairs permitted. Alexander was well pleased, convinced that Demetrius was leaving not in hostility but of his own free will; he escorted him on his way as far as Thessaly.

When they came to Larissa, once more they exchanged invitations to banquets as each plotted against the life of the other. This, more than anything else, put Alexander into the power of Demetrius. For Alexander refrained from precautions in order not to teach Demetrius to counter him; since he delayed measures to prevent his adversary from slipping through his fingers, he was first to meet the doom he was himself devising. When Demetrius rose up from table before supper was over, Alexander, filled with fear, rose up also and followed close on his heels toward the door. Demetrius, on reaching the door where his body-guards stood, said simply "Smite anyone who follows me," and quietly went out. Alexander was cut down by the guards, together with those of his friends who came to his aid. One of these, we are told, said as he was struck that Demetrius had anticipated them by a single day.

[37] That night, naturally, was full of tumult. But with the day, the Macedonians, in confusion and afraid of the forces of Demetrius, found that no enemy came against them; instead Demetrius sent a request for a parley and an opportunity to explain what had been done. They therefore took heart and promised to receive him in a friendly spirit. When he arrived, there was no need of long speeches, but because of their hatred

* On the southern border of Macedonia.

of Antipater (who had killed his own mother) and their lack of anyone better, they proclaimed Demetrius king of the Macedonians and at once brought him back to Macedon.* To the Macedonians at home the change was not unwelcome, for they remembered with hatred the crimes Cassander had committed against the line of Alexander the Great.† And if any kindly memories of Antipater the Elder's moderation and justice still remained,‡ Demetrius reaped the benefit of these too, since he was the husband of Phila, Antipater's daughter, and had a son by her to be his successor—a son who was already a young man and was serving in the army under his father.

[38] While Demetrius was enjoying such illustrious good fortune, he had news that his children and his mother had been set free§ and that Ptolemy had given them gifts and honors besides; he had other news concerning his daughter who was wedded to Seleucus, namely, that she had now become the wife of Antiochus—Seleucus' son—and had the title "Queen of Upper Asia." For it seems that Antiochus had fallen in love with Stratonicē,¶ who was young and already mother of a little boy by Seleucus. Antiochus was distressed and resorted to many means of fighting down his passion, but at last, condemning himself for his inordinate desires, for his incurable malady, and for the subjugation of his reason, he determined to escape from life and destroy himself gradually by neglecting his person and abstaining from food under pretense of having some disease. But Erasistratus, his physician, perceived quite easily that Antiochus was in love, and wishing to learn the object of his passion (a

---

* Further evidence of how confused the Greek world had become in the age of the Successors. Up until the death of Alexander the Great, the Macedonians had been ruled by a single dynasty for three centuries. Following the death of Alexander they'd seen a succession of would-be monarchs come and go, often amid violent clashes, and finally reached out to Demetrius—who hadn't set foot on their soil since he was a young child and had no claim on the throne—in hopes of regaining stability. The ousted Antipater (son of Cassander) went into exile at the court of Lysimachus, as we learn from other sources, where he was murdered seven years later.

† These crimes included the murders of Alexander's mother, widow, and son. Many even suspected him of having poisoned Alexander.

‡ Antipater had governed Macedonia on behalf of Alexander the Great during the time of Alexander's Asian campaign and for several years thereafter. He was the grandfather of the Antipater mentioned above (the man who had murdered his mother).

§ Apparently a chivalrous gesture like that discussed in chapter 5 above.

¶ His stepmother. The story of the illicit love that became licit was very popular in antiquity, and Plutarch retells it with obvious enjoyment of its salacious aspects. We may guess that the handoff of wife by father to son was motivated more by politics than passion.

matter not so easy to determine), he spent day after day in the young man's chamber; if any of the beauties of the court came in, male or female, he would study Antiochus' face and watch the movements of his body and those parts that nature has made to respond most to the inclinations of the soul. When anyone else came in, Antiochus showed no change, but whenever Stratonicē came to see him, as she often did, either alone or with Seleucus, those telltale signs of which Sappho sings* were all there in him—stammering speech, fiery flushes, darkened vision, sudden sweats, irregular palpitations of the heart, and finally, as his soul was taken by storm, helplessness, stupor, and pallor.

Besides all this, Erasistratus reasoned further that in all probability the king's son, had he loved any *other* woman, would not have persisted to the death in refusing to speak about it. He thought it a difficult matter to explain the case fully to Seleucus, but nevertheless, relying on the father's kindly feelings toward his son, he took the risk one day and told him that love was the young man's trouble, a love that could neither be fulfilled nor cured. The king was amazed and asked why his son's love could not be fulfilled. "Because," said Erasistratus, "he is in love with *my wife*." "In that case, Erasistratus," said Seleucus, "since you're my son's friend, can't you give him your wife in addition to your friendship—especially when you see he is the only anchor of our storm-tossed house?" "You're his father," said Erasistratus, "and yet *you* wouldn't do this for him, if he had fallen in love with Stratonicē." "My friend," said Seleucus, "if only someone in heaven or on earth might speedily turn his passion in this direction! I would gladly let my kingdom go, if I might keep Antiochus." Thus spoke Seleucus with deep emotion and many tears. Erasistratus promptly clasped Seleucus by the hand and told him he had no need of Erasistratus, for as father, husband, and king *he* was also the best physician for his household.

Seleucus called an assembly of the people and declared it to be his wish and purpose to make Antiochus king of all Upper Asia and Stratonicē his queen, once the two were wed. He also said he thought that his son, accustomed as he was to being submissive and obedient in all things, would not oppose him in this marriage; and that if his wife were reluctant to take this extraordinary step, he called on his friends to instruct and persuade her to regard as just and honorable whatever seemed good to

---

* Plutarch alludes to a poem by Sappho, the Greek poetess of the seventh century BC, in which the speaker describes the physical sensations of agitated love.

the king and beneficial. That's the reason, we are told, Antiochus and Stratonicē became husband and wife.

[39] As for Demetrius: After Macedonia he became master of Thessaly also. And now that he had most of the Peloponnese and (north of the Isthmus) Megara and Athens, he turned his arms against the Boeotians.* They at first made friendly agreements with him on reasonable terms, but afterward, when Cleonymus the Spartan† made his way into Thebes with an army, the Boeotians' spirits were raised; and since at the same time Pisis of Thespiae,‡ who was foremost in reputation and influence, added his instigations to the step, they revolted. But when Demetrius brought up his siege engines against Thebes and laid siege to the city, Cleonymus took fright and stole away, and the Boeotians, in terror, surrendered. Demetrius put garrisons in their cities, fined them large sums, and left as their overseer and governor Hieronymus the historian.§ His actions gained him a reputation for mercy—particularly his treatment of Pisis. For after capturing him Demetrius did him no harm but actually greeted him, showed him kindness, and appointed him polemarch in Thespiae. A short while later, however, Lysimachus was taken prisoner by Dromichaetes,¶ and in view of this Demetrius set out with all speed for Thrace, thinking he would get control of the region while it was empty of defenders. At that the Boeotians revolted again, and at the same time word arrived that Lysimachus had been set free. Quickly, therefore, and in a rage, Demetrius turned back. Finding that the Boeotians had been defeated in battle by his son Antigonus, he once more laid siege to Thebes.

[40] Pyrrhus now overran Thessaly and was seen as far south as Thermopylae. Demetrius therefore left his son Antigonus in charge of the siege of Thebes and set out against this new foe. Pyrrhus made a swift retreat; Demetrius stationed ten thousand hoplites and a thousand horsemen in Thessaly and once again concentrated on Thebes. He brought up

---

* By "Boeotians," Plutarch principally refers to the Thebans. They, like the Athenians, continued to grasp at liberty whenever Demetrius was far off the scene.

† A Spartan royal who had left his city and become a condottiere, or mercenary captain, leading a crew of soldiers for hire.

‡ Little is known about Pisis beyond this passage. Thespiae is a town in Boeotia.

§ Hieronymus of Cardia composed a history of this period that was well regarded in its own day but has since become lost.

¶ A king of the Getae, a Thracian people.

against the city his famous City-taker, but this was so laboriously and slowly levered forward owing to its weight and size that in the space of two months it hardly advanced two stades.* The Boeotians too mounted a strong resistance, and Demetrius many times, out of stubbornness rather than need, forced his soldiers to risk their lives in battle. Antigonus saw them falling in great numbers and in grave concern said "Why, father, should we let these lives be squandered needlessly?" Demetrius was furious and said "Why do you take it so hard? Do you owe food rations to the *dead*?"[†] Yet, wishing not to be thought reckless only of others' lives but also to share the perils of battle, he was pierced through the neck by a catapult-bolt. Badly wounded as he was, he did not give up, but captured Thebes a second time.

His entry into the city filled the citizens with fear; they thought they were going to suffer the most dreadful punishments, but he put to death only thirteen, banished a few, and pardoned the rest. And so it was the fate of Thebes, which had been occupied for less than ten years, to be captured twice during this time.

Furthermore, since the time for the Pythian games[‡] was now at hand, Demetrius did something unprecedented. The Aetolians occupied the passes around Delphi, so he conducted the games and the festival, in person, at *Athens*. He declared it especially fitting that Apollo be honored *there*, being that Apollo was a patron deity of the Athenians and said to be the founder of their race.

[41] From Athens, Demetrius returned to Macedonia. He was not prone to staying idle, and he saw that his followers were more devoted to him while on campaign but at home grew turbulent and made trouble, so he launched an expedition against the Aetolians. After ravaging the country he left Pantauchus there with a large part of his forces and moved against Pyrrhus. Pyrrhus also moved against him, but they missed each other on the march. Demetrius plundered Epeirus while Pyrrhus fell upon Pantauchus, and after a battle in which the two commanders

---

* The Greek stade varied in measure but generally averaged a bit over six hundred feet. The City-taker mentioned here is a different machine than the one earlier used against Rhodes, but built on the same design.

† The point of the cutting remark seems to be that the king and prince would save on supply expenses if more men died.

‡ The quadrennial Pythian games, in honor of Apollo—a festival not quite as splendid as the one at Olympia—were normally held at Delphi.

fought hand to hand and wounded each other, routed him, took five thousand of his men prisoners, and slew many of the rest. This did the greatest harm to the cause of Demetrius. For Pyrrhus, who was not so much hated for what he had done as he was admired for what he had achieved by his own hand, got from this battle a great and splendid name among the Macedonians. Many were moved to say that in him alone of all the kings they saw an image of Alexander's daring, while the others, particularly Demetrius, only acted out, as though on stage,* Alexander's majesty and pomp.

There was in truth much of the theatrical about Demetrius. He was not only clothed and adorned extravagantly—double-mitered broad-brimmed hats and purple robes shot with gold—but also shod with gold-embroidered shoes of richest purple felt.† One cloak, woven for him over a long span, was a magnificent work that depicted the world and the heavenly bodies. This was left behind half-finished when the reversal of his fortunes came; no succeeding king of Macedonia ventured to use it, although not a few of them were given to pomp and luxury.

[42] Not only by such displays did Demetrius vex a society unused to them, but his luxurious ways of living were also offensive, above all his remoteness and inaccessibility. Either he made no opportunities to hear petitions or else he was stern and harsh with those he met with. For two years he kept waiting for an embassy from the Athenians—the people whose favor he sought more than any other Greeks. When a single envoy came to him from Sparta, he thought he'd been disrespected and grew angry. He cried, "What are you saying? Have the Spartans sent *one* envoy?"; then got the clever reply—typical of a Spartan—"Yes, to speak with *one* man." Another time, when he was out riding in public and seemed to be open to chance encounters, a group of people came up to him with written petitions. He received them all and folded them away in his cloak; the people were delighted and escorted him on his way, but when he came to the bridge over the Axius,‡ he shook out the folds of his cloak and threw the petitions into the river. This was a great vexation to the Macedonians, who thought themselves insulted, not ruled; they re-

---

* This is the third time Plutarch has employed an analogy from theater when discussing the pretensions of the Successors. He goes on to expand the analogy below.

† Purple robes and elaborate shoes were, in the Greek world, properties of the tragic stage. Tyrants in various Greek cities had begun wearing such gear in the preceding century in order to awe their subjects.

‡ A river in Pella, the capital of Macedonia.

called, or listened to those who recalled, how reasonable and accessible Philip* used to be in such matters.

An old woman once assailed Demetrius as he was passing by and demanded many times that he give her a hearing. "I have no time," said Demetrius. "Then don't be king," screamed the old woman. Demetrius was stung to the quick and, after thinking about the matter, went back to his house, postponed everything else, and for several days gave himself entirely to those who wanted to meet with him, beginning with the old woman who had rebuked him.

Surely nothing befits a king as much as the work of justice.† For "Ares is tyrant," in the words of Timotheus, but "Law is king of all things," according to Pindar.‡ Homer speaks of kings as receiving from Zeus, not City-takers nor bronze-beaked ships, but "ordinances of justice," for protection and safe-keeping; and he calls the most just king, not the most warlike or unjust or murderous, a disciple and "confidant" of Zeus.§ Demetrius, on the contrary, was delighted to receive a surname most unlike those given to the king of the gods; for Zeus is called City-guardian or City-protector, but Demetrius was known as City-besieger. Thus power without wisdom advances evil to the place of good and puts injustice cheek by jowl with fame.

[43] Demetrius, lying dangerously ill at Pella, almost lost Macedonia when Pyrrhus swiftly overran it and advanced as far as Edessa. But as soon as Demetrius had somewhat recovered his strength, he easily drove Pyrrhus out and then came to a kind of agreement with him, not wanting constant collisions and local conflicts with this opponent to defeat his set purpose. This purpose was nothing less than the recovery of all the realm that had been subject to his father.¶

His preparations were fully in line with his hopes and undertakings.

---

* Philip II, father of Alexander the Great, had been dead almost half a century by this time.

† Plutarch here pauses the narrative to make his own moral observations.

‡ The two phrases, taken from the works of two classical poets, pose a contrast between tyranny—autocratic, illegitimate power, associated by Timotheus with Ares, i.e., war and violence—and kingship, linked by Pindar to the norms enshrined in law.

§ The quotes are from the *Iliad* and *Odyssey* respectively. The "most just king" in the second passage is Minos, who became a judge of souls in the Underworld.

¶ By "the realm that had been subject to his father," Plutarch means the greater part of Asia, a far wealthier continent than Europe. Demetrius might easily have held his Macedonian seat had he not tried to regain the lost Asian territories.

He had already gathered an army that numbered ninety-eight thousand infantry and nearly twelve thousand horsemen. At the same time he had laid the keels for a fleet of five hundred ships, some in Piraeus, some at Corinth, some at Chalcis, and some at Pella. He would visit all these places in person, showing what was to be done and aiding the plans, while all men wondered not only at the number but at the scale of the works. Up to this time no one had seen a ship of fifteen or sixteen banks of oars. At a later time Ptolemy Philopator* built one of forty banks of oars, over four hundred feet long and seventy-two feet high to the top of the stern, manned by four hundred nonrowing crewmen and four thousand rowers, and besides these had room on gangways and decks for nearly three thousand hoplites. But this ship was merely for show; since it differed little from a fixed structure, being meant for exhibition and not for use, it was moved only with difficulty and danger. But Demetrius' ships' beauty did not get in the way of their fighting strength, nor did their magnificent construction rob them of usefulness. Their speed and effectiveness was more remarkable than their size.

[44] While this great force, the like of which no one had seen since Alexander, was getting under way to invade Asia, the three kings, Seleucus, Ptolemy, and Lysimachus, formed a league against Demetrius. They sent a joint embassy to Pyrrhus urging him to attack Macedonia and not to respect the truce by which Demetrius had not promised to leave Pyrrhus in peace but had reserved the right of pre-emptive attack on whomever he chose. Pyrrhus granted their requests, and a great war encompassed Demetrius before his preparations were completed. In a coordinated movement, Ptolemy sailed to Greece with a great fleet and raised a revolt while Lysimachus invaded Macedonia from Thrace and Pyrrhus from neighboring Epirus, and both plundered the land. Demetrius left his son Antigonus in charge of Greece while he himself, hastening to the rescue of Macedonia, set out first against Lysimachus.

But news came to him that Pyrrhus had taken Beroea.† The report quickly came to the ears of the Macedonians, and then Demetrius could no longer maintain discipline; his camp was full of lamentations and tears coupled with anger and curses against himself, and the soldiers

---

* Great-grandson of the Ptolemy who contended with Demetrius, Ptolemy IV Philopator was king of Egypt in the late third century BC.

† A town in southwest Macedonia.

would not stick together but insisted on going away, ostensibly to their homes but in reality to Lysimachus.

Demetrius therefore determined to put as much distance as possible between himself and Lysimachus and to turn his arms against Pyrrhus, thinking that Lysimachus, one of his own nation, was congenial to many Macedonians because of Alexander,* while Pyrrhus was a new-comer and a foreigner and would not be preferred by them before himself. In these calculations, however, he was greatly deceived. For he drew near and pitched his camp by that of Pyrrhus, but his soldiers had always admired Pyrrhus' brilliant exploits in arms; they had always considered the man who was mightiest in arms also the most kingly. Besides, they now learned that Pyrrhus treated well his prisoners of war. They were seeking to be rid of Demetrius whether they went to Pyrrhus or to another, so they kept deserting him, at first secretly and in small companies; then the whole camp was in open turmoil and disorder. At last some of the soldiers dared to go to Demetrius, bidding him get away and save himself, for the Macedonians, they said, were tired of waging war in support of his luxurious way of living. Demetrius thought this was very moderate language compared with the harshness of the rest; so he went to his tent and, as if he were an actor and not a real king, put on a dark cloak in place of the one befitting the tragic stage and stole away unnoticed.

Most of the soldiers at once fell to pillaging and tearing down his tent, fighting with one another for the spoils. But Pyrrhus came up, mastered the camp without a blow, and took possession of it. And all Macedonia was divided between Pyrrhus and Lysimachus, after Demetrius had reigned over it securely for seven years.

[45] Demetrius thus lost his power and fled for refuge to Cassandreia.† His wife Phila was full of grief and could not endure to see her husband, that most afflicted of kings, once more in private status and in exile. She gave up hope, and, hating his fortune, which was more secure in adversity than prosperity, she drank poison and died. Demetrius, determined to cling still to what was left of his wrecked fortunes, went off to Greece and tried to assemble his friends and generals there.

---

* Lysimachus, unlike either Pyrrhus or Demetrius, had fought under Alexander the Great.

† A city on the Pallene peninsula of the Chalcidice, founded by Cassander (as the name implies).

In the *Menelaus* of Sophocles,* the title character applies this simile to his own fortunes:

> *But my fate on the swiftly turning wheel of the god*
> *Goes whirling round forever and ever changes shape,*
> *Just as the moon's appearance for two kindly nights*
> *Could never be identical and show no change,*
> *But out of darkness first she comes forth young and new,*
> *With face that ever grows more beautiful and full,*
> *And after the largest and most ample of her phases,*
> *Again she flows away and comes to naught.*

This simile might be better used of the fortunes of Demetrius, now waxing and now waning, now full-orbed and now diminished; even at this time, when his power seemed gone and extinguished, it shot forth new rays of light, and pockets of strength little by little filled out the measure of his hopes.

At first he went about visiting the cities in the garb of a private man and without the insignia of a king, and one who saw him thus at Thebes applied to him, not inaptly, the verses of Euripides:[†]

> *Exchanging now the form of god for that of man,*
> *He visits Dirce's rivulets and Ismenus' flood.*

[46] But soon he had set his foot on the path of hope as if on a kingly road, and had gathered about himself a body and form of sovereignty. He restored to the Thebans their constitution; the Athenians, however, revolted from him.[‡] They voted to elect archons as was their ancient custom and took away from Diphilus, priest of the Savior-gods, the privilege of giving his name to the current year.[§] When they saw that Demetrius had more strength than they expected, they summoned Pyrrhus to their

---

* A play now lost, and perhaps not actually by Sophocles. Menelaus, legendary king of Sparta, endured many travails on his voyage home from the Trojan War.

† Lines 4 and 5 of Euripides' *Bacchae,* in which Dionysus returns to his native Thebes in disguise as a mortal man.

‡ This rebellion (287 BC) is today known in part from a long inscription honoring its principal military chief, Callias of Sphettus.

§ See note to chapter 10.

aid from Macedonia. Demetrius came against them in a rage and began a forceful siege of the city. But the people sent as ambassador Crates the philosopher,* a man of great repute and influence, and Demetrius, in part induced to grant what Crates asked on behalf of Athens and in part convinced that what the philosopher taught could benefit him, lifted the siege. After assembling all the ships he had and putting on board eleven thousand soldiers together with his cavalry, he sailed for Asia Minor to wrest Caria and Lydia from Lysimachus.

He was met at Miletus by Eurydicē, a sister of Phila, who brought with her one of her daughters by Ptolemy, Ptolemaïs, who had been betrothed to Demetrius before this through the agency of Seleucus.† Demetrius married her now, and Eurydicē gave the bride away. After the marriage, Demetrius at once turned his arms against the cities; many came over to him of their own accord and many were forced into submission. He took Sardis also, and some of the generals of Lysimachus defected to him, bringing money and troops. But when Agathocles, son of Lysimachus, came against him with an army, Demetrius retreated into Phrygia. He had determined, if he could reach Armenia, to bring Media to revolt and make for the upper satrapies,‡ where someone who was tossed out of his homeland could find many refuges and retreats. Agathocles followed him, and though Demetrius had the advantage in their clashes, he was cut off from provisions and forage and in dire straits; his soldiers were suspicious that he was trying to make his way toward Armenia and Media.§ And not only did famine press them harder but also some mistake was made in crossing the river Lycus and a large number of men were carried away by the current and lost. Nevertheless the men did not refrain from jokes. One of them wrote up in front of the tent of Demetrius the opening words of the Oedipus play,¶ slightly changed:

* Not the more famous Crates (who was Theban) but an Athenian thinker who was at this time head of the Platonic Academy.

† See note to chapter 10.

‡ Chiefly Bactria and Sogdiana (modern-day Afghanistan and parts of neighboring lands).

§ These provinces belonged to Antiochus, husband of Demetrius' daughter, so the troops may have feared some sort of betrayal.

¶ According to our modern title, *Oedipus at Colonus*. The lines quoted here are the opening lines, with a substitution of *Antigonou*, "of Antigonus," for *Antigonē*, "O Antigone." Oedipus, blind and wandering, asks his daughter where they have come to.

O child of blind and aged Antigonus, what are
These regions whither we are come?

[47] But at last sickness assailed them as well as famine, which often happens when people have recourse to foods they need to save their lives. After losing no less than eight thousand in all, Demetrius retraced his steps with the rest and came down to Tarsus.

Here he would gladly have spared the country*—it was then under Seleucus—and given its ruler no ground of complaint, but this was impossible. His soldiers were suffering extreme privations and Agathocles had fortified the Taurus passes against him. He therefore wrote a very long letter to Seleucus, bewailing his misfortunes and begging and beseeching him to take pity on a man who was allied to him by marriage[†] and had suffered enough to win sympathy even from his enemies.

Seleucus was somewhat softened by this appeal and wrote to his generals in that province that they should furnish Demetrius with royal maintenance and his troops with abundant supplies. But Patrocles, a man known for wisdom and a trusted friend of Seleucus, came to him and told him that the expense of maintaining Demetrius' army was a very small matter, but that it was unwise to allow Demetrius to remain in that country; he had always been the most violent of the kings and the most given to grand designs, and he was now in a state of fortune in which even moderate men are led to take risks and do harm. Roused by this advice, Seleucus marched into Cilicia with a large force. Then Demetrius, filled with amazement and alarm at Seleucus' sudden change of attitude, asked that he might be permitted to acquire some small realm among the free barbarians in which he might end his days without further wanderings and flights; but if this might not be, he begged Seleucus to give his troops food for the winter there and not drive him out, stripped of all things and in need, and cast him into the hands of his enemies.[‡]

[48] But Seleucus was suspicious of all this and told Demetrius that he might, if he wished, spend two months in winter quarters in Cataonia,[§]

---

* "Sparing" in this context means refraining from plunder and stripping of crops.

† Formerly Seleucus' father-in-law, Demetrius was now father-in-law to Antiochus, Seleucus' adult son. Seleucus' young son by Stratonicē was also Demetrius' grandson.

‡ The "enemies" Demetrius feared included, principally, Lysimachus.

§ The northern part of Cappadocia. A ring of mountains here might serve to pen Demetrius in.

provided he gave his chief friends as hostages. At the same time he fortified the passes into Syria against him. Then Demetrius, like a wild beast,
hemmed in and attacked on all sides, was driven to defend himself. He
overran the country, and when Seleucus attacked him, engaged with him
and always had the advantage. Once in particular, when the scythe-
bearing chariots* were dashing down on him, he avoided the charge,
routed his assailants, and drove away those fortifying the Syrian passes,
thus gaining control of them. And now he was completely lifted up in
spirit. Seeing that his soldiers had recovered their courage, he made
ready to fight Seleucus to the finish for the supreme prizes.

Seleucus was at this point at a difficult juncture. He had refused the
assistance offered by Lysimachus, whom he distrusted and feared, but he
hesitated to join battle with Demetrius by himself, fearing the man's desperation and the perpetual change that brought him from the worst destitution to the greatest good fortune. But a grievous sickness seized
Demetrius at this juncture; it wrought terrible harm to his body and utterly ruined his cause. Some of his soldiers went over to the enemy and
others dispersed. At last, after forty days, he recovered, and, taking the
soldiers that remained, he set out, as far as his enemies could see or guess,
for Cilicia; then, in the night and without trumpet signal, he struck out
in the opposite direction, crossed the range of Amanus, and plundered
the lower country as far as Cyrrhestica.

When Seleucus made his appearance there and encamped nearby,
Demetrius set his army in motion by night and advanced against him. For
a long time Seleucus was ignorant of his approach and lay sleeping. But
some deserters came and told him of his peril. He was astounded, and
leaping up, ordered the trumpets to sound, pulling on his boots and
shouting to his companions that a terrible wild beast was upon them.
Demetrius, perceiving from the noise his enemies made that they'd
learned of his approach, drew off his troops with all speed.

When day came, with Seleucus pressing him hard, Demetrius sent
one of his officers to the other wing and partly routed the enemy. But at
this point Seleucus himself dismounted from his horse, removed his helmet, took up a light shield, and went to meet Demetrius' mercenaries,
showing them who he was and exhorting them to come over to him, judg-

* A weapon adopted by the Successors from the Persian war machine. The chariots were
designed to break apart phalanx lines by charging into them with blades protruding from
the wheels.

ing that they must for some time have been aware that he had held back his attack so long for their sake, not that of Demetrius. Consequently they all welcomed him, hailed him as king, and went over to his side.

Demetrius, perceiving that the last of many reversals of fortune was now upon him, left the field and fled to the passes of Amanus. He plunged into a dense forest along with a small group of friends and followers and waited for the night. He wished, if possible, to take the road to Caunus and make his way to the sea, where he expected to find his fleet. But when he learned that the party had not provisions enough even for the coming day, he tried to think of other plans. At this point, Sosigenes came up, a companion of his, with four hundred pieces of gold in his belt. Hoping that with this money they could get through to the sea, the party set out toward the passes in the dark of night. But in the passes the enemy were burning fires, so the fugitives gave up on this road and returned to their place in the forest—not all, for some ran away, and those who remained were not as willing as before. When one of them ventured to speak out and say that Demetrius ought to surrender to Seleucus, Demetrius drew his sword and would have killed himself, but his friends surrounded him and with encouraging words persuaded him to do as the man had said. So he sent a message to Seleucus and put himself at his disposal.

[50] When Seleucus heard of this, he declared that it was not by Demetrius' good fortune but his own that Demetrius had been kept safe—a good fortune that, along with other blessings, gave Seleucus the chance to show generosity and kindness. Then he called his overseers and ordered them to pitch a royal tent and make all other preparations for a magnificent reception and entertainment.

With Seleucus was a certain Apollonides, formerly an intimate friend of Demetrius. He sent this man at once to Demetrius to give him cheer and confidence, reminding him that he was coming into the presence of a friend and relative. When Seleucus' plans became clear, first a few of his friends, then the greater part of them, went off immediately to Demetrius, competing in their efforts to reach him first, for it was expected that Demetrius would immediately become a great personage at the court of Seleucus.

But this behavior of Demetrius' friends turned Seleucus' pity into jealousy and gave malicious and mischievous persons a chance to thwart and end his generosity. They frightened him by their insinuations that at the first sight of Demetrius there would be a great revolution in the camp. And so it came to pass that at the moment when Apollonides had come to Demetrius with a joyful face, and while the other courtiers were coming up telling wonderful tales about Seleucus and his generosity, and when Demetrius, after all his disasters and misfortunes, even if he had once thought his surrender a disgraceful act, had now changed his mind as a result of new courage and hopefulness—suddenly up came Pausanias* at the head of a thousand soldiers, infantry and cavalry together. With these he surrounded Demetrius, and after sending off everyone else, conducted him, not into the presence of Seleucus, but away to the Syrian Chersonese.†

Here, for the rest of his life, a strong guard was set over Demetrius. Attendants sufficient for his needs were sent to him by Seleucus, and a decent amount of money and maintenance were provided for him. Royal courses for riding and walking, and parks with wild game in them, were set apart for his use. Any friend who shared his exile and wished to visit him could do so, and despite his captivity, people kept coming to him from Seleucus bringing kindly messages and exhorting him to be of good cheer, since as soon as Antiochus arrived with Stratonicē, he was to be set free.

[51] Demetrius, finding himself in this plight, sent word to his son and the friends and commanders who were at Athens and Corinth. He bade them put no trust in any letter or seal that seemed to be his but to treat him as dead, and to preserve for Antigonus his cities and the rest of his power. When Antigonus learned of his father's capture, he was deeply distressed, put on mourning apparel, and wrote to the other kings, and especially to Seleucus, supplicating him and offering to surrender whatever was left of his own and his father's possessions. Above all he volunteered to be a hostage for his father. Many cities and many rulers joined in these supplications, but Lysimachus did not; he sent to Seleucus the promise of a large sum of money if he killed Demetrius. But Seleucus, who had always had an aversion to Lysimachus, thought him all the more abominable and barbarous for this proposal and continued to keep Demetrius under watch and ward for Antiochus his son and Stratonicē, that the favor of his release might come from them.

[52] Demetrius at first bore up under his misfortune and soon grew

* Clearly a general serving under Seleucus, otherwise unknown.

† The city of Apamea seems to be meant. It occupied a peninsula formed by a deep bend in the Orontes River, and Greeks tended to label such promontories "the — Chersonese" after the more familiar Chersonese in Thrace (modern-day Gallipoli).

accustomed to it, enduring his situation with a better grace. He exercised his body in one way or another, resorting to hunting (so far as he could) or riding; then, little by little, he became indifferent and averse to these sports. He took to drinking and dice and spent most of his time at these. This was perhaps because he wanted to escape from thoughts about his present condition that tormented him when he was sober, and tried to smother his reflections in drunkenness. Or perhaps he had convinced himself that this was the real life he had long desired and striven to attain but had foolishly missed through folly and empty ambition, thereby bringing many troubles on himself and many on others; he had sought in arms and fleets and armies to find the highest good, but now, to his surprise, had discovered it in idleness and leisure and repose. For what other goal than this can worthless kings seek to attain by their wars and perils? Wicked and foolish indeed are they, not only because they seek luxury and pleasure instead of virtue and honor, but because they do not even know how to enjoy real pleasure or true luxury.

So then Demetrius, after an imprisonment of three years in the Syrian Chersonese, through inactivity and excess of food and wine, fell sick and died in his fifty-fifth year. Seleucus was in ill repute for this and regretted bitterly having held such suspicions against Demetrius, thus allowing himself to be outdone even by Dromichaetes, a barbarous Thracian, who had given Lysimachus, his captive, royal and humane treatment.*

[53] There was something dramatic and theatrical even in the funeral ceremonies of Demetrius. His son Antigonus, when he learned that his father's remains had been sent home, put to sea with his entire fleet and met the funeral ship off the islands.† The remains were given to him in a golden urn, and he placed them in the largest of his admiral's ships. The cities where the fleet docked during its voyage either brought garlands to adorn the urn or sent men in mourning attire to escort it home and help bury it. When the fleet put in at Corinth, the funeral urn was conspicuous on the vessel's deck, adorned with royal purple and a king's diadem, and armed young men stood about it as though forming a body-guard. The most celebrated flute-player then living, Xenophantus, sat near, and with the most solemn melody accompanied the rowers on his instrument; the oars kept perfect time, and their splashing, like funereal beatings of the breast, answered to the cadences of the flute's notes.

* See p. 396 above.
† Presumably the Cyclades in the mid-Aegean are meant.

Among those who came in throngs to the sea-shore, the sight of Antigonus, bowed down and in tears, aroused the greatest pity and lamentation. After garlands and other honors had been bestowed on the remains at Corinth, they were brought by Antigonus to Demetrias for burial—a city named after his father, who had founded it from the small villages near Iolcus.

The children who survived Demetrius were: Antigonus and Stratonicē, by Phila; two named Demetrius, one surnamed the Thin, by a woman of Illyria, and the other Demetrius who ruled Cyrene, by Ptolemaïs; and, by Deïdameia, Alexander, who lived and died in Egypt. It is said that he also had a son, Corrhagus, by Eurydicē. His line came down in a succession of kings to Perseus, the last, in whose reign the Romans subdued Macedonia.

Appendix

Warfare and Battle in the Greek World

Jon E. Lendon

"Putting shields against shields they pushed, they fought, they killed and were killed" writes the ancient Greek historian Xenophon, in the infuriating confidence that his intended audience, who had been in battles themselves, would know what he meant. We, who have (thankfully) not experienced ancient Greek battles, must reconstruct Greek combat from brief flashes in surviving writings and pictures on cracked vases.

The chief variety of warrior in Greece from the seventh through the fourth century BC was called the hoplite, or "heavy-armed" man, equipped (at minimum) with spear, helmet, and (this was what set him apart from the other warriors of his day) a three-foot-diameter shield with a double grip, hand and elbow. This shield extended considerably to the left of the warrior and was intended to overlap the shield of the man standing to his left, just as the shield of the man to the right overlapped the shield of our warrior. The "phalanx," or "roller," the body of men in which the hoplite fought, was therefore fronted by a shield wall similar to those used by the Vikings, the Anglo-Saxons, and any number of other folk who have historically chosen to wield large shields. One usual way of fighting will have been for the two embattled forces to stand a spear's length apart and prod for openings in the opposing shield-wall. When a lucky spear met flesh and a man went down, he was dragged back out of the mêlée, and the man standing behind him advanced to take his place; the phalanx was conventionally seven or more ranks deep. Curiously, however, spear fighting in the phalanx appears to have become less common over time. This we can tell from the fact that between the seventh and fifth centuries, armor that would have been useful in such a fight—

especially leg-protecting greaves and the all-encompassing so-called Corinthian helmet—became less common, and the hoplite was left with his legs bare and wearing a metal cone, which did not protect his face, on his head. The bronze cuirass, which had provided such excellent protection to the chest, was also replaced by armor made of fabric or, no less usually, abandoned entirely.

What evolutionary force in combat would lead to this lessening of the hoplite panoply of equipment? Is it perhaps related to the great mystery of hoplite warfare, which pertains to the "pushing" of shield against shield described by our author above? Was this pushing actual or metaphorical? The factual reality of the pushing seems to be favored by historians who have engaged themselves in this almost century-old controversy. We know that opposing phalanxes usually met at a run: Stopping at spear's length will have been impossible (given the ranks running behind and crashing into the backs of the first) and inevitably shield will have collided with foe's shield (thus the "roller" of the name). The piling up of the ranks behind will, in the nature of things, have led to a pushing contest. The "push" of the phalanx, then, was not what we might call a tactic, but the natural result of how opposing phalanxes usually crashed into each other. In such a push, the shield (bowl-shaped so that a shoulder could take as much of the pressure as possible) became the weapon; the spear could hardly be used; and so there was less reason for greaves or a fully protective helmet (the face being withdrawn behind the shield) or a heavy chest-protecting cuirass. The push might continue until the exhaustion of the parties, whereupon they would pull back and fight with spears, or even, we speculate, pull back beyond spear length and rest; or one party might push upon the other until those pressed backward finally broke and fled. The flight was the killing time in a hoplite clash, because when defeated hoplites turned to run, their shields (which they often dropped anyway, so as to run faster) no longer protected them, and the victors could spear them in the back. Over time, however, the natural "push" of the charge of phalanxes did develop an element of calculation. It appears to have been the Thebans who had the idea to deepen the section of their phalanx expected to strike the decisive blow, first to twenty-five ranks, then to fifty. How much forward pressure the man in the fiftieth row could usefully convey to the man in the first is a mystery; all we know is that these deeper phalanxes reliably prevailed over shallower ones.

Returning to the origins of the phalanx, if it began (as seems likely from images on Greek vases) only one or two ranks deep, the pressure of numerous rear ranks will not have rammed the opposing front ranks together willy-nilly. Spear fighting will therefore have been more common, and the heavier equipment that protected the spear fighter (full helmet, greaves, bronze cuirass) will have been more necessary than it became in later times when pushing became the more usual style of phalanx fighting.

Surrounding the actual clash of hoplites was elaborate ritual. As hoplites advanced to contact, they sang the paean, a hymn to Apollo, and then uttered a cry begging the help of Ares, the god of war. Finally came the actual battle cry, *eueueueu!* to Greeks of the Ionian tribe (including the Athenians) and *alalalalalai!* to Dorians (including the Spartans). And after the battle there was ritual as well. Once fatigue put an end to the pursuit, the losers sent a herald under divine protection to ask that the bodies of their dead be returned (thereby formally admitting defeat), a request that the winners, after stripping the corpses of their equipment, granted. Upon the battlefield the victors built a trophy—a token of thanks to the gods for their victory—from some of the captured equipment. And then both sides in most instances carried their dead home for burial.

The hoplite was the king of the Greek battle, but he did not bestride the field alone. Where the land allowed it, as in Thessaly and Macedonia in the north, horses were bred, and cavalry played their role in battle. Those who could not afford hoplite equipment (and even the reduced panoply of the late fifth and fourth centuries would cost a laborer months' worth of pay) might follow the army as "light troops," which is how we translate the more evocative Greek *gymnetes*, "naked ones." They tended to fight similar rivals on the flanks of the hoplite battle, throwing javelins, shooting arrows (although a few states had formal corps of archers), and throwing stones. Higher quality mercenary light infantry might also be hired from barbarian Thrace in the north—"peltasts," they were called, from their crescent-moon-shaped shields—and eventually Greek states fielded their own peltasts as well. But in the south of Greece at least, both horsemen and light infantry were scorned as cowards (Sparta, for example, had a "cavalry" of three hundred, who, however, fought on foot as hoplites), and a strong prejudice insisted that battles should be fought by hoplites alone, who were regarded as the avatars of courage. And so it was that in southern Greece this prejudice sidelined light troops and cavalry (especially in formal battles, when hoplites were present) into the fourth century BC, regardless of the advantages in combat that creative use of them might have yielded. It was the Macedonians who developed the first efficient "combined arms" system of using infantry, cavalry, and light troops in coordination, and that development was in no little degree responsible for their success in reducing the Greeks to subjection.

If Greek land combat was a lumbering, elephantine, pushing affair, Greek sea battles were as fast as the flash of a school of fish trying to evade the jaws of a dolphin. The Greeks claimed to have invented the battleship of the classical era, what we call the trireme (from the Greek *trieres,* or "three-er"), but they might equally well have adopted it from some other Mediterranean seafaring folk. This was a galley manned by one hundred and seventy hired—and so usually not slave—rowers stacked three high within the hull, both port and starboard. It was a long, slender ship without a keel and with a ram in front, and every comfort and convenience was sacrificed to pushing that ram through the water as fast as possible, and to undertaking the deftest maneuvers, in order to plant the ram in the vulnerable side or stern of an enemy trireme. A hole having been smashed, the victorious trireme would then back water, leaving the victim to swamp (triremes were too lightly built to sink). It would then form, with its crew clinging to the wreckage, an item of loot for the trireme fleet that proved victorious. Triremes made passages under sail when the wind favored, but they left their masts and sails on the shore, if they could, before a battle, to lighten the ships for speed; for the same reason, they carried little water or food, and there was nowhere for the rowers to sleep but at their oars, and so triremes would put in to a friendly port or unfriendly beach for the night, to buy what they needed at a market or plunder the surrounding territory.

For battle, triremes lined up side by side (sometimes in several rows), but necessarily some hundreds of feet apart, so that the vagaries of wind and water would not send them sliding sideways into their comrades (everybody remembered what had happened to the Persian fleet at the Battle of Salamis in 480 BC when their ships got too close together). The large gaps between triremes in order of battle were the basis of sea-battle tactics, as enemy triremes tried to get between them, turn, and ram the enemy's side, or row all the way through the opposing line, turn, and ram the adversary's stern. Naturally such maneuvers were not regarded with complacency by their intended victims, who would turn with all speed to direct their own rams at their antagonists. We are therefore to imagine a battle that began with relatively well-disciplined parallel lines of triremes quickly becoming a chaotic swirl of opposing ships, many in pairs, trying to turn faster in a smaller radius to ram their chosen opponents, while others rowed opportunistically through the turmoil in search of a distracted enemy to ram; this was a contest of well-trained rowers and experienced steersmen. Earlier in their history, triremes had been apt to become entangled as they collided with their competitors, and so they had carried significant forces of hoplites and archers, to fight on deck. It was the well-practiced Athenians, we believe, who reduced these forces to a minimum (ten hoplites, four archers) and who first came to rely exclusively on ramming speed and maneuver.

Of attacks on fortified places—sieges and assaults on cities—there is surprisingly little to say. Never in the history of the West has the advantage of the fortified, behind his high walls of neatly trimmed rectangular stones, so exceeded the means of the besiegers: Until the late fourth century BC the machinery of siege (rams, rolling towers, catapults, tunnels), many of them used for centuries in the Near East, were essentially unknown in metropolitan Greece. Thus only the smallest and weakest places could be taken by assault, by laying ladders against the walls and climbing up them. The alternative technique—starving the defenders out—worked and was used, but so primitive were Greek logistics that the besieger often ran out of supplies before the besieged.

SUGGESTIONS FOR FURTHER READING

Useful surveys of Greek military techniques include Hans van Wees, *Greek Warfare, Myths and Realities* (2004); Louis Rawlings, *The Ancient Greeks at War* (2007); and Matthew Sears, *Understanding Greek Warfare* (2019). For the Spartans in particular, see J. F. Lazenby, *The Spartan Army* (1985 and 2012). For the hoplite, the classic, evocative account remains Victor Hanson, *The Western Way of War* (1989); for the controversies about how hoplites fought, see Christopher Matthew, *A Storm of Spears* (2012). For the trireme and its construction, see J. S. Morrison, J. F. Coates, and N. B. Rankov, *The Athenian Trireme* (2nd ed., 2000). For the Athenian navy, see John Hale, *Lords of the Sea* (2009).

ACKNOWLEDGMENTS

We would like to thank all those who helped make this book possible: Agent Glen Hartley; Random House editors Molly Turpin and Samuel Nicholson; production editor Nancy Delia; text designer Simon Sullivan; production manager Samuel Wetzler; cover designer Rachel Ake; publicist Erin Richards; indexer Charlee Trantino; and proofreader Lucy Haydn. Among our friends and collaborators, special thanks go to translator Pamela Mensch and test reader Jim Ottaway, Jr., supporters of all modern efforts to reconnect with the Greeks.

INDEX

Page numbers of illustrations appear in italics.

Gaugamela, battle of (*cont'd*):
the Persians retreat from, 342; Persian weapons used in, 340; Plutarch's account of, 342n

Gaza, battle of, xxx, 364–65, 365n, 366n

Gedrosia, xxiii, 351, 351n

Gongylus, 208

Granicus, battle of, 333–35, 333n, 334n; Alexander sends spoils of war to Athens and his mother, 335, 335n; Alexander's horse killed during, 335; casualties of, 335, 335n; Greek mercenaries fight with Persia in, 334, 334n, 335n

Greece, Greeks, *290;* Alexander and the transformation of, 329; allied states of fight against Xerxes, 97; ancient kings of, 134–35; cities of run by tyrants, 138, 138n; comic drama versus tragedy in, 385n; Common Peace of, 289; described by Demaratus to Xerxes, 92–94, 92n; dialects of, 227, 227n; division between those accepting Persian rule and those ready to fight, 94–95; early land wars in, 137; fertile land of, 133; first naval battle of, 136; first navy of, 134; the flute (*aulos*) of, 361, 361n; form of oath-taking in, 21; geography and ethnic divisions of, 79n; growth of cities and tyrannies of, 136; as Hellenes, 134; Hellenistic age of, 359; Homer's references to the people of, 134; Ionian troops of fighting for Persia, 91, 91n; lack of hegemony in, 248; libations of, 196, 196n; male beauty prized in, *376;* mercenaries in, 295n; military alliances of, 134; national growth and, 137; navies of, 137; night warfare and, 221–22, 221n; paean of, 196, 196n; Persian invasion of, first (490 BC), 63–74; Persian invasion of, second (480 BC), 74–123, *76–77;* political and military culture of, 92–94; victors of kill the males and enslave the women and children of a conquered city, 161n, 179n; pre-Hellenic populations, 133, 133n; Roman Empire and, 318; split between pro-Sparta and anti-Sparta states of, 301; Successor era of, 359–60, 363–66, 389n, 394, 394n; term "tyrants" used in, 138n; Thebes as the leading power of, 308, 320; as a "three-headed monster," 296; Thucydides' history of earliest times of, 132–41; typical

infantryman in, *68;* universal use of the name "Greece," 133; war as transformative in, 127; Wars of the Successors and, 359–60; Xenophon's *Hellenica* and, 248. *See also* Athens; *Hellenica; Peloponnesian War, The;* Persian Wars; Sparta; *specific cities*

Greek historical writing: authors' selections of, xi–xii; awareness of or inclusion of the gods in, x; the divine's role in human history and, x–xi, 3; Greek epic poems and, x; Herodotus as the first practitioner of, x; human beings at the center of, x, 4; human nature at the center of, ix; overlap with Greek tragic drama, xi; role of, versus today's histories, x; those who "took up the sequel" from Xenophon, 313; time spans covered by selections from, xii; use of speeches, conversations, and dialogue in, ix–x, 4, 92, 172, 173n, 279, 318; written for future ages, ix

Gyges, 8–10

Gylippus, xxiii; addresses his troops in Syracuse, 228–30; commands the Spartans in Syracuse, 207–11, 219–20, 221, 223; fights a naval battle against the Athenians in Syracuse, 228–33; Nicias surrenders to, 240–41; prevents the Athenians' retreat from Syracuse, 234–41

Halicarnassus, xvii; Artemisia as queen of, xvii, 117–19, 119n

Harmodius and Aristogeiton "tyrant slayers," 68, 68n

harmost (garrison commander), 281, 281n

Harpalus, xxiii, 352n

Helen of Troy, 135, 135n

Hellenes, 133, 133n, 134, 134n, 219; original, 134

Hellenica (Xenophon), xxxiii; as a continuation of Thucydides' history, 279; the divine's role in, xi; ending of, 313, 313n; introduction to, 279–80; use of diplomatic speeches in, 279

—The Fall of Theramenes (Athens, 403 BC), xii, 280–91, *290;* Critias as leading member of the Thirty, 281, 281n; dissolution of democracy in Athens, 282–83; the Eleven (enforcement squad), 287, 287n; exiles oppose the Thirty, 286–87, 286n; Sparta installs the Thirty to rule

Athens, 280; Theramenes argues against the Three Thousand, 281–82; Theramenes defends himself against Critias, 285–87; Theramenes is condemned to death, 288–89; Theramenes is plotted against, 282–84; the Thirty arrest and punish unjustly, 280, 281, 282, 285–86; the Thirty commit violence and murder, 282; the Thirty enlist the Three Thousand, 281–82; the Thirty hire a Spartan garrison, 280–81, 286; the Thirty raise funds to pay the Spartan garrison, 282; Thrasybulus leads the overthrow of the Thirty, 286, 286n, 289, 290
—The Last Campaign of Epaminondas of Thebes, (Mantinea, in the Peloponnese, 362 BC), 308–13; Archidamus leads the Spartans against Epaminondas, 309; Athenian horsemen rescue the Mantineans from Epaminondas' forces, 310, 310n; the Athenians return the Theban corpses, 310, 310n; both sides erect trophies, claim victory, 312–13; Epaminondas' forces march from Tegea to Sparta, 308, 308n; Epaminondas has a time limit for his campaign, 310, 310n; Epaminondas mounts a final assault on Sparta, 310–12; Epaminondas receives a fatal wound, 312, 312n; Epaminondas uses "cut off the snake's head" strategy, 311, 311n
—The Retaking of Thebes (379 BC), 279, 290–96, *293;* Athenians troops aid the Theban rebellion, 294, 294n; the coup to retake Thebes is planned for the Aphrodisia holiday, 290–91, 292, 292n; Melōn and six exiles secretly enter Thebes, 292, 292n; Phillidas aids the Theban rebels in exile, 291–92; Phillidas and his men join Melōn in the retaking of Thebes, 293, 294, 294n; Sparta controls Thebes with puppet rulers (polemarchs) and garrison troops, 290, 291, 291n, 292; Sparta gets help from Plataea and Thespiae, 294; the Spartan garrison asks to depart, 294, 295, 295n; the Spartan garrison with its Theban collaborators are slaughtered, 294–95, 294n; the Spartan king Cleombrotus fails to recapture Thebes, 295–96, 295n, 296n

—Thebes Confronts Sparta (Leuctra, near Thebes, 371 BC), 301–8, *303;* Agesilaus refuses to change the Panhellenic peace treaty for the Thebans, 301–2, 302n; the Battle of Leuctra pits Sparta against the Boeotians led by Thebes, 305–7, 306–7n; legitimacy of the Boeotian League is at issue, 302, 302n; rape of the Leuctridae, 304–5, 304–5n; Sparta keeps a garrison in Phocis, 302, 302n, 303; Spartan king Cleombrotus is defeated during battle, 303–6, 305n; Sparta recovers its dead, 307, 307n; Sparta's allies respond to defeat, 307, 307n; Theban cavalry and infantry are contrasted with those of Sparta, 305–6; the Theban victory is foretold by portents, 304–5, 305n; Thebes uses the strategy called "cut off the snake's head," 306, 306n; *to theion* (collective will of the gods), 303, 303n; Xenophon's prejudice against Thebes, 302n
—A Thessalian's Plea for Help (Sparta, 375 BC), 297–301; Jason of Pherae poses a threat to Thessaly, 297–99, 300; Polydamas asks Sparta for aid, 297–300; Polydamas presents himself to Sparta's general assembly, 297; Sparta declines to go to Thessaly's aid, 300
Hellenic League (League of Corinth), 329, 332, 332n, 335n, 382n
Hellespont (modern strait of Dardanelles), xxiii, 78, 81; Alexander crosses, 333; Demosthenes drives Philip II out of, 324–25, 324n; Persian ships sent to protect, 120; Xerxes bridges, 86; Xerxes crosses with his forces, 91–92
helots, 108, 108n, 299, 300, 300n, 361, 361n
hemlock, 371, 371n, 378; Theramenes drinks, 289
Hephaestion, xxiii
Heracles (Hercules), xxiii, 346; Battle of Marathon and, 67, 71; Leonidas of the house of Heracles, 101, 102; Lydia and the Heraclids, 8, 8n; temple of, in Thebes, 305
Herodotus, xxiv, xxxi, xxxiii, 3–5; anti-Theban bias of, 101n; cites sources for implausible stories, 27n; contradictions in the writing of, 43, 43n; Croesus and, 4; dubious stories repeated by, 4, 5; exploration of the upper Nile by, 34; eyewitness accounts in his writings, 4–5; as the first

Herodotus (*cont'd*):

Greek historian, x; as friend of Sophocles, xi; gods investigated by, 5, 81; *Histories,* xxiv, *6,* 7–123, 127; history is akin to myth in writings of, 4; hometown of, 117n; human beings central to writings of, 4; on the Hyperboreans, 5; the *Iliad* as a model for, x, 106n; influence of the divine on human life explored by, 3, 5; insight into scientific questions in writings of, 32–33, 34; *logoi* of, 3–4; luxury-loving aggressors versus poorer, tougher adversaries as theme of, 20n; neutral tone of the ethnographies of, 44, 44n; origin of dreams discussed by, 5; the Persian Wars and, 3, 127; phrase "at the ends of the earth" used by, 37n; phrase "total destruction" of Troy used by, 242n; priests of Hephaestus at Memphis are informants for, 32, 32n; retribution for wrong over time as theme of, 61; stress on personal knowledge in the writings of, 4; Susa known to, xxxi; use of speeches and conversations by, x, 4, 48–49, 48n, 75–83, 90; the word "history" and, 3; writing of, versus Thucydides, 127, 128, 129, 140, 140n. *See also Histories*

Hieronymus of Cardia, 396, 396n

Hippias, 63, 63n, 65n, 67; dream of, 67; as guide for Persians at Marathon, 67

Hippocleides, 72, 73; "What does Hippocleides care?" proverb, 73, 73n

Histiaeus, 81

Histories (Herodotus), xxiv, *6,* 7–123; as compendium of geography, anthropology, and narrative history, 4; ethnographies of, 30–36; idea of a jealous god and, 15–18, 82n; Introduction to, 7; organizing pattern of Persian expansion used in, 31, 36–37

—The Edges of the World (excerpt): Arabia, 50; Ethiopia, 51–52; Europe, 52; hares and lions, 51, 51n; India, 50, 50n

—The First Persian Invasion of Greece (490 BC) (excerpt), 63–74, 137n; Alcmaeonid family history, 71–74; Athens sends Philippides with a message to Sparta for help, 66–67, 67n; the Battle of Marathon pits Athens, aided by the Plataeans, against a Persian force, 65–70, 79; Darius invades the Aegean, 55, 60,

63–74, 137n; Delos and, 64; generals Datis and Artaphernes are appointed to attack Eretria and Athens, 63, 79, 81; Hippias dreams of the future and loses a tooth, 67; Hippias guides the Persians, 65n, 67; Miltiades becomes one of ten generals of the Athenians, xix, 65–69, 65n, 66n, 74; the Persians subjugate Eretria, 65, 66; the Persians subjugate Naxos, 63–64

—A Greek Tyrant, Polycrates of Samos and The End of Polycrates (excerpts), 44–46, 52–54; Amasis of Egypt dissolves his alliance with, 44–45; aspires to be master of the seas, 53; calamity befalls, 46, 46n, 52–54; cannot be saved from his destiny, 46; casts his ring into the sea, 45, 52; commits fratricide, 44; companion of, Democedes of Croton, 54, 54n; crucifixion of, 54; daughter's vision as a warning to, 54; Oroetes plots to seize and kill him, 52–54; successful military campaigns of, 44–45; as a *tyrannos,* 54, 54n

—Leadership Crisis in Sparta (excerpt), 55–62, 56n; Cleomenes, coregent of Sparta, works to remove coregent Demaratus, 56, 56n, 57, 58, 59; Cleomenes goes mad and dies, 61–62, 62n; Cleomenes marches against Aegina, 61; Cleomenes questions Demaratus' legitimacy of birth, 57–59, 57n, 61; Demaratus conspires with Crius of Aegina, 56, 56n; Demaratus defects to the Persians, 60; Demaratus is deposed, replaced by Leotychides, 58, 59; Leotychides is punished, 60–61; origin of dual kingship, 56–57, 56n; the truth of Demaratus' birth, 59–60

—Lydia (excerpt), 30–31; colonization of Tyrrhenia by, 30–31; games invented in, 30–31; prostitution of daughters in, 30; silver and gold coinage of, 30, 30n; tomb of Croesus' father, Alyattes, in, 30–31, 30n

—The Marvels of Egypt (excerpt), 4, 31–36; Amasis and the oracles of, 36; Amasis' fart and the deposing of Apries, 35; Amasis' golden statue made from a footbath, 35–36; Amasis rules, 31; Amasis speaks about human conduct, 36; antiquity of, 32; Apries rules, 35; customs and ways of life in, 34–35; formation of land of, 33–34, 33n; Herodotus' insight into scientific

Persian Empire (*cont'd*):
343n; Alexander campaigns against, xxviii, 329, *330–31,* 332; Alexander fights at the Battle of Granicus, 333–35, 333n, 334n; Alexander proclaimed king of Asia, 342; annual revenue of, 50; Artaxerxes II as king of, xvii, xxiv (*see also* Artaxerxes II); Cambyses as king of, 36–44; conquests of, 4; controls coast of Asia Minor, 289; Darius I as king of, xxi, 50, 74; Darius II as king of, xxi; Darius III as king of, xxi; Debate on Government in (Constitutional Debate), 47–49; destruction of, at Gaugamela, 342; Egypt conquered by, 4, 31, 37; Greek mercenaries fighting for, 334, 334n; Greeks conscripted in the military of, 39n, 40; Herodotus' analysis of, 75; *Histories* and, xxiv, 36–44; Magian rule of, 46–47; messengers of, horse-relay system, 120, 120n; navy of, 89n, 338; Persepolis and, xxviii; Persians called "Medes," 58n; plague of 430 and, 154n; political and military culture of, 92–94; provinces, or "satrapies," of, 50; rise and fall of, 4; slaves and slavery in, 299; Spartan alliances with, 128, 289; survey of, under Darius, 50; Themistocles as satrap of, xxxii; typical infantryman of, *68;* Xerxes and, xvi, xvii, xxiii, xxvi, xxviii, 5, 64, 74–123, 154. *See also* Persian Wars; specific regions
Persians, The (play by Aeschylus), 116n
Persian scythe-bearing chariots, 249, 249n, 252, 254, 405, 405n
Persian Wars, xix, 3; assault by Persia on Athens and Eretria, 62–63; assault by Persia on Athens fails after Marathon, 70–71, 70n; Battle of Artemisium, 140, 140n; Battle of Marathon, 65–70; Battle of Plataea, xxi, xxvii, xxxiii, 108, 109n; Battle of Pteria, 22; Battle of Salamis, *III,* 116–19, 140, 140n; Battle of Thermopylae, xxv, xxxii, 100–109, 140, 140n; commanders of Persia whip their men to make them fight, 93, 93n; confrontations between Persians and less "civilized" peoples, 85n; Croesus and, 18–29, 18n; Croesus invades Cappadocia, 20–22, 20n; Cyrus overthrows Astyages of Media, 20–21, 20n; Greek revolt of 499, 55; the Immortals, 103; Persian invasion of Greece, first (490 BC),

63–74, 128, 138, 138n; Persian invasion of Greece, second (480 BC), 74–123, *76–77,* 128, 138n; Sardis besieged, 23n, 24; Sardis sacked and burned, 55, 62; Thucydides' summary of, 140; typical Persian infantryman contrasted with Greek infantryman, *68. See also Histories:* The First Persian Invasion of Greece; *Histories:* The Second Persian Invasion of Greece
phalanx, xxviii, 191n; in battle, 260, 305, 306, 306n, 311, 312, 334, 341, 347, 386, 387, 387n; billowing of, 255; hoplite warfare, "pushing" of shield, and, 412; origins, 412–13; Philip's weaponry against, 320; scythe-bearing chariots used against, 405n
Pharsalus, Pharsalians, 297–301
Phila (daughter of Antipater), xxviii, 360, 373, 373n, 379, 385, 389, 389n, 394, 401, 403, 409
Philip II of Macedon, xv, xvi, xix, xxii, xxviii–xxix, xxxii–xxxiii, 248, 279, 301, 313, 379; assassination of, 328, 328n, 332; defeats Thebes, xxxii; fights the Greeks at the Battle of Chaeronea, 327, 327n, 328; is opposed by Demosthenes and Athens, 324–26, 324n; organizes the League of Corinth, 382n; reorganizes the army and introduces new weapons, 320; rise of, 319–20, 322–28; as ruler, 399, 399n; seizes Elatea, 326, 326n; wife of, Olympias, xvi, xix, xxvii, 356, 356n, 379
Philip III of Macedon, 357, 357n
Philip V of Macedon, 363, 363n
Philippics (Demosthenes), 321, 321n, 324
Philippides, comic playwright, 371–72, 371n, 384, 384n
Philippides (or Pheidippides), Athenian courier, 66, 66n
Phillidas, 291–94, *293,* 294n. *See also Hellenica:* The Retaking of Thebes
Philotas, xxvii, xxix
Phocion, xxix, 320, 322, 322n, 323
—The Fall of Phocion (excerpt, Plutarch), 356–59: brought with his friends to Athens as a captive, 356–57; faces calls for his torture, 357–58; is admired for his impassivity and greatness of heart, 358; is given a death sentence, 357–58; is forbidden a funeral pyre, but receives one, 358; pleads for his friends, 357; statue dedicated to after reburial, 359

ABOUT THE EDITORS

MARY LEFKOWITZ is the Andrew W. Mellon Professor in the Humanities, emerita, at Wellesley College. A recipient of the National Humanities Award, Lefkowitz is the author and editor of numerous articles and books, including *Greek Gods, Human Lives: What We Can Learn from Myths*; *Women in Greek Myth*; and *Women's Life in Greece and Rome*.

JAMES ROMM is the James H. Ottaway Jr. Professor of Classics at Bard College and the author of several books, including *Dying Every Day: Seneca at the Court of Nero* and *Ghost on the Throne: The Death of Alexander the Great and the War for Crown and Empire*. He has edited numerous translations of ancient Greek texts, including the *Anabasis* of Arrian for the volume *The Campaigns of Alexander* in the distinguished Landmark Series of Ancient Historians.

jamesromm.com
Twitter: @JamesRomm